S0-BCX-342

# Group Counseling

### Second Edition

## Merle M. Ohlsen
**Indiana University**

**HOLT, RINEHART AND WINSTON**
New York  Chicago  San Francisco  Atlanta  Dallas  Montreal  Toronto  London  Sydney

The following publishers or journals have given permission to quote from their publications on the pages designated:

American Psychiatric Association: E. Lindeman, Symptomatology and management of acute grief. *American Journal of Psychiatry* 1944, *101*, 141–148. Pages 199–200.

Basic Books, Inc., Publishers: *Encounter groups: First facts* by Morton A. Lieberman, Irvin D. Yalom and Matthew B. Miles, © 1973 by Morton A. Lieberman, Irvin D. Yalom and Matthew B. Miles. Basic Books, Inc., Publishers, New York. Pages 3, 4, 36, 113.
*The theory and practice of group psychotherapy,* second edition, by Irvin D. Yalom, © 1975 by Basic Books, Inc., Publishers, New York. Pages 112–113, 118, 126–127, 217.

*British Journal of Guidance and Counselling,* 1974, *2,* 15–26: J. Wilson, Transference and counter-transference in counselling. The *British Journal of Guidance and Counselling* is published by Hobson's Press (Cambridge) Ltd. for the Careers Research and Advisory Centre. Page 115.

M. Evans and Company, Inc.: *Shifting gears: Finding security in a changing world,* by Nena O'Neill and George O'Neill. Copyright © 1974 by Nena O'Neill and George O'Neill. Reprinted by permission of the publisher. Pages 236–237.

Grove Press, Inc. William C. Schutz, *Joy: Expanding human awareness.* Copyright © 1967 by William C. Schutz. Reprinted by permission of Grove Press, Inc. Pages 138–140.

Houghton Mifflin Company: Carl R. Rogers, *On becoming a person.* Copyright © 1961 by Carl R. Rogers. Used by permission of Houghton Mifflin Company. Pages 73–74.

*International Journal of Group Psychotherapy:* M. Goodman, M. Marks, and H. Rockberger, Resistance in group psychotherapy enhanced by countertransference reactions of therapist (1964, *14,* 332–343). Pages 123–124.
H. C. Kelman, The role of the group in the induction of therapeutic change (1963, *13,* 399–432). Pages 62–63, 68–69.
I. Ziferstein and M. Grotzahn, Group dynamics of acting out in analytic group psychotherapy (1957, *7,* 77–85). Page 229.

*Journal of Individual Psychology:* R. Dreikurs, Technology of conflict resolution (1972, *28,* 203–206). Page 243.

Macmillan Publishing Company, Inc., and Tavistock Publications, Ltd.: Elisabeth Kubler-Ross, *On death and dying.* Copyright © 1969 by Elisabeth Kubler-Ross. Reprinted by permission. Pages 199, 201.

**Library of Congress Cataloging in Publication Data**

Ohlsen, Merle M.
  Group counseling.

  Bibliographies.
  Includes index.
  1.  Group Counseling.  I.  Title.
BF637.C6048  1977        158        76-51307

**ISBN 0-03-089848-X**

# Preface

The second edition of *Group Counseling* has been written to help prospective and practicing counselors improve their understanding of the therapeutic forces within a counseling group and to help them to manage these forces. Counselors are also encouraged to facilitate the learning of desired new behaviors by clients, and to inspire their continuing growth subsequent to treatment.

Throughout the book case study materials have been used. The studies illustrate the kinds of assistance required by human beings, how persons can be helped by competent professionals, and why professional organizations must act more responsibly to ensure the chances that clients are helped rather than hurt.

In addition to making a conscientious effort to review the research findings on group dynamics, social psychology, group counseling, and group psychotherapy, I have tried to draw upon my professional experiences as a counselor; counselor educator; and consultant to schools, colleges, and community mental health centers to provide this practical case material for my readers.

Unique features of this edition include Chapter 13, "Marriage Counseling in Groups," and the three chapters on challenging clients: 10, "The Emotionally Debilitated" (griever, dying, anxious, hostile, depressed, and learning disabled): 11, "The Other-Controlled" (silent or withdrawn, scapegoat, socializer, dependent, and advice giver); and 12, "The Reluctant" (nonclient, disruptive client, drug addicted, monopolist, and acting-out client). These chapters are down to earth and highly practical, yet they are firmly based on research findings.

The book stresses helping clients to learn to take responsibility for themselves as decent human beings. Clients should be able to discuss their problems openly, define precise behavioral goals, identify criteria that each can use to appraise his or her progress, and learn how to enlist the assistance of significant others in encouraging each to put desired new behaviors into practice and to reinforce these behaviors when they do occur. Increasingly over the past decade I have tried to teach my clients to function effectively as both clients and peer helpers—discussing their therapeutic material openly, detecting others' therapeutic material, encouraging peers to discuss their material openly, sharing goals, and taking the necessary risks to implement desired new behaviors.

Prior to asking my prospective clients whether or not they want to join a counseling group, I try to convey what they can expect from each other, to help them make commitments to help each other and to learn new behaviors, and to assist them in establishing therapeutic norms. They are encouraged to explore how this very accepting temporary relationship in the group differs from their relationships with significant others and why they must complete their unfinished business with significant others or develop new relationships with new significant others rather than merely rely on their therapeutic group for warm, peak experiences.

Within the counseling profession there are many who have the potential to do effective group counseling. Some have even mastered the theoretical background and a knowledge of the techniques, but they lack the required supervised practice and the known support of their supervisors and colleagues that they feel they require in order to initiate group counseling. I have tried to provide practical suggestions on how to introduce group counseling, and to propose ways in which fellow counselors can provide peer supervision and at the same time cooperate in developing a strong support system.

This book is designed to encourage counselor educators to develop the best possible professional preparation, to enhance their growth during professional preparation, to encourage them to accept responsibility for selecting the best possible candidates for preparation in group counseling, and to invite counselors to develop new treatment methods and appraise their worth. In order to achieve these goals counselor educators must be able to appraise the worth of their treatment procedures, to exhibit their own commitment to improve their helping skills, and to encourage their students to continue growth on the job.

My editor and I have struggled with the use of third person singular general pronoun in this text where the universal "he" stands for all human beings as a result of the structure of the English language. I hope that we have handled it satisfactorily, and not just to please sensitive readers or even my partner, Helen, and my three assertive daughters. I want to encourage competent women as well as competent men to lead groups.

This book is the product of over thirty years of doing group counseling, teaching didactic courses, and supervising students in practica. I have been fortunate to have had excellent students and colleagues who were highly motivated to grow and help me to grow, who challenged me, who helped me revise and clarify my ideas, who provided helpful feedback on my counseling tapes and demonstrations, and who encouraged me to experiment with new techniques,

Fortunate as I have been to have had such rewarding students and colleagues, none have influenced me as deeply as my wife, our daughters, and our son. They have given me unselfish love, rich companionship, encouragement, and quality feedback when I have required it most. Therefore, I dedicate this book to Helen, Marilyn, Linda, Barbara, and Ron.

*Terre Haute, Indiana*                                                                              —*M.O.*
*January 1977*

# Contents

# Group Counseling

# 1

# The Helping Process

Counseling is an accepting, trusting, and safe relationship in which clients learn to discuss openly what worries and upsets them, to define precise behavioral goals, to acquire the essential social skills, and to develop the courage and self-confidence to implement desired new behaviors. They can learn to make future plans, to appraise their progress toward their goals, to cope with conflict, and to enrich the various facets of their lives—such as family, politics, recreation, religion, and work.

When clients successfully implement desired new behaviors, they report their successes to fellow clients and when they fail, they feel sufficiently secure within their counseling group to review frankly what happened, to solicit feedback from the others, to decide whether to try a new solution or to figure out how to make the unsuccessful one work. Though a client succeeds in implementing desired new behaviors, relatives, friends, teachers, or co-workers may not notice the change and therefore fail to reinforce the desired new behaviors. Even when successful a client often requires assistance from his fellow clients in deciding how to present his goals to his significant others, in soliciting their encouragement, in teaching them to reinforce desired new behaviors, and in helping them adjust to his new desired self.

Clients learn to help fellow clients and to accept assistance from them: to develop the courage to act while they are exploring alternate solutions and learning new interpersonal skills, and to accept and give frank, yet considerate, feedback to fellow clients. When a client discovers that he can trust his counselor and fellow clients, and that they try to be considerate while providing genuine feedback, he gives up his facades, talks openly about himself and his problems as he sees them, learns to accept himself, dares to implement desired new behaviors, and encourages others to take such risks too. During this process the counselor supplements what he tried to communicate to prospective clients while describing group counseling and selecting clients for the group, clarifies what clients may expect from him and from each other, teaches them to be helpers as well as helpees, reinforces client modeling of both behaviors, and conveys his commitment to help them change. As the therapeutic potency of the counseling group increases, the clients' personal respect for each other grows, and consequently they learn to tolerate individual differences and to accept different solutions to similar problems. They also learn to accept responsibility for their own growth and for helping their counselor develop and maintain a therapeutic climate.

Many clients, especially adolescents, find it easier to discuss their problems openly in group counseling than in individual counseling. Within counseling groups adolescents think that their adult leader is more inclined to listen to them and help them discover their own solutions than to manipulate them or even to put pressure on them to do what their parents or teachers would prefer that they do. When a client observes others discuss their problems openly, senses others' acceptance of those who can talk openly, and realizes the extent to which his peers can understand and help each other, he is encouraged to discuss his problems too. He values their feedback, and they value his. He is even more encouraged when he notices their behavior changes. On the other hand, he notes that members can put pressure on those who talk but fail to act. Nevertheless, the reluctant client does not seem to react as negatively as he does when teachers and parents exert pressure to behave differently. Perhaps it is because fellow clients seem to push him toward his own goals rather than others' goals for him. His fellow clients accept him, including his faults, and seem to believe that he can learn his desired new behaviors. Hence, he can accept the pressure they exert on him. Furthermore, they encourage him and reinforce his desired behaviors rather than nag at him for his faults. Members enjoy the satisfaction that accrues to them in helping others in this very personal way. They enjoy seeing others grow and contributing to their growth. Adolescent clients in particular enjoy helping their peers. Perhaps it is because they rarely feel needed to the extent that their parents felt needed as adolescents.

From the previous paragraphs some readers may conclude that these treatment groups develop into continuing relationships. Some authors such as Bach (1954) and Mowrer (1973) encourage continuing relationships, but most writers agree that memberships in a counseling group should be looked upon as a temporary relationship. These groups are formed to help clients learn to solve their problems, including the ability to develop and maintain meaningful relationships with significant others, and, where desirable, to select and develop new relationships. Though they learn to care for fellow clients, successful clients recognize that fellow clients cannot and should not be substituted for their significant others outside of counseling. When they fail to develop meaningful relationships outside of counseling, clients tend to seek group treatment periodically for their peak experiences. Instead, they must use their time spent in counseling to cope with the forces within their real world—whether it be adjusting to them, working for change, or both.

Three of Lieberman, Yalom, and Miles's (1973) findings indicate that those who profited most from their groups applied outside what they learned in their treatment groups, and furthermore, that they seemed to perceive therapeutic relationships as temporary ones:

> Our investigation of the maintenance of learning revealed that change is more enduring if it is practiced outside the group (p. 150).
>
> Although many participants reported in their interviews that they felt good in meeting, even months later, someone from their group, or that they felt a special kind of bond with fellow members, not one reported a single, meaningful, enduring friendship which had issued from the encounter groups (p. 151).
>
> Patients may report that they are better, but cite a number of external or environmental ameliorating factors: new friends, new social groups, a love relationship, greater satisfaction and greater achievement at work, etc. We cannot suggest that the factors were unimportant in the positive change that occurred, but we must not ignore the fact that the potential friends, the new social groups, the work satisfaction were always "out there" waiting for the individual. Not until the group experience mobilized him to take advantage of these resources was he able to exploit them for his satisfaction and personal growth (p. 151).

Lieberman, Yalom, and Miles (1973) portray such groups as a social oasis where people can drop the facade of competence demanded by a fast moving, competitive society, and discuss their doubts, fears, and disappointments. Their most successful clients learned to be more trusting, open, honest; to give and accept forthright feedback; to recognize the curvilinear nature of openness—when and with whom too much as well as too little openness jeopardizes human relationships; and to apply more consistently a humanistic view of man in order to encourage personal development. Though models discovered in their treatment groups, including the leader, had a great impact upon them, clients tended to become more inner-directed; perhaps they developed more confidence in their own judgments and used models selectively—consciously copying primarily their models' desirable behaviors rather than unknowingly copying their undesirable as well as desirable behaviors.

What clients discuss in their groups is a function of their previous group experiences, their preparation for their group, the way fellow clients react to them and what they disclose, and the counselor's ability to detect and reflect what they are feeling and to enlist other members' assistance in making it safe to discuss their feelings. Ohlsen and Oelke's (1962) findings support these observations. Talland and Clark (1954) discovered that those topics which their patients described as most helpful were also the topics which were judged to be most painful. Although their patients reported that no topics were judged as entirely worthless, some seemed to be more therapeutic than others. Thus, the counselor must be able to detect when a client is troubled, guess what a client may be troubled about (including the fear of discussing a painful topic), and encourage open discussion of it (and teach clients to do it too). Very early in the relationship every client should discover that others want to and can help him learn to discuss whatever is bothering him. By detecting and reflecting accurately what a client is feeling, the counselor (and even another client) conveys caring and confidence in a client's ability to face and cope with his problems.

Lieberman, Yalom, and Miles (1973) found that their clients used their group experiences to get in touch with persons whom they trusted, to validate themselves, and to experiment with new behaviors:

> Am I okay? Am I acceptable? Am I lovable? Many people have not found an opportunity or the audience to whom to address these questions since leaving their family (p. 157).
>
> Some High Learners stressed the opportunity for experimentation. They were encouraged to take risks, to say things and do things which in their wildest dreams, they never envisaged doing. One member who had difficulty expressing himself with any spontaneity was helped, he claimed, by being given certain tasks in the group such as going around the group and giving each member a compliment (p. 159).

## Unique Features of Group Counseling

Frank (1952) reported that, unlike the experience in individual counseling, group clients tended to focus attention on each other rather than upon their history or upon persons outside their group. Durkin (1964) also found that group patients tended to discuss the here and now more than those treated individually. Joel and Shapiro's (1950) and Lieberman, Yalom, and Miles's (1973) patients used the group to do reality testing. The latter's patients also used the groups to develop the courage and skills to take risks. Powdermaker and Frank (1953) noted that their patients were responsive to the problems which they had in common with fellow patients. Lindt (1958) stressed the importance of patients learning to listen and to react to each other therapeutically. He reported that those who profited most from his groups invested in fellow clients and made a genuine effort to help at least one other patient.

Group counseling also differs from other types of group techniques. In order to highlight precise ways in which group counseling differs from other group techniques a number of questions are raised concerning the major differences:

1. *Where does group counseling fall on the continuum of the learning or educational model versus the medical treatment model?* Group counseling is based upon the learning model. Those who accept and use the treatment model described in this book believe that their clients seek assistance when they recognize that their learned behaviors are not enabling them to function satisfactorily or that they are confronted with developmental tasks with which they have not learned to cope. The counselor encourages significant others such as teachers and parents to become sensitive to children's and youths' need for assistance with developmental tasks and helps them teach children and youth to cope with these tasks. He also helps them to recognize children's and youths' self-defeating behaviors and to seek essential remedial treatment for them.

Thus, he enlists their assistance in furthering students' normal social, emotional, and intellectual development. Although this book is primarily concerned with helping reasonably well-adjusted persons, the writer agrees with Szasz (1973) that it is a mistake to look upon treatment of the emotionally disturbed as only medical treatment. Disturbed persons have learned to cope inappropriately with their problems. They must learn new and more appropriate behaviors to develop and maintain satisfying relationships with friends, relatives, and co-workers and to achieve their goals.

2. *How does counseling differ from psychotherapy?* Whereas counselors devote most of their time to helping clients learn to recognize and cope early with self-defeating behaviors and to master developmental tasks (consequently to obviate the development of serious problems), psychotherapists devote most of their time to remediation for emotionally disturbed persons. Psychotherapists also tend to rely on elaborate diagnosis for classification of their clients' problems, whereas counselors merely try to assess whether the clients who seek their assistance are persons whom they can help. Though counselors usually encourage clients to discuss only that part of their history and to uncover those repressed materials which they feel have relevance for their present problems, they tend to focus on the here and now and to help their clients implement desired new behaviors.

In general, the writer agrees with Gazda's (1973) discussion of this problem with reference to treating children:

> . . . My preference is to view the group procedures as falling along a continuum from those that are preventive-oriented to those that are remediation-oriented. Thus, on the remedial pole, I place group psychotherapy (including play-group therapy) because it is a mode of treatment that is applied to those

children who are already emotionally disturbed or behaviorally disoriented to the degree that rehabilitation or behavioral modification are the prime goals of treatment.

Within the middle of this continuum I place group counseling (including play-group counseling) which is preventive-remedial. It is preventive to the degree that children are experiencing difficulty in mastering coping behaviors for given developmental tasks and, given timely assistance in the way of accurate information and/or new modes of behavior, could achieve mastery within normal developmental levels. It is remedial to the extent that a child has begun to enter into spiral self-defeating behavior that requires intervention of the type which includes first stopping of the maladaptive behavior and then the introduction of and subsequent mastery of appropriate modes of behaving, which in turn will enable the child to cope successfully with a given developmental task.

The preventive end of the continuum includes group procedures such as group guidance and human relations training with its many variations—all a part of the human potential movement characterized by basic encounter groups and laboratory training groups . . . (p. 119).

3. *To what extent does a counselor try to help his clients understand why they behave and feel as they do?* Rather than encourage clients to try to understand why they feel and behave as they do (the search for insight), he helps them discuss openly how they feel, learn to accept themselves, recognize and use their potentialities to define meaningful goals, and implement desired new behaviors. Even so, some clients will want to discuss history. Carefully stated, accurate reflections on a client's current worries and desired new behaviors tend to limit such discussion and shift emphasis from intellectual topics to affective ones. Lewis's findings (1959) support this practice. His better-adjusted research subjects experienced more need satisfaction but not a better understanding of their needs than less well-adjusted subjects. Hobbs (1962) concludes that insight follows changed behavior rather than precedes it. Nevertheless, some counselors and psychotherapists are exhibiting increased interest in techniques that stress cognitive development and longer-term treatment.

4. *How long does it take?* Many counselors have demonstrated that clients can be helped in eight to ten weekly sessions of approximately ninety minutes. Younger clients tend to profit from shorter sessions scheduled two or three times a week. Both counselors and psychotherapists are coming to accept the notion that clients who are ready for treatment can be helped in six months or less. In contrast, more analytic psychotherapies that stress insight tend to take several years.

Nevertheless, most counselors and psychotherapists tend to endorse short-term treatment (for example, Adler, 1972; Ansbacher, 1972; Alexander & French, 1946; Barten, 1971; Bellak & Small, 1965; Buda, 1972; Carney, 1971; Godbole & Falk, 1972; Mann, 1973; Oxley, 1973; Phillips &

Wierner, 1966; Reid & Shyne, 1969; Rhodes, 1973; Schafer, 1973; Sifneos, 1972; Stewart, 1972; Thomas, 1973; Torre, 1972; Wolberg, 1965). In general, length of therapy does not influence results (Carney, 1971). "With the development of health insurance programs to finance a limited number of psychotherapeutic sessions, interest is being focused on short-term treatment methods. This economic stimulus merely highlights a growing conviction among many psychotherapists that there are disadvantages in long-term approaches in many cases. Indeed short-term therapy may be the treatment of choice (Wolberg, 1965, p. 4)."

5. *To what extent do counselors who apply the methods endorsed in this book try to convey expectations to prospective clients?* Unlike leaders of analytic therapy groups, T-groups, and encounter groups, who prefer to do minimal structuring, these counselors try to convey precisely what will be expected of clients (including what choices they have in structuring relationships), what they can expect of their counselor, and how clients like themselves have been helped. This is done to provide them with the essential data that they must have in order to decide for themselves whether or not to participate, to prepare them to accept their responsibility for developing a therapeutic climate, and to ensure "truth in packaging."

6. *How much responsibility should a counselor give his clients?* Counselors who endorse the methods advocated here have a great deal of confidence in their clients' ability to learn to play the client and helper roles, to accept responsibility for talking therapeutically and for implementing their desired new behaviors. As clients learn to function responsibly they experience quality participation in the therapeutic process. When the counselor discovers clients who cannot accept responsibility he teaches them to do so and reinforces them for doing so. On the other hand, most analytic therapists tend to be protective and to encourage their clients to be dependent upon them and to look upon them as experts who will diagnose and prescribe, whereas counselors who use the methods endorsed here begin at once to develop a structure in which clients can learn to accept primary responsibility for their own growth.

7. *To what extent does the counselor expect his clients to define precise behavioral goals and to use their behavioral goals to define criteria they can use to appraise their own therapeutic progress?* These notions are central to the treatment process discussed in this book. The counselor takes great care to ensure that the goals are really his clients' goals.[1] Some therapists and leaders of sensitivity and encounter groups reject the need for any

---

[1] How this is done is discussed in considerable detail in the next section of this chapter and in Chapter 4.

goals. Others merely reject the need for precise behavioral goals. Consequently, they are forced to accept vague, general criteria to appraise their clients' growth.

8. *Are clients merely encouraged to adjust to their environment?* For counselors, helping clients adjust to their environment is necessary but not sufficient. Sometimes they must learn to change their environment or move. However, most therapists help their clients understand themselves and their environment and adjust to it. Some, and especially encounter-group leaders, encourage their clients to accept responsibility for correcting social injustices as well as for improving their own ability to adjust to their situations.

9. *How are clients selected for group counseling?* In organizing groups most leaders ask themselves these questions as they select each member: What assistance does the client want and require? Is the client the type of person who tends to be helped or hurt by the technique for which I am selecting members? How do I feel toward the client? Who needs whom for what?

Group counseling is usually offered to reasonably healthy persons who are allowed to decide whether or not they want to participate.[2] Prospective members are expected to convince themselves and the counselor that they are committed to discuss their problems openly, to define precise behavioral goals, to implement these desired new behaviors, and to help fellow clients do the same before they are accepted into the group. Consequently, clients feel responsible for helping to develop and maintain a therapeutic climate and readily accept responsibility for recognizing and coping with their own and their fellow clients' resistance.

Other leaders of groups vary markedly on this issue. Whereas some encounter-group leaders question the value of any screening, and even object to any structuring for prospective members, some analytically oriented therapists require elaborate diagnostic testing and complete case histories.

10. *How is resistance perceived by those who use this model of group counseling?* They perceive it as a natural reaction—an intrapersonal conflict that arises out of a client contracting for assistance, but then, during the process of being helped, questioning whether the desired new goals are worth the pain required to achieve them, or whether the goals can be achieved even if he discusses his problems openly and genuinely tries to implement desired new behaviors. A counselor who follows this model recognizes that although resistance usually has its roots within the client, a counselor may enhance it by his own inappropriate professional behaviors and by countertransference reactions. When a counselor recognizes either of these he must try to cope with it during the sessions. He also reviews the crucial session with a trusted colleague (Chapters 2 and 5). Where the

---

[2] Clients' participation in the selection process is discussed later in this chapter.

problem is primarily an intrapersonal conflict, the counselor tries to detect and reflect accurately what the resisting client is feeling, to enable him to own and discuss these feelings, and to teach other clients to recognize resistance and to cope with it (Chapter 6). Those who differ most sharply with this point of view tend to be encounter-group leaders, who use feedback to confront the resisting member with his unproductive behavior, and psychoanalysts, who use interpretations to explain to the resisting client why he is behaving as he is (and both tend to perceive it as personal reaction against them more than does the counselor).

11. *How is the transference phenomenon dealt with by counselors who use this treatment model* (Chapter 5)? Most client-centered counselors and encounter-group leaders do not perceive transference to be important in their treatment. Most psychoanalysts, on the other hand, look upon the development of transference, the opening up of these feelings to interpretation, and the patient's learning to reevaluate and to cope with these feelings as central to the treatment process.

When a client experiences a transference reaction he assigns another the role of a significant other with whom he has some unfinished business and treats this person (the transference object) as though he were that significant other. When this occurs in the group the counselor helps the client express his feelings toward his transference object and resolve any problems that result from it. If the transference object appears to be confused, the counselor helps him discuss how it feels to be treated inappropriately and to convey how he wants to be loved or rejected for what he really is rather than for what someone inappropriately perceives him to be. Usually he also helps the original client in the interaction to explore with whom it is outside the group that he has similar problems, to decide what unfinished business he must work through with that significant other (and if necessary, to practice desired new behaviors), and to implement the new behaviors.

12. *Who decides when a client terminates?* What criteria are used to make the decision? Are rituals used in the termination process? Clients use their own behavioral goals, and the criteria they developed during the intake interview, to appraise their progress. Most counselors terminate the relationship whenever a majority of the clients decide either that they have achieved their goals or that they have accomplished all they can at this time. Individuals realize that they can drop out of the group whenever they choose, but those who achieve their goals early in the life of the group usually elect to continue membership in order to help fellow clients achieve their goals. Finally, closing rituals are used to give members a chance to learn to say their goodbyes, to appraise their progress, to identify the unfinished business on which they will continue to work on their own, and to plan their follow-up session and/or report.

Rarely do encounter groups, T-groups, or therapy groups have specific goals they can use to appraise their progress. Some encounter and sensitivity-type groups use a closing ritual, but do not relate it directly to personal growth, continuing growth, and follow-up appraisal. Psychoanalytic-group members can drop out, but usually the therapist decides when members are ready to terminate.

## Elements in the Helping Process[3]

**developing the relationship**   The extent of a client's recognized need for assistance, his understanding of the helping process, the counselor's reputation as a helper, and the counselor's initial responses to the client can all contribute to or interfere with building a counseling relationship. A counselor begins developing a counseling relationship at his first contact. It may be a casual meeting; a discussion that follows a formal description of the treatment process for prospective clients; or endorsement by a former client who profited from counseling. Wherever or however clients meet the counselor they should find in him the personal qualities that enable them to accept and trust him. They must believe that he can keep confidences, that he can listen to them and not be shocked by anything they tell him, and that he can help them work out their own solutions rather than exhibit doubts about their ability to solve their problems by giving advice or using some other protective tactics.

During this process of developing a relationship a counselor tries to convey to prospective clients who he is, what he does to help them, what he expects from them, what they can expect from each other and him, and how counseling helps them. The counselor listens to each, gives each individual attention, expresses caring, suffers with each, all without becoming un-wholesomely involved with the client. He helps his clients realize that they can talk about anybody or anything with the expectation that confidences will be kept. He detects how his clients feel and is able to reflect and help them discuss these feelings. When, for example, an adolescent wonders whether he can discuss his feelings of hate toward his father, whom he also loves very much, the counselor enhances the relationship by reflecting how deeply he hurts with the client, by helping the client discuss his deep desire to improve his relationship with his father, and by noting his fellow clients' compassion for him as he struggles with the problem.

**beginning the first private conference**   For those who volunteer for group counseling the first private meeting will be the intake interview.[4] Most clients speak first—especially when they seek counseling after having heard

---

[3] Practicing and prospective counselors like to know precisely how they should go about helping their clients. Though they vary in their life style, the writer describes the components that most can use in helping their clients.

[4] The intake interview will be discussed in a later section of this chapter.

their counselor describe the process and what is expected from them. When a client does not talk, the counselor tries to determine whether the client knows what is expected from him or her and with what he would like help. The clients' readiness to discuss some difficult topics is enhanced by helping them explain to the counselor why the topics are threatening or embarrassing to discuss. Shyness, lack of trust, and doubts about being able to be helped also may explain failure to talk openly. In any case, detecting what the client is experiencing, reflecting accurately what he feels, and encouraging him to discuss it enhance openness. As the client learns to talk openly she is helped to accept responsibility for talking about whatever worries and upsets her, for defining behavioral goals, and for learning new and more appropriate behaviors. For most clients, but especially adolescents, precise behavioral goals enhance open discussion, and consequently the counseling relationship. With their search for identity (Erikson, 1953), adolescents are very wary of therapy that stresses basic personality change (Holmes, 1964). They can accept their need for learning new behaviors more easily than they can cope with further confusion in their identity crisis. Moerover, most clients react positively to a helping relationship for which they volunteer and in which they are expected to accept responsibility for learning their own desired new behaviors.

**detecting a client's feelings**    In order to detect what a client is feeling a counselor must try to sense what that client is experiencing, to empathize with him, to feel what he feels, and to perceive what is happening as he perceives it (the counselor also teaches clients to do this). If he is to be therapeutic the empathizer must try to guess precisely how the client is hurting, or what he would like to do about it, or what he wishes he had the courage or the interpersonal skills to do about it. The sources of data are the client's struggle to express himself on certain topics, the way he exhibits approach-avoidance to them, his speech patterns, and his communication of emotions by facial expressions, laughing, crying, and use of emotionally loaded words. Moreover, different clients may use similar behavior to express very different emotions. What for some would be hostility for others would be efforts to convey affection, and vice versa (for example, some tease or make sarcastic remarks when they really want to convey affection). When some clients feel hostile they attack; others act bored or indifferent or defensive. In any case, the counselor recognizes that in order to understand a client's behavior he must take cognizance of everything he has learned about that particular client. Every client has his own life style, and consequently his own unique ways of revealing his true inner feelings. Thus, the counselor realizes that a client may even wish to convey something very different from what his words communicate. He may mask his real feelings because he is ashamed of how he feels or of what he has done, or he is not certain that he can trust the counselor or some fellow clients.

In addition to uncovering essential data for an accurate reflection, the counselor's effort to detect his client's genuine feelings conveys caring; it also conveys the counselor's respect for the client and his desire to help the client accept responsibility for his own personal growth. Though external sources such as case histories and intensive interviews with significant others (teachers, parents, spouse, employers, and so on) can provide useful data to enrich his understanding of a client, the counselor tends to be most productive when he encourages his clients to accept primary responsibility for revealing the relevant data that will be required to help them implement desired new behaviors.

**reflecting a client's feelings**    From what was presented in the previous section, it is evident that the modern therapies described above call for less use of interpretation and more use of reflection. In order to use either method a counselor must understand the client's behaviors, feelings, and frustrations, and be able to communicate these understandings accurately to the client.

There are two primary distinctions that differentiate interpretation and reflection: the extent to which the counselor (1) assumes the expert role and (2) assumes responsibility for his clients. When a counselor interprets a client's behavior ("Because your teacher embarrassed you, and you didn't know what else to do at that time, you talked back to him and got kicked out of class."), the counselor assumes the expert role. He thus encourages his client to feel increasingly dependent and to expect advice. Furthermore, most clients, and especially adolescents, tend to perceive interpretation as attack (Dougherty, 1974; Helner, 1972; Katz, Ohlsen, & Proff, 1959). Nevertheless, Helner's fourth and tenth grade subjects preferred advice giving and probing to both reflection and interpretation. Dougherty's fourth graders and tenth graders also preferred advice giving to both Adlerian interpretation and traditional analytic interpretation. Although a majority of Taylor's (1974) tenth grade subjects reacted with approach to all four of the techniques he studied, they reacted significantly differently to the techniques. Their ordered preferences were: content probing, affect probing, reflection, and advice giving. There are at least three possible explanations why Taylor's adolescent subjects may have reacted less favorably to reflection than to probing: (1) reflection is not a response with which they have had much experience; (2) they recognize and react somewhat fearfully to the underlying responsibility associated with a reflection; and (3) the reflections with which Taylor's subjects were confronted may have been somewhat too deep for them in that experimental setting.

When a counselor notes a client's uneasy or uncomfortable reaction to a reflection, it does not mean that he should discontinue its use. Instead, he should try to detect and reflect his client's underlying feelings, explain why he uses the technique, and what it reveals about the counselor's or a fellow client's feelings toward the client: for example, "Perhaps that made you feel a little uncomfortable or made you wonder what I was trying to do. That kind of a helping response is called reflection. When I use it I am trying to guess where you are and make it safe for you to talk about what is troubling you. In other words, it is meant to be an encouraging response; you will discover that you and your fellow clients can learn quickly to use it to help each other too. When any of us use it here, we are saying we care about you, we want to help you, and we believe you have what it takes to solve this problem."

If the counselor's response to the boy who was criticized in front of the other students had been a reflection, he would not have tried to explain why the boy felt and behaved as he did. Instead he would have merely tried to detect and mirror back what the boy felt. He also could have moved the boy toward some action with a reflection such as: "Your teacher embarrassed you. As you think about it now perhaps you would like to discuss how you could resolve your conflict with your teacher, and even role play how you could go about talking to him about it." Thus, the counselor reacts more as an equal who is trying to sense what the client is experiencing, to communicate with him in order to help him discuss his feeling openly, to identify desired new behaviors, and to implement them. Such a reflection tends to be most productive when its focus is just a little deeper and a little ahead of where the client is.

**relating discussion of feelings to behavioral goals**     As a counselor listens to a client discuss what worries and upsets him, he tries to decide when the client has talked sufficiently and obtained adequate feedback (especially in group counseling) to be ready to define behavioral goals. If a client feels pressured to define goals before he has talked out his feelings, he may conclude that fellow clients either do not care or that they have not obtained enough data to help him. When, therefore, the counselor wonders whether a client is ready to define behavioral goals, he can make a reflection that checks out where the client is: "I think we understand how you feel about ————; perhaps you are ready to discuss what you would like to do differently with ———— in order to improve things for you." He also may incorporate in a reflection a desired new behavior, as the counselor did in the illustration of a reflection in the previous section. Early in the life of a group, a counselor may use his clients' own case materials to teach them to expect and to facilitate the definition and implementation of behavioral goals. He also helps understand why it is better for one of them rather than the counselor to ask, "What can or do you want to do about this situation now? What are your long-term goals and with what can you begin today?" For example, in a marriage counseling group (in which both spouses were present) a male client had talked several times about how deeply he loved his wife and yet at the same time how much he seemed to want to hurt her, but had never exhibited any inclination to change his behavior. After one such speech about his wife another male client frowned, paused a moment, and then responded as follows: "I can see how you are hurting, but all you do is talk about hurting. I cannot seem to grasp what you want to do about it. I cannot tell whether you want to continue to live in misery, split, or change your behavior. In any case, you must learn to behave differently or you will repeat the same mistakes with some other woman. What new behaviors must you learn to develop a good life with your wife, or with some other person?"

Sometimes a client is ready to move from discussion of feelings to discussion of goals, but doesn't know how to do it. On such an occasion a counselor may say, "It sounds like you believe that you have the interests, abilities, and aptitudes to be an electrician. I am wondering whether you would like for us to help you talk about what you must do to become an electrician or help you figure out how to tell your parents that you don't want to go to college." On the other hand, it may be better to say nothing. The client may be pleased to discover that his counselor and fellow clients can listen to him patiently while he wrestles with conflicting feelings and motivations. He may be even more pleased to discover that other clients are simultaneously struggling with similar problems, that they will own up to their problems, and that they can discuss their problems.

Sometimes, however, a counselor allows clients to wallow needlessly in painful material. He permits them to achieve catharsis to the point where they lose much of their motivation to change. Rather than encourage clients to purge themselves of all of their painful feelings related to their unsolved problems, the counselor may do better to help clients define feasible behavioral goals and discover and practice new behaviors as they discuss their problems. In this way clients experience success from implementing some new behaviors while they are experiencing relief from talking openly about other problems.

**defining behavioral goals**     Counselors are increasingly accepting the notion of helping their clients define precise behavorial goals. Beginning with the description to prospective clients of group counseling, counselors review what similar clients have discussed and how they have changed their behaviors; they thus create the expectation of specific goals. During the intake interview counselors encourage prospective clients to define idiosyncratic goals and the criteria that they can use to appraise their own growth during counseling and subsequent to it. Throughout treatment they listen carefully to clues revealed by clients in order to detect how their clients would like to change old behaviors or learn new ones.

As reported earlier, the discussion of behavioral goals makes sense to most clients and enhances the attractiveness of group counseling. They want to learn how to accept responsibility for changing their behaviors. A reflection such as the following one encourages self-disclosure and opens up examination of desires to learn new behaviors: "You really like her—I bet you wish you knew how to tell her. Perhaps you didn't know that is one of the things that clients learn to do in group counseling. We also give you the chance to practice talking to your special people. We call it role playing, and we will teach you how to do it." Inasmuch as most clients' problems involve learning to express a feeling toward, developing a relationship with, or resolving a conflict with significant others, a response such as the following often opens up a discussion of goals: "With whom do you want to learn to do what? With what do you feel you are ready to begin now?"

Clients' tendency to want to settle for vague, general goals may show a lack of readiness for group counseling, and reluctance to define precise behavioral goals usually indicates resistance. Rather than interpret their lack of readiness or resistance (Chapter 6), counselors are encouraged to try to capture precisely what the client is feeling and reflect the underlying resisting feelings as accurately as possible. This tends to bring the discussion of underlying feelings out into the open where they can be explored and accepted. Fellow clients also tend to give recognition for the courage exhibited by the resisting client's struggle to discuss his problem openly and to reinforce his self-disclosures. Fellow clients also tend to be more productive than the counselor in helping the reluctant client explore the natural consequences of his failure to define and implement desired new behaviors.

**helping clients define criteria to appraise their own growth**    When the counselor can enlist his clients' assistance in defining criteria for appraising their own growth subsequent to defining behavioral goals, they learn to use these criteria to appraise their own progress. Clients' discovery of specific ways in which they are growing encourages further growth and reinforces desired new behaviors. These discussions also provide a natural setting for teaching clients to generalize to significant others outside their counseling group—to teach clients how to communicate their goals to significant others and to teach significant others precisely how they can reinforce clients' desired new behaviors.

Definition of criteria to appraise clients' achievement of their goals also can be used to clarify treatment goals. When, for example, a junior high school boy indicated in the intake interview that his primary goal was to learn to get along with classmates, the counselor said, "With whom would you like to learn to do what?" The boy's response to that question was a long one, including the names of two boys and one girl with whom he would like to develop a close friendship. A further clarification response opened up the topic even more and identified the need to practice relationship building and maintenance skills. Consequently, the counselor responded as follows: "That helps. Now I know with whom you would like to develop special friendships. You would like to learn how to tell them how you feel toward them, check out whether or not they think they could like you, and for those who also think that they could like you, figure out how to encourage growth of the friendship. Perhaps that is a skill that we could practice in the group [and if this was the first time role playing had been introduced the counselor would have described it and told briefly how it is used in group counseling]." Such discussion opens the way for another counselor response which helps clients formulate criteria for appraising their own growth: "How will you know when you have learned to do that? How will you behave differently? How will your family and friends perceive you differently? Precisely how will you feel differently about yourself?" Thus, even prospective clients learn in the intake interview how to formulate precise goals and to appraise their achievement of such goals. DeEsch (1974) concludes that clients' experiences in formulating behavioral goals and criteria for appraising their own growth may account for the fact that his control subjects achieved almost as much growth as his experimental subjects did.

A client's criteria for appraising his own growth also can be used by the counselor to determine whether a client is being helped by a treatment, can be helped at this time, or should be treated by some other method or be referred to someone else for treatment (or whether one of the client's significant others should be treated instead or with him).

**helping clients define mini-goals**    Once clients have defined their goals, most profit from breaking up their goals into mini-goals, or at least from deciding with what they feel most confident to begin implementing desired new behaviors. Some like to break their long-term goals into steps and order these steps. The way the counselor helped the junior high school boy I have cited, who requested assistance in getting along with classmates, illustrates how a counselor uses reflections and clarification responses to help a client do two things simultaneously: defiine a more precise goal with specific target persons and break his big goal into mini-goals he tackles one at a time.

**teaching a client good client and helper behaviors**    Basically, teaching behaviors is a part of structuring, and it is begun when the counselor first tells a prospective client about group counseling and answers his questions about the process and what will be expected from him. The better a client understands what is expected from him before he gets into the group and the more committed he is to join a group, the better he functions and the more eager he is to learn to function effectively as client and helper. Nevertheless, most clients at one time or another will exhibit some uncertainty about how to act. When this occurs the counselor tries to detect and reflect what the client wants to know, to encourage a fellow client to explain what is expected and—better still—to demonstrate it. The counselor also should watch from the beginning for specific instances in which clients functioned especially well as helpers as well as clients and should call these behaviors to the attention of the entire group. When, for example, the counselor observed that Jack had detected how Sally was feeling and had made it safe for her to share her feelings he called it to the attention of the group. A counselor also can replay recordings of counseling sessions in order to point out good examples of group members' performances in both roles. Such counselor behavior tends to reinforce a member's desired behavior and encourage others to use him as a model. Hilkey's (1975) results suggest that even poor treatment risks (incarcerated criminals), treated in groups in which they were taught client and helper roles through use of fellow prisoner models recorded on video recordings, profited more from group counseling in the first few sessions than did similar clients who were counseled by the same counselors, but without being systematically taught these two roles.

**teaching clients the necessary interpersonal skills required to implement desired new behaviors**   Although films and video recordings can be used for this purpose, most counselors tend to prefer the use of role playing[5] to teach skills. In addition to teaching the required skills, the helpee's description of the situation in which he is expected to perform, of the other principal actors, and of his fears, together with his struggles in casting for the essential roles, help members of the group understand him and his situation; and these experiences enable fellow clients to provide better feedback.

**teaching clients to communicate their goals to significant others and the precise type of reinforcement which they will require to implement and sustain desired new behaviors**   Usually clients want to practice in their counseling groups what they want to say to their families, friends, or co-workers (or to write what they wish to convey and get feedback on the letter before they mail it). Frequently, they prefer to select actors, to role play the scene, and to solicit feedback from fellow clients before they attempt either oral or written communication with significant others. In any case, they require and appreciate assistance in formulating and in communicating the precise message they require.

**sharing successes**   When clients decide on precise things to do between sessions they learn quickly how to share the success they experience in implementing the behaviors. Gradually they learn to differentiate between bragging to impress someone and sharing real successes, first with fellow clients and then eventually with those significant others who care deeply about helping them implement desired new behaviors. Increasingly they learn to celebrate successes; and they also learn to admit their failures and

---

[5] Chapter 7 is devoted to helping clients use these techniques effectively in group counseling.

analyze them for the purpose of deciding how to revise unsuccessful tactics and try other approaches.

**termination**  Termination of a course of group counseling sessions can teach clients how to conclude a temporary relationship, appraise its worth, identify each one's unfinished business, and plan for follow-up. During the first or second session members should be encouraged to decide on starting and closing times, how and under what conditions members may arrange for individual sessions, approximately how many group sessions they will have, how they will decide on termination, and how the counselor will provide for those who are not ready to terminate counseling when their group disbands.

Sometimes clients resist termination because the group is providing them with some of the best relationships they have ever experienced and they do not want to give them up. When the counselor senses such feelings he reflects them in order to help clients acknowledge them, discuss them, explore what they must do to develop more satisfying relationships with friends, relatives, and co-workers and/or develop new and more meaningful friendships, and say their goodbyes to their fellow members. With the frequent moves most clients will be expected to make, they must learn to terminate some meaningful relationships, to sustain others despite separation, and build new relationships quickly.

The use of a closing ritual by counselors of groups has become markedly more popular recently. Several sessions prior to termination those counselors who favor the idea encourage each client to review which goals he has achieved, which still require additional work, whose assistance he will require to make the desired changes or to reinforce the changes already achieved, and what problems he envisions in implementing and maintaining his new behaviors. Each client also is directed to give the group feedback on those instances in which he was helped and hurt most. After each client reviews his own gains and describes his unfinished tasks he is asked to stand before each of the others to receive two final messages: (1) a statement concerning what each liked about him, and in particular about what he accomplished in the group and (2) an "I urge you" message in which each notes some specific area of growth on which he would like to encourage this particular client's further growth. In order to preserve these messages for each client, the counselor assigns each a partner who records the first of the two messages on the front side of a sheet of paper and the second message on the back of it.

**follow-up and encouragement for continuing growth**  Even the counselor who questions his ability to appraise his treatment with systematic research can combine clients' goals for each group into a behavior inventory he has each client complete for himself and for each of the other clients immediately following termination and immediately following the follow-up sessions (Chapter 14). Some counselors offer to review these findings with each client. They tend to encourage continuing growth.

When such an evaluation instrument is used, some counselors prefer to send clients a copy of it a few days prior to the follow-up to encourage them to review their own and others' goals and to review for each what his unfinished business items are. Some also request each client to complete one inventory for himself and for each of the others early enough so that the counselor is able to summarize the results prior to the follow-up meeting.

Nevertheless, the primary purpose of the follow-up session is to review the degree to which each has maintained the gains he or she made during counseling and has completed his or her unfinished business. Where it is difficult or impossible to reassemble the group for a follow-up session, the counselor can request a follow-up letter from each, with a carbon of his letter to the others. Clients commonly comment on the fact that even though some at first failed to work on unfinished business, the prospect of the follow-up encouraged them to do so.

## Who Profits from Group Counseling?

Most who are willing to learn new behaviors can profit from counseling when they are troubled by problems or confronted with developmental tasks with which they feel they cannot cope by themselves or even with the assistance of friends, relatives, or co-workers. For example, an individual may have been hurt or let down by someone whom he loves; he doubts the love from someone he loves very much; he feels guilty about hurting someone; he is grieving for someone; he is conscious of a problem for which he lacks the courage, self-confidence, or skills to attack; he is confronted with a problem for which he has the essential knowledge, abilities, and skills to solve, but he does not realize it; or he is confronted with a problem for which he has a good solution but implementing it will disappoint or hurt someone whose acceptance he values very much.

Consequently, even similar personality types seek assistance for quite different reasons. Some require assistance in identifying and clarifying their problems. Others require information and feedback on themselves and their environment, training in decision making, skill building, and increased confidence in themselves. Those who require feedback from others, opportunities to give help to others and to accept help from others and to practice interpersonal skills can be helped best in groups.

Those who seek assistance on their own are easier to help than those who are coerced into treatment by relatives and friends (Beck, 1958; Ewing & Gilbert, 1967; Johnson, 1963; Rickard, 1965). Lieberman, Yalom, and Miles's (1973) clients who profited most from treatment were open and trusting. They gave others frank but considerate feedback and requested feedback from others. On the other hand, they recognized the curvilinear nature of openness—with whom and under what conditions it is appropriate to be open. The authors' successful clients also took risks in implementing desired new behaviors outside their counseling groups. Stranahan, Schwartzman, and Atkin (1957) found that those who profited most from their group treatment had some capacity for insight, a degree of flexibility, a desire for growth, and some wholesome experiences early in life with an authority figure who possessed some measure of steadiness, helpfulness, direction, and maturity. Allport (1960) decided that ability to become ego-involved is an essential characteristic of any good group member. Such a member is able to invest in helping others and to reap satisfaction from seeing others solve their problems. Ryan (1958) reported that clients' ability to become meaningfully involved in a treatment group seems to be related to a member's ability to empathize with others, to delay gratification of one's own needs, and to derive satisfaction from helping others gratify their needs. On the other hand, Sethna and Harrington (1971) established that those who failed to disclose and to become meaningfully involved early in the life of the group tended either to lapse from treatment or to become non-participating members. Spielberger, Weitz, and Denny (1962) decided that those who profited most from group counseling had the personality characteristics which enabled them to participate fully (and possessed the commitment to attend counseling sessions regularly). Lindt (1958) found that those who were helped were able to make an emotional investment in helping at least one other client. Finally, the author has found that those who are able to define precise behavioral goals are most apt to be helped (and those who cannot or will not do so are most apt to become resisting clients). Bach (1954) questioned the wisdom of including the decidedly resisting types of client: the culturally deviant, the chronic monopolist, and the impulsive.

Possibly most of those characteristics which McClelland (1971) discovered that differentiate achievers from others also describe good bets for counseling: (1) they are challenged by the opportunity for growth and are willing to work hard to achieve some clear goals; (2) they prefer to work at a problem rather than to leave the outcome to chance or to others; (3) they require clear goals and criteria for growth in order to use their feedback to assess their own growth; and (4) they habitually spend time thinking about doing things better.

Many clients who at first appear to be poor bets (and have not volunteered) can become good treatment risks when the treatment is described for them; their questions about it are answered; they are encouraged to explore alternative sources for help; they are permitted to decide for themselves whether to participate; and they accept the responsibility for convincing themselves and their counselor that they can discuss their problems openly, define precise behavioral goals, and encourage fellow clients to learn desired new behaviors. Perhaps even the reluctant client, including the resisting type, can be helped when he or she is included in a group in which most clients are strong enough to prevent her from interfering with the development of (or from destroying) therapeutic group norms. If, however, she is to profit from counseling she must not be forced to participate.

## The Presentation

The presentation is a description of the treatment process for prospective group counseling clients. It also includes a discussion of what is expected of clients and what they can expect from their counselor and from fellow clients and of examples of the kinds of concerns that similar clients commonly discuss, of previous clients' goals, and of how previous clients were helped. For example, a counselor began his presentation to a college freshmen psychology class as follows:

> Students like you join a counseling group to discuss with peers the problems that really worry and upset them. They soon discover that a counseling group is a safe place in which to talk about anybody or any topic that worries them. They learn to share with fellow clients how they really feel, to decide precisely what new behaviors they want to implement, to listen to others, and to help them learn the new behaviors they require to cope with life more effectively. They also learn that when the problem involves conflict with someone the purpose of the discussion is not to determine who is at fault, but to discover what the problem is, what new behaviors must be learned to solve it, whose cooperation is required to solve it, how that cooperation can be elicited, and if it cannot be obtained how the problem can be solved without it.

Included among the expectations is a description of the intake interview.[6] Its purpose and how it is scheduled is discussed at the end of the presentation, after prospective clients' questions have been answered.

Though the presentation is designed to provide prospective clients with the information they require to decide whether to volunteer for a counseling group, it also achieves several additional purposes: (1) It encourages clients to accept responsibility for getting themselves ready to talk openly about their problems and for learning precise new behaviors; (2) It helps ensure truth in packaging for the services; and (3) To the degree that the presenting counselor is able to answer prospective clients' questions nondefensively, to give examples of meaningful problems that similar clients have discussed in groups, and to include some examples of problems of prestigious clients, it increases the attractiveness of group counseling.[7] Some counselors have achieved these goals with the assistance of successful former

---

[6] See the next section of this chapter for a more detailed description of this process.
[7] More will be said about this matter in Chapter 3.

clients. They make a video tape of the first session of a role-played counseling session, which the counselor plays for prospective clients. This approach enables former clients to produce on the basis of their own experiences as clients a highly realistic first session without running the risk of breaking confidences. It also provides prospective clients with a chance to quiz this particular counselor's previous clients and to obtain from them the answers to their questions.

Prospective clients' questions tend to deal with the degree of privacy in discussion topics, membership, expectations, and confidentiality. For example, "Will we feel really free to discuss anything that bothers us?" "How do we learn to do that?" "How will we behave differently in a counseling group than we do in a bull session with a group of friends . . . than participants do in an encounter or sensitivity group?" "How will you decide with whom you place me?" "How can we help others when we are upset ourselves?" "What can a counseling group do for persons like us?" "What can't or won't group counseling do for us?" "To what extent am I running a risk of being hurt in group counseling?" "Will I be permitted or encouraged to have individual counseling sessions with you between group sessions?" "How have others like us been helped?" "Where will the group meet?" "How often will it meet?" "Is attendance required?" "For how many sessions do such groups usually meet?"

When prospective clients seem to have their questions answered the counselor distributes slips of paper to everyone. Each prospective client indicates whether he wants to participate in group counseling by selecting one of these three answers: (1) yes, definitely; (2) no, not interested; or (3) maybe. In addition to his name, where he can be reached most easily, and the extent of his interest in participation, each also records: (1) the best meeting times for him; (2) with whom would he like to be placed for group counseling; and (3) with whom he would prefer not to be placed.

Those who write "yes" are contacted first and scheduled for intake interviews. In the meantime some who wrote "maybe" will seek out the counselor to indicate that they are definitely interested, and consequently are scheduled for intake interviews. Of course, others will report that they are no longer interested, or at least are not interested for the present.

Presentations are made whenever counselors meet their clients. Some of a counselor's individual clients are introduced to the idea during individual counseling. Others are introduced to the idea when they are referred for counseling. Group presentations have been made in classes, churches (especially for marriage counseling and parent education groups), special group outreach meetings scheduled by community mental health staff members, special after-work meetings scheduled in industrial plants, and special meetings called for this particular purpose for persons in mental hospitals and prisons. When such presentations are first proposed for inmates of mental hospitals and prisons, some staff members tend to be threatened by the idea until they can observe how it is done and discuss why it works.

## The Intake Interview

In this example, the individual intake interview occurred a few days after the counselor had made a presentation to a group of eleventh graders. The counselor reviewed the highlights of his presentation and structured for the intake interview as follows:

> When I visited your class I described what goes on in a counseling group, gave you a number of examples of what students your age talk about in counseling groups, reviewed how they were helped, and answered your questions. I also indicated that I schedule these intake interviews to give you a chance to practice talking about what worries and upsets you, to help you decide precisely how you would like to change your behavior [goals for counseling], and to help you decide precisely how you will be able to recognize when you have achieved your goals for counseling [criteria for evaluating personal growth]. Although I try very hard to help everyone who requests counseling, I accept for group counseling only those who can convince themselves and me that they are ready for group counseling—that they are committed to discuss from the beginning what really worries and upsets them, to learn desired new behaviors, and to help fellow clients learn and implement desired new behaviors. The more carefully we select clients the better are the chances that each will be helped. [Here I often give examples of who needs whom for what—both as models and as characters to role play significant others.] Tell me about you, what is worrying you right now? I will listen very carefully, guess how you feel in order to help you talk, and try to determine what you seem to be ready to deal with now.

For most this is sufficient. For those who require more help in getting started I often use one of these two approaches: (1) "Perhaps it would help if you could tell me what you wish you could share with me and what is keeping you from doing it"; or (2) "Close your eyes, think about your earliest memories that you can visualize vividly, and tell me about them."

Besides clarifying clients' expectations the counselor uses the intake interview to help each prospective client assess his commitment to talk openly about his problems and to implement desired new behaviors, define specific goals (and criteria to appraise his own growth with reference to each), identify those significant others whose assistance and reinforcement would enhance his chances for success, and decide how their assistance may be elicited. A few must be re-interviewed to help them define more precise behavioral goals or develop the courage to make a commitment to speak first at the first meeting of the group and to begin their discussion with their most difficult problems. Obviously, such interviews take considerable time (30–60 minutes), but they are worth it. Consequently, even before clients join these counseling groups they are motivated to talk openly at a productive level and to accept considerable responsibility for helping to develop therapeutic norms and to enhance and maintain their own personal growth.

For those prospective clients who are not ready for group counseling, the counselor may help them decide whether it would be a good future source for assistance, and if so, what they may do to get themselves ready for a future group. When they decide that group counseling does not show promise as a source of help for them, he helps them look at other sources for assistance. Thus, he exhibits genuine caring for them and helps them learn to accept responsibility for their growth.

## Structuring

The purpose of structuring is to provide a framework within which clients can learn their desired new behaviors, develop therapeutic group norms, make input into their group, revise the structure when desirable, and use it to enhance their own growth. With the preparation used in this treatment model most clients realize before the first counseling session how therapeutic talk differs from social conversations and classroom discussions, and how expectations in group counseling differ from those of other groups. Each learns that he must accept responsibility for developing trust and for preventing those situations in his group in which members may be tempted to break confidence. From the very beginning of the first session good client and helping behaviors are recognized and reinforced. Thus, clients learn quickly to discuss genuine feelings openly and to accept them. Gradually they also learn to manage and enjoy them.

Some school counselors have failed to differentiate clearly between the teacher's function and the counselor's function in a group. In these schools counselors must communicate these differences, and, more importantly, exhibit these differences in their daily relationships with clients. The real structuring is done by the way the counselor lives his professional role and responds to his clients' behavior—knowingly encouraging certain behaviors and discouraging others. The way in which a counselor participates and encourages clients to participate, especially during early sessions, affects the amount and the nature of clients' participation throughout the life of the group (Psathas, 1960).

The more deep and meaningful group relationships clients have had and the safer they feel with their counselor the easier the structuring will be. Similar previous experiences provide a base from which the counselor can generalize and differentiate to convey the unique nature of clients' expectations and responsibilities in group counseling. Even within the best working climate the counselor must be sensitive to detect and clarify inaccurate communications—to ensure that his intentions are imparted in understandable language, taking cognizance of his clients' maturity and cultural, ethnic, and racial backgrounds. Nevertheless, clients may understand their stated responsibilities and limits, but have difficulty accepting them genuinely. For these clients he must be able to detect such feelings, reflect them accurately, and help them explore whether they are committed to implement the essential norms for their own growth.

The primary structuring for this group counseling approach is done during the presentation. Expectations are further clarified during the intake interview. From time to time the need for further structuring occurs whenever clients are either not certain what is expected or sense the need for new operating guidelines. Though it is appropriate for the counselor to describe the conditions under which he has been best able to help clients within a group setting, he also should encourage clients to define those guidelines that they feel they need. Effective structuring contributes to the therapeutic climate; overstructuring and rigid rules interfere with it.

## Selecting Clients for a Group

A counselor should be allowed to select only those clients who he feels reasonably certain can be helped by his methods within his setting. Rather than sit back and wait for clients to seek assistance or be referred, Wattenburg (1953) encourages school counselors to describe for teachers and administrators (and the writer does it for clients too) who can be most readily helped by counseling. In other words, Wattenburg believes that counselors should know whom they can help and should solicit the assistance of relevant persons in attracting such clients. When, on the other hand, poor bets are referred he believes that the counselor should accept them on a trial basis after communicating to the referrer why this particular client is a poor bet. When the referrer and the counselor decide cooperatively that the client cannot be helped by counseling, the counselor should help the referrer to explore other sources of assistance. Wattenburg notes that when counselors fail to follow this recommendation two harmful side effects result: (1) the counselor is discouraged with his poor results and (2) referrers tend to judge counselors' worth on the basis of their poorest treatment risks.

The methods described in the two previous sections tend to attract good bets for successful treatment. The literature reviewed in the section "Who Profits Most from Group Counseling" suggests that the counselor ask himself the following questions in selecting each prospective client for a group and in deciding to what group each should be assigned (and preferably these decisions should be made with the assistance of a trusted colleague): Is he able to talk openly about what worries and upsets him? Is he willing to do so in a group? Has he defined some specific new behaviors he is committed to learn and implement in daily living outside his counseling group, and is he committed to help his fellow clients to do the same? Is he committed to attend counseling sessions regularly and to work on his problems? Does he understand and accept his responsibilities for helping to develop and to maintain therapeutic group norms? Has he developed criteria for each of his goals that are precise enough to enable him to appraise his own progress during treatment? Does he seem to be the type of person who has the courage to take the risks required to implement desired new behaviors? Is he capable of becoming ego-involved in helping fellow clients? Can he delay gratification of his immediate personal needs in order to help others? Can he reap satisfaction from observing others achieve their goals? Is he challenged by his problems and is he willing to work hard to solve them? Does he prefer to work out his own solutions rather than let others solve them for him? Who needs whom for what?

Of all those criterion questions listed above perhaps the most important criteria pertain to clients' commitment to discuss their problems openly beginning with the first session, to define specific behavioral goals, and to implement desired new behaviors. They also must be able to become involved in helping fellow clients and possess the courage to expect fellow clients to implement their own desired new behaviors.

From their review of the literature Peck and Stewart (1964) concluded that most therapists who provide group play therapy preferred homogeneity with reference to sex and age; 76 percent considered intellectual level important, but less than 50 percent considered religion or socioeconomic status important. Except for extremely withdrawn children—who they concluded should be treated by themselves—most therapists preferred heterogeneity with reference to personality or diagnostic types. Bach (1954) argued for heterogeneous personality types on the grounds that they provide patients with the opportunity to learn to relate to and to aid persons different from themselves. Freedman and Sweet (1954) found that when they chose patients who were homogeneous in diagnosis they tended to reinforce each other's defenses. For example, in the school setting a counselor can counteract this problem by placing gifted underachievers in groups with peers whom they admire, who are searching for ways to improve their academic performance and who are highly motivated to adjust to their situation rather than to rebel against it; or by placing young drug addicts with attractive peers who can experience peak moments without drugs; or depressed persons with their spouses for group counseling. In the latter instance the spouse discovers how he or she contributes to the depression, and what he or she can do to help the spouse cope with depression and reinforce the desired new behaviors.

On the other hand, clients can be assigned to groups with persons who have common problems. Clients can sense genuine affiliation feelings when they have assigned a problem the same name and still have very different underlying causes for it or its diagnosis. Observing others openly discuss similar problems, fellow clients' efforts to empathize, and fellow clients' encouraging those who implement new behaviors motivates even the one who is holding back, trying to decide whether to disclose and to learn new behaviors. Recognizing and reflecting affiliation feelings is highly therapeutic counselor behavior (Powdermaker & Frank, 1953). Discovering other clients with problems to which they have assigned the same name tends to make all clients feel that they belong and that they are understood, but it is especially potent for adolescents.

Most counselors prefer to counsel in a group of clients of approximately the same age, but the crucial factor is social maturity rather than chronological age. Even for his adult therapy groups Bach (1954) selected patients with similar problems as well as similar social maturity:

> For example, with respect to age and maturity, we find it necessary to exclude very young with little sexual and social experience from more experienced adult groups. While we definitely like to mix married and unmarried members in the same group, we see to it that we have at least two of each category in the same group. In general, we limit excessive heterogeneity by trying to place a patient in a group when he can find at least one other patient in circumstances which are similar with respect to some other central phase of his own life (p. 26).

Ginott (1961) reported that the prevailing practice in clinics is to separate boys and girls for treatment during the latency period. Ohlsen and Gazda (1965) noted that in their fifth grade groups girls were more mature, showed more interest in boys than boys did in girls, tended to handle topics related to sex better than boys, were more verbal, and tended to dominate the discussion. Consequently, Gazda tended to prefer to separate boys and girls at this age while Ohlsen preferred to treat them together. Although there are difficulties in treating them together, perhaps the counseling group is one of the better places in which to help them face and deal with their differing rates of sociosexual development. Moreover, most counselors agree that for adolescents both sexes should be treated within the same group. Whereas adolescents tend to be very sensitive to opposite sex peers' evaluations of them and have a very strong need to prove themselves (Ackerman, 1955), they want very much to learn to relate to the opposite sex. They also learn quickly to discuss their sociosexual development problems frankly and to practice skills required to help each other in role-played scenes, with less need to use language that they think may be offensive to the counselor and/or to some fellow clients, than when they are assigned to groups composed of only boys or girls.

Bach found that the less educated and less intelligent adults tend to feel out of place and reluctant to participate with persons much brighter and better educated. Perhaps those who work with children having a wide range of verbal fluency should take cognizance of Bach's recommendation of some homogeneity concerning verbal fluency. When most clients have better verbal fluency than a given client, they tend to talk over his head. When, on the other hand, a client talks down to the rest of the group, he often rejects, and in turn is rejected by, his fellow clients. Granted that a client's ability to profit from counseling is determined in part by his communication skills. Nevertheless, persons with a wide range of verbal fluency can learn to communicate, and the group can be the source of motivation for improving communication skills. Furthermore, bright adolescents who want to become leaders must learn to communicate with a wide range of persons, and a counseling group can be a place in which they begin this process.

For those who use the methods endorsed here, prospective clients are the primary source of data. Though the elaborate type of diagnostic testing used by Bach is rarely required by those who counsel normal clients, there are occasions when a counselor may wish to supplement the intake interview with other sources of data (and of course only with a prospective client's permission): the cumulative folder and case conference (Ohlsen, 1974) and interviews with teachers, relatives, friends, or employers. From such data a counselor can learn what primary roles the prospective client plays in various settings, the ways he attempts to solve his problems, the way he relates to his significant others, and significant others' perceptions of his problems.

Once a counselor has the essential data, he selects from his pool of clients the best possible combination for each group. Best results tend to be obtained when several counselors assist each other in selecting clients and supervise each other during counseling (especially for their first several groups).

## Group Size

Loeser (1957) concluded that four to eight clients are ideal for group counseling and group therapy, and that such a size is the largest that can function without a leader and some strong rules. As groups increase in size above this, transference tends to become weaker and weaker until members have little meaningful, involved relationships with each other; the group tends to function as a collection of subgroups; members tend to develop meaningful relationships only with the leader, speaker, or performer; and members tend to function like a class with increasing dependence on the leader. The extent to which the leader is able to establish meaningful relationships with members determines the degree to which he can arouse emotion for action or quiet unrest.

Psathas's (1960) review of the literature also indicated that with increased group size, members experience less direct involvement and participation. Instead of interacting with each other they tend as the group gets larger to direct their communications to the highest-ranking initiator, who in turn responds to them as a group rather than as individuals. Most communications in larger groups flow through a selected or appointed leader.

When making a decision on group size, a counselor must consider clients' maturity, attention span, and ability to invest in others. Each client must feel that he is allocated adequate time during each session, that he does not have to wait too long to get the floor, and that the group is small enough for him to get to know the other clients and for them to know him. Those who counsel children in groups tend to schedule shorter sessions for smaller groups and to meet with them more frequently than those who counsel adolescents and adults. Usually adolescents are counseled in groups of six to eight. In order for clients to function effectively, a client must be able to capture others' attention, to feel safe, to interact meaningfully with others, and to give, solicit, and accept feedback.

## Group Setting

Effective group counseling can be provided with minimal space and equipment: adequate space for a circle of nine chairs in a room in which clients can speak freely without being overheard. An attractive, spacious, well-equipped group room indicates institutional support for the service (and a successful practice for the private practitioner). Furthermore, a carpeted floor encourages clients to move back their chairs and to sit on the floor when they feel that it is appropriate. A more spacious room is essential for those who use play techniques, informal exercises (such as trust walk), dance, music, and role playing (Chapter 7) as a basic part of their treatment process (Ohlsen, 1973). Regular audio recordings are essential in order to enable clients to review what happened in any given session, to criticize a proposal or role-played action, and to help an individual, including the counselor, to appraise his impact on others. Video recordings are even better for these purposes; often they are essential in order to help a member recognize his own unproductive behavior and unverbalized needs. Increasingly counselors are learning to use video recordings to solicit feedback from their clients. Even young children can review a video tape and react to the following directions: (1) watch for specific instances in which you were helped or hurt; (2) for each indicate whether you were helped or hurt; and (3) watch for and tell us what helped or hurt you.

## Beginning the First Session

Clients come to the first counseling session expecting to talk openly about what worries and upsets them and to explain to fellow clients precisely how they plan to change their behavior. Those who may otherwise be inclined to speak last are prepared by the intake interview to speak first and to begin with those problems that they think may be most difficult to discuss. For this courageous behavior they are reinforced by the counselor and fellow clients.

As a consequence they tend to be pleased with their behavior, to feel that they have passed their most difficult test within their group, to conclude that they can cope with their problems, and to sense fellow clients' genuine acceptance of them. They recognize that their openness and courage helps others too.

Early in the first session the counselor comments very briefly on the importance of everyone being given a chance to talk about his problems and goals. Usually he also asks his clients to help him manage the use of time in order to give everyone a chance to talk, and finally to agree on operation guidelines. After each has discussed his major concerns and described his desired new behaviors, clients are encouraged to ask any questions they may have concerning expectations and to agree on any essential operation guidelines. Most groups develop some agreements on confidentiality, meeting time, attendance, approximate number of meetings, scheduling of individual sessions, and termination. Whenever the counselor notices, especially during the first several sessions, a client functioning especially well as a client or helper, he reinforces it by calling attention to the productive behavior. Some counselors even make video recordings of early sessions and criticize them, looking for specific instances in which individuals were good clients or good helpers. When the need for a new operating guideline surfaces the counselor reflects the need for it and helps the clients define it. When they have a guideline but seem to be waiting for him to enforce it the counselor tries to help them detect and accept their responsibility for maintaining their own guidelines: for example, "You seem to be annoyed with Jack's walking around the room when you'd like him to listen. I guess you wish I'd make him sit down and help Jane decide what she would like to tell her teacher." Thus, the counselor conveys to clients that they must accept responsibility for maintaining a working atmosphere which enhances their chances for being helped.

## Summary

Group counseling is a special relationship in which clients feel safe to discuss what really worries and upsets them, to define desired new behaviors, to practice essential interpersonal skills, and to implement new behaviors. Precisely how it differs from other group relationships and why each must demonstrate commitment to change and to help others change are discussed in this chapter.

Besides reviewing characteristics of those who tend to profit from group counseling, the chapter stresses why good prognosis for treatment is not sufficient. Clients must convince themselves as well as the counselor that they are ready for group counseling and committed to help develop and maintain the necessary and sufficient conditions for client growth.

Prior to being asked to decide whether they wish to participate in group counseling, a presentation is made to convey what clients can expect, what will be expected from them, and how they may be helped. The presentation also encourages clients to accept responsibility for getting themselves ready for group counseling and for defining behavioral goals and criteria that they can use to appraise their own growth. In addition, it tends to make the group experience more attractive. It is followed by an intake interview in which each prospective client is helped to define behavioral goals and criteria for appraising his own growth, to assess his readiness for counseling, and to clarify expectations.

The primary structuring for group counseling is done in the presentation and the intake interview prior to the first counseling session. Further structuring occurs whenever clients are either uncertain what is expected or sense the need for new operational guidelines. Nevertheless, verbal structuring alone does not convey what is really expected. At least the counselor's expectations also are communicated by the way he behaves in the counseling group—knowingly encouraging certain behaviors and discouraging others.

## Discussion Questions

1. What criteria would you use to screen clients for group counseling? Defend each. Include in your defense what each criterion contributes to the development of a therapeutic group and the readiness of the client for change.
2. What are the counselor's facilitative behaviors that contribute most to clients' growth?
3. How can a counselor determine when adequate structure has been provided for a group?
4. How does group counseling differ from individual counseling? . . . from effective classroom discussions? . . . from encounter-group experiences?
5. To what extent and in what ways may precise behavioral goals for clients enhance clients' open discussions?
6. Why should a counselor encourage simultaneous treatment of several clients by the group rather than counseling one individual at a time in the presence of others?
7. What are affiliation responses? For what purposes may they be used in a counseling group?
8. How may a counselor help clients recognize therapeutic material and use it in the group?
9. How does reflection differ from confrontation? . . . from interpretation? . . . from a request for information? . . . from inferred advice? What makes reflection more productive than any of the others?
10. How may a counselor differentiate in a counseling group between therapeutic interaction and mere talking?

# References

Ackerman, N. W. Group psychotherapy with a mixed group of adolescents. *International Journal of Group Psychotherapy,* 1955, *5,* 249–260.

Adler, K. Techniques that shorten psychotherapy illustrated with five cases. *Journal of Individual Psychology,* 1972, *28,* 155–168.

Allport, G. W. *Personality and social encounter.* Boston: Beacon Press, 1960.

Ansbacher, H. Adlerian psychology: The tradition of brief psychotherapy. *Journal of Individual Psychology,* 1972, *28,* 137–151.

Alexander, F., & French, T. M., *Psychoanalytic therapy.* New York: Ronald, 1946.

Bach, G. R. *Intensive group psychotherapy.* New York: Ronald, 1954.

Barten, H. H. *Brief therapies.* New York: Behavioral Publications, 1971.

Beck, D. F. The dynamics of group psychotherapy as seen by a sociologist. *Sociometry,* 1958, *21,* 98–128, 180–197.

Bellak, L., & Small, L. *Emergency psychotherapy and brief psychotherapy.* New York: Grune & Stratton, 1965.

Buda, B. Utilization of resistance and paradox communication in short-term psychotherapy. *Psychotherapy and Psychosomatics,* 1972, *20,* 210–211.

Carney, F. J. Evaluation of psychotherapy in maximum security prison. *Seminars in Psychiatry,* 1971, *3,* 363–375.

DeEsch, J. B. *The use of the Ohlsen model of group counseling with secondary school students identified as being disruptive to the education process.* Doctoral dissertation, Indiana State University, 1974.

Dougherty, A. M. *A study of the effects of two types of interpretation on subjects of different personality types from two education levels.* Unpublished doctoral dissertation, Indiana State University, 1974.

Durkin, H. E. *The group in depth.* New York: International Universities, 1964.

Erikson, E. H. *Childhood and society.* New York: Norton, 1953.

Ewing, T. N., & Gilbert, W. M. Controlled study of the effects of counseling on scholastic achievements of students of superior ability. *Journal of Counseling Psychology,* 1967, *14,* 235–239.

Frank, J. D. Group methods in psychotherapy. *Journal of Social Issues,* 1952, *8,* 35–44.

Freedman, M. D., & Sweet, B. S. Some specific features of group psychotherapy and their implications for selection of patients. *International Journal of Group Psychotherapy,* 1954, *4,* 355–368.

Gazda, G. M. Group procedures with children: A developmental approach. In M. M. Ohlsen (Ed.), *Counseling children in groups: A forum.* New York: Holt, Rinehart and Winston, 1973.

Ginott, H. G. *Group psychotherapy with children.* New York: McGraw-Hill, 1961.

Godbole, A., & Falk, M. Confrontation-problem solving therapy in the treatment of confusional and delirious states. *Gerontologist,* 1972, *12,* 151–154.

Helner, P. A. *The effects of the use of interpretation as a counseling technique.* Unpublished doctoral dissertation, Indiana State University, 1972.

Hilkey, J. H. *The effects of video-tape pretraining and guided performance on the process and outcomes of group counseling.* Unpublished doctoral dissertation, Indiana State University, 1975.

Hobbs, N. Sources of gain in psychotherapy. *American Psychologist,* 1962, *17,* 741–747.

Holmes, D. J. *The adolescent in psychotherapy.* Boston: Little, Brown, 1964.

Joel, W., & Shapiro, D. Some principles and procedures for group psychotherapy. *Journal of Psychology,* 1950, *29,* 77–88.

Johnson, J. A. *Group therapy: A practical approach.* New York: McGraw-Hill, 1963.

Katz, E. W., Ohlsen, M. M., & Proff, F. C. An analysis through use of kinescopes of the interpersonal behavior of adolescents in group counseling. *Journal of College Student Personnel,* 1959, *1,* 2–10.

Lewis, W. A. Emotional adjustment and need satisfaction of hospital patients. *Journal of Counseling Psychology,* 1959, *6,* 127–131.

Lieberman, M. A., Yalom, I. D., & Miles, M. D. *Encounter groups: First facts.* New York: Basic Books, 1973.

Lindt, H. The nature of therapeutic interaction of patients in groups. *International Journal of Group Psychotherapy,* 1958, *8,* 55–69.

Loeser, L. H. Some aspects of group dynamics. *International Journal of Group Psychotherapy,* 1957, *7,* 5–19.

Mann, J. *Time-limited psychotherapy.* Cambridge, Mass.: Harvard University Press, 1973.

McClelland, D. C. That urge to achieve. In D. A. Kalb, I. M. Rubin, & J. M. McIntyre, (Eds.), *Organizational psychology: A book of readings.* Englewood Cliffs, N. J.: Prentice-Hall, 1971.

Mowrer, O. H. Group counseling in the elementary school: The professional vs. the peer model. In M. M. Ohlsen (Ed.), *Counseling children in groups: A forum.* New York: Holt, Rinehart and Winston, 1973.

Ohlsen, M. M. (Ed.), *Counseling children in groups: A forum.* New York: Holt, Rinehart and Winston, 1973.

Ohlsen, M. M. *Guidance services in the modern school.* New York: Harcourt, 1974.

Ohlsen, M. M., & Gazda, G. M. Counseling underachieving bright pupils. *Education,* 1965, *86,* 78–81.

Ohlsen, M. M., & Oelke, M. C. An evaluation of discussion topics in group counseling. *Journal of Clinical Psychology,* 1962, *18,* 317–322.

Oxley, G. Short-term therapy with student couples. *Social Casework,* 1973, *54,* 216–233.

Peck, M. L., & Stewart, R. H. Current practices in selection criteria for group-play therapy. *Journal of Clinical Psychology,* 1964, *20,* 146.

Phillips, E. L., & Wierner, D. N. *Short-term psychotherapy and behavior change.* New York: McGraw-Hill, 1966.

Powdermaker, F. B., & Frank, J. D. *Group psychotherapy.* Cambridge, Mass.: Harvard University Press, 1953.

Psathas, G. Phase, movement and equilibrium tendencies in interaction process in psychotherapy groups. *Sociometry,* 1960, *23,* 177–194.

Reid, W. J., & Shyne, A. W. *Brief and extended casework.* New York: Columbia University Press, 1969.

Rhodes, S. L. Short-term groups of latency age children in a school setting. *International Journal of Group Psychotherapy,* 1973, *23,* 204–216.

Rickard, H. C. Tailored criteria of change in psychotherapy. *Journal of General Psychology*, 1965, *72*, 63–68.

Ryan, W. Capacity for mutual dependencies and involvement in group psychotherapy. *Dissertation Abstracts*, 1958, *19*, 1119.

Schafer, R. The termination of brief psychoanalytic psychotherapy. *International Journal of Psychoanalytic Psychotherapy*, 1973, *2*, 135–148.

Sethna, E. R., & Harrington, J. A. A study of patients who lapsed from group psychotherapy. *British Journal of Psychiatry*, 1971, *119*, 59–69.

Sifneos, P. E. *Short-term psychotherapy and emotional crises.* Cambridge, Mass. Harvard University Press, 1972.

Spielberger, C. O., Weitz, H. & Denny, J. P. Group counseling and academic performance of anxious freshmen. *Journal of Counseling Psychology*, 1962, *9*, 195–204.

Stewart, H. Six months, fixed-term, once weekly psychotherapy: A report on twenty follow-ups. *British Journal of Psychiatry*, 1972, *121*, 425–435.

Stranahan, M., Schwartzman, C., & Atkin, E. Group treatment for emotionally disturbed and potentially delinquent boys and girls. *American Journal of Orthopsychiatry*, 1957, *27*, 518–527.

Szasz, T. S. *Age of madness.* New York: Doubleday, 1973.

Talland, G. A., & Clark, D. H. Evaluation of topics in a therapy group discussion. *Journal of Clinical Psychology*, 1954, *10*, 131–137.

Taylor, H. E. *A study of a comparison of reactions to four types of counselor response on the dimension of the locus of responsibility.* Unpublished doctoral dissertation, Indiana State University, 1974.

Thomas, M. R. An investigation of two different processes in short-term psychotherapy. *Dissertation Abstracts*, 1973, *33*, 5527.

Torre, J. De La. The therapist tells a story: A technique in brief therapy. *Menninger Clinic Bulletin*, 1972, *36*, 609–616.

Wattenburg, W. W. Who needs counseling? *Personnel Guidance Journal*, 1953, *32*, 202–205.

Wolberg, L. R. *Short-term psychotherapy.* New York: Grune & Stratton, 1965.

# 2

# The Counselor

The counselor is an approachable, committed person who has mastered essential helping skills. Those who train professional group counselors face common problems with those who prepare other professionals: (1) helping to develop primary professional affiliations; (2) defining the treatment processes; (3) determining precisely what facilitative skills a helper must possess in order to provide each of his services; (4) deciding how to organize these skills and knowledges into instructional units; (5) selecting good prospects for professional preparation; (6) developing a plan for periodic appraisal of the program; and (7) developing some means for encouraging continuing growth following graduation from the program. Good professional preparation enhances both an individual's personal and professional development.

## Professional Affiliation

Members' services and the conditions under which those services can best be provided are defined by a profession. Entry to a profession is usually controlled by the profession, and is based upon a common body of professional knowledge and skills specified by a commission named by the leaders in the profession. Therefore professional schools and colleges must try to admit to the program only those who would profit from professional preparation and qualify for a license upon completion of the program.

Standards of professional performance are also determined by the profession. Therefore only a qualified member can evaluate a practitioner's performance for salary increases, promotions, or tenure. For many school counselors this has been a problem because educators who are not qualified as counselors have been allowed to define their responsibilities and evaluate their performance. Consequently, other professionals question the professional status of such counselors.

Those who provide leadership for various group procedures have a similar problem in community agencies. Persons from other disciplines (and sometimes without adequate professional preparation) present themselves as qualified to lead various types of personal growth groups. Usually, the unqualified, irresponsible leaders do not belong to any professional organization. Consequently, no professional group tends to accept responsibility for screening, for licensing, or for appraising the quality of these unqualified leaders' services, or for ensuring that they function ethically.[1] When there is no one to protect the clients' welfare the odds are greatest that clients will be hurt rather than helped.

Participants have criticized incompetent leaders for attacking and confronting and for encouraging members to attack and confront each other; for forcing them to reveal hurtful material; for not being able to help them deal with hurtful material after they have exposed it; and for pressuring them to deviate from their personal moral code.

Although they were not discussing unethical and unqualified leaders, Lieberman, Yalom, and Miles's (1973) interviews with casualties revealed that the leaders of groups in which clients were frequently hurt shared several common characteristics:

> An unwavering faith in themselves, their product, and their technique, a sense of impatience—changes must be made now—a tendency to impose their values on their subjects, a failure to recognize signals that vital defenses are prematurely crumbling, and a failure to differentiate between individuals; they operated as though all individuals needed to make the same changes (p. 436).

Professional leaders have criticized irresponsible leaders for failures, which must be questioned from the point of view of ethics: (1) to screen participants; (2) to help prospective members define specific, behavioral goals; (3) to help participants generalize from what they learned in groups and apply it in their daily lives rather than return repeatedly to groups for peak experiences; and (4) to evaluate systematically the worth of their services.

Fortunately, a number of professional organizations have developed ethical guidelines for group procedures to protect the public, to com-

---

[1] Rather than to devote one section to leaders' ethics this topic is discussed throughout the book.

municate that there are competent professionals doing group work, and to offer support for their qualified leaders of groups: American Group Psychotherapy Association, American Personnel and Guidance Association, International Association of Applied Social Psychologists, Inc., National Training Laboratories, and University and College Counseling Center Directors. Eventually each relevant professional organization must answer the following questions for its members (Ohlsen, 1975):

1. For which of the group procedures does its organization have something to offer professionals?
2. For whom will it assume primary and/or shared responsibility?
3. Who can be served best by each technique, with whom, and under what conditions? How does the treatment differ from other accepted group techniques?
4. What competencies must a person possess to lead each type of group for which it assumes responsibility? What criteria may it use to appraise a leader's performance during treatment and the worth of the service following treatment? What criteria may it use to accredit and/or endorse institutions for professional preparation?
5. How may one differentiate between a leader's ethical and unethical behaviors?
6. What can it do to encourage practitioners to evaluate their services, to experiment with and adequately evaluate new procedures, and to stimulate professional growth on the job?
7. What legislations must it initiate to ensure that only qualified persons are licensed or certified?
8. What provisions has it made for identifying, investigating, and disciplining unethical behavior?

Professional counselors are usually members of either the American Personnel and Guidance Association or the American Psychological Association. Increasing numbers of those counselors who do group counseling are also members of the American Group Psychotherapy Association.

## Professional Services and Competence

Prior to the development of a professional organization most professions have defined their professional services and qualifications for membership. Periodically they review and revise these, and where appropriate decide which phases of their work they can assign to paraprofessionals who work under their supervision. Increasingly, designated members of the profession are selected to do a taxonomy of their professional work in order to determine what knowledge, skills, attitudes, and values are required for quality services (for example, Krathwhol, Bloom, & Masia, 1964). For determining performance requirements for competence in orthopaedic surgery, Miller, McGuire, and Larsen (1965) used the critical incident technique and endorsed it as a valid and reliable technique. This latter technique has been used successfully to screen prospective counselors (Carr, Merz, Peterson, & Thayer, 1972). It also looks promising for assessing performance requirements for counselors. Moreover, Dash (1975) notes the similarities between competency-based counselor education and the revised *Standards for the Preparation of Counselors and Other Personnel Service Specialists* of the American Personnel and Guidance Association (Aces, 1972).

Professionals who do group counseling recognize that there are a number of other effective group techniques. After the profession has defined the basic competencies for a counselor, some group must define the performance requirements for competence in each speciality—for example, group counseling. Since each group technique was designed for somewhat different purposes and consequently requires different competencies, precise endorsement requirements are essential for each. On the other hand, all leaders of groups must be able to describe the treatment process for prospective participants, the potential benefits for them, and the expectations of them so that they can decide whether or not to participate. Each leader also must believe in himself, have confidence in the technique, possess the competence required for its use, realize who profits from the technique (or may be hurt by it) with whom and under what conditions (recognize the limitations of the technique), and select only those participants who he believes can be helped by it.

Committees that develop preparation standards for a profession usually develop criteria that are used to evaluate the caliber of the faculty and students, the intellectual climate, the laboratories, the library, and the other teaching facilities of professional colleges within universities. These standards are then published by the profession for use by faculties for self-appraisal and by visiting teams that evaluate programs for accreditation.

## The Counselor's Facilitative Behaviors

The approach used by the Association for Counselor Education *Sub-Committee on Preparation of Standards for Preparation of Elementary Counselors* (ACES, 1968) may be used by a profession in determining performance requirements for those who do group counseling. They identified outstanding practitioners, involved them in identifying performance requirements, and solicited their evaluation of the components of their professional preparation. Perhaps even better results could be achieved by identifying outstanding counselors of groups, having them make video recordings of a number of groups, having them select their most successful groups, and having another group of competent counselors study the tapes with care to identify precise facilitative counselor behaviors. They also could notice how those clients who were helped least (or were hurt) were treated differently from those who were helped most.

Since the work suggested above has not been done, the writer is forced to rely on related published literature. Much of that relevant literature on the counselor's facilitative behaviors has already been reported in the first chapter. Hence, only the highlights on the counselor's facilitative behaviors are reviewed here.

**developing readiness**    The counselor: (1) communicates what will be expected of prospective clients; (2) helps them develop the expectation that they can change; (3) helps them accept their responsibility for convincing themselves that they are ready to discuss their problems openly and to learn desired new behaviors; (4) motivates them to think about their goals and the criteria they can use to appraise their progress even before they begin counseling; (5) answers clients' questions concerning expectations clearly and nondefensively; and (6) encourages them to think about what they require of others and how they may help others to encourage their mutual growth. Most of these facilitative behaviors are exhibited first in the presentation and in the intake interviews. Obviously, the counselor must be competent to do both.

**relationship building**    Merely being a decent person is not enough:

> Research into the interaction between technique and relationship variables in therapy has shown that an effective therapist must be more than a nice guy who can exude prescribed interpersonal conditions—he must have an armamentarium of scientifically derived skills and techniques to supplement his effective interpersonal relations. Deliberately excluded from the present formulation is the empathic, nonjudgmental warmth, wit and wisdom which characterize those therapists who help rather than harm their clients. If this were an article on surgical techniques and procedures, we would presuppose that individuals who apply the prescribed methods are free from pronounced tremors and possess more than a modicum of manual dexterity. Thus, it is hoped that multimodal behavioral procedures will attract nonmechanistic therapists who are flexible, empathic and genuinely concerned about the welfare of their clients (Lazarus, 1973, p. 405).

In order to develop a therapeutic relationship with a client and to enlist his assistance in developing and maintaining therapeutic norms for a group, the counselor must be able to convey that he is concerned about each client's welfare. He must select clients who are ready for counseling, exhibit confidence in each client's ability to learn, listen, detect and reflect accurately what the client is experiencing, sense when the client is threatened and enable him to discuss simultaneously his source of threat and his need for support, empathize with each client as he suffers and struggles with problem identification, goal formulation, and development of courage to act, and help each client formulate precise behavioral goals. As a client comes to feel that the counselor cares about him, seems to understand him, believes that he can be helped, and is really an expert in helping people help themselves, a counseling relationship is developed. Most clients recognize and value competent professional services from a counselor who seems to know what he is doing, is willing to answer his client's questions concerning his helping behaviors, and is able to enlist clients' genuine participation in learning to profit from the therapeutic experience.

**relationship maintenance**    Relationship maintenance requires commitment and hard work in counseling as it does in daily living. In order for a person to take the risks required to discuss his problems openly, admit where he needs help, define desired new behaviors, and implement them, he must believe that his counselor and fellow clients will keep confidences and provide essential support when he requires it. These others enhance a therapeutic relationship by empathizing with him, suffering with him, encouraging him, sensing when he needs support, and providing it (without pity and reassurances), providing genuine and considerate feedback, helping him define specific goals, helping break his goals into mini-goals, helping him implement his goals, helping him discover where he has grown and where he needs to continue grow, teaching him to share successes and enjoy others' successes, and learning to touch him helpfully. Moreover, fellow clients must be able to convey that they will stick with him and help him see it through. They must be able to help him realize that he does not have to change his entire life style—to lose his identity. Their task is to merely help him learn and implement his own desired new behaviors. They also help him realize how he can apply these new maintenance skills with significant others in his daily life. Thus, it is not sufficient for the counselor to master these facilitative behaviors; he must also teach them to clients. Perhaps the single, strongest maintenance experience for a client is to detect his own growth.

**problem identification**    Problem identification is begun when the counselor describes group counseling for prospective clients and reviews what similar clients discussed previously and how they were helped. It is continued during the intake interview and encouraged throughout the counseling process. Not only must the counselor be able to listen carefully, to detect and reflect therapeutic material, to relate the pain and unfinished business to specific behavioral goals, to decide when the client is ready to formulate goals, and to help the client define behavioral goals and criteria for appraising his own growth, he must also be able to teach clients to assist him in these tasks. The sensitivity to detect and the courage to reflect painful material are essential counselor qualities. Lazarus (1973) believes that faulty problem identification is probably the greatest impediment to successful counseling and therapy.

**definition of counseling goals**    Definition of goals is encouraged from the first contact. Though it should be conveyed as an expectation, the counselor must be very sensitive to when the client has explored a problem sufficiently to formulate treatment goals. On the other hand, when the counselor permits unnecessary suffering other clients' readiness to discuss their problems may be decreased, and when he allows a client to achieve catharsis for too long a time that client may experience sufficient relief to lose some motivation to learn new behaviors. Inasmuch as a reflection that relates a client's present suffering to a goal tends to be the better way to err, the counselor should make such a reflection when he is in doubt as to whether the client has discussed the problem sufficiently. For example, after a young woman had discussed how she had been hurt by her husband's neglect and his admission of a homosexual love affair, she cried and continued to deprecate herself. Although the counselor was uncertain whether he should encourage her to explore further her self-doubts as a worthy lover, he elected to make a goal-related reflection as follows: "Then you want to decide what you must do to make yourself more attractive to men and to talk to your husband about what your primary marriage problems are and how (or whether) you can help each other solve them." When she said that she was ready to do the former, but was not certain she could do the latter, the counselor was tempted to step aside and let her talk about her marriage failures and cry it out, but he didn't do that. Instead he said, "Perhaps we could help you get ready to face that problem now. What do you wish you could say to your husband? What do you wish you could ask him? Which male client in this group would you like to take your part while you take your husband's part first, and then take your husband's part while you take your own and role play the scenes? Which would you like to do?" At first she pulled back, but was encouraged by fellow clients, especially those who had been helped by role playing. Although such actions can be threatening, clients tend to reduce resistance and increase the will to change. Certainly, such actions are preferred to merely allowing a client to achieve catharsis or to talk about why they are afraid to do anything now.

**definition of criteria to appraise client's growth**   As each goal is defined the counselor helps the client explore how he will know when he has achieved it. As the client does this, goals are clarified and stated more clearly in behavioral terms. A client also may be encouraged by a counselor to make a written record of each goal and to record parenthetically the criteria to appraise his own progress. When these are shared with fellow clients, they usually sharpen the goal statements and improve the criteria—pushing the client to state his criteria in more precise, measurable, and objective terms.

**resistance**   A counselor must be able to detect the early signs of resistance and to teach clients to recognize and cope with it. In effective counseling groups clients also learn to detect their tendencies to interfere with their own and others' growth and to discuss their fear of change, their doubts about their ability to change, and their fears that they may be hurt without achieving their goals. When a counselor discovers clients coping with their own resistance he detects it, reinforces it, and calls it to the attention of other clients. He helps clients experience the pleasure of managing their own resistance (Chapter 6).

**countertransference**   The counselor must recognize countertransference, learn to disengage himself, reengage himself therapeutically, and examine his relationships with the transference object (preferably by analyzing a video recording of the counseling session) with the assistance of a trusted colleague or supervisor (Chapter 5).

**feedback**   The counselor must be able to teach clients to detect when they require feedback, to solicit it, to use it, and to provide it in a helpful, considerate manner for others. They also must be taught to detect and to communicate when another client requires feedback. The counselor must possess the knowledge and skills required to help his clients obtain the information they require about themselves, their opportunities, and their environments to appraise their opportunities (for example, to evaluate job offers or to compare colleges to which they have been admitted), to identify alternative choices, and to make essential decisions (he must be adept in teaching clients decision-making skills). He must be sensitive to the impact of feedback on the one for whom it is given and be quick to detect the receiver's underlying feelings, reflect them, and help him discuss his difficulties in accepting certain feedback (including what he wishes he were like, why it is important to be that way, and whether he can or is willing to learn the new behaviors to become more like his wished-for self). In order for feedback to facilitate a client's growth, the giver of feedback must be perceived by the receiver as caring about him and wanting to help him learn his desired new behaviors. The giver of feedback must be genuine, neither overpraise nor give phony praise, be considerate, be congruent and able to enhance the receiver's congruence, be sensitive to the receiver's needs, be able to detect and reflect the receiver's underlying feelings and to help the receiver discuss these underlying feelings.

**termination**   Termination is important to enhance a client's continuing growth following counseling. Whenever a client feels that he has achieved his goals or that he will not achieve them he should be encouraged to discuss termination. Whenever the counselor believes that a majority of the members have achieved their goals, that they seem to lack therapeutic discussion topics, or that they are not going to achieve their goals, he may ask questions such as: "Which of your goals have you achieved?" "What do you have left to do?" "Whose help do you require to learn and to implement your desired new behaviors?" "What assistance do you require to enlist these significant others' aid?" And for those who have achieved few, if any, of their goals, "What other sources of assistance are available to you and what must you do to obtain it?" The counselor's failure to discuss these questions can result in merely letting a group die. When groups die because of a counselor's failure to deal with resistance or to convey clients' responsibility for taking initiative to complete their unfinished business or continue longer than necessary, some of the group's positive impact is lost. Moreover, those who are not helped tend to conclude that they cannot be helped. Even those who are helped tend not to realize precisely how they were helped and how they can use what they learned to cope with other similar situations outside of counseling. Furthermore, they do not endorse group counseling for others who could profit from it.

Both the clients and the counselor profit from the feedback they obtain in answering the questions listed above. They profit from learning to express their feelings toward each other and from saying their goodbyes. Not only the clients but also the counselor should be sensitive to his own separation feelings and deal with them. Finally, systematic plans for prescribed follow-up sessions enhance continuing growth and provide essential feedback both for clients and the counselor.

Fortunately the facilitative counselor behaviors described above can be stated in behavioral terms so that an observer can determine how often each behavior is displayed, for whom it is displayed, and whether it is exhibited when it is needed most (Winborn, Hinds, & Stewart, 1971). For example, after the first group session a counselor can criticize a video tape of the session and determine precisely what he did for each client to increase readiness for growth, to enhance the therapeutic relationship, to uncover new problems, to identify new goals or clarify old ones, to clarify criteria for appraising growth, and to maintain a quality therapetuic relationship: He can, for example, ask himself, "Did anyone exhibit any concern about what was expected of him in the counseling group?" If so, precisely what did he do to clarify expectations? Better still, he can enlist the help of a trusted colleague or supervisor to observe and discuss the video tape. He also can ask his clients to criticize the tape with him and note specific instances in which: (1) he helped them, (2) he interfered with their talking about their problems openly or with their learning new behaviors, (3) he hurt them, or (4) he missed an opportunity to help them. With a carefully prepared check list of facilitative counselor behavior, even upper-grade elementary school children can provide even more useful feedback to counselors.

## Professional Preparation

Professional preparation is designed to enable those who do group counseling to master essential professional knowledge and facilitative behaviors. The revised *Standards for the Preparation of Counselors and Other Personnel Service Specialists* (ACES, 1972) are concerned with the philosophy and objectives of a program, the way in which a program should be developed, its staff competencies, the quality of instruction, its program of studies, its supervised experiences, and the methods used by the staff to select, retain, endorse, and place students. The minimum one-year graduate program includes philosophy and principles of guidance, use of appraisal and measurement techniques, statistics and research methods (including data-processing and computer-programming techniques), career development, counseling theory and practice, group guidance procedures, professional relationships and ethics, coordination and administration of guidance services, and supervised experiences in all essential components of the counselor's work. Most professional organizations now endorse a minimum two-year graduate program for counselors. Usually it includes some preparation in group counseling techniques. For carefully screened, practicing counselors who had completed at least the minimum one-year graduate program and were endorsed by their counseling practicum supervisor Ohlsen (1975) describes a twelve-semester-hour program which has been designed to prepare successful practicing counselors to do group counseling: (1) group dynamics laboratory— 3 semester hours, (2) group counseling—3 semester hours, and (3) group counseling practicum—6 semester hours. The fourth component was participation as a client in a counseling group.

**client experience in a group**    Enrollees select their counselor from those available each term, schedule their intake interview, and demonstrate their readiness for group counseling. In other words, procedures described in Chapter 1 are followed. Perhaps the counselors devote a more than usual amount of attention to the extent of the client's interest in having experience as a client, its potential benefits for him, and his commitment to talk openly about what really bothers him.

**group dynamics laboratory**    Group dynamics laboratory is designed to increase enrollees' sensitivity and improve their interpersonal skills. Intensive small group experiences, including an off-campus weekend retreat, are supplemented by skill-building activities to promote increased knowledge of group dynamics theory and to encourage enrollees to explore the relevance of their knowledge for their personal as well as their professional lives.

**group counseling**    The group-counseling course includes considerable reading in the professional journals as well as in texts. This text covers the basic topics of the course. Class discussions focus on clarifying and implementing ideas. Case materials, recordings, and demonstrations are often used.

**practicum**    Each enrollee describes group counseling for prospective clients, conducts his intake interviews, and selects the best combination of clients for two counseling groups with the assistance of his supervisor and playback partner (a fellow enrollee selected by him). Besides weekly supervision (twice weekly during a summer session) by both his supervisor and playback partner he is supervised at least twice during the term by guest supervisors. Moreover, every enrollee is expected to come to practicum prepared to present a critique of a recorded session and solicit feedback on particular parts of that session. Although audio recordings are usually used for supervision, enrollees are expected to submit periodically a video recording of their counseling sessions.

For the above program (designed for successful, practicing counselors) a follow-up evaluation was developed to solicit trainees' appraisal of each component of the program. Their responses clearly indicated that the program improved their counseling skills and personal adjustment (Ohlsen, 1975).

Most graduate professional programs appraise enrollees' mastery of professional knowledge. It is more difficult to evaluate their mastery of helping skills. It is even more difficult to evaluate the extent to which enrollees implement their new professional knowledge and skills. Nevertheless, those who prepare counselors must assess the impact of their programs on enrollee's attitudes, values, professional skills, and on their commitment to implement their new knowledge and skills on the job. An adequate evaluation of counselors' preparation includes periodic appraisal of knowledge and skills by carefully constructed achievement and performance tests during preparation; periodic interviews with enrollees during preparation to appraise their progress, to identify problems with which they would like assistance, and to help them identify resources for assistance; end-of-preparation appraisal to evaluate adequacy of various components of the program, working relationships, teaching materials, facilities, and the degree to which program objectives were achieved; and follow-up visits to each enrollee's place of employment. Perhaps the follow-up visit is the most important of all. It provides feedback on the value of specific components of the training from a practitioner. Furthermore, when counselors know that they are going to be visited on the job they tend to be more highly motivated to implement their new helping skills and to be more innovative—knowing that they can count on support and consultant help from the follow-up visitor.

Finally, there can be no substitute for staff members in counselor preparation programs who are enthusiastic about their profession, who possess good helping skills and keep up to date, who can teach, who are allocated adequate time to supervise, who have the knowledge and courage to screen applicants, who know how to encourage students and can motivate them to learn, who care about the students, and who can do research which contributes to improving helping skills.

Effectiveness=Effective People+Effective Programs+Effective Organizations . . . Effectiveness is a function of interpersonal skills and speciality program skills. . . . The helper[2] not only relates to where the helpee is "coming from" but he also establishes himself as having something that the helpee wants. The helper can function effectively in interpersonal areas where the helpee cannot. Given that the helper has related to the helpee's frame of reference, this desirable qual-

[2] Whether he is the counselor educator or the counselor (M.O.)

ity constitutes the basis for the helpee's motivation: the helpee knows that he is understood at the level that he is functioning and he sees before him a person whom he wants to emulate and imitate. What theories of motivation have never comprehended fully is that people motivate people: it is the helper and the level of skills that he has and the helpee needs and wants that motivates the helpee to learn. Motivation is reinforced when the helper understands the helpee and the level of skills that he has and when the helper is committed to bridge the gap between them (Carkhuff, 1972, pp. 14–15).

Increasingly those who prepare counselors are being asked to endorse graduates of their programs for certification or licensing. Certainly, they learn many things about these prospective professionals in teaching and supervising them in practice and internships that are not assessed on the usual licensing examination. Whether or not formal examinations are required by the state for certification or licensing, this practice makes those who prepare counselors accept responsibility for their products. Perhaps this procedure also will encourage counselor educators to screen candidates more carefully and assess their growth during training with greater care.

A technology allows us to grow. The choice is ours. We can continue to live like fools producing unmotivated counselors with 13% success rates or motivated counselors with 25% success rates or even 50% or 67% success rates. Or we can demand of ourselves and the counselors we train a level of skill acquisition necessary for success rates closer to 100%. And in those instances where we fall shy of our goal we can determine the reason why. We can choose, as our helpees, between the resisting growth and growing. When we choose for ourselves we choose for mankind. If we cannot choose to grow, then there is no future for us, our profession or our world (Carkhuff, 1972, p. 29).

## Selective Admission-Retention

After counselor educators and practitioners decide what competencies are required for effective practice, they must determine by research who can profit from professional education and qualify for a license. Counselor educators must apply their findings to practice humane selective admission-retention procedures, including special encouragement for the most promising and assistance for the least promising in finding another career. However, many have difficulty discouraging poor prospects, and this is understandable. Counselor educators prefer to help persons achieve their goals rather than act as gate-keepers for the profession. On the other hand, admitting poor risks and ignoring their early unsuccessful efforts in helping others is not being kind either. The more time, effort, and money the poor prospect invests before he is dropped (or admits to himself that he will not obtain a counseling position) the greater is his loss of self-respect. Some individuals also rationalize their failures on the grounds that selection procedures are far from perfect (and this is true, but even the instruments available can be used to identify the persons who are the very poorest risks).

Difficult admission requirements, good pay, and good job opportunities make a profession attractive. When, however, a profession makes admission too difficult, many good prospects will perceive admission as impossible and not even apply. Consequently, admission requirements must be reasonable and relevant to success in practice. Unfortunately, some professional colleges weigh too heavily those data obtained from criterion measures that predict success in professional preparation and fail to give sufficient weight to the data obtained from those measures that discriminate between the most and the least successful practitioners.

Good mental ability and demonstrated success in using it are, of course, essential. Undergraduate grade point average, the Graduate Record Examination, and the Miller Analogies test are most often used to assess this ability. Although such data can be used to predict academic success in graduate education, they rarely predict counseling effectiveness (Blocher, 1963; Callis & Prediger, 1964; Ohlsen, 1967; Patterson, 1967; Stefflre, King, & Leafgren, 1962; Wasson, 1965; Whitely, Sprinthall, Mosher, & Donaghty, 1967; Wittmer & Lister, 1971). Nevertheless, Jansen, Robb, and Bonk's (1970, 1972) two studies indicate that high-rated, female, master's degree candidates earned higher scholastic aptitude scores than the lowest-rated ones (1970) and that the most effective male practicum students also earned higher scores than the least-effective ones (1972). For both studies the most effective counselors also were younger, less anxious, and generally better adjusted.

Peer ratings have been widely used as criterion measures for validating screening measures for selection of counselors (Blocher, 1963; McDougall & Reitan, 1961; Ohlsen, 1967; Stefflre, King, & Leafgren, 1962). McDougall and Reitan also argue the case for their use during counselor education to provide: (1) periodic feedback on growth, (2) feedback on behaviors that the enrollee himself may not recognize, (3) ratings against which an enrollee may compare his self-ratings, (4) desensitization against external ratings, and (5) feedback against which the instructor may validate his evaluations. Research findings indicate that these ratings are reliable and valid (Blocher, 1963; Dilley, 1964; Gade, 1967; Jansen, Robb, & Bonk, 1973; Jones & Schoch, 1968; Ohlsen & Dennis, 1951; Stefflre, King, & Leafgren, 1962; Wicas & Mahan, 1966). Although such sociometric ratings have also been used frequently to screen prospective counselors, Stevens's (1970) results suggest that the sociometric items she used are not valid for screening.

Most professionals agree that personality traits influence counselor effectiveness, but few personality tests have proven to contribute useful data for screening counselors. Inasmuch as the Minnesota Multiphasic Personality Inventory has been widely used with counselors Heikkinen and Wegner's (1973) review of research is quoted:

> Overall, we conclude tentatively that on the MMPI, counselors appear
> more extroverted (low Si) and perhaps more defensive (high K), more calm

and efficient (lower Ma), and more honest (low L) than other professional groups. Effective counselors, in turn, show some lowered tendency to daydream or to be verbally angular (Sc) and appear more calm and efficient (lower Ma) than ineffective counselors. . . . At this point, we simply cannot say that the MMPI is a proven discriminator between effective and ineffective counselors. It may not even be worthwhile to undertake further MMPI research in light of the appearance of more promising instruments (Walton & Sweeney, 1969), for example, the Wisconsin Relationship Orientation Scale and the Rokeach Dogmatism Scale (pp. 277-278).

Wasson (1965) found that scores on the Wisconsin Relationship Orientation Scale correlated higher with his three criterion measures (rated counseling segments .61, staff ratings .54, and peer ratings .61) than with Minnesota Multiphasic Personality Inventory, Edwards Personal Preference Scale, Miller Analogies, Strong Vocational Interest Blank, and NDEA Comprehensive Examination. As a matter of fact, none of the other measures correlated significantly with criterion measures. Moreover, at the end of the institute, those with ratings in the top third earned significantly higher scores on the Wisconsin Scale than did those with the lowest-third ratings.

Effective counselors score significantly lower on Rokeach Dogmatism Scale than ineffective counselors (Kemp, 1962; Russo, Kelz, & Hudson, 1964; Stefflre, King, & Leafgren, 1962). However, Palmer (1975) found that the Rokeach Scale failed to predict with statistical significance on Carkhuff-Berenson scales.

The Sixteen Personality Factor Questionnaire shows some promise as a screening device for prospective counselors. Miller's (1965) independent ratings of male university student advisers correlated with 16PF scores. Helpers who werere perceived to be most helpful scored significantly higher than the least helpful in the following factors: F+ (enthusiastic, happy-go-lucky), G+ (super-ego strength), and C− (emotional, immature, unstable). Obviously, one must not conclude that helpees preferred unstable helpers; perhaps they looked upon the preferred helpers' more emotional behavior as indicative of them being more open and genuine. Myrick, Kelly, and Wittmer (1972) found that 16PF differentiated between effective and ineffective counselors on the following scales: F+ (outgoing, happy-go-lucky), A+ (warm), E+ (assertive), C+ (stable), G− (casual), H+ (adventuresome), and I+ (sensitive). Female counselors were more casual and imaginative than males, whereas males were more conscientious, persistent, and practical. The authors endorse the 16PF questionnaire for selection and for helping trainees to set goals for their growth during their professional preparation.

Hubele (1970) identified four significant discriminant functions, but only the first and fourth appear to be useful in screening counselors: (a) factors making contributions to function one are A+ (warm, sociable), B+ (general intelligence), and I+ (sensitive, effeminate); and (b) major factors for the fourth were F− (sober, serious), I+ (sensitive, effeminate), and M+ (unconventional, imaginative). The principal loadings for the two remaining functions tended to be negative: second, primarily B− (less intelligent) and C+ (ego strength); and third primarily A− (aloof), M+ (introverted), and $Q_2$+ (self-sufficient). Counselors who earned A in practicum had the highest scores for both first and fourth functions. Group B counselors (earned B in practicum) and Group C counselors (did not take practicum) scored above all three noncounselor groups (school administrators, teachers, and students not in the helping professions) on the first function, but below them on the fourth function. Obviously, all three studies identified some common factors that differentiated between counselors.

For the Edwards Personal Preference Scale individual researchers (Demos & Zuwaylif, 1966; Stefflre, King, & Leafgren, 1962; Truax, Silbre, & Warge, 1966) have identified scales that differentiate between effective and ineffective counselors, but their findings tend to contradict one another. Truax, Silbre, and Warge (1966) found that students who profited most from their professional preparation began it with significantly higher autonomy scores and raised them, whereas those who profited least from it began with lower autonomy scores and lowered them. During graduate education Ohlsen's (1967) select groups of prospective elementary school counselors raised their heterosexuality and autonomy scores and lowered their abasement scores.

Carkhuff's (1969) scales show possibilities for screening counselors. Carkhuff believes that level of communication is the best single index of a person's helping skills. McNally (1972) used counselors', clients', and an objective judge's responses to a modified form of the Counselor Behavior Inventory to identify characteristics predictive of effective counseling for junior high, secondary school, and college counselors. Carkhuff's scales and two scales from the Personal Orientation Inventory (counselor synergy and acceptance of aggression) were the best predictors. Carkhuff's communication and discrimination model of counseling was of limited value.

A very different type of screening device that is rarely mentioned for screening counselors is assessment of physiological reactions. Gellen (1970) makes a case for the notion that empathic persons should exhibit more physical reactions to affect-arousing stimulation than their opposites. For only one of the four physical tests (finger blood volume) did counselors respond differently from noncounselors.

Simulated tests are commonly being used today to screen persons, and to train them, for business and industrial positions. For some time counselor educators have asked enrollees to respond to clients' written, audio, and video statements (both in and out of context). Stevens (1970) used two methods for scoring counselors' responses to a video tape of critical incidents in counseling (Carr, Merz, Peterson, & Thayer, 1972) and found that results from both scoring methods clearly differentiated between levels of counseling competency. The tape shows promise for both screening and training counselors. Use of coached clients is another simulated technique that shows promise for both screening candidates and for training them. For example, a practicum supervisor can use a coached client to incorporate into a counseling session (video-taped outside of class) agreed-upon critical incidents, and then as these tapes are all criticized in class practicum enrolleees can discover how they responded differently to similar stimuli. Moreover, for practicum classes the writer has found that even primary school children can be trained to function as coached clients and to give very helpful feedback to counselors (of course, for group practicum the counselor would be expected to make a video recording with a group of clients). Similar video tapes with coached clients incorporating critical incidents into the session and scored by techniques such as Carkhuff's scales can also be used to screen counselor-education candidates. Moreover, Mc-Ilvaine (1972) found that coached clients are competent raters of counselors' effectiveness.

Finally, the intake interview can be used to help counselor-education candidates explore their interests, aptitudes, and abilities, their motivation for wanting to be counselors, unsolved problems that may interfere with their success as counselors, their commitment to master essential helping skills, and their goals for professional and personal growth during counselor preparation. Such interviews may be structured as follows:

> I would like to get to know you better in order to help you evaluate your potential for counseling, review your motivation for wanting to be a counselor, assess your commitment to master essential helping skills, and make the most of your opportunities to grow personally while you are here. Try to trust me as you have never trusted anyone before and tell me about yourself. Start with your earliest memories. Tell me about those memories that you can visualize vividly before age ten, and the persons who have had the greatest impact upon your life, especially your career development. As you talk I will give you my undivided attention, try to detect and reflect how you feel, and help you explore what will contribute to or interfere with your success as a counselor.

After such structuring the candidate is encouraged to carry the interview, and most do find that they can talk about themselves and feel reasonably comfortable. If, during the course of the interview, a candidate does not mention parents, siblings, early childhood, school experiences, adolescence, sex, personal convictions, or career development, the counselor asks an ambiguous question such as "You never mentioned anything about your early school experiences," leaving it up to the candidate to develop it as he wishes.

Failure to develop generally accepted criteria for assessing counselors' effectiveness has been a major obstacle to developing adequate measures for screening counselor-education candidates. Furthermore, performance during counselor education has usually been used to validate screening instruments. Obviously, really effective screening devices must differentiate between those who will be effective and ineffective on the job. Counselor educators also require better means for assessing personal and professional growth during professional preparation and for using these data to encourage the most promising and discourage the least promising (and with the ethical commitment to help the latter discover new, and more promising careers).

> . . . There are some individuals who simply do not have the resources necessary for the helping role, and we would do best to treat such persons as helpees rather than as helpers. Others can see but cannot or will not translate what they see into constructive action. More rare are those who can see and do but who do not consistently employ their resources for constructive purposes. Whatever the degree of investment, it is as important to exclude those who cannot utilize their resources from assuming helping positions as it is to populate the world with those who can (Carkhuff, 1969, p. 145).

## Continuing Growth

The kind of person the counselor is determines both his counseling style and his motivation for continuing growth. For both it is important that he try to see himself as he really is and use his assets to become the best possible counselor. For example, some counselors care deeply about their clients and possess the skills to help them, but are not able to use their skills effectively because they try to use a counseling style that is not congruent with their life style. If, therefore, a counselor is to be effective he must understand his own life style and select or develop techniques that are appropriate for him. The way he answers questions such as those listed below (and preferably while criticizing a recorded session) determines the extent to which he can either enlist clients' assistance in therapeutic process or function as an expert who diagnoses and prescribes activities for learning new behaviors.

> Can and will clients talk openly about the problems that worry and upset them?
> Do I believe that my clients can define precisely the new behaviors they desire and are committed to implement?
> Do I believe that my clients possess the potential for learning their desired new behaviors?
> What have I done to enhance each client's learning to function increasingly independently? How do I really feel when a dependent client no longer seems to need me? . . . to admire me?
> What have I done to help each client to accept responsibility for learning new behaviors? . . . to teach clients to recognize and reinforce each other's independent, responsible behaviors?
> What do I do when I feel I know what is best for a client and he is tempted to do something else?
> What do I do when a client appeals to my need for power and control?

Similarly, the extent to which a counselor can open himself up for continuing growth is determined by his honest answers to these questions:

What do I like most about myself? How can I use these assets to improve my counseling?
What aspects of myself do I have greatest difficulty accepting? How do these interfere with my effectiveness as a counselor?
With whom would I be willing to discuss these weaknesses, play recordings, and enlist assistance in learning desired new behaviors?
Do I really have the potential to counsel clients in groups? What competencies have I already mastered? What new ones must I develop?
Am I really committed to learn the essential new behaviors and to continue essential on-the-job professional development to ensure continuing growth?

True professionals make the most of their opportunities for personal and professional development during graduate education and continue their growth on the job. Employers who are interested in providing good counseling services employ competent counselors who have the potential for growth, intellectual curiosity, and the commitment to grow and provide them with the type of supervision that enhances growth.

Even where good supervision is provided, the professional counselor must take initiative to ensure his continuing growth. To do this he must believe in himself and the techniques he uses, sense support from his colleagues and supervisor, and realize to whom he can turn for assistance when he needs it. He requires at least one trusted colleague with whom he can discuss cases, solicit feedback on ideas, and criticize audio and video recordings (and even better results are achieved when three or four counselors can meet regularly for these purposes and help each other grow). Best results are obtained when the counselor and his colleagues use some guidelines for criticizing a recording. A six-column worksheet on which the counselor records the following data has been helpful for many: (1) the significant feelings expressed by each client, (2) responses, if any, that the counselor made to each feeling, (3) alternate or perhaps more productive responses that he could have made, (4) possible behavioral goals for each feeling, (5) mini-goals or immediate actions that the client could take to implement his goals, and (6) feelings experienced by the counselor at that moment in the interaction.

Usually, the counselor is encouraged to listen to the entire tape, complete as many of the columns as he can, and note specific spots where he would like his colleagues' assistance prior to his meeting with them. Beginners often request help in completing columns 1, 2, and 3. If, however, the counselor is to help his clients learn new behaviors, he must also give attention to columns 4 and 5; and if he is to discover how and where his own needs may be interfering with his effectiveness as a counselor, he must direct attention to column 6. The worksheet can be used to help the counselor identify significant new therapeutic material (1), to improve his responses to that material (2 and 3), to help clients formulate new goals and clarify old ones (4), to help clients decide where to initiate new behaviors (5), and to be open to his own feelings and needs and to use them therapeutically (6)—to ask himself why a given client is causing him to feel and react as he does and also to ask himself how he can use his responses to better understand and respond to that client.

Such experiences with trusted colleagues help provide the basic support system that everyone requires for personal and professional growth. It provides encouragement and feedback when it is needed. It encourages professionals to implement new practices, to define precise new professional goals, to discover and develop new and improved criteria for appraising their professional services, and to explore new and improved ways of serving their clients.

Good supervision enhances continuing growth on the job. Best results tend to be achieved when the supervisor looks upon supervision as a leadership rather than as a regulatory function. The former stresses support, encouragement, and reinforcement of desired new behaviors, whereas the latter stresses judgment, criticism, and enforcement of policies. Counselors must believe that their supervisor respects them, genuinely wants to help them, and is competent to do so. Besides exhibiting caring for them, a supervisor can aid them best by helping them define specific behavioral goals, recognize and build upon their own professional strengths, and develop a support system for themselves (both a group of colleagues such as described above and a support system of friends and relatives for an enriched personal life). Under such circumstances counselors feel sufficiently secure to request assistance and to discuss openly specific incidents for which they desire help. They can recall how they felt about the troublesome incidents, admit their mistakes, suggest what they would like to say or do the next time a similar situation occurs, and select from the supervisor's suggestions those they can adapt to their life style. With a favorable psychological climate and the precise kind of feedback provided by a device like the worksheet described earlier, a counselor can discover his own deficiencies and uncover ways of correcting them. Although the very best counseling programs do provide good supervision and a climate in which growth is encouraged, every professional counselor must accept responsibility for his own growth even when his local situation does not encourage it.

## Summary

The counselor is a qualified professional who possesses special helping skills. Quality professional preparation enhances both his personal and his professional development. Those who prepare counselors must accept the responsibility for selecting promising candidates, for preparing them well, and for encouraging their growth in practice. Techniques for screening candidates are reviewed and evaluated in this chapter. However, screening candidates with even the best available instruments is not sufficient. In order to help prospective counselors grow and develop as professionals these instruments must be interpreted for them in a manner that encourages them to identify and use their strengths and sources of personal satisfaction and to detect and cope with those unresolved problems that may interfere with their effectiveness as counselors. Participation in group counseling as a client is one of the best ways of enhancing this personal development.

The kind of person the counselor is determines both his counseling style and his motivation for continuing growth. For both it is important that he see himself as he really is and be committed to use fully his potentialities in becoming the best possible counselor that he can. Employers who are interested in providing good counseling services employ competent counselors who have the potential for growth, intellectual curiosity, and the commitment to continue their growth, and provide them with the type of supervision that enhances this growth.

Competent counselors are participating members of their professional organizations. Increasingly, designated members of the profession are assigned the responsibility for analyzing the duties of the practitioner to determine what knowledge, attitudes, and skills are required for each technique (such as group counseling) used within the profession. Once the essential components have been identified for a technique, members of the professional university staff must develop a sequence of didactic and laboratory experiences for each component and develop techniques for evaluating the impact of their program on their students. They also must do systematic follow-up studies of their graduates and encourage continued growth on the job.

The profession is still confronted with the problem of what to do about the incompetent who pose as experts and lead groups. Most such leaders do not belong to any professional organization. Eventually the various helping professions must cooperate in defining ethical standards and methods for screening candidates for licensing which include performance tests as well as tests that assess mastery of professional knowledge.

Good didactic instruction, clear expectations for professional development, a meaningful therapeutic experience in a counseling group as a client, and even good supervised practicum and internship experiences are not sufficient. These must be supplemented by encouraging meaningful relationships with fellow prospective counselors and staff during professional preparation and by colleagues' encouragement on the job. Even when these are missing, a professional must accept responsibility for his own continuing growth. If he is to provide quality services for his clients he must continue to grow as a person and as a professional.

## Discussion Questions

1. What criteria may a prospective client use to determine whether the professional offering him group-counseling services is competent to provide them? For what questions should the client try to obtain answers? How would the competent counselor of groups answer these questions differently from the incompetent one?
2. What are the counselor's essential facilitative behaviors for group counseling? How do these essential professional competencies differ from those that are essential for leadership training? . . . for personal growth groups? . . . for parent education? . . . for group psychotherapy?
3. What facilitates the maintenance of a therapeutic relationship in a group?
4. What is the rationale for encouraging those who wish to do group counseling to participate in a counseling group as a client? . . . for encouraging the prospective counselor to include his or her spouse in the counseling group?
5. How does the counselor's need for nurturance and affiliation affect his ability to deal with hostility in a group?
6. If you were a member of the state licensing board for counselors, what criteria would you use to screen counselors who applied for the right to do group counseling? From what sources would you obtain your data?
7. Why should practicum supervisors be expected to endorse (or refuse to endorse) prospective counselors for license and placement?
8. How may those with whom you studied improve their selective admission-retention policies?
9. What conditions are essential for a professional counselor's continuing growth on the job?
10. Let us suppose that you are a member of a state ethics committee who was assigned the task of determining whether a group leader charged with unethical conduct is guilty as charged. What questions would you ask the defendant?

## References

ACES *Sub-Committe on Preparation of Elementary School Counselors*. Washington, D.C.: American Personnel and Guidance Association, 1968.
ACES *Standards for the Preparation of Counselors and Other Personnel Service*

*Specialists.* Washington, D.C.: American Personnel and Guidance Association, 1972.

Blocher, D. H. A multiple regression approach to predicting success in a counselor education program. *Counselor Education and Supervision,* 1963, *3,* 19–22.

Callis, R., & Prediger, D. J. Predicators of achievement in counseling and guidance. *Counselor Education and Supervision,* 1964, *3,* 63–69.

Carkhuff, R. R. *Helping and human relations: A primer for lay and professional helpers* (Vol. I). New York: Holt, Rinehart and Winston, 1969.

Carkhuff, R. R. New directions in training for the helping professions: Toward a technology for human and community resource development. *The Counseling Psychologist,* 1972, *3,* 12–30.

Carr, E., Merz, D., Peterson, J. V., & Thayer, L. Development of a critical incident tape. *Journal of Counseling Psychology,* 1972, *19,* 188–191.

Dash, E. F. Counselor competencies and revised ACES standards. *Counselor Education and Supervision,* 1975, *14,* 221–227.

Demos, G. D., & Zuwaylif, F. H. Characteristics of effective counselors. *Counselor Education and Supervision,* 1966, *5,* 163–165.

Dilley, J. S. Supervisory ratings of counselor trainees in a simulated work setting as compared with peer and instructor's ratings of some trainees in an academic setting. *Counselor Education and Supervision,* 1964, *3,* 70–73.

Gade, E. M. The relationship of sociometric indices and counselor candidate effectiveness. *Counselor Education and Supervision,* 1967, *6,* 121–124.

Gellen, M. I. Finger blood volume responses of counselors, counselor trainees, and non-counselors to stimuli from an empathy test. *Counselor Education and Supervision,* 1970, *10,* 64–74.

Heikkinen, C. A., & Wegner, K. W. Minnesota Multiphasic Personality Inventory studies of counselors: A review. *Journal of Counseling Psychology,* 1973, *20,* 275–279.

Hubele, G. E. *An investigation of personality characteristics of counselors, administrators, teachers, and non-helping professionals.* Unpublished doctoral dissertation, University of Illinois, 1970.

Jansen, D. G., Robb, G. P., & Bonk, E. C. Characteristics of high-rated and low-rated Masters' degree candidates in counseling and guidance. *Counselor Education and Supervision,* 1970, *10,* 162–172.

Jansen, D. G., Robb, G. P., & Bonk, E. C. Differences among male A, B, and C Masters' degree candidates in a counseling practicum. *Counselor Education and Supervision,* 1972, *12,* 24–30.

Jansen, D. G., Robb, G. P., & Bonk, E. C. Peer ratings on twelve bipolar items of practicum counselors ranked high and low in competence by their peers. *Journal of Counseling Psychology,* 1973, *20,* 419–424.

Jones, J. E., & Schoch, E. W. Correlates of success in MA level counselor education. *Counselor Education and Supervision,* 1968, *7,* 286–291.

Kemp, C. G. Influence of Dogmatism on training of counselors. *Journal of Counseling Psychology,* 1962, *9,* 155–157.

Krathwohl, D. R., Bloom, B. S., & Masia, B. B. *Taxonomy of educational objectives: The clasification of educational goals, Handbook II, Affective domain.* New York: McKay, 1964.

Lazarus, A. A. Multimodal behavior therapy: Treating the basic id. *The Journal of Nervous and Mental Diseases,* 1973, *156,* 404–411.

Lieberman, M. A., Yalom, I. D., & Miles, M. D. *Encounter groups: First facts.* New York: Basic Books, 1973.

McDougall, W. P., & Reitan, H. M. The use of peer rating technique in appraising selected attributes of counselor trainees. *Counselor Education and Supervision,* 1961, *1,* 72–76.

McIlvaine, J. F. Coached clients as raters of counseling effectiveness. *Counselor Education and Supervision,* 1972, *12,* 123–129.

McNally, H. A. *An investigation of selected counselor and client characteristics of possible predictors of counseling effectiveness.* Unpublished doctoral dissertation, University of Maine, 1972.

Miller, G. E., McGuire, C. H., & Larsen, L. B. The orthopaedic training study— A progress report. *Bulletin of American Academy of Orthopaedic Surgery,* 1965, *13,* 8–11.

Miller, T. K. Characteristics of perceived helpers. *Personnel and Guidance Journal,* 1965, *43,* 687–691.

Myrick, R. D., Kelly, F. D., & Wittmer, J. The sixteen personality factor questionnaire as a predictor of counselor effectiveness. *Counselor Education and Supervision,* 1972, *11,* 293–301.

Ohlsen, M. M. *Final technical report on Institute for Elementary School Counselors.* Urbana: College of Education, University of Illinois, 1967.

Ohlsen, M. M. Group leader preparation. *Counselor Education and Supervision,* 1975, *14,* 215–220.

Ohlsen, M. M., & Denis, C. Factors associated with education students' choices of classmates. *Educational Administration and Supervision,* 1951, *37,* 277–290.

Palmer, C. J. *Characteristics of effective counselor trainees.* Unpublished doctoral dissertation, Ball State University, 1975.

Patterson, C. H. The selection of counselors. A paper read at Washington University Conference on Research in Counseling, St. Louis, Missouri, January 10–13, 1967.

Russo, J. R., Kelz, J. W., & Hudson, G. R. Are good counselors open minded? *Counselor Education and Supervision,* 1964, *3,* 74–77.

Stefflre, B., King, P., & Leafgren, F. Characteristics of counselors judged effective by their peers. *Journal of Counseling Psychology,* 1962, *9,* 335–340.

Stevens, H. L. *The validation of a sociometric test for counselor education students.* Unpublished doctoral dissertation, University of Illinois, 1970.

Truax, C. B., Silbre, L. D., & Warge, D. G. Personality change and achievement in therapeutic training. Fayetteville: Arkansas Rehabilitation Research and Training Center, University of Arkansas, 1966.

Walton, F. K., & Sweeney, T. J. Useful predictors of counseling effectiveness. *Personnel and Guidance Journal,* 1969, *48,* 32–38.

Wasson, R. M. The Wisconsin Orientation Scale in the assessment of applicants for counselor education. *Counselor Education and Supervision,* 1965, *4,* 89–92.

Whiteley, J. M., Sprinthall, N. A., Mosher, R. L., & Donaghty, T. A. Selection and evaluation of counselor effectiveness. *Journal of Counseling Psychology*, 1967, *14*, 226–234.

Wicas, E. A., & Mahan, T. W. Characteristics of counselors rated effective by supervisors and peers. *Counselor Education and Supervision*, 1966, *6*, 50–56.

Winborn, B. B., Hinds, W. C., & Stewart, N. R. Instructional objectives for professional preparation of counselors. *Counselor Education and Supervision*, 1971, *10*, 133–137.

Wittmer, J., & Lister, J. L. The Graduate Record Examination, 16 P.F. Questionnaire, and counseling effectiveness. *Counselor Education and Supervision*, 1971, *10*, 293–296.

# Therapeutic Forces in
a Counseling Group

The counselor is a powerful therapeutic force in a counseling group. With every new group he must be able to help prospective clients decide whether to participate, to define specific behavioral goals, to make essential commitments as clients and helpers, and to accept responsibility for helping to develop and maintain a therapeutic climate. Clients' faith in the healer is an important variable in developing and maintaining a therapeutic group climate (Frank, 1961). Even the clients' introduction to this artificially structured, temporary subculture in which change is expected, supported, and reinforced not only encourages them to learn new behaviors but also breaks down the resistance to change experienced in other groups (Beck, 1958).

Every effective leader tries to understand the forces within his group that contribute to or interfere with the group achieving its goals. The extent to which he trusts members and shares leadership functions with them determines the extent to which he can enlist their assistance in identifying the group's leadership resources, in uncovering the problems which interfere with the group's success, in diagnosing these problems, and in taking action to solve them. To do this leaders of counseling groups require background in group dynamics and leadership development (see Argyris, 1970; Cartwright & Zanders, 1968; Golembiewski, 1972; Gordon, 1955; Luft, 1969).

Lewin (1944) was a central figure in the early research on T-groups.

His findings as well as those of his associates support democratic leadership. Some of their findings are particularly relevant for leaders of counseling groups: (1) a discussion can clarify issues better than a lecture, but it does not necessarily produce either a decision or action; (2) improved production (and/or changed behavior) follows meaningful participation in defining specific production goals; (3) a we-feeling (belonging) is experienced in a democratically led group; and (4) friendliness and cooperative behaviors tend to replace in democratic groups much hostility and competition experienced in autocratically led groups.

As free men most current writers in counseling support Lewin's stance on democratic leadership. Citizens must be given opportunities to participate democratically for our nation to identify and use its much needed human resources to solve its problems. Gordon's (1955) perception of this leadership model can be readily applied by leaders of counseling groups. He believes that the leader must respect members, trust them, exhibit confidence in their ability to achieve their goals, recognize each member's unique contributions, and find relevance in each member's contributions. The leader listens empathically, tests his understandings, tries to discover relevance in each one's contributions for solving the problems being discussed, detects and conveys linkage to contributions from others, and helps members learn to function with increasing independence. He recognizes members' leadership skills and encourages members to use these skills. By his example, and perhaps by teaching, Gordon helps members develop leadership skills as he helps them achieve their group goals.

Likewise, a counselor must understand, recognize, and know how to use the therapeutic forces within a counseling group, and he teaches his clients to accept responsibility for the management of these forces. He also must recognize and feel competent to cope with the antitherapeutic forces, and teach his clients to recognize, cope with, and accept responsibility for dealing with these forces. Intelligent management of therapeutic forces tends to prevent the negative consequences of antitherapeutic forces.

Expecting persons to change in a group is threatening (Cartwright, 1951). The mere goal of change does not suggest respect for values or ensure positive change. Some clients wonder whether they may be hurt or at least not helped sufficiently to be worth the pain they experience. On the other hand, the techniques for selecting clients, for helping them define their own desired new behaviors, and for helping them define criteria for appraising their own growth described in Chapter 1 can allay much of this threat concerned with change. The client's security is further enhanced by the way the counselor detects the hurt one's feelings and helps him learn to manage them.

Whenever an individual joins a group, accepts its norms and its goals (and this is expected), makes a commitment to help its members achieve their goals, and invests of himself genuinely, he can expect, even in a short-term, task-oriented group, that he will have some impact on the other members, and they upon him. This notion holds even more strongly for a counseling group, but it poses less threat because each member knows more clearly what to expect and how to change the group norms when they no longer meet members' needs.

Some counselors are deeply bothered by the notion of the counselor's management of the therapeutic forces to achieve change. They are bothered by the authoritarian connotations, and they are appropriately concerned by counselors' potential misuse of power. Each must be cautious lest he encourage clients to implement the counselor's desired new behaviors or lest clients may be pressured to implement other clients' goals. When clients are given the kinds of responsibilities described in Chapter 1 and are taught how to use them as helpers as well as clients, clients help the counselor insure that the group helps each member implement his or her own new desired behaviors, use feedback, and celebrate successes. Clients become increasingly tolerant of others' values and own unique ways of solving their problems. Moreover, they learn to recognize and to manage the therapeutic forces discussed in this chapter: attractiveness of the group (including its prestigious members), acceptance by the group, expectations, belonging, security within the group, client readiness, client commitment, client participation, client acceptance of responsibility, congruence, feedback, openness, therapeutic tension, and therapeutic norms.

## Attractiveness of the Group

"The more attractive the group is to its members, the greater is the influence that the group can exert on its members (Cartwright, 1951, p. 388)." A group's attractiveness is determined by the importance of its perceived goals, the extent to which it meets its members' needs, whether its members are liked, and whether it includes prestigious members (Cartwright, 1951). Even a dull group is more likely to be attractive when admittance to it is difficult than when admittance requires little or no effort (Festinger & Aronson, 1960).

From their review of the research Cartwright and Zanders (1968) later concluded that a group is attractive when (1) its members are valued and accepted (Dittes, 1959); (2) its members are similar (Newcomb, 1953; Festinger, 1954); (3) it is small enough to enable members to communicate and relate effectively (Porter & Lawler, 1965); (4) it provides opportunities for social life and close personal associations (Hagstrom & Selvin, 1965); and it provides at least two of these three sources of satisfaction: personal attraction, task attraction (attractive goals), and prestige from membership (Back, 1951). Cartwright (1951) concluded from Back's research that:

> When cohesiveness was based on personal attractions among members, they made their discussion a long, pleasant conversation in which they expected to be able to persuade one another easily. When cohesiveness was based on effective performance of the task they were given to do, the members wanted to complete the activity quickly and efficiently and discussed only those matters which they thought were relevant to achieving their purposes. And when cohesiveness was based on the prestige obtainable from membership, the members acted cautiously, concentrated on their own actions, and in general were careful not to risk their status. (p. 106)

Back's findings are supported by Kelman (1963).

> On the consequent side, the framework proposes that the changes produced by each of the three processes [compliance, identification, and internalization] tend to be of a different nature. The crucial difference in nature of change between the three processes is in the conditions under which the newly acquired behavior is likely to manifest itself. Behavior accepted through compliance will tend to manifest itself only under conditions of surveillance by the influencing agent, that is, only when the person's behavior is observable (directly or indirectly) by the agent. The manifestation of identification-based behavior does not depend on observability by the influencing agent, but it does depend on the salience of the person's relationship to the agent. That is, the behavior is likely to manifest itself only in situations that are in some way or other associated with the individual or group from whom the behavior was originally adopted. Thus, whether or not the behavior is manifested will depend on the role that the individual takes at any given moment in time. While surveillance is irrelevant, identification-based behavior is designed to meet the other's expectations for the person's own role performance. The behavior, therefore, remains tied to the external source and dependent upon social support. It is not integrated with the individual's value system, but rather tends to be isolated from the rest of his values, to remain encapsulated. In contrast, behavior accepted through internalization depends neither on surveillance nor on salience but tends to manifest itself whenever the values on which it is based are relevant to the issue at hand. Behavior adopted through internalization is in some way, rational or otherwise, integrated with the individual's existing values. It becomes part of a personal system, as distinguished from a system of social-role expectations. It becomes independent of the original source and, because of the resulting interplay with other parts of the person's value system, it tends to be more idiosyncratic, more flexible, and more complex. (p. 402)

Therefore, it may be appropriate to include prestigious members initially in a counseling group to encourage change, but such persons tend to create only external motivation for quality participation and implementation of new behaviors. For real lasting change, clients must be helped to develop the internalized motivation for change.

Moreover, the greater the prestige of a group member in the eyes of group members, the greater is his influence within the group (Cartwright, 1951). When, therefore, a counselor selects a prestigious figure for a group, he must be certain that the client is admired by prospective clients rather than by only the institution's staff. He also must be certain that the prestige figure is sincerely committed to being both client and helper, and that he understands both roles.

Finally, in his presentation and intake interviews the counselor can increase a counseling group's attractiveness by (1) involving attractive previous clients (for example, use of video tapes, Chapter 1); (2) using as illustrative material client problems which convey that reasonably healthy prestigious persons participate in group counseling; (3) giving precise examples of behavioral goals and describing the extent to which each was achieved; and (4) explaining why clients are selected with such care.

## Acceptance by the Group

Genuine acceptance by his fellow clients enhances self-esteem and provides quality support for behavior change. When a client discovers that he has been accepted for treatment in a group whose members expect to profit from counseling, try to detect how he feels, and reflect those feelings in order to encourage him to talk openly, to convey support, to express confidence in his ability to face the surfacing problems, and to invite him to implement desired new behaviors, he is better able to accept himself, including his problems. Kelman (1963) described the impact of peer acceptance in therapy groups as follows:

> . . . While acceptance from the group is not as predictable nor as unconditional as that from the therapist, when it does occur it is likely to have a powerful impact. For here is acceptance not by a professional, who has been trained to take this role and is being paid for it, but by the person's own peers who, despite their deviancy, are more representative of society at large. (p. 413)

## Expectations

In even a task-oriented group members must hammer out agreements on the following topics in order to function effectively (Thelen & Stock, 1955): (1) To whom will essential operational roles be assigned? (2) How will these assignments be made and by whom? (3) What common and unique responsibilities are expected of each member? (4) How freely are feelings to be expressed (and today the question probably would be the degree and nature of self-disclosure)? (5) What behaviors are to be rewarded and punished? (6) How will disputes be settled, and by whom? and (7) How will norms be established and changed? Until these are settled, spontaneity is limited, members are self-conscious, and any efforts of members to initiate action or influence the group's direction are perceived by members to be loaded with risks.

From their research on therapy groups with out-patient World War II veterans Powdermaker and Frank (1963) drew similar conclusions: When there was too little structure, intense competition developed among patients, and when there was too much structure patients tended to become too inhibited and to spend too much energy in trying to please the therapist.

A productive group must be a safe place in which members can express their ideas and expect honest feedback. Members must be able to convey acceptance of an individual even when they cannot accept some of his ideas or behavior and to exhibit tolerance for individual differences and values (Lifton, 1966).

For Bradford and Mial (1963) a group exists when (1) it knows why it exists; (2) its members have established an atmosphere in which its work can be done; (3) its members realize how decisions are made; (4) each member is encouraged to make his own unique contributions; (5) its members have learned how to request, accept, and give help; (6) its members have learned how to diagnose problems and improve its functioning; and (7) its members have learned to cope with conflict.

Clients profit most from a counseling group when they understand what will be expected from them and what they can expect from others prior to deciding whether to participate in group counseling. When clients realize under what conditions the counselor functions best, what decisions they can make, and how they may initiate changes in group norms they tend to accept more responsibility for developing a therapeutic climate and for maintaining group norms. Techniques for structuring and for preparing clients to achieve these objectives were discussed in Chapter 1. To profit most from the group clients must learn to function both as good clients and as good helpers, to admit when another's problem is relevant for them (and to share time and work simultaneously on their common problems), and to use models wisely (rather than blindly copying bad as well as good behaviors). On the other hand, the counselor must realize that his behavior in the early life of the group tends to be established as a norm. Therefore, whereas it is important for him to teach clients to function effectively as clients and as helpers, he must establish himself primarily as a helper (Chapter 1) rather than as an information giver and as a teacher.

Counselors who have well-established reputations as helpers in effective programs have a decided advantage in introducing group counseling within an institutional setting. They have developed working relationships and have established lines of communication with the staff which enable them to convey to the staff what will be expected of clients in the counseling groups. Even here best results are achieved when the counselor is able to make a presentation to the staff and answer their questions in order to help them describe the service accurately and to make good referrals for group counseling. For institutions like schools, colleges, mental hospitals, and prisons the counselor also can use these staff contacts to arrange for presentations to prospective clients in organized groups.

When the above procedure is followed, prospective clients tend to come to intake interviews with a better understanding of what is expected in the group and with specific questions to clarify those expectations. Thus, insofar as it can be done in advance, prospective clients have an opportunity to learn what is unique about interpersonal relationships within a counseling group, what they will be expected to do to develop and maintain such relationships, and what they will be expected to discuss. They come to the group prepared to participate meaningfully, to use its resources, and contribute to others' growth.

## Belonging

Both those who are to be changed and those who influence change must sense a strong feeling of belonging in their group (Cartwright, 1951). When a client feels that he belongs to a counseling group, he feels accepted, needed, and valued; he accepts the group's norms, makes a commitment to learn new behaviors and to help others learn new behaviors; and gives of himself genuinely.

The rootlessness of many Americans has deprived them of the emotional support formerly provided by the large and close family. With their competition for status and prestige at work, school, and social clubs, these associates have not proven to be adequate substitutes for former close family ties. In fact, conflict within many of these very primary groups (and especially the family) from which persons expect genuine belonging and support has motivated prospective clients to seek group counseling. Such therapeutic experiences enable clients to be themselves, discuss their problems openly, heighten hopes, and increase self-esteem. They learn how to escape from their devastating loneliness, to develop improved relationships with their relatives, friends, and co-workers, and to seek out and build meaningful new relationships.

For a client to be open, to look at himself as he really is, to lower his defenses, and to search for more appropriate goals, he must feel that he truly belongs; he must experience within his treatment group genuine human fellowship in which individuals give of themselves without ulterior motives: "unlike any other group, here, individual differences and particular deficiencies do not lower the patient's status (Dreikurs, 1957, p. 374)."

The presence of persons with shared problems increases clients' identification with the group and their commitment to the therapeutic situation (Kelman, 1963). Moreover, the feeling of belonging is enhanced by the counselor's affiliation responses, emphasizing the similarity among individual clients' problems and experiences, and generalizing from one client's remarks to help others see the implications for them (Powdermaker & Frank, 1953).

Hobbs (1962) argues that because the neurotic has learned from early associations that other people cannot be trusted and that it is dangerous to be open treatment should be designed to enable him to learn to be close to others without being hurt. Human intimacy is necessary for his survival. Intimate discussion with the support of fellow clients in a group bolsters this needed feeling of belonging (Kelman, 1963). This crucial feeling of belonging for neurotics applies to reasonably healthy clients too, and to adolescents in particular. When a counselor tries to communicate to adolescents what they can expect before they elect to join a group, helps them define their desired new behaviors, encourages them to set up operational guidelines, helps them understand that the group will be made up of others like themselves, and expects them to help develop and maintain a therapeutic climate, the adolescents sense genuine membership in their counseling group—they feel that they belong.

As the feeling of belonging increases, clients become more ego-involved in the interaction, participate more meaningfully, and increase their commitment for change. Belonging to a group in which a client experiences intimacy desensitizes him to the fear of intimacy, teaches him relationship skills, and provides experiences that reinforce his efforts to achieve such meaningful relationships. However, it is not sufficient to experience these relationships only in counseling. A client also must learn to relate successfully to significant others outside of counseling (Hobbs, 1962; Lieberman, Yalom, & Miles, 1973). His investment in the other clients, their investment in him, his commitment to change, their expectations for him to change, and his experiences in relating meaningfully to varied personalities in his group convey to him that he can belong and develop the will and self-confidence to change his behavior outside his counseling group. His membership in a safe group in which its members implement new behaviors encourages him to apply in daily life outside the group what he has learned in it, to celebrate his successes, and to learn from his failures.

## Security Within a Counseling Group

When clients come to feel reasonably secure within their counseling group, they can be themselves, give up their facades, discuss their problem openly, accept other persons' frank reactions to them, and express considerately their own genuine feelings toward others. With a clear understanding of what is expected of them and a commitment to deal openly with their problems clients who have been processed by the methods described in

Chapter 1 accept considerable responsibility for helping to make the group a safe place in which they can achieve their goals. They expect their group to provide security, they have high hopes for success, and they realize that they must accept considerable responsibility for developing trust. When their security is threatened their counselor recognizes the threat, reflects it, and helps them decide what to do about it. He also teaches them to recognize threat in others, to encourage them to discuss it openly, and to resolve it. Learning to recognize sources of threat, to discuss them openly, and to learn to cope with threat desensitizes clients to common sources of threat.

The counselor's reputation as a helper, a keeper of confidences, a selector of clients who are helped, and a manager of threat and conflict among clients facilitates development of a feeling of security within the group (Chapter 1). The way he copes with threat to clients' security, particularly early in the life of the group, and the confidence he exhibits in dealing with these instances also contribute to clients' security. Where coping with threat requires learning to cope with specific persons and situations, role playing and the critique of the role scene played can be used to enhance feelings of security within the counseling group. Although such realistic interaction can surface the pain and frustration of human conflict, it also tends to enhance clients' hopes for success. It introduces them to change in their own real world, encourages them to discuss their problems openly, helps them practice new ways of behaving, and enables them to obtain helpful feedback on their proposed new behaviors before they actually implement them with significant others outside of counseling.

These are a number of additional reasons why the counseling group is a safe place for self-revelation (Beck, 1958): (1) it is more easily learned with peers; (2) untrained peers provide uncensored, more realistic response to it; (3) peer feedback tends to be less threatening and consequently tends to lower a client's defenses; and (4) peers listen, accept one's problems as real, and offer helpful assistance. Moreover, each learns readily from fellow clients how to be client and helper and that others have problems as bad or worse than one's own, and that they expect to be helped by their counseling group.

## Client Readiness

The more clients understand what is expected, adopt the expectations, accept the responsibility for convincing themselves and the counselor that they are committed to discuss their problems openly, to define specific behavioral goals, to learn and implement their desired new behaviors and, where necessary, to pressure fellow clients to implement new behaviors, the more ready they feel for group counseling. Although a counselor can facilitate this readiness, he must convey to prospective clients that it is their responsibility to get themselves ready. When a counselor achieves this objective, clients not only increase their readiness for counseling but increase their self-esteem. They also come to feel more potent and optimistic.

The fact that clients are told in the presentation that they are expected to assume responsibility for readying themselves for counseling prior to the intake interview increases a client's readiness. They are told to think about what really worries and upsets them, to come to the interview prepared to discuss these worries and concerns, to think about how they would like to behave differently, and to come to the interview prepared to convince themselves and their counselor that they are committed to learn and implement new behaviors. As they meet these commitments in the intake interview, in the counseling sessions, and in applying their new learnings they feel good about themselves and are reinforced by their fellow clients and counselor. Clients enjoy their own increased self-respect; their own early minor successes (and management of failures); their group's support and encouragement; and the support system that they learn to develop outside the group enables them to maintain a commitment to continued growth. Even children often comment on how good it feels to experience success in meeting these responsibilities within a supportive climate in which others believe in them sufficiently to help them do it for themselves.

## Client Commitment

Those who profit most from group counseling recognize and accept the need for assistance and are committed to talk openly about their problems, to implement desired new behaviors, and to help others learn desired new behaviors. In addition to selecting motivated volunteers, three other criteria have been identified by Beck (1958) which support the necessity for clients' commitment: (1) their awareness of their own emotional difficulties, (2) their open admission of their need for help, and (3) their surrender of their defenses. From her review of the relevant research she concluded that good treatment prospects must want assistance, accept it as relevant for them, and want to improve their adjustment.

Kelman (1963) also agreed that clients must be committed to treatment norms and to the process until they achieve their goals:

> If the patient, then, is to continue in therapy long enough so that he can get to the point of having corrective emotional experiences, he must develop commitment to the therapeutic situation as one that is potentially beneficial to him and to which it is worth making certain sacrifices.... When he is asked to conform to the therapeutic norms by exposing himself and expressing his feelings

without censorship he is placed in a very difficult situation. He runs the risk of criticism, rejection and condemnation after he has divested himself of his defenses and laid himself bare before others. If the patient is to feel free to engage in the therapeutic process and talk about himself, then he must regard the situation as one in which he is safe from attack and condemnation and in which he can afford to relax his customary protective mechanisms. In short, then if the patient is to engage himself in the therapeutic process and open himself to the possibility of therapeutic experiences, he must develop a commitment to the situation: an attitude of trust and a willingness to accept its terms, based on his conviction that he will be protected in this situation and that he will benefit from it. (p. 410)

When patients fail to disclose and become meaningfully involved in the therapeutic process early in the life of the group, they tend either to lapse from treatment or to become nonpatient members (Sethna & Harrington, 1971). Therefore, clients must accept therapeutic norms, accept considerable responsibility for making their group a safe place and for coping with their own resistance, and expect to be helped. The intake interview and the approaches used by the counselor to help clients learn to recognize and deal with lack of commitment during counseling reinforce clients' commitment.

Where prospective clients have many opportunities to get to know the counselor, to learn from him, from the staff, and from their peers what he does, and to learn from peers how he has helped them, the counselor should be able to obtain committed clients somewhat more easily than other counselors who do not have such exposure to prospective group counseling clients. When, however, he selects clients who are not committed and fails, his failures also haunt him.

## Client Participation

A human being wants to become meaningfully involved in solving his own problems, in improving society, and in making the decisions that affect him. When he is not allowed to participate meaningfully or does not know how to participate adequately, he tends to become reactive. He attacks, complains, looks for a scapegoat, and also becomes an easy prey for a demagogue (Allport, 1945). On the other hand, when he can help shape the events which influence his life, he finds life more meaningful and hence more readily accepts responsibility for himself and for improving the conditions within his environment:

> Friendly, unaffected social relations are the most indispensable condition. Patronizing hand-outs and wage-incentive systems alone do not succeed. Opportunities for consultation on personal problems are, somewhat surprisingly, found

to be important. And as members of this society have shown, group decision, open discussion, and restraining of leaders in accordance with democratic standards yield remarkable results. . . . In other words, a person ceases to be reactive and contrary in respect to a desirable course of conduct only when he himself has had a hand in declaring that course of conduct to be desirable. . . .

In insisting that participation depends upon ego-development, it would be a mistake if we were to assume that we are dealing with a wholly self-centered and parasitic ego that demands unlimited status, and power for the individual himself. Often, indeed, the ego is clamorous, jealous, possessive, and cantankerous. But this is true chiefly when it is forced to be reactive against constant threats and deprivations. We all know "power people" who cannot, as we say, "submerge their egos." The trouble comes, I suspect, not because the egos are unsubmerged, but because they are still reactive toward some outer or inner features of the situation which are causing conflicts and insecurity. Reactive egos tend to perceive their neighbors and associates as threats rather than as collaborators. (Allport, 1945, pp. 122–123)

Strong pressure for change can be developed in a group by creating a shared perception of the need for change, and thus pressure for change comes from members rather than the leader (Cartwright, 1951). For example, Marrow and French (1945) demonstrated that other persons alone supporting data for change cannot produce change; the decision-makers must participate in solving their own problems. In this case, on the grounds of absenteeism and poor training risks, management defended a policy of not hiring women over the age of thirty. Even though the staff psychologist presented convincing contrary evidence from other studies management refused to change their policy until data were colleced within their own plant (with assistance from management) that justified the need for a new policy.

When clients are given a chance to decide whether they participate in group counseling, to demonstrate their own readiness for counseling, to define their own behavioral goals, to develop criteria which they can use to appraise their own progress, and to develop operational guidelines, they recognize that they are given real responsibility and they like it. Clients' participation in developing and in revising group norms is one of the most effective elements in producing group cohesiveness (Bach, 1954). Moreover, those who most readily accept responsibility for helping others as well as themselves tend to profit most from the therapeutic experience (Lindt, 1958).

## Client Acceptance of Responsibility

Increased responsibility for themselves and the therapeutic process increases clients' chances for growth within a counseling group. When prospective clients are allowed to decide whether to participate and are expected to ready themselves for treatment, they feel respected and encouraged to improve themselves. They learn to help others as well as to obtain help for themselves.

Hobbs (1962) argued that the locus of control must be placed with the clients rather than with the counselor and that clients must accept responsibility for developing and modifying their cognitive structure in order to make personal sense out of the world (and that insight as it is usually perceived probably follows rather than precedes changed behavior). He said that emphasis must be placed upon clients' immediate experiences and their learning new behaviors. Clients must practice making decisions, learn to accept responsibility for themselves, learn new ways of relating to others, and discover that they are capable of managing their own lives.

Acceptance of responsibility for formulating and maintaining their group norms does not mean that even norms so developed will never be ignored or challenged. From time to time individuals do have difficulty disciplining themselves, listening to others, and suppressing their own immediate needs in order to help others. When this happens, and clients do not recognize and manage the problem, the counselor teaches clients to recognize and to cope with the problem rather than coping with it for them. A reflection of the distracting client's underlying feeling is usually sufficient: "Joe seems to be unhappy with the idea that he is expected to _____." Occasionally the counselor may find that it is necessary to ask the group to review what is expected and to decide whether or not they wish to change the group norms. Though it may be difficult for a client to accept some particular working agreement that he does not like or to listen when he wants to talk, he eventually learns to do so because he has learned the rationale for the guideline during his participation in its formulation and he realizes that reasonably soon he will be given a chance to talk.

Unfortunately current practices in mental hospitals, prisons, and courts that excuse irresponsible behavior actually encourage and reinforce it—for example, a plea of not guilty on the basis of insanity relieves a person of the responsibility for his acts. Instead, patients (and clients) must accept responsibility for their irresponsible past behaviors and for learning new appropriate behaviors (Glasser, 1965). The irresponsible person must learn to satisfy his needs in a responsible way.

Whenever a person is faced with debilitating emotions (intense anger, despair, distrust, embarrassment, fear, grief, guilt, jealousy, loneliness or feelings of inadequacy) he may be tempted to behave irresponsibly and excuse himself.

For such clients the counselor tries to detect and reflect the debilitating emotion. He helps the client discuss the debilitating emotion, reflects the temptation to feel helpless and do nothing, explores the consequences of such a conclusion, and helps him decide what he can do about it: to face up to the problems involved, to define new behavioral goals including discovering what precipitates these feelings and how they can be prevented, to learn new desired behaviors, and to implement them. As he implements the new behaviors he encourages the client to share his success with his counseling group and helps him explore how these new more daring behaviors have changed his view of himself. For these clients especially the counselor also encourages (and teaches) the other clients to be active helpers during this entire process and encourages them to discuss what they experienced emotionally in helping such a client. Usually most of these other clients admit and learn to deal with their own debilitating emotions.

Sometimes a person also behaves irresponsibly when he wants something very much and feels that he cannot obtain it through normal responsible behavior, and either consciously or unconsciously learns to behave irresponsibly (by acting insane or taking drugs, including alcohol) to free himself of the controlling inhibitions of his conscience or punishment under the law or even to free himself from subsequent guilt. Everyone has read about such persons who have learned insane behaviors to kill someone who has hurt them or is blocking their progress to achieve a goal and about the person who gets drunk (or pretends to get drunk) in order to tell off someone who has hurt him (and tries later to excuse his behavior on the basis of not knowing what he was doing). Within a counseling group a counselor can detect such feelings, help clients own them, discuss them, and decide how to manage them (and teach clients to do these things for each other). From their participation in such discussions clients discover many instances in which they have behaved irresponsibly, why they did so, and what were the consequences of such behavior. When, for example, a reasonably healthy college male discovered how he had behaved irresponsibly, he was reluctant to stop because it seemed to work well for him. The other clients did not argue with him, but they asked whether he may eventually be faced with serious negative consequences. He reluctantly explored what was the impact upon the target person (his girl friend) and himself. The more he talked about the lack of genuineness in his crazy behavior, how it eroded his self-respect, and how she probably really felt toward him, the more he became frightened. Consequently, he decided to stop, role played how he really felt toward her and why he wanted to change his behavior in order to build their relationship on a sounder basis, and defined several new counseling goals for himself. His changed behavior and his success encouraged the others to explore where they behaved irresponsibly and what new behaviors they were willing to learn in order to function more responsibly, especially with significant others. The three who suffered from test anxiety concluded that this "crazy" behavior was exhibited to avoid facing their self-doubts, and where necessary, they defined new career plans which were more congruent with their abilities, aptitudes, and interests. They also concluded that even when crazy, irresponsible behavior enabled them to achieve their goals, it eroded their own feelings of self-respect.

For most clients, and especially for adolescents who have been pressured to accept counseling because of some conflict with important others such as parents and teachers, voluntary participation enables them to accept more responsibility for developing and maintaining a therapeutic group climate and for implementing their desired new behaviors. Moreover, giving every client the right to decide whether he elects to participate and the responsibility for convincing himself and his counselor that he is ready for counseling and committed to its objectives tends to enable him to be a better client and helper. It also makes it safer for him to explore other sources for help and the consequences of doing nothing to solve his problems.

## Congruence

Congruence is essential for effective communication within a group. It is the accurate matching of those feelings of which an individual is aware with those which he is experiencing (Rogers, 1961). To illustrate lack of congruence Rogers used the example of a man whose flushed face, angry tone of voice, and pointing finger clearly suggested anger, although his words denied his anger:

> What is happening here? It seems clear that at a physiological level he is experiencing anger. This is not matched by his awareness. Consciously he is not experiencing anger, nor is he communicating this (so far as he is consciously aware). There is a real incongruence between experience and awareness, and between experience and communication.
>
> Another point to be noted here is that his communication is actually ambiguous and unclear. In its words it is a setting forth of logic and fact. In its tones, and in the accompanying gestures, it is carrying a different message—"I am angry at you." I believe this ambiguity or contradictoriness of communication is always present when a person who is at the moment incongruent endeavors to communicate.
>
> Still another facet of the concept of incongruence is illustrated by this example. The individual himself is not a sound judge of his own degree of incongruence. Thus, the laughter of the group indicates a clear consensual judgment that the man is experiencing anger, whether or not he thinks so. Yet in his own awareness this is not true. In other words it appears that the degree of congruence cannot be evaluated by the person himself at that moment. We may make progress in learning to measure it from an external frame of reference. We have also learned much about incongruence from the person's own ability to recognize incongruence in himself in the past. (Rogers, 1961, pp. 339–340)

On the basis of his knowledge of the research evidence and his experience as a therapist Rogers presented a tentative statement of a general law:

> Assuming (a) a minimal willingness on the part of two people to be in

contact; (b) an ability and minimal willingness on the part of each to receive communication from the other; and (c) assuming the contact to continue over a period of time; the following relationship is hypothesized to hold true.

The greater the congruence of experience, awareness and communication on the part of one individual, the more the ensuing relationship will involve: a tendency toward reciprocal communication with a quality of increasing congruence; a tendency toward more mutually accurate understanding of the communications; improved psychological adjustment and functioning in both parties; mutual satisfaction in the relationship.

Conversely the greater the communicated incongruence of experience and awareness, the more the ensuing relationship will involve: further communication with the same quality; disintegration of accurate understanding, less adequate psychological adjustment and functioning in both parties; and mutual dissatisfaction in the relationship. (Rogers, 1961, pp. 344–345)

If, therefore, the sender is to send a clear message, he must experience congruence while he is sending his message, and if the receiver is to receive the message clearly and accurately, he must be congruent while he is receiving. Good communication between congruent individuals is essential for a quality relationship.

Roger's general law on congruence seems to apply to both task-oriented groups and counseling groups. In fact, members' failure to experience the kind of congruence described by Rogers, the openness described by Shaw and Blum (1965), and the quality of participation described by Allport (1945) may explain, at least partially, why subgroups and distracting side conversations develop within a group. Even when members are invited to participate in solving problems, they may appear to accept the leader's proposals, but feel uncertain that they can really trust everyone; consequently, they meet later in an informal, safer group in which they can gripe and state somewhat more honestly what they really think. These persons tend to be cautious; they do not want to be hurt as they had been previously when they were let down. To involve them the leader must convince them that their assistance is required and that members can afford to disagree with the leader and each other.

Whenever an individual accepts employment in or joins an organization, he gives up some aspects of personal freedom for the rewards provided by the organization. Sometimes an informal organization or subgroup develops to help members restore some of the personal freedom they surrendered for group membership. It also may develop because members' needs are not being met in the way they expected. A subgroup also may develop to rally around a splinter group when there are basic differences in opinion concerning what is best for the entire group. When these events occur, the leader must be able to enlist members' assistance in diagnosing the group's problems and in developing strategies to solve them. With such leadership behavior the leader enhances individuals' openness and congruence, recognizes that cohesiveness can be maintained even with conflict among members, and exhibits confidence in members' ability to assume responsibility for solving their problems. With the orientation described in Chapter 1, group-counseling clients tend to recognize their own lack of congruence, and to solicit feedback on behavior which suggests lack of congruence, more quickly than do members of most other groups.

## Feedback

Effective feedback encourages a client to listen, to explore its implications for learning new behaviors, to define new behavioral goals, to clarify what was communicated, to react to the feedback, and to solicit further feedback with reference to new goals and proposed actions.

Everyone has blind spots. Golembiewski (1972) believes that feedback can be used to decrease an individual's blind spots:

> Feedback is the process by which Self learns how he appears to Others. And feedback is one thing we cannot do for ourselves, no matter what our skills and resources. Our fellow men must help us intricately adjust our actions and behaviors, as they report on whether our actions are having the consequences for others that we intended. (pp. 25–26)

Bradford, Gibb, and Benne's (1964) definition further clarifies the purpose of feedback:

> Feedback, as used here, signifies verbal and nonverbal responses from others to a unit of behavior provided as close in time to the behavior as possible, and capable of being perceived and utilized by the individual initiating the behavior. Feedback may serve a validating function with respect to subsequent behavior. It may also serve to stimulate changes in the behavior, feeling, attitude, perception, and knowledge of the initiator. (p. 24)
>
> They gradually look at what they do and its consequences for the group and for individual members. They develop a willingness to receive feedback from the group. They learn to check what other people say about them against their own self-perception. They come to see that feelings and perceptions represent information important to individual and group performance. They see that improvement can occur only if information is reported, listened to, and tested. (p. 204)

It is important for members of T-groups to learn to give feedback very soon after the behavior occurs, to describe what happened in behavioral terms (and with minimal moral and judgmental terms), to describe the impact of specific behaviors, to suggest specific alternate behaviors, and to give feedback in an emotional tone that leaves the individual free to accept or reject reactions and to request clarification concerning the communication (Mead, 1973).

There is a considerable body of research on feedback. Most of the group experiments have been conducted with T-groups. Even before the most relevant of these are reviewed, a summary of the findings on use and interpretation of tests (as a source for feedback) is reviewed:

> Those who use tests must take account of the clients' maturity, clients' perceptions of the relevance of the test information for them, clients' readiness to accept and use the information, the extent of the clients' participation in the interpretation of their tests, and the counselor's professional skills. The counselor must be able to detect a client's feelings toward himself and his test results, to reflect these feelings back to his client, to help his client accept and interpret the new data, and to incorporate the new data into his behavior or new educational and vocational plans. (Ohlsen, 1974, p. 201)

> Even when a counselor tries to understand his client's reactions to test results and is competent to help him discover their implications for him, a client may distort or reject that information that is not congruent with his current self-image. (Ohlsen, 1974, p. 197)

Increasingly those who assist youth in formulating educational and vocational plans are coming to obtain first their clients' perceptions of their interests, abilities, and aptitudes before they help them decide for what questions they would like more information about themselves. Where tests appear to be a good source for their desired information, counselors take account of the research findings which encourage them to involve their clients in the selection and interpretation of the tests. Recent findings suggest that test results have much more emotional impact on clients than counselors previously realized. Therefore, the counselor must be very sensitive to the emotional impact of test results and help clients deal with it. Not only must the client be congruent to accept and use the results, the counselor must be congruent to communicate the results meaningfully. As with any other feedback, the counselor must be very sensitive to conditions which suggest that either he or his client is not congruent and be able to respond helpfully to this lack of congruence. Within a counseling group he also must be able to teach the other group members to recognize it and cope with it. Where the group can become a safe place for self-disclosure, as a counseling group is, the group leader encourages clients to participate in the feedback process—to identify areas for which feedback may be helpful to a client and then draw upon the research findings from use and interpretation of tests and vocational counseling to solicit the client's participation in the feedback process for himself with the use of a technique such as self-appraisal (Ohlsen, 1974, pp. 196–204; 334–356).

On the other hand, many group leaders today, and especially encounter-group leaders, encourage clients to give spontaneous, basic reactions to each other. Consequently, a number of studies have focused upon the impact of positive and negative feedback as well as the nature of the feedback: factual, behavioral, or emotional. A few of the most relevant results for group counseling are summarized here: (1) Perhaps information which disconfirms self-concepts should be presented prior to positive feedback (Stoller, 1968); (2) positive feedback is rated as more credible and desirable than negative feedback, and both were readily accepted when positive preceded negative feedback (Schaible, 1970); (3) positive feedback is better accepted, and feedback which focuses on feelings is more effective than that which focuses on tasks (Gibb, 1971); (4) feedback to an individual is more effective than feedback to a group (Smith, 1972); (5) successful clients learn to give frank and genuine, but considerate feedback to fellow clients (Lieberman, Yalom, & Miles, 1973); (6) positive feedback is more credible and desirable than negative feedback to recipients (Jacobs, Jacobs, Gatz, & Schaible, 1973); and (7) it is more important for the deliverer of positive feedback to be known than it is for negative feedback (Jacobs, Jacobs, Cavior, & Burke, 1974).

Quotations from two of the studies suggests that group leaders reexamine with care the ways in which they encourage members to give positive and negative feedback:

The major findings of these studies may be summarized as follows: (a) Positive feedback is rated as more credible, more desirable, and as having greater impact than negative feedback. (b) Negative feedback that is behavioral is more credible than negative emotional feedback. (c) Feedback that has an emotional component is negative, and is rated as lower in impact than other types of feedback. (d) The impact of feedback varies with the sex of S and the valence of the feedback. In particular, highest impact ratings come from males receiving positive feedback, and lowest ratings come from males receiving negative feedback. (e) People receiving negative feedback rate their groups as less cohesive. (f) People receiving combined behavioral-emotional feedback rate their groups as less cohesive. (g) There is a trend toward the Ss who were in the behavioral conditions to rate the laboratory as significantly more effective in promoting behavior change.

Assuming that a primary goal of most personal growth and psychotherapy groups is to change some aspects of the behavior of its members, current findings would suggest that the credibility of positive behavioral feedback is enhanced by the addition of positive emotional feedback concerning the reactions of the giver of feedback. Negative behavioral feedback is best delivered in the absence of negative emotional reactions. In other words, the most credible of positive feedback is something like, "You were very helpful to group members (behavioral) and that makes me feel warm toward you (emotional)." However, negative feedback should be limited to, "You talk too much in groups (behavioral)"; adding "and that makes me angry" makes it less credible. (Jacobs, Jacobs, Feldman, & Cavior, 1973, p. 222)

Positive emotional feedback, which was the most believable when the critic was known, became the least credible of the positive feedbacks when delivered anonymously. Negative emotional feedback, which was least believable when the critic was known, became the most believable negative feedback when delivered anonymously. The anonymous delivery of feedback might have reduced the emotion-arousing aspects of the situation and the feedback became more impersonal, almost abstract. As a consequence there was less need to distort feedback that was emotional in content; the differences in ratings of credibility between positive emotional and negative emotional feedback were small and not significant when the feedback was delivered anonymously. (Jacobs, Jacobs, Cavior, & Burke, 1974, p. 109)

Pulvino and Sanborn (1972) make another good point concerning the use of positive and negative feedback by spotters for guiding artillery fire (helical feedback):

> He (the spotter) provides gunners with negative feedback (corrections in range and aim) or positive feedback (burst on target) to improve the effectiveness of the artillery. In this interaction both negative and positive feedback are constructive, since they are used to determine how well behavior and outcomes are related to intentions: Neither sender nor receiver regards negative feedback as destructive criticism; their lives depend on their functioning apppropriately with a functional feedback system. (p. 16)

Perhaps the disagreements in the research literature on the impact of positive and negative feedback could be explained by the definition and the person who decides what is positive and negative feedback. What may have seemed positive feedback to a researcher could be perceived by the receiver as negative feedback and vice versa. When, for example, a test interpreter reports that a client's mental test score is much higher than the client estimated prior to testing, the test interpreter tends to perceive the feedback as positive. If she had known that the client had been trying to deny good mental ability in order to avoid pressure to accept either an educational or vocational goal which he felt was inappropriate for him, the test interpreter would have perceived the higher test score as negative feedback too. Thus, only the receiver can really tell whether feedback is positive or negative. Its acceptance is also determined by the receiver's perception of the giver of the feedback, the setting in which it is given, and the emotional state of the receiver. At the conclusion of an excellent paper in which he describes ten different types of feedback Dyer (1972) supports the views expressed here as follows:

> Supportive or rewarding feedback is important not only in reinforcing behavior we want to persist in others, but in improving our relationships. Such feedback may also be just a spontaneous expression of good feeling toward another person. Examples would be:
> "That was a great idea."
> "When you supported my position, I really felt good and I appreciated it."
> "I want you to know that I like you and appreciate your work."
> It would seem that such positive feedback would be most welcomed and people would want to hear such reactions. However, there are people who find it difficult to share such feedback with others. There are also people who accept such feedback reluctantly and some are always suspicious of the motives of people who give them supportive data.

. . . A critical factor that influences the impact that the feedback has on the other person is the motivation of the person giving the data. A person giving feedback to someone should also examine not only his method but his motivation. The form may be correct but if the motivation is to punish or put down the other person, the impact may not be positive. (p. 11)

Within the type of group atmosphere described in Chapter 1 clients learn to request specific feedback with reference to characteristics, behaviors, and proposed actions. For example, Ralph (member of a counseling group made up of undergraduate college students) enlisted Sally's assistance to role play a scene with his girl friend (Jill). After a few minutes he stopped the role playing and said: "Please help me. I am not sure what is happening. What Sally is saying is upsetting me even more than when I try to talk to Jill. I want to learn from her but I don't seem to be able to do so. What do the rest of you think is going on? What do you think I'd like to say to Sally—or to Jill? I can't tell whether I am reacting to Sally as Sally or to Sally as Jill. I can't tell whether she is putting me down, or I am setting her up to put me down, or what she is saying and doing is so threatening that I can't learn from it." The group reacted very sincerely to his genuine request and gave him feedback. Then they helped him to decide how he felt toward Sally and to express these feelings. Finally, they helped him clarify what he wanted to say to Jill and to decide to what extent the problems he had in expressing his feelings toward Sally were symptomatic of the way he related to females his own age.

Clients profit most from feedback from others whom they trust and perceive as motivated to help them. The better the feedback giver accepts the receiver and the better the feedback giver has exhibited caring and support for him previously as well as at present, the more credible the receiver perceives his feedback. First with the members of their counseling group and then gradually with their significant others clients learn to request and to give feedback. They also learn to express their feelings *when they first experience them* rather than either miss the expression of a tender feeling when it can best be shared or try to ignore a growing conflict until angry, hurtful feelings burst forth.

## Openness

Those who profit most from group counseling are committed to discuss their problems openly and to help fellow clients do likewise (Chapter 1). They feel that discussing their deficiencies and deciding what to do about them enhances their acceptance in the group.

On the other hand, when members of a group accept a decision that only a few believe is best for them because each feels that he alone is displeased with the decision (pluralistic ignorance), open communication is difficult. Though Shaw and Blum (1965) agreed on the desirability of open feedback, their research subjects were more likely than Shaw and Caron's (1965) subjects to signal their true feelings when they reported them anonymously. When members are secure, they can afford to discuss issues as they perceive them. When they are not secure, they tend to report their satisfactions and to withhold reporting their dissatisfactions.

Does expecting clients to talk openly from the beginning seem to be invasion of privacy? It does when clients are coerced into counseling and when the counselor uses power techniques such as interpretation and confrontation to uncover repressed material, but not when the counselor communicates expectations and each client is given the right to decide for himself whether he participates.

Successful clients self-disclose (Lieberman, Yalom, & Miles, 1973; Truax, 1968; Truax & Carkhuff, 1965). Certain counselors believe that the counselor's modeling of self-disclosure enhances clients' self-disclosure (Jourard & Jaffe, 1970; May & Thompson, 1973; Myrick, 1969; Truax & Carkhuff, 1965). Others question the value of counselor self-disclosure. The self-disclosing therapist violates the clients' role expectations for his behavior and tends to make them wonder about his mental health (Weigel, Dinges, Dyer, & Straumford, 1972). Self-disclosing leaders also were perceived by clients as more trusting and friendly (Dies, 1973), but Dies is not able to endorse it without qualifications. Perhaps it is the nature and extent of counselors' self-disclosure that accounts for the apparent disagreement among these findings. If the counselor discusses a painful problem with much weeping and disorganized behavior (appears to be falling apart), clients will be threatened. They will question his stability and wonder whether he will be available to help them when they need him. If, on the other hand, he merely owns a problem (and especially one that a client has just discussed) he encourages others to be open, too. He also may enlist their assistance when he finds it difficult to help a client who is struggling with a problem that the counselor is still struggling with or with whom the counselor is experiencing countertransference. Consequently, he shares his feelings briefly and precedes with counseling as follows: "What Jerry is discussing is still painful for me. Your assistance in helping Jerry is needed here more than it usually is." or "Jerry reminds me of a friend with whom I am trying to resolve a similar problem. I'd appreciate your help here." Such behavior conveys that the counselor is human, too. Even though he requires special assistance at special times, he is able to cope with the situation even under stress. Carkhuff and Berenson (1967) offer considerable evidence to support the idea that when the counselor offers empathy, warmth, and genuineness he facilitates clients' self-disclosure. Stone and Gotlib's (1975) principal finding was that both instructional and modeling procedures increase clients' self-disclosure. Like Whalen (1969) they also concluded that a combination of modeling and specific instructions would encourage more self-disclosure than if either is used alone. Dreikurs (1957) concluded that talking openly in a group enhances a client's status. Weigel, Dinges, Dyer, and Straumford (1972) found a positive relationship between liking fellow clients and the extent of their self-disclosure. Their clients also tended to rate their self-disclosing peers as healthier.

Perhaps nothing is as powerful in encouraging self-disclosure, especially for adolescents, than for clients to discover that they are a member of an attractive group in which everyone seems to accept the idea that self-disclosure is essential to get help and everyone seems to be willing to discuss their problems openly, to learn new behaviors, and to help each other change. They have good peer models for self-disclosing, for exhibiting willingness to change, for developing specific behavioral goals out of their confusion and pain, and for observing others implement desired new behaviors. When they are able to talk openly they sense increased personal acceptance and as they listen they discover that these fellow clients whom they admire have problems as difficult to solve as their own and that they are not giving up. They are discussing their problems and doing something to solve them.

## Therapeutic Tension

Clients must experience some tension and dissatisfaction with their present state to be motivated to learn desired new behaviors.

> In a well-planned therapeutic group, tension will be present from the beginning, because the patients have been so selected as to stimulate each other and to maintain interpersonal exchanges of material loaded with affect. Tension is the motor which keeps the therapeutic group going; anxiety is the fuel that makes the motor run. The group therapist becomes the responsible conductor of this vehicle. (Hulse, 1950, p. 834)

When the counselor is most effective clients also learn to detect and reflect therapeutic material, and thereby help each other recognize their problems, own them, and solve them. Clients recognize that helping each other face their problems can be painful, but they also realize that it is essential in order to change. Furthermore, they learn to give each other the support which is required (and encourage each other to solicit such support from significant others outside their counseling group) to discuss their problems and take the risks which are required to implement desired new behaviors. They discover the real difference between a quality support system and a rescue service.

On the other hand, excessive anxiety and tension can debilitate clients to such an extent that they cannot use their own resources to learn their desired new behaviors. Usually this occurs when the counselor uses, and encourages clients to use, confrontation and interpretation to tear away a client's defenses. Though most clients who are really helped usually experience pain as they face their problems and decide what they must do with whom to improve the quality of their daily lives, they rarely, if ever, are debilitated to the extent that they cannot discover and use their own resources to solve their problems when their counselor and fellow clients help them uncover painful material by detecting and reflecting their feelings.

Even when clients discover and use their own resources as suggested above they may merely cathart, experience relief, and consequently lose some motivation to learn new behaviors. Instead each client must be helped to define precise goals and to implement new behaviors as he discusses his problems—experiencing pleasure from learning and implementing new behaviors as he experiences relief from catharsis.

## Therapeutic Norms

When a client understands and accepts what is expected from him in order to achieve his goals he helps develop and maintain therapeutic norms for his group. Prior to deciding whether to participate in a group he learns what will be expected from him, what decisions the group will be expected to make with reference to norms, and how norms can be changed during counseling. Each tends to perceive his counseling group as an attractive source for help; he does not want to be a deviant in it. Consequently, therapeutic norms tend to be reinforced.

Important as it is for the counselor to encourage genuine client participation in establishing and maintaining therapeutic group norms and in the helping process itself, the counselor is still a special group member. He is a qualified professional with a reputation for helping people. He initiates group counseling, describes the process (including describing the conditions under which he functions best in helping his clients), answers clients' questions concerning the selection process, treatment process, and outcomes of treatment, and selects clients for each group. By his reputation and his ability to communicate what the treatment process is like, he develops expectations, reinforces them, and helps clients learn to function as clients and as helpers. He is a special helper, and as Bach (1954) stressed he has special professional responsibilities for helping clients develop and maintain therapeutic norms.

During the course of treatment the counselor also has special responsibility for helping clients deal with their resistance to change and for helping them enlist the assistance of their significant others to reinforce desired changes and to ensure that desired new behaviors are not extinguished by their environment. When, for example, juvenile delinquents have been removed from their neighborhoods and counseled they have often responded well to the treatment, but have not been able to maintain their gains when they return to their old neighborhoods. Hence, treatment must be continued in their old environment while they are learning to solicit reinforcement from old associates, to develop new relationships from which they can expect reinforcement of new behaviors, or move into a new neighborhood. If such assistance is not provided, few such clients are able to prevent their environment from extinguishing their desired new behaviors.

Thus, the problem which was noted for clients also applies for professionals. Even counselors who develop new skills and perceptions of their role may not be reinforced for implementing them when they return to their jobs. Being able to help clients in new ways and being willing to teach colleagues their new skills can cause conflict even with colleagues with whom they previously worked well. Counselors also must be helped, and preferably on the job, to cope with those blocking forces on the job which tend to extinguish their desired new behaviors.

## Summary

Every effective leader helps members understand and manage the forces which contribute to and interfere with members achieving their goals. He must be able to help members identify and use group resources effectively, to recognize behavior which suggests difficulty, and to involve members in diagnosing and treating the difficulty. In addition, the counselor must be able to select clients, to describe the treatment process for prospective clients, to help them decide whether to participate, to help them demonstrate their commitment to participate as clients and as helpers and to learn new behaviors, and to teach them to function as clients and as helpers.

A group's therapeutic potential is most fully realized when clients: (1) perceive their group to be attractive; (2) feel genuinely accepted in their group; (3) know what is expected from them and what they can expect from others; (4) feel that they truly belong; (5) feel safe enough within their group to discuss their problems and to solicit feedback whenever they feel that they require it; (6) accept responsibility for getting themselves ready for group counseling; (7) enter counseling with a commitment to discuss their problems openly, to define precise behavioral goals, to implement desired new behaviors, and to help and even pressure fellow clients to do the same; (8) experience meaningful participation; (9) accept responsibility for developing and maintaining a therapeutic climate within their group and for their own growth; (10) communicate best and develop best relationships when they are congruent and those with whom they are trying to communicate are congruent; (11) obtain considerate feedback to recognize their blind spots and their problem-solving resources; (12) discuss their problems openly; (13) experience sufficient tension to be motivated to change, believe that they can manage the tension, and are convinced that the outcomes are worth the pain and tension they experience in achieving their goals; and (14) understand and accept the group's norms.

## Discussion Questions

1. What criteria may an observer use to determine whether or not a counselor is functioning as a democratic leader in the group?
2. In what way does the leader's acceptance of responsibility for formulating norms and for facilitating behavior change influence a client's behavior? How does a leader's acceptance of responsibility for clients interfere with their growth?
3. What are the primary advantages of democratic leadership in a counseling group? For whom is such leadership most essential? Why?
4. How do you feel about the idea of managing the therapeutic forces within a counseling group?
5. Explain how a client gets himself ready for group counseling and develops the essential trust. What does the counselor do to facilitate each?
6. Explain how congruence contributes to improved communication, self-disclosure, and readiness for growth within a counseling group.
7. What criteria may a counselor use to assess a client's readiness for group counseling?
8. How do the problems for the counselor change as the size of a counseling group increases? How does it change for members?
9. When is structuring done most effectively for group counseling? What questions must be answered for clients in order for a group to function effectively?
10. Let us suppose that you are asked to look through a one-way mirror (with sound piped through to you) and determine whether the group you are observing is a guidance group, a T-group, a counseling group, or a graduate seminar. What criteria could you use to differentiate group counseling from each of the other three?
11. What may the counselor do to facilitate warm, caring feelings in a group?
12. Of what does meaningful participation in a counseling group consist? How does it encourage clients to assume responsibility for their own and their fellow clients' growth?
13. What would you do if your clients decided to allow one client to continue membership in an observer role without any substantial self-disclosure (to participate vicariously)?
14. Of all the therapeutic forces discussed in this chapter, which do you feel are most potent? Which would be most difficult for you to manage?

15. What would be the impact of admitting a client to a group on probation status and of putting a fully admitted client on probation?
16. How may a counselor determine whether the tension that is evident in a group (and/or primarily evident in an individual) is enhancing open communication and behavior change or is debilitating?
17. What may a counselor do to enhance the development of therapeutic group norms?
18. What are the precise differences between activity and meaningful participation in a group?
19. Under what conditions may feedback be best accepted and used? How does confrontation and interpretation influence the acceptance and use of feedback?
20. Bill has always been perceived as a weak person by his junior high school gang. At a recent meeting he surprised everyone and took a strong stand against a proposed plan for stealing a car. How do you think the members responded to his stand?
21. A group of six college friends (3 women and 3 men) witnessed a group therapy session on a TV program. The next day they asked a member of the counseling center staff to provide group counseling for them as a group. One of the women is president of the student body and one of the men is captain of the football team.
    a. To what extent do you think self-disclosures will be influenced by membership of friends? By the TV program?
    b. What may the counselor do to increase his chances for success with this group?

# References

Allport, G. W. The psychology of participation. *Psychological Review*, 1945, *52*, 117–132.

Argyris, C. Conditions for competence acquisition and therapy. In R. Golembiewski & A. Blumberg (Eds.) *Sensitivity training and the laboratory approach*. Itasca, Ill.: F. E. Peacock, 1970.

Bach, G. R. *Intensive group psychotherapy*. New York: Ronald, 1954.

Back, K. Influence through social communication. *Journal of Abnormal and Social Psychology*, 1951, *46*, 9–23.

Beck, D. F. The dynamics of group psychotherapy as seen by a sociologist: Part I, The basic process and the dynamics of group psychotherapy as seen by a sociologist: Part II. Some puzzling questions on leadership, contextual relations, and outcomes. *Sociometry*, 1958, *21*, 98–128, and *21*, 180–197.

Bradford, L. P., Gibb, J. R., & Benne, K. D. *T-group theory and laboratory method*, New York: Wiley, 1964.

Bradford, L. P., & Mial, D. When is a group? *Educational Leadership,* 1963, *21,* 147–151.

Carkhuff, R. R., & Berenson, B. G. *Beyond counseling and therapy.* New York: Holt, Rinehart and Winston, 1967.

Cartwright, D. Achieving change in people: Some applications of group dynamics theory. *Human Relations,* 1951, *4,* 381–392.

Cartwright, D., & Zanders, A. *Group dynamics: Research and theory.* New York: Harper & Row, 1968.

Dies, R. R. Group therapist self-disclosure: An evaluation by clients. *Journal of Counseling Psychology,* 1973, *20,* 344–348.

Dittes, J. Attractiveness of group as function of self-esteem and acceptance by group. *Journal of Abnormal and Social Psychology,* 1959, *59,* 77–82.

Dreikurs, R. Group psychotherapy from the point of view of Adlerian psychology. *International Journal of Group Psychotherapy,* 1957, *7,* 363–375.

Dyer, W. G. Forms of interpersonal feedback. *Training and Development Journal,* 1972, *8,* 8–12.

Festinger, L. A theory of social comparison process. *Human Relations,* 1954, *7,* 117–140.

Festinger, L., & Aronson, E. The arousal and reduction of dissonance in social contexts. Chapter 12 in D. Cartwright & A. Zander, *Group dynamics: Theory and practice.* New York: Harper & Row, 1960.

Frank, J. D. *Persuasion and healing.* Baltimore: The Johns Hopkins Press, 1961.

Gibb, J. R. The effects of human relations training. In A. E. Bergin & S. L. Garfield (Eds.) *Handbook in psychotherapy and behavior change: An empirical analysis,* New York: Wiley, 1971.

Glasser, W. *Reality therapy.* New York: Harper & Row, 1965.

Golembiewski, R. T. *Renewing organizations: The laboratory approach to planned change.* Itasca, Ill.: F. E. Peacock, 1972.

Gordon, T. *Group-centered leadership.* Boston: Houghton Mifflin, 1955.

Hagstrom, W. O., & Selvin, H. C. The dimensions of cohesiveness in small groups. *Sociometry,* 1965, *28,* 30–43.

Hobbs, N. Sources of gain in psychotherapy. *American Psychologist,* 1962, *17,* 741–747.

Hulse, W. C. The therapeutic management of group tension. *American Journal of Orthopsychiatry,* 1950, *20,* 834–838.

Jacobs, A., Jacobs, M., Cavior, N., & Burke, J. Anonymous feedback: Credibility and desirability of structured emotional and behavioral feedback delivered in groups. *Journal of Counseling Psychology,* 1974, *21,* 106–111.

Jacobs, A., Jacobs, M., Feldman, G., & Cavior, N. Feedback II: The credibility gap: Delivery of positive and negative emotional and behavioral feedback in groups. *Journal of Consulting and Clinical Psychology,* 1973, *41,* 215–223.

Jacobs, A., Jacobs, M., Gatz, M., & Schaible, T. Credibility and desirability of positive and negative structured feedback in groups. *Journal of Consulting and Clinical Psychology,* 1973, *40,* 244–252.

Jourard, S. M., & Jaffee, P. E. Influence of an interviewers' disclosure on self-disclosing behavior of interviewees. *Journal of Counseling Psychology,* 1970, *17,* 252–257.

Kelman, H. C. The role of the group in the induction of therapeutic change. *International Journal of Group Psychotherapy,* 1963, *13*, 399–432.

Lewin, K. The dynamics of group action. *Educational Leadership,* 1944, *1*, 195–200.

Lieberman, M. A., Yalom, I. D., & Miles, M. D. *Encounter groups: First facts.* New York: Basic Books, 1973.

Lifton, W. M. *Working with groups: Group process and individual growth.* New York: Wiley, 1966.

Lindt, H. The nature of therapeutic interaction of patients in groups. *International Journal of Group Psychotherapy,* 1958, *8*, 55–69.

Luft, J. *Of human interaction.* Palo Alto, Calif.: National Press Books, 1969.

Marrow, A. J., & French, J. P. R. Changing a stereotype in industry. *Journal of Social Science,* 1945, *1*, 33–37.

May, O. P., & Thompson, C. L. Perceived levels of self-disclosure, mental health, and helpfulness of group leaders. *Journal of Counseling Psychology,* 1973, *20*, 349–352.

Mead, W. R. Feedback: A how to primer for T-group participants. In R. T. Golembiewski & A. Blumberg (Ed.), *Sensitivity training and the laboratory approach,* Itasca, Ill.: F. E. Peacock, 1973.

Myrick, D. Effect of a model on verbal behavior in counseling. *Journal of Counseling Psychology,* 1969, *16*, 185–191.

Newcomb, T. M. An approach to the study of communication acts. *Psychological Review,* 1953, *60*, 393–404.

Ohlsen, M. M. *Guidance services in the modern school.* New York: Harcourt, 1974.

Porter, L. W., & Lawler, E. E. Properties of organization structure in relation to job attitudes and job behavior. *Psychological Bulletin,* 1965, *64*, 23–51.

Powdermaker, F. R., & Frank, J. D. *Group psychotherapy.* Cambridge, Mass.: Harvard University Press, 1953.

Pulvino, C. J., & Sanborn, M. P. Feedback and accountability. *The Personnel and Guidance Journal,* 1972, *51*, 15–20.

Rogers, C. R. *On becoming a person.* Boston: Houghton Mifflin, 1961.

Schaible. T. *Group cohesion, feedback acceptance and desirability.* Unpublished master's thesis, West Virginia University, 1970.

Sethna, E. R., & Harrington, J. A. A study of patients who lapsed from group therapy. *British Journal of Psychiatry,* 1971, *119*, 59–69.

Shaw, M. E., & Blum, J. M. Group performances as a function of task difficulty and group awareness of member satisfaction. *Journal of Applied Psychology,* 1965, *49*, 151–154.

Shaw, M. E., & Caron, P. Group effectiveness as a function of the group's knowledge of member dissatisfaction. *Psychonomic Science,* 1965, *2*, 299–300.

Smith, K. H. Changes in group structure through individual and group feedback. *Journal of Personality and Social Psychology,* 1972, *24*, 425–428.

Stoller, F. H. Marathon group therapy. In G. M. Gazda, *Innovations in group psychotherapy.* Springfield, Ill.: Charles C Thomas, 1968.

Stone, G. L., & Gotlib, I. Effects of instructions and modeling on self-disclosure. *Journal of Counseling Psychology,* 1975, *22*, 288–293.

Thelen, H. A., & Stock, D. Basic problems in developing a mature and effective group. *National Education Association Journal*, 1955, *44*, 105–106.

Truax, C. B. Therapist interpersonal reinforcement of client self-exploration and therapeutic outcome in group psychotherapy. *Journal of Counseling Psychology*, 1968, *15*, 225–231.

Truax, C. B., & Carkhuff, R. R. Client and therapist transparency in the psychotherapeutic encounter. *Journal of Counseling Psychology*, 1965, *12*, 3–9.

Weigel, R., Dinges, N., Dyer, R., & Straumford, A. A. Perceived self-disclosure, mental health, and who is liked in group treatment. *Journal of Counseling Psychology*, 1972, *19*, 47–52.

Whalen, C. Effects of a model and instructions on group verbal behaviors. *Journal of Consulting and Clinical Psychology*, 1969, *33*, 509–521.

# Clients' Counseling Goals

When clients seek assistance they are usually troubled about something with which they hope to learn to cope. More often than not they require help in learning to relate to some significant others (relatives, friends, classmates or co-workers, or authority figures). Beginning with the intake interview each client is helped to define specific, idiosyncratic goals which are clarified and restated in more precise, behavioral terms during counseling. In an effective counseling group each member discovers that he can face and cope with crises as he meets them. He learns to accept himself and others, to give and to accept love, to build meaningful relationships with his significant others, to work and play with others, to find meaningful work, to recognize reality, and to change what he can change or learn to live with those disturbing situations which he cannot change (or are not worth the effort to change). He gradually discovers who he is; what he can do; what gives him greatest satisfaction; what he would like to do; how to recognize, express, learn to manage, and enjoy his feelings; how to recognize sources of conflict early; and how to cope with conflict (rather than ignore or deny it). With his improving adjustment he recognizes that he is gradually becoming his wished-for self. He experiences increasing congruence between his real and wished-for self as he redefines his perception of ideal self and learns the desired new behaviors which enable him to be more like his ideal self. In other words, therapists' and counselors' general counseling goals tend to reflect their perception of the good life.

For example, Adlerians (Sonstegard & Dreikurs, 1973) help their clients give up the faulty premises that have produced their guilt feelings, their feelings of inferiority and isolation, and their desire for prestige. By helping their clients experience genuine feelings of belonging and a meaningful exchange of ideas they help their clients discover their real goals and the consequences of their behavior and goals, teach them to cooperate with others, to relate more wholesomely, to seek healthier sources of satisfaction, to experience increased self-esteem (or remove feelings of inferiority), and to take life in stride.

Like Adlerians Glasser (1965) stresses the importance of his clients' learning to accept responsibility for their behavior:

> Therapy is a special kind of teaching or training which attempts to accomplish in a relatively short, intense period what should have been established during growing up. The more irresponsible the person is, the more he has to learn about acceptable, realistic behavior in order to fulfill his needs. However, the drug addict, the chronic alcoholic, and the severely psychotic are examples of deep irresponsible people with whom it is difficult to gain sufficient involvement so that they can learn or relearn better ways to fulfill their needs. (Glasser, 1965; pp. 20–21)

Glasser is concerned about helping each client satisfy two basic needs: (1) the need to love and be loved and (2) the need to feel worthwhile in his own as well as others' eyes. In his discussion of the process he delineates how he tries to help each take cognizance of others' needs in fulfilling his own. Like Adlerians he uses encouragement to reinforce desired behaviors, and natural consequences to extinguish undesirable behaviors. To that extent (and perhaps, as they perceive it, with more human compassion for their clients) Glasser and the Adlerians are behavioral therapists.

Bross (1959) states quite different goals for her analytically oriented groups: to develop ego resources, to improve functioning as a group member, to resolve transference and resistence, to gain pleasure from purposeful activities, to develop self-confidence, greater assertiveness, and greater self-realization with contemporaries, and to formulate and implement one's plans.

Both Frank (1957) and Kelman (1963) also take cognizance of clients' need for improved interpersonal skills. Frank's general treatment goals are: (1) to facilitate constructive release of feelings, (2) to strengthen patients' self-esteem, (3) to encourage patients to face and resolve their problems, (4) to improve their skills for recognizing and resolving both interpersonal and intrapersonal conflicts, and (5) to fortify them to consolidate and to maintain their therapeutic gains. Kelman's goals are: (1) to overcome feelings of isolation, (2) to enhance self-esteem and increased acceptance of self, (3) to develop hope for improved adjustment, (4) to help each client learn to be himself and to express his feelings, (5) to accept responsibility for himself and for solving his problems, (6) to develop, practice, and maintain new relationship skills, and (7) to enhance his commitment to change his attitudes and behaviors, and to generalize his insight and skills by implementing them in daily life.

Such goals are desirable, but more precise behavioral goals are required to encourage client growth, to appraise counseling outcomes, and to help counselors determine whether to continue a given client's treatment, to change the treatment, or to terminate treatment and/or refer the client for more appropriate treatment. The recent influence of behavioral therapists has caused even some of their critics to adapt behavioral techniques for their use. In particular, early in the therapeutic relationship more counselors are helping their clients define behavioral goals. Some critics of counseling practices recognized this need some time ago:

> Brayfield (1962) argued that counseling psychologists had placed undue emphasis on egocentric self-regarding internal states and should instead use a performance criterion which would stress dependability, accountability, obligation and responsibility. Similarly, Samler (1962) cited three instances in which problems of prejudice, self-pity and poor workmanship were brought to the counselor. In each case, Samler argued the important objective was that the client change his behavior in relevant ways whether or not his subjective feelings changed. Such logic finds a foundation in the concept of efficiency as advocated by Wishner (1955) and the concept of competence which was brilliantly developed by White (1959). . . . Ultimately counselors of all persuasions look to client behavior changes as justification for their procedures.
>
> . . . The use of behavioral goals would result in (a) a clearer anticipation of what counseling could accomplish, (b) a better integration of counseling psychology with the mainstream of psychological theory and research, (c) a facilitation of the search for new and more effective techniques for helping clients and (d) the use of different criteria for assessing the outcome of counseling with different clients. (Krumboltz, 1966; p. 153)

## Clients' Need for Behavioral Goals

Before we consider counseling research findings let us consider a few of the principal findings concerning goals and industrial production. Locke's (1968) summary of findings is:

> (1) hard goals produce a higher level of performance (output) than easy goals; (2) specific hard goals produce a higher level of output than a goal "do your best"; and (3) behavioral intentions regulate choice behavior. The theory also views goals and intentions as mediators of the effects of incentives on task performance. Evidence is presented supporting the view that monetary incentives, time limits, and knowledge of results do not affect performance level independently of the individual's goals and intentions. (p. 157)

In most real life work situations a combination of all of these incentives is employed. A worker is hired and instructed on what to do and how fast to do it; he is given or gets knowledge of performance either from others or from the task itself; he may compete with others for promotion; he is paid for working, he is evaluated by his supervisor, and sometimes he participates in decision making. (p. 185)

The issue of goal commitment has not been dealt with in any of the research discussed above, but it is no doubt an important factor in performance. The subject's degree of commitment to his goal may play an important role in determining how easily he will give up in the face of difficulty, how likely he is to abandon hard goals, and how prone he will be to "leave the field" (i.e. the job) in the face of stress. (p. 186)

McClelland (1971) also found that motivated workers like to be challenged. They set moderately difficult, but potentially achievable goals for themselves, and they work hard to achieve their goals.

Locke, Cartledge, and Knerr (1970) concluded from their review of five studies concerned with satisfaction, goal-setting, and performance that:

(a) satisfaction was predicted from value judgments; (b) goal-setting was predicted from satisfaction; and (c) performance was predicted from goals. In nearly all cases the correlations were both high and/or significant. It was found, however, that in some cases the level of performance that yielded satisfaction in the past was not necessarily that which produced it in the future. In these cases it was the individual's anticipated (rather than past) satisfaction that best predicted subsequent goal-setting. (p. 135)

Several of Steers and Porter's (1974) conclusions from their review of the literature on employees' performance may apply to clients' participation in group counseling:

The general consensus of laboratory findings then strongly indicate that setting specific goals can serve to focus attention and effort and lead to improved task performance at least in the short run. Whether sustained results can be achieved over longer periods of time remains to be demonstrated. (pp. 436–437)

More difficult goals (up to some point) may lead to increased performance, [but] significant exceptions . . . are noted. . . . Such goals may lose their sustaining power when they are not properly reinforced. Past failures on previous goals may negate the effects of setting difficult goals. (p. 444)

For his review of the research on work motivation Notz (1975) relates the findings to deCharms' (1968) hypothesis that man's primary motivation is to be effective in producing changes in his environment:

Because of the desire to be the "origin" of his behavior, man is constantly struggling against the constraint of external forces—against being moved about like a pawn. Thus, deCharms hypothesized that when a man perceives his behavior as stemming from his own choice (i.e., sees himself as an origin), he will cherish that behavior and its results; when he perceives his behavior as stemming from external forces (i.e., sees himself as a pawn), that behavior and its results, though identical in other respects to behavior of his own choosing, will be devalued. (p. 884)

More theoretical and empirical work needs to be done on specifying the properties of tasks that bring forth intrinsic motivation. Presumably, the extent to which a task offers a challenge to valued abilities, provides feedback, relates to a meaningful whole, etc. are variables which may be related to intrinsic motivation (see Hackman & Lawler, 1971; Staw, 1975). Similarly, the degree to which the person performing the task feels that he has had freedom of choice and the opportunity for self-investment or commitment to the task may be related to his feelings of personal causation and intrinsic motivation. (Notz, 1975, p. 889)

Notz's review lends credence to the emphasis presented in Chapter 1 for describing counseling, letting clients decide if they participate, making them feel and truly be responsible for getting themselves ready for treatment, encouraging their full participation in defining behavioral goals, and making them responsible for implementing their desired new behaviors. These conditions also tend to contribute to a client's intrinsic motivation.

Perhaps the following generalizations from all of the findings presented above on employees' behavior apply to clients' behavior in group counseling: (1) specific goals serve to focus a client's behavior on learning specific new behaviors; (2) commitment to goals enables a client to sustain his efforts at times when otherwise he may be tempted to stop; (3) the expectation of succeeding (anticipation) may enhance a client's chances for achieving his goals; (4) a client wants to be challenged, but he can be discouraged by unrealistic goals; (5) the definition of goals must enhance a client's intrinsic motivation; and (6) encouragement and reinforcement are required to maintain a client's motivation to achieve his goals.

Though a number of studies have attempted to assess the impact of counselors' goals and clients' awareness of goals on counseling outcomes for clients, no research was identified which focussed on either the impact of clients' participation in formulating their counseling goals or on each defining his own idiosyncratic goals. Four studies using the model described in Chapter 1 determined that the clients did make significant growth with reference to clients' defined goals (Bartell, 1972; Bush, 1971; De Esch, 1974; Hilkey, 1975).

The threat of change and what may be done to reduce this threat for clients was discussed in Chapter 3. Several of the elements which reduce the threat of change associated with counseling pertain to a client's participation in deciding whether (1) to volunteer for group counseling, (2) to accept responsibility for learning to trust the counselor and the other clients, (3) to cooperate in formulating specific, behavioral goals, and (4) to cooperate in defining criteria which enable him to appraise his own progress during counseling. With the definition of behavioral goals clients discover that group counseling is designed *to help each learn his own desired new behaviors.* This is much less threatening than the inferred need for basic personality change—something which threatens most clients, and especially adolescents who tend to wonder whether treatment will disrupt their search for identity.

## Counselors' Need for Precise Behavioral Goals

Every profession is obligated to appraise the worth of its services. Specific goals stated in precise, measurable, or observable terms are necessary in order to appraise treatment outcomes, whether the purpose is to assess a client's progress or a service systematically. Even the practitioner who does not feel that he has the time or inclination to do research must accept the ethical responsibility to seek the necessary data to answer questions such as: which members of this group are profiting most and least (and/or are being hurt most) by this treatment? Which goals has each achieved? For which of his goals has each discussed related painful material openly? For which of those problems discussed does each require mini-goals, training in interpersonal skills before he can implement the desired new behaviors, or assistance in determining how to request (or practice in requesting) reinforcement of desired new behaviors from significant others? For those who do not or cannot profit from the treatment (or are hurt by it), what changes may enable them to profit from it? What other sources of help are available? Beside his own case notes in which he records descriptions of specific behavior, he can ask his clients and their significant others to note specific behavior changes and/or evidence concerning implemented desired new behaviors.

A practicum student's request for help from his supervisor with a countertransference problem (Chapters 5 and 6) can be used to illustrate how a counselor helps his client develop behavioral goals for the purposes discussed above. When his supervisor reflected the student's reluctance to respond therapeutically to one particular client's painful feelings (as the supervisor had done several times previously) the student discussed his reluctance to expose this client's painful material. Without going into all the details of the conference it will suffice to review the primary topics which they discussed: How does he feel toward this client? What feelings does he experience when this client approaches therapeutic material? Why has he (the counselor) avoided earlier treatment opportunities? What is the impact of his fear of being a client on his counseling behavior? What unfinished business does he have with the person of whom this special client reminds him? Following the conference the student sought membership in a counseling group at the counseling center. With the assistance of his counselor he defined the following goals for group counseling (and for each his criteria for appraising growth with reference to it is added parenthetically): (1) to volunteer to play his recorded counseling sessions during class supervision, to solicit feedback from peers, and to use their feedback for improving his counseling skills (come to every practicum class session with a tape marked at the spots where he'd like help, and following the criticism of the tape, to solicit feedback from his peers on the extent to which he listens to their feedback and uses it to improve his counseling in the specific ways expressed in his goals); (2) to determine of whom this particular client reminds him, what his unfinished business is with this person, and finish it (identify the person on or before the close of the third counseling session, decide what must be done, and begin work on the problem with the target person immediately); and (3) to examine whether he really wants to be a counselor, and if he cannot be satisfied with his level of success in practicum, to define a new career goal (sources of data for adequacy of counseling performance will be peers', practicum professor's, and another professor's [selected cooperatively by student and professor] rating on their standard practicum rating sheet). Of course, another criterion is whether he makes the decision to stay in counseling or to leave it and define a new career goal. With these goals and criteria for appraising his growth, this client and his counselor were able to determine to what extent he was helped by group counseling. He also was able to use his criteria to appraise his growth during treatment. His successes encouraged him to work harder on goals not yet achieved. With such criteria a counselor can discover growth in his clients and solicit better feedback from his clients and their significant others.

## Formulating Clients' Goals

For the model described in this book clients define their initial goals with the assistance of their counselor in the intake interview. Additional goals are often developed during counseling with the help of fellow clients and counselor.

When a client learns from the presentation what is expected from him in group counseling he comes to the intake interview prepared to discuss what worries and upsets him and to define desired new behaviors (goals for counseling). Even when a client has learned about group counseling from a friend or relative, or is referred by someone, and has not heard a presentation, he learns to discuss what bothers him. His counselor helps him develop specific behavioral goals out of his therapeutic material (Chapter 1). As the counselor listens emphatically he tries to decide when the client has discussed a problem in sufficient detail and experienced sufficient relief to decide precisely what he must do with whom to improve his adjustment—what desired new behaviors he must learn. On the other hand, the counselor must not permit a client either to wallow needlessly in painful material or to cathart to such an extent that catharsis alleviates both the pain and the motivation to change. Instead, clients are helped to define and implement behavioral goals at the earliest possible moment to achieve some goals while they are still discussing and formulating relevant goals for other painful material.

During the course of treatment when clients uncover additional therapeutic material, fellow clients help them define new goals. Frequently, such new goal material surfaces as another client struggles with a similar problem. In any case the client wants fellow clients *to listen* carefully and allow him to share what worries him. When he feels they push him toward precise goals too quickly, he tends to wonder whether they care or whether they have obtained enough data about him to help him. Like the counselor they must listen, win his trust, help him develop his own idiosyncratic goals, and see that he perceives his goals as stemming from his own needs and desire to change.

With reference to the points just made, Melby (1972) found that: (1) appraisal instruments should be designed to measure growth in terms of individuals' goals, (2) mean change scores on common goals were significantly higher than mean change scores on individual goals, and (3) significantly more change was reported on items which were selected by individuals as goals than on items not selected by individuals.

Usually counselors ask: "What about clients who develop unrealistic goals?" Schwartz (1974) found that subjects with higher depression scores were less accurate in setting goals than subjects with lower depression scores. His more depressed subjects tended to set unrealistically high goals:

> Dreikurs (1962) spoke of vertical competition in which the person sets unattainable goals in order to fail. This built-in reinforcement allows the person who feels inferior to experience failure and reinforce his feelings of inferiority.
>
> Unlike Dreikurs' view of self-defeating reinforcement Bieliauskas (1966) sees unrealistic goal setting as a compensatory reaction on the unconscious level for a lack of value. In compensating, the individual exaggerates his value by over aspiring.
>
> The goal-setting strategies associated with feelings of inferiority and with depression are quite similar. In both cases, the aspirations are unrealistic, and the trend is one of overestimation. (Schwartz, 1974, p. 309)

Setting unrealistic goals tends to be a part of such clients' life style. Krumboltz and Thoresen (1969) describe them as follows:

> The problem of unrealistic high aspirations is a difficult one. High aspirations are undoubtedly instilled at an early age by perfectionistic mothers, fathers, and teachers as well as mass media. . . . The difficulty is that they compare their own successes with those of the most successful people in each field of endeavor. (p. 13)

For such clients, best results tend to be achieved when they are placed in a group with at least one or two clients whom they admire and who have had the same weakness to a lesser degree. Such peers model more realistic goal setting and are able to react frankly and considerately, but bluntly if necessary, to their unrealistic goals and generally self-defeating behavior. Clients with unrealistic goals also witness these models openly discussing painful material and getting real help.

When a counselor discovers such a client, even in his first contact in the intake interview, he tries to convey caring and willingness to help the person become the best he can with reference to his most cherished goals without setting himself up for failure. As he listens to such a client discuss unrealistic goals he may say, "Jack, it is really important for you to please ————. I guess you feel that you just about have to be perfect to please him (her)." Within the counseling group he also often detects and reflects other clients' feelings toward such a client as follows: "Jack seems to feel like a failure at times when you think he should feel OK. Perhaps you feel that he is already doing as well as he should expect himself to do. His goals for himself could not be achieved even by a superman." Such a reflection enables other clients to respond in a caring, empathic manner; to express admiration for motivation to do well; and to encourage him to explore whether his unrealistic goals are essential. They encourage him to explore what else he may do to build the kind of relationship that he would like with the target person. Sometimes a client who seems to have unrealistic goals learns that some goals could even be achieved if he were to correct deficiencies such as learning disabilities which block his progress toward goals. Eventually the client with unrealistic goals learns with peers' assistance either to define more realistic goals or to correct deficiencies which make some of his goals unachievable. Such discussions also often surface into awareness of other valued goals which have been neglected. This encourages him to examine how he wants to spend his time and energy—whether he is willing to continue to ignore valued goals now that he is no longer possessed by certain goals.

Even for such a client some realistic, behavioral goals can be defined in the intake interview. The counselor helps develop his goals in terms of specific attitudes, behaviors, and skills and helps him define precise criteria (Chapter 1) to determine whether, and to what extent, he is being helped. They also discuss what data they must collect from whom to help them appraise his growth during and after counseling. In other words, the counselor merely helps each client define his or her own goals. Moreover, when for any reason he questions whether goals are his client's or his own, he examines that particular recorded session with great care. He ensures that he helps his clients define their own desired new behaviors.

Krumboltz (1965) answers two related questions for counselors: Whose criteria shall be used to evaluate counseling? What may a counselor do when he feels that a client's goals seem to call for unethical or immoral behavior?

Some people may be offended by the notion that we should permit the wishes of our clients to determine the criteria of our success and would prefer to establish universal criteria applicable to all clients. It should be remembered that all professional groups and all professional persons are ultimately evaluated by the extent to which they bring about the conditions desired by their clientele. When a client requests his lawyer to write out a last will and testament, the client expects the lawyer to write the document in such a manner that the client's requests will eventually be executed in precisely the manner that he wishes. In a like manner a physician is successful if, let us say, a patient with a broken leg can walk normally again as he desires. In the case of both the lawyer and the physician there come times when the professional man cannot carry out the wishes of his client either because the request is not within the scope of his interests, or because it is beyond his power, or because it violates his ethical standards. In such cases the professional man explains the reasons why he cannot carry out the specific requests of the client, perhaps indicating alternate courses of action including referrals when appropriate. When a professional man does accept a client, however, he is implicitly agreeing to exert whatever efforts he can to accomplish what his client requests. The use of clients' requests as a basis for generating the criteria of success is as appropriate for counselors as it is for lawyers and physicians. In the case of counselors it means that the same criterion measures cannot be applied to evaluating all counseling contacts. (pp. 383–384)

To what extent is a counselor free to respond to new therapeutic material during counseling, and thereby infer the need for new goals? Fellow clients also will detect new therapeutic material and respond to it. Both are appropriate. As long as each client realizes that he can decide whether he adds new goals and how he ranks his goals (either for the order in which he works on them or on the level of relative importance to him) the counselor has protected his client's rights.

And finally, what happens when a majority of the group elect to terminate? Does it make any difference whether those voting for termination have achieved their goals? What about those who have not achieved their goals? Unless the group is not functioning therapeutically, most who support termination will have achieved their goals. When, on the other hand, the counselor senses that someone who is suggesting termination has given up or is confronted with goals which are very difficult to handle, he reflects these feelings and helps the client discuss them. Sometimes this discussion produces either new goals or mini-goals for the old goals. If, nevertheless, such a client still elects to terminate, he is permitted to do so. Often the other clients encourage him to explore the natural consequences of running away from unresolved problems. In any case clients decide when they terminate. When they decide to terminate each is usually helped to explore: What he has accomplished? What does he still have to do? Whose help will be required to do it? How can he enlist the assistance of significant others in reinforcing gains and in helping him complete his unfinished business? Among those who achieve their goals first there is usually considerable commitment to help the others achieve their goals. Nevertheless, groups often terminate before everyone achieves his goals. These clients are either counseled individually or referred to other groups.

## Evaluation of Clients' Goals

Once clients have defined their goals and developed criteria to appraise their own growth the counselor examines their goals to ensure that the clients' best interests can be served. A few criteria which he may use for that purpose are discussed here.

*Is this the client's goal for himself?* To what extent does it reflect the counselor's values and ambitions for his client? Walker and Peiffer (1957) believe that counseling goals are influenced too much by the counselor's middle-class values. Krumboltz (1966) on the other hand contends that a client's goal must at least be compatible with, though not necessarily identical to, the counselor's values. Most counselors agree that it would be unethical to accept a client whose goal involves breaking a specific law, but many have great difficulty deciding whether they should be expected to accept a client for counseling whose goal involves actions which they perceive to be immoral: for instance, a request for assistance in planning a robbery vs. a request for help in deciding whether to seek an abortion. If he feels that he cannot help a client achieve his goals, a counselor must refuse treatment, give his reasons for refusal, and help the client find other resources for help. Perhaps the danger comes when the counselor thinks he accepts the client's goals, but unconsciously reinforces behaviors which divert the client away from his goal. Wolberg (1954) believes that even when a therapist is objective and tries to help a patient plan action consistent with the patient's values, the patient tends to be influenced by the therapist's values—to use the therapist as a model.

Because counselors exhibit tolerance for values different from their own, and not usually accepted in the community, does not mean as some critics have suggested, that either they or their clients condone unlawful or irresponsible behavior. It does mean that members of a counseling group can accept others' goals which are not appropriate for themselves. When there is eminent danger that someone may be hurt by a client's anticipated plans, usually fellow clients encourage him to examine the consequences of such behavior. When they don't, the counselor may do so; he also may ask permission of the group to take action to protect the person who may be hurt. Very, very rarely are those who only do individual counseling required to break confidence for such reasons. It is even less likely that group counselors would be required to do so.

*Does the goal statement convey that client's unique, idiosyncratic need?* Krumboltz (1966) contends that the unique feature of counseling is the individualization that it provides and consequently counselors must be willing to help each client state and work for his own unique objectives. For treatment purposes alone Krumboltz is correct. When, however, a counselor sets out to appraise the worth of a technique he usually finds it necessary to paraphrase and combine very similar goals into common, behavioral statements just to reduce the number of goal statements on the Q-sort or behavior inventory (Bartell, 1972; Bush, 1972; De Esch, 1974; Hilkey, 1975). Furthermore, such common behavioral goal statements so developed tend to be perceived as clearly their own. Most clients also adopt and work on others' goals.

*Are the goals stated in clear, precise, behavioral terms for which a client and his counselor can readily obtain essential measures and/or observations to appraise outcomes?* Do the goals focus attention on specific desired new behaviors? Though Walker and Peiffer (1957) endorse the need for specific goals they still warn counselors about the dangers of symptom removal and substitution. Few counselors are bothered about the latter point today. They don't believe that symptom substitution occurs when symptoms are removed by effective counseling. Ample support for this point of view is provided by the behavior therapists (for example, Ullman & Krasner, 1965).

*Do the goals reflect the client's language and thereby enhance the client's sense of ownership and anticipation?* When a client truly believes that the goals arise out of his own needs and unresolved problems, he invests more fully of himself to achieve them. He realizes that he participated fully in their development. He makes a greater commitment to achieve them.

*What observations of the client's behavior suggest that he believes that his goals can be achieved—that he anticipates success?* His expectation of succeeding enhances his chance for success.

*Are the goals challenging to him and still perceived as achievable?* The case was made earlier for both this criterion and the previous one.

Perhaps some readers will be concerned because none of the criteria dealt with what is good for society. Well-adjusted persons are concerned about what is good for society as well as for themselves; they work very hard to correct social injustices. They accept the need for a balance between what is required of them for self-actualization and what must be done to improve society. Some learn to express genuine concern for others as they learn to help fellow clients achieve their goals.

## Summary

Group counseling is designed to help reasonably healthy clients recognize their problems, seek help with them, define precise new behaviors that they would like to learn, and implement their new learnings in daily living. When a counselor accepts a client's reasons for seeking counseling and can involve each client in stating clearly and simply the changes in behavior and attitude that he or she desires, he facilitates clients' readiness for counseling and commitment to change.

More often than not clients want assistance in improving their relationships with relatives, friends, or co-workers. Consequently, they require help in deciding what they want to learn to do with whom. During counseling they often have to break their goals into mini-goals: "Tomorrow I will talk to my husband about————. After we decide what we are going to do about ————, I can talk to my mother about ————." Frequently a single problem has several facets. A client requires help in deciding where he will begin with whom for each.

Most counselors have general goals for their treatment, but they are not sufficient. Precise, behavioral goals are needed to focus a client's attention and energy on learning desired new behaviors. Genuine participation in the development of the goals is necessary for a client to develop acceptance of the goals and the commitment required to sustain his efforts when he might be tempted to stop. Criteria for appraising growth with reference to each goal also enhance further growth.

## Discussion Questions

1. What is your perception of the good life? How could these ideas be expressed as general goals for group counseling? Select one that most clearly relates to one of your client's problems and help him develop it into a goal for counseling.
2. What is the rationale for helping a prospective client define behavioral goals before he is admitted to a group?
3. Let us suppose that your practicum supervisor questioned the extent to which your own personal values and problems were incorporated into one of your clients' goals for counseling. How could you check whether his accusations were true?
4. What do Adlerians do that makes them good behavior therapists?
5. Why isn't increased acceptance of self an adequate goal for clients?
6. What does reluctance to develop precise, behavioral goals imply about a client? How would you expect this behavior to influence his subsequent behavior in a counseling group? Explain.
7. What may a counselor do to insure a client's participation in defining goals for group counseling?
8. How can a counselor tell when a client has talked through his problems sufficiently to define goals for counseling? What are the consequences of letting him talk too long before he defines goals?
9. With what major difficulties is a counselor faced in helping a client develop criteria to appraise his own growth?

10. How can a counselor assess when a client's goals are challenging but not overwhelming and discouraging?
11. How may a counselor help a client who sets unrealistic goals?
12. Threat of change is real for clients. What may a counselor do to minimize that threat for clients?
13. How may a counselor defend selecting for counseling only those who volunteer for a group and those who can define behavioral goals for counseling? What does it do for the image of counselors? for attracting clients who normally do not seek counseling?
14. What are the primary advantages of precise, behavioral goals for clients? for counselors?
15. How may a counselor determine whether or not a client's goals for group counseling are realistic?
16. Give some examples to illustrate how a client's goals for group counseling differ from a T-group member's goals and from encounter group member's goals.
17. How did you react to the way the supervisor and counselor tried to help the practicum student who was experiencing countertransference? What would you have done differently?

# References

Bartell, W. *The effect of the intake interview on client perceived outcomes of group counseling.* Unpublished doctoral dissertation, Indiana State University, 1972.

Bieliauskas, U. J. Shifting of the guilt feelings in the process of psychotherapy. In J. L. Moreno (Ed.), *The international handbook of group psychotherapy.* New York: Philosophical Library, 1966.

Brayfield, A. H. Performance is the thing. *Journal of Counseling Psychology,* 1962, *9,* 3.

Bross, R. B. Termination of analytically oriented psychotherapy in groups. *International Journal of Group Psychotherapy,* 1959, *9,* 326–337.

Bush, J. *The effects of fixed and random actor interaction on individual goal attainment in group counseling.* Unpublished doctoral dissertation, Indiana State University, 1971.

deCharms, R. *Personal causation: The internal affective determinants of behavior.* New York: Academic Press, 1968.

De Esch, J. B. *The use of the Ohlsen model of group counseling with secondary students identified as being disruptive to the educational process.* Unpublished doctoral dissertation, Indiana State University, 1974.

Dreikurs, R. *Fundamentals of Adlerian psychology.* Jamaica, W. I.: Spaeleng, K.E.S., 1962.

Frank, J. D. Some determinants, manifestations, and efforts of cohesiveness in therapy groups. *International Journal of Group Psychotherapy,* 1957, *7,* 53–63.

Glasser, W. *Reality therapy.* New York: Harper & Row, 1965.

Hackman, J. R., & Lawler, E. E. Employee reactions to job characteristics. *Journal of Applied Psychology,* 1971, *55,* 259–289.

Hilkey, J. H. *The effects of video-tape pretraining and guided performance on the process and outcomes of group counseling.* Unpublished doctoral dissertation, Indiana State University, 1975.

Kelman, H. C. The role of the group in the induction of therapeutic change. *International Journal of Group Psychotherapy,* 1963, *13,* 399–432.

Krumboltz, J. D. Behavioral counseling: Rationale and research. *Personnel and Guidance Journal,* 1965, *44,* 376–382.

Krumboltz, J. D. Behavioral goals for group counseling. *Journal of Counseling Psychology,* 1966, *13,* 153–159.

Krumboltz, J. D., & Thoresen, C. E. (Eds.), *Behavioral counseling: Cases and techniques.* New York: Holt, Rinehart and Winston, 1969.

Locke, E. A. Toward a theory of task motivation and incentives. *Organizational Behavior and Human Performance,* 1968, *3,* 157–189.

Locke, E. A., Cartledge, N., & Knerr, C. S. Studies of the relationship between satisfaction, goal setting, and performance. *Organizational Behavior and Human Performance,* 1970, *5,* 135–158.

McClelland, D. C. That urge to achieve. In D. A. Kalb, I. M. Rubin, & J. M. McIntyre (Eds.), *Organizational psychology.* Englewood Cliffs, N.J.: Prentice-Hall, 1971.

Melby, D. J. *Individual and Common Goals: An analysis of the criterion problem in group counseling.* Unpublished doctoral dissertation, Southern Illinois University, 1972.

Notz, W. W. Work motivation and the negative effects of extrinsic rewards. *American Psychologist,* 1975, *30,* 884–891.

Samler, J. An examination of client strength and counselor responsibility. *Journal of Counseling Psychology,* 1962, *9,* 5–11.

Schwartz, J. L. Relationship between goal discrepancy and depression. *Journal of Consulting and Clinical Psychology,* 1974, *42,* 309.

Sonstegard, M. A., & Dreikurs, R. The Adlerian approach to group counseling of children. Chapter 3 in M. M. Ohlsen (Ed.), *Counseling children in groups: A forum.* New York: Holt, Rinehart and Winston, 1973.

Staw, B. M. *Intrinsic and extrinsic motivation.* Morristown, N.J.: General Learning Press, 1975.

Steers, R. M., & Porter, L. W. The role of task-goal attributes in employee performance. *Psychological Bulletin,* 1974, *81,* 434–452.

Ullman, L. P., & Krasner, L. (Eds.), *Case studies in behavior modification.* New York: Holt, Rinehart and Winston, 1965.

Walker, D. E., & Peiffer, H. C. The goals of counseling. *Journal of Counseling Psychology,* 1957, *3,* 204–209.

White, R. W. Motivation reconsidered: The concept of competence. *Psychological Review,* 1959, *66,* 297–333.

Wishner, J. A. Concept of efficiency in psychological health and in psychopathology. *Psychological Review,* 1955, *62,* 69–80.

Wolberg, L. R. *The technique of psychotherapy.* New York: Grune & Stratton, 1954.

# 5

# Transference

Laymen as well as counselors and therapists must comprehend the phenomenon of transference to understand their own and others' behavior and to develop meaningful relationships. Because practitioners tend to define the term differently, some common definitions are reviewed before it is defined as it is used in this text. Topics such as the implications of transference for daily living, its use in facilitating clients' behavior change, its enticement for the therapist and counselor, and its influence on the counselor's effectiveness (countertransference) are then discussed.

## What Is Transference?

Transference is a displacement of affect from one person to another; it is the process whereby a patient shifts affects that are applicable for a significant other onto the analyst (English & English, 1958). Freud first used the term to describe one of the major impediments to the development of a good therapeutic relationship between patient and therapist. He also recognized quickly that the therapist could use it productively.

Projecting unconsciously and inappropriately onto another the very traits that keep a patient from relating effectively to some significant other is transference (Wolf, 1963). It is an unreasona reaction that may be exhibited by some affective disturbance such as mild anxiety, irritability, depression, and fearfulness. Because the patient is unable to control his response despite its drawbacks, Wolf characterizes the transference response as excessive beyond what one would expect from the provoking circumstances.

Glatzer (1965) portrays transference as symptomatic of the conflict between id, ego, and superego. Like English and English she describes transference as an unconscious attempt to imbue current relationships with old attitudes that are inappropriate for those present. She also points out that positive transference may be a cover-up for negative feelings for significant others. She says that deeply neurotic patients are unable to love tenderly because their unconscious fantasies are so centered around the oedipal and preoedipal figures that they feel guilty about these fantasies. Their transference love objects are both loved and feared. A therapeutic group enables them to work through these feelings so that they can learn to give and accept mature love. On the other hand, Glatzer also acknowledges that transference is not confined to the analyst and the analytic hour. It occurs with fellow patients in the therapeutic group as well as others outside the group.

Fried (1971) explains transference in group psychotherapy as follows:

> Transferences occur in groups when feelings and defenses (largely unconscious) and other behavior patterns (character traits) or isolated acts (acting out behavior), formerly directed at and associated with primary figures of childhood, are repeated toward the therapist and group members without being related to ongoing stimuli.
>
> . . . The transference neurosis occurs in classical analytic treatment partially because the analyst makes a point of remaining neutral and, indeed, becoming a silent screen for the patient's responses. The point can be strongly made that intense and prolonged feelings of love, hate, etc. are clearly the result of distortions on the part of the patient who has entered the transference neurosis. . . .
>
> In groups, where the therapist's expressive movements are seen, where his behavior—of necessity more active—is observed to reflect some of his predilections and opinions, where his personality in general is more bound to show, it is naturally more difficult to evoke and sustain the classical transference neurosis.
>
> . . . Transference feelings become interrupted or fragmented due to interruptions of others, who react with their own concerns and feelings, but the frequency with which identical feelings return, regardless of present-day reality, does convince many members that they are stuck in a rut that was imprinted in the soil of the personality long ago and from which an exit must be sought. (p. 60)

There are many and varied transference objects within a treatment group; the range depends, at least in part, on the counselor's criteria for selecting clients. Freedman and Sweet (1954) note that in group counseling transference also tends to be experienced differently than in individual therapy because of the multiplicity of transference objects and because transference objects do not regulate their reactions as does the therapist. In the group, too, the therapist is observed relating to others and thereby becomes less of a "blank screen."

Because patients do react to each other, Durkin (1964) concluded that transference must be analyzed in piecemeal fashion in groups, rather than systematically as a therapist would do in individual analysis:

> The repeated interruptions which inevitably occurred as one member or another brought his ideas, his feelings, his problems, or his interpretation to the others, could not be avoided without sacrificing full member participation. The effect was kaleidoscopic. To avoid it, the therapist would have had to conduct a leader-centered group in which he made all the interpretations and did not give the members a chance to come to grips on their own with whatever problem was brought up. . . . (p. 149)

From Bach's (1957) frame of reference, transference is a particular type of interpersonal contact in which *unfulfilled* regressive needs seek to fulfill themselves with objects unsuited for these activated infantile motivations. Clients set each other up to activate and release wishes and fantasies. However, they do not necessarily limit themselves to reexperiencing early childhood experiences; they also entice each other into dealing with their here-and-now unfulfilled needs or unfinished business with significant others. Individuals may express love, hate, or anger; may relive hurtful experiences; or may exhibit readiness to resolve conflict. Unlike the therapist in individual treatment, clients react when they are bombarded with transference demands. They also learn to discuss how it feels to be used as a transference object and to use others as transference objects, and they discover why individuals want to be loved or rejected for what they are and for what they have done rather than as transference objects.

Moreover, classic analytic explanation of transference can account for only part of what appears to be transference. Much of the interaction within a counseling group is reaction to reality. The transference object may look like, and even behave much like, a client's significant other. When, therefore, a female counselor (or a female client) responds to a shy, naive college male with understanding and acceptance and enables him to discuss his feelings of inadequacy with minimal threat this is the most wholesome interaction he probably has ever experienced. Naturally, he develops genuine tender feelings for such a female.

Bach's research suggests that, in part at least, clients do react to other members' characteristics such as size and body build and to their real behavior. Within a therapeutic group clients also learn to give and solicit genuine feedback. Consequently, Bach noted that the interchange is so vivid that it is very difficult for even the therapist alone to distinguish between unreal projections and justified reactions, between healthy self-assertions and the acting out of infantile wishes.

When the counselor encourages clients to take considerable responsibility for developing a therapeutic climate within their treatment group, for improving their *own* mental health, and for helping fellow clients change their behavior and attitudes, transference interactions will be interrupted. Fellow clients discourage intellectualization and encourage clients to express their real feelings for each other. By reacting openly and honestly, they learn to express positive feelings as well as negative ones, to recognize conflict and to cope directly with it rather than trying to ignore it or deny it. After a client has expressed his feelings toward a transference object and they have learned to deal with these feelings, the one experiencing transference is prepared to generalize to the relevant significant other outside the group.

For our present purposes, whenever a client assigns another the role of a significant person in his life with whom he has unfinished business and then treats the transference object as though he were that significant other, he is experiencing transference. Usually he is not aware of what he is doing, and the role which he projects unto the other tends to be that of a relative or close friend, but he can recognize what he is doing when the counselor says something to him such as: "And now that you have worked out your problem with Barbara, I would guess, Jim, that Barbara reminds you of someone with whom you have a similar problem. If my guess is correct, perhaps, you would like to tell us about that problem. Perhaps also, after you have prepared her for the role, you would like to ask Barbara to play that person's part and practice in role playing what you would like to say to that person."

Furthermore, that significant other need not necessarily be someone from his early childhood. It may be a spouse, a friend, a lover, a fellow worker, a supervisor, or a teacher as well as a parent or sibling. When transference is exhibited it almost always means that the client has some unfinished business with that significant other. It may be that he failed to say important goodbyes; that he let a relationship die that means much to him, and he wants to revive it; that he has failed to convey that he deeply appreciates a relationship and/or something a valued person has done for him; that he loves someone deeply and does not feel that he has expressed his feelings adequately; that he has unfinished business with someone whom he has hurt or been hurt by; or that he wants to resolve a problem with someone with whom he is at odds. Since clients are encouraged to empathize with each other, to express and cope with their feelings for each other, and to help each other face and resolve their problems, group clients' interactions tend to focus on the here and now. Even more traditional group therapists have noticed this tendency for group clients to focus on the present. Perhaps this is why some therapists have concluded that adolescents rarely experience transference in group counseling or therapy. Adolescents' primary focus is on the present and future. Although they frequently exhibit transference in groups, the problems with which they deal tend not to come from early childhood. Their projections tend to involve significant others with whom they are having current problems.

## Implications for Daily Living

Unfinished business with significant others influences the way individuals relate. Under the right circumstances perhaps everyone is inclined to assign someone the role of a significant other and relate to him as though he were that significant other. This is probably why a person might like *some* new acquaintances immediately and dislike others. On the other hand, Bach (1957) found that these transference objects usually looked like or behaved like, at least in a limited way, the relevant significant other. There was some realistic basis for the response.

Inasmuch as persons usually try to fulfill the roles assigned to them, both in treatment groups and in daily living, transference objects tend to become uncomfortable, or even angry, when they are assigned roles which they cannot fulfill or which they feel are inappropriate for them. Adolescents, for example, often complain that peers, parents, teachers, and even employers unexpectedly assign them responsibilities which thrust them into inappropriate roles—or at least roles for which they feel that they are not adequately prepared. Even if a role reflects favorably on them, everyone requires help in living a new role for which he has not been adequately prepared. If he understands the phenomenon of transference, and why it occurs, he finds it easier to accept those roles which enable him to help someone he cares about to complete important unfinished business.

## Use of Transference in Group Counseling

Classic analysis encourages transference with the therapist, and to a lesser degree with the other members of the group, and makes interpretation of transference a central element in treatment. Glatzer (1965) succinctly describes this process as follows: "As the patient repeats his infantile relationships in his relationship to the analyst, his buried feelings emerge and become accessible to interpretation. The repetition of the infantile conflicts under controlled analytic conditions enables the maturing ego to reevaluate and handle more objectively the early repressed conflicts." (p. 167)

For Fried (1965) psychoanalytic group psychotherapy tries to improve patients' emotional-mental functioning by helping them to recognize the unsuitability of archaic emotions transferred indiscriminately and automatically onto present-day figures who do not warrant them. Patients also come to understand the nature of their defenses and the ways in which they try to manage their emotional turmoil.

It is important to note that there exists a rather pronounced tradition among group therapists to select as the focus of their attention among transferred emotions, defenses, and transferred objects the third category, namely, the transference objects. I question the usefulness of this particular emphasis upon transference objects since I believe that the recognition of the transference object is of limited dynamic value. Understanding of the emotions that are being transferred, and particularly of the defenses that are being used as part and parcel of an emotional-mental approach that has become so firmly entrenched as to constitute an essential core of personality and character, is of highest dynamic importance. While it is often vividly clear and amusing to see how, given the cast of a therapy group, a person will focus on a certain member as though he or she were, say, a domineering intolerant older sibling, and it is tempting to point this out, such recognition of transference object is of lesser value than understanding of the transferred emotions and defenses against them. If someone discovers that he falsely equates an older woman in the group with his mother, he will find this interesting, but, in and of itself, such insight will not prompt new reactions and actions inside or outside the group. It is more important that the patient find out what emotions he transfers to the transference objects and what defenses and adaptations he uses in dealing with these emotions. And, above all, the patient must genuinely discover that both the old emotions and the defenses and adaptations can be replaced by truly up-to-date reactions. This last step is the one that clears the road for new behavior. (Fried, 1965, pp. 49–50)

Undoubtedly, many patients have been helped by psychoanalytic methods, especially when the therapist encourages patients to focus on transferred emotions and to learn essential new behaviors to relate more meaningfully to relevant significant others. On the other hand, this method tends to extend the length of treatment needlessly, to encourage dependency and acting out, and to threaten and/or hurt transference objects.

Naturally clients feel somewhat dependent when they seek help. For many it is a new experience and they feel insecure. When the counselor and his services are not known and understood by clients and the counselor provides minimum structuring, he elicits projection. To the degree that he remains a blank screen, an expert, and authority figure, the counselor further encourages transference responses.

Use of interpretation encourages unproductive intellectualization and hence tends to lengthen the treatment period unnecessarily. Some clients react to interpretation as though they were attacked. They also may change their behavior without achieving insight (Chapter 1).

Clients often find it easier to discuss their past, to discover crucial elements that shaped their behavior, and to understand the sources of their behavior than to identify improved ways of behaving and put them into practice. As a matter of fact, persons often enter group treatment knowing that they should do many things differently, and knowing why, but lack the self-confidence, the courage, and the interpersonal skills to behave differently. These qualities must be developed during treatment. Acceptance, support, and pressure from group members can encourage a client to experiment with new behaviors and help him convey his new self to significant others. Others' confidence in his ability to change and his observation of good models also motivate change. Though the counselor may allow clients to search for and share insights, he should not encourage it. Instead he should help clients discuss the problems that bother them and their doubts about their ability to change their behavior, encourage them to explore what they can do to resolve their problems, to take action, and, when they fail, to appraise their action.

When transference is elicited, clients are more apt to *act out* impulses toward the transference object (for example, verbally or even physically attack a foreman who is a hurtful authority figure). If they believe it appropriate within the safety of their group to assign a fellow client the role of a significant other and respond to him spontaneously as though he were that other, some clients may act irresponsibly and justify it as experimentation with new behaviors. Obviously, when transference is dealt with adequately, such tendencies to act out can be recognized and dealt with before the client acts out.

Acting out does reveal therapeutic material that can be dealt with afterwards; nevertheless, it should be prevented whenever possible. Such efforts protect the transference object, and/or significant other, from being hurt and the client himself from the subsequent guilt and natural consequences. If these complications are avoided, it is also easier to help the acting-out client express his feelings for the transference object, discover new ways of relating to him, and even practice these in role playing.

Finally, some counselors are concerned about the impact of transference on the transference object. Being treated as though he is someone else may be disturbing. Though he may be confused or hurt or frightened, he certainly can cope with these feelings as well as the problems uncovered in a sensitive, understanding, and accepting group. When the counselor discovers that the transference object has difficulty accepting the role he has been assigned, he tries to reflect the client's feelings with a comment such as: "You're confused. You can't understand why he responded to you as he did—it doesn't seem to make sense; his responses don't seem to be appropriate for what you have done and feel." In other words, the counselor helps the persons involved deal with their feelings for each other without even labeling the phenomenon as transference. When the counselor does open up discussion to help the transference object cope with the feelings projected on him, he merely alerts him to what is happening. In the instance above he might add: "It's almost like he has assigned you someone else's role—treating you as though you were that other person." This helps the transference object accept the projecting client's feelings toward him and makes it easier for him temporarily to play the assigned role. In order to encourage generalization beyond the treatment group, and to avoid intellectualization, the counselor may follow with a response such as: "Perhaps it would help if he could tell you of whom you remind him, so that we can set up a role-playing situation in which you can play the part and help him complete his unfinished business with that person. Naturally, we want to help him apply what he learns here to improve his relationship with this other person outside our group." Since another chapter is devoted to use of role playing in treatment groups, we note here simply that this approach focuses on the transferred emotions, on the learning of new human-relations skills, and on generalization outside the treatment group rather than intellectual discussion of the transference object.

With clear expectations, minimal use of interpretation, more focus on the present, greater effort to empathize with the client as he is, and the expectation that he can act more independently, much of this dependency can be prevented. A client is less inclined to become dependent if the counselor believes in his ability to solve his problems and expects him to take responsibility for doing so, expects his fellow clients to help him without letting him lean on them, is able to identify dependency feelings (and teach fellow clients to identify these feelings) and help him cope with his dependency feelings. Group members also can encourage the dependent client to learn new and more independent ways of behaving, reinforce independent behavior, provide support and assistance in analyzing the failure he experiences when he takes independent action, and encourage him to try again.

Less dependency also tends to develop when a client is encouraged to express his real feelings toward the transference object in his counseling group (and more often than not these feelings are positive ones) and deal with the consequences of responding genuinely toward him. When the feelings involve conflict, the client is helped by fellow clients as well as the counselor to determine what the problem is; to decide whether both are ready to resolve it or whether at least one prefers to express more revenge; and to decide how they can help each other learn essential new behaviors required for them to relate better (Chapter 13). After he has dealt directly with his transference object in the group, and at least begun to resolve their problems, he is encouraged to explore what his unfinished business is with the relevant significant other of whom the transference object reminds him. Often he elects to role play with the transference object the scene in which he practices communicating important feelings or practices communicating what he thinks their problem is and requests the significant other's assistance in solving the problem. Throughout the process the client learns to cope with the transference object and to develop readiness to deal with his significant other rather than to understand merely why he failed to complete his unfinished business with that significant other.

Transference will be exhibited in group counseling even when the counselor does not specifically encourage it. On such occasions the counselor should help clients express their feelings for each other, and when conflict arises to face up to it and deal with it. Unfortunately, too many clients are inclined to deny or ignore conflict rather than cope with it directly. Many also need to learn to express and accept others' positive feelings for them. Even reasonably healthy clients who try to learn to live more richly with significant others experience some of the deprivation of neurotics. To more fully actualize themselves they must learn to recognize and enjoy positive reactions as well as to cope with negative reactions and conflict.

Transference problems can be treated without formal recognition or interpretation of the underlying transeference dynamics. The clients' learning to cope with each other within the counseling group usually generalizes outside the group. Although this should not be forced, the counselor should use the therapeutic forces within the group to encourage clients to apply outside the group what they learned from counseling—to help them expect to behave differently outside their counseling group as well as within it.

## Eliciting Transference

Patterson (1959) concludes that ambiguity evokes projection and transference. The more unstructured or ambiguous the situation is and the more the counselor is perceived as an all-powerful expert, the more clients are inclined to project.

Even in groups in which the counselor does not try to be a blank screen and tries to involve members in establishing group norms, the counselor continues to be a special member:

> Every patient, to a great or lesser degree, perceives the therapist incorrectly because of transference distortions. Few are conflict-free in their attitudes toward such issues as parental authority, dependency, God, autonomy, and rebellion—all of which often come to be personified in the person of the therapist. (p. 195)

> As a result of transference the therapy group may grant the leader superhuman powers. His words are given more weight and imbued with more wisdom than they possess. . . . Groups, including groups of professional therapists, overestimate his presence and knowledge. They believe that there are great calculated depths to each of his interviews, that he predicts and controls all the events of the group. Even when he confesses puzzlement or ignorance, that too, is regarded as part of his technique, deliberately intended to have a particular effect in the group. (Yalom, 1975, pp. 198–199)

> The leader looms very large in the emotional life of the group. Try as he will he cannot shirk all the irrationally based trappings of his role. . . . Interviews with learners indicated that the leader's support and acceptance was of considerable value for some individuals in helping them to increase their evaluation of self-worth. Other members, through their constructive interaction with the leader, were able to reevaluate and to alter their relationships with parents or parental surrogates. Others identified strongly with the leader's world view and modus operandi; for example, even months later they might deal with a personal dilemma by trying to remember how the leader would have considered or handled a similar situation.

Conversely, strong criticism, negative judgment or rejection by the leader was received by some members as an exceedingly important indictment. Recall that the majority of the Casualties reported having been deeply affected by an attack or rejection by the leader. Some of the Casualties recalled months later some of the negative statements of the leaders with extraordinary vividness. (Lieberman, Yalom, & Miles, 1973, p. 436)

Thus, a counselor must seriously consider whether he can ever be a blank screen for a client. In group counseling clients observe how the counselor reacts to others as well as how he attempts to help them. They recognize that he is a real person with his own feelings, values, needs, and expectations. Where the counselor sits and what he does, as well as his words, determine what clients expect from him. If he sits in an open circle of chairs, occupies a chair like the clients, and encourages clients to react to him as well as to fellow clients, he will be perceived more as a true member than if he maintains his distance by sitting behind a desk and enhances his status by assuming the primary responsibility for helping individuals deal with transference. On the other hand, even a group-centered counselor is someone special whose words and actions are valued more than those of other members. Clients do, and should, expect him to describe treatment conditions within which clients seem to be most effectively helped. The roles he plays determine the degree to which he makes clients dependent upon him and himself a primary transference object.

Because of his many and varied contacts with clients outside of the counseling relationship a counselor who has varied contacts with clients in an institution certainly will not be seen as a blank screen. Clients get to know him as a person, and they will be confused about what they should expect from him in various contexts. Nevertheless, he can still be effective, provided that he does not have responsibility for evaluating or disciplining them and that he takes special care to distinguish clearly the purpose for which each group is organized and how it differs from groups in which counselors function as the counselor.

Can a counselor ever be completely objective? Probably not, but having had the experience of being a client in a group can increase his awareness of his own needs, values, expectations of clients and of himself, and his unresolved problems; help him understand how these factors influence his effectiveness as a counselor; and help him learn to function more effectively. Goodman, Marks, and Rockberger (1964) also made a strong case for cooperative supervision among colleagues on the job to minimize interference by these elements with the counselor's effectiveness.

A counselor's own needs, his clinical experience, and his professional preparation all influence the degree to which he elicits transference. Very likely, and perhaps unconsciously, he reinforces certain behaviors and discourages other behaviors. The nature and extent of the transference elicited in his groups seems to depend on his honest responses to the following questions: Does he believe he knows what most of the clients should do to improve their adjustment? To what extent should he encourage them to decide what they should do? How do dependent clients make him feel? Is it important for him to impress his clients with his insightful interpretations? Does he believe that most clients must understand why they behaved as they have in the past before they can change their behavior? Does he encourage clients to use him, or other members of the group, as transference objects? Does he encourage his clients to express their feelings for each other, to try to cope directly with the conflicts that arise, and, where appropriate, to generalize to significant others outside the treatment group? To what extent does he encourage them to focus discussion on their present problems and specific changes in their behavior? Does he encourage his clients to focus on early childhood experiences, or rather to deal only with the part of their history that has relevance for their current problems?

In sum, the counselor's needs, values, and expectations help determine the extent and nature of transference reactions within the treatment group —not only the extent to which the counselor is the primary stimulus for transference, but the degree to which other members become transference objects.

## Countertransference

When the counselor assigns a client the role of a significant other in his own life and treats that client as though he were a significant other, the counselor is experiencing countertransference. In order to prevent this phenomenon from interfering with his effectiveness the counselor must be able to recognize when it occurs. Korner (1950) lists the following reactions of the counselor (or therapist) when he is experiencing countertransference: his thoughts wander away from the interaction; he has difficulty focusing attention on a client's communications; he feels insensitive to a client's needs; he has difficulty comprehending what a client is trying to convey; suddenly he is distracted by thoughts unrelated to a client's words; he becomes impatient with a client's progress or feels at a loss in how to help him; or he feels too protective of a client. Similarly, Cohen (1952) describes the following clues which suggest countertransference: unreasoning dislike, inability to feel with him, overemotional reaction to his troubles, excessive liking for him, dreading the treatment period with him, undue concern about him between sessions, defensiveness, argumentativeness, indifference, inattentiveness, impatience, and feeling angrily sympathetic with him. Whenever a counselor notices any of these behaviors, he should listen to a recording of that counseling session (preferably with a trusted colleague) to determine the nature of his participation, to detect and analyze his own emotional needs, and appraise his management of the therapeutic forces within the group. Goodman, Marks, and Rockberger (1964) contend that counter-transference distorts the counselor's communications and interferes with his ability to manage resistance within a counseling group.

Whether the feelings are very positive or negative (or even make the counselor feel confused and/or powerless), the counselor must be able to sense countertransference and ask himself: "Why does he make me feel this way?" "How can I use these feelings to detect how my client must be feeling and respond to his feelings productively?"

> Patients naturally produce feelings in their analyst: some make them feel uncomfortable or anxious, induce feelings of exasperation, annoyance and even anger; others can stimulate erotic feelings or arouse over-determined sympathy. Some of these feelings may be due to conflicts within the analyst which have not been sufficiently resolved in his own personal analysis, with the result that the patient's unconscious needs and difficulties provoke those of the analyst. But positive use can be made of the countertransference. There is for instance the patient who manages to induce in the analyst a feeling of being rendered use-less and expendable: the analyst can usefully ask whether, if he feels this way about the patient, the patient might make others feel like this, and if so, why. Similarly, when the analyst feels that he is really wanted by and useful to the patient, he must not only guard against enjoying the enlargement of his own ego, but also find out if the patient has an unconscious need to make the analyst feel this way. (p. 17)
>
> A start in training could perhaps be made by helping counsellor-students to understand their own counter-transference, so that they learn how all kinds of feelings can be utilized towards therapeutic ends. Wood (1970) instances a group of social workers who were frustrated by their clients and made to feel helpless, angry and hostile. The social workers felt that they were falling short of what an ideal social worker should be: namely one who is genuine, accepting, warm, completely tolerant, whose business is always to care. They held to the faith that if enough is given, then favourable response is bound to result—and it did not. The real breakthrough came when they were helped to understand the counter-transference, and to accept their hostility with their clients rather than maintain an idealized role. They had been denying their normal human responses instead of using them as pointers towards under-standing their clients' problems. (Wilson, 1974, pp. 24–25)

Suicidal patients, in particular, tend to arouse in their therapists counter-transference hatred (Maltsberger & Buie, 1974). As Wilson indicates above, they conclude that a therapist's awareness of his patient's impact, and per-haps understanding and acceptance of it, are essential to cope with it thera-peutically. When a counselor (or a therapist) denies or distorts counter-transference hatred he increases the danger of a patient's suicide.

The counselor (or therapist) must recognize and accept the fact that he does not have to be perfect—functioning perfectly in his ideal role al-ways. He is a human being with unfulfilled needs and unresolved problems, and consequently his countertransference reactions can interfere with his effectiveness (and clients' effectiveness in helping each other). Periodic therapy (especially in a group with other counselors) and good supervision are essential to alert the counselor to his unfulfilled needs and unresolved problems (and to enhance his personal growth). Such experiences also enable him to increasingly use his countertransference reactions to understand his clients and to use these new insights to help his clients develop new goals during treatment.

There also is much to be said in favor of Korner's argument for recognition of countertransference and disengagement. Occasionally the counselor discovers his feelings toward a client so distracting that he must clear the air in order to make the rest of the treatment hour productive. Bob's behavior in a parent group illustrates such a case. These parents sought help with their underachieving, uncooperative ninth- and tenth-grade children. Though Bob was hostile and had difficulty discussing his own pain and his wife refused to accept counseling, he convinced the counselor that he should be admitted to the group. The men were skilled craftsmen and factory workers; only Chuck had attended college (and he dropped out at the end of his second year). Most of the women were college graduates. During the first eight sessions all except Bob had openly discussed their problems. Bob had severely criticized the others for wanting their children to do well academically so that they could go to college. He belittled the value of education and resented his college-professor wife's ambition for their son, an only child. In spite of these attitudes he often requested the counselor to advise the others: "Tell them what to do and insist that they do it." At the beginning of the ninth session two of the women and one of the men shared some success experiences. Then Chuck said, "I can't seem to get my kid to do good school work. He just doesn't seem to give a damn. He is doing the same thing I did when I was in high school. I don't mind working two jobs to get enough money ahead to send him to college, but it sure as hell gripes me that he doesn't have the good sense to see the good of it." When the counselor said, "You'd like for him to have something better than you have had," Bob said, "So you think that college is great too—that college graduates are better than the rest of us—that you are better than I am. If you are so damn good why don't you tell Chuck what to do." After a painful pause of a minute or two (during which he tried to formulate what to say) the counselor said, "I guess that you don't think that we try to understand how you feel—that we put you on the spot like your wife does." This evoked Bob's attack on counseling and his second threat to quit the group, and for the first time the others were not bullied by him. They told him off.

After a rough 15-minute interchange in which the counselor was more quiet than usual and seemed to be pondering what to say, the counselor responded to Bob as follows: "I can understand why the others responded to you as they just did. In fact, I am pleased to see that they are strong enough not to be bullied by you any more, but I would like for you to stay if you are willing to try to talk about the things that really bother you—if you are willing to accept responsibility for working on your problem. I'd like for all of us to try to capture how you feel, help you express these feelings, and figure out what you can do. It has been difficult for me to like you, but I'll try. It has been difficult for me to help you too. When I try to guess how you feel and to help you express your feelings, you deny them. When I try to help others discuss their feelings, you criticize them for having these feelings. Little wonder that they attack you. On the other hand, I feel that they will try to help you too, when you are willing to discuss what really bothers you, to decide what precise new behaviors you must learn, and learn them."

Here the counselor was discussing his own feelings, and hence for that moment was a client, but he quickly got out of the role. What he said cleared the air for himself so that he could focus better on his client's needs. It also let Bob know that the counselor wanted him to stay, it structured relationships, and it provided new material for discussion. After a brief discussion of their feelings for Bob and his for them, the group asked Bob to try to discuss what really bothered him. Had they dwelt on the counselor's feelings for clients, he would have indicated that the time was for them— that he discussed his feelings for them only when he felt that he must to clear the air and maintain his effectiveness.

The case above illustrates one way a counselor can cope with a distracting client. Korner recommended that when a counselor recognizes countertransference, he proceed cautiously the rest of that treatment session— that he limit his interpretations and reflections and that he resist the temptation to push the client. Finally, he urged the counselor to consult with associates concerning that particular session. If a counselor records every treatment session, he can preserve the raw data for critical analysis whenever countertransference is suspected. He also should video-record the session that follows the suspect one to pick up subtle nonverbal clues that may be influencing the relationship.

Frequently, when the counselor detects countertransference in groups he can merely sit back for a moment and listen to the interaction until he tunes in again. Sometimes it is necessary for him to ask the group to review what occurred during the period in which he was distracted by countertransference. Occasionally he may need to admit that he was distracted and to request a review of the interaction. Such behaviors enable him to disengage himself from the countertransference object and tune in to the interaction so that he can function more effectively for the rest of the counseling session. Careful study of the recording between sessions helps him prepare to cope with the problem better for the next session.

The more effectively the counselor involves clients in the helping process and solicits their feedback on his efforts to help them, the more readily do they respond to him openly. As clients become increasingly aware of the phenomenon of transference, they also detect when the counselor appears to be assigning a role out of his life to a group member. On the one hand, clients can become very upset when they believe that the counselor has favorites:

> [A rule that] the leader shall have no favorites seems to be essential for the stability of every working group. . . . If one could not be the favorite, then there must be no favorite at all. Everyone is granted an equal investment in the leader and out of this demand for equality is born what we have come to know as group spirit. (Yalom, 1975, p. 197)

On the other hand, when clients detect countertransference they can accept that as part of his being human—a real person with problems and unfinished business with significant others. Some counselors contend that at such times the counselor should be a client and enlist clients' assistance. The research on self-disclosure for the counselor is not conclusive on this point (Openness, Chapter 3). However, it seems relatively clear that it is sufficient for a counselor to own the problem, and without going into the details share what new behaviors he is learning to cope with it. He also may wish to enlist clients' special assistance while he is disengaging himself and becoming once again primarily a helper. Moreover, clients can accept his countertransference better than they can his caring more for one client than the rest.

## Summary

An individual is exhibiting transference when he assigns another the role of a significant other and treats him as though he were that significant other. Transference occurs even within normal interactions in nontherapeutic relationships. The counselor's perception of the treatment process, his role in it, his response to transference, his own needs, his expectations for his clients, his criteria for selecting members of a treatment group, and the needs of his clients determine the extent to which the counselor becomes the primary transference object, and the extent to which members use each other as transference objects.

Those counselors and therapists who use transference as a primary vehicle for treatment do many things to induce it. Although undoubtedly many patients have been treated successfully by this method, the writer does not recommend it for his clients because it makes them unnecessarily dependent, encourages intellectualization, extends the length of the treatment process, precipitates acting out, and possibly could hurt or confuse the transference object. Anyway, the classic analytic explanation of transference can account for only part of such interaction. Much of the interaction within a counseling group is reaction to reality. What a client says and does precipitates genuine reaction from another—not transference or counter-transference.

Instead of inducing transference and interpreting it, the counselor encourages clients to empathize with each other, to discuss problems openly, to seek and try out solutions, and to learn new behaviors and attitudes. Clients tend then to face up to the conflicts that arise among individuals within their counseling group. The counselor encourages clients to express their feelings for each other, and when conflicts arise to resolve them. When he feels that a client is exhibiting transference he also helps that client explore with whom he may have unfinished business and decide whether he would like to practice a proposed solution with the assistance of the transference object in role playing.

When a counselor assigns the role of a significant other from his own life to a client and treats him as though he were that person, the counselor is exhibiting countertransference. Such distortions interfere with the counselor's effectiveness. Clues that may help a counselor recognize this condition are reviewed in the text. When he recognizes countertransference he asks himself, "Why is this client affecting me as he is and how can I use this information to detect therapeutic material and respond to it?" Sometimes he also must step back emotionally, disengage himself, and decide how to reengage into the therapeutic interaction.

## Discussion Questions

1. What are the consequences of building relationships on transference responses in daily life?
2. What are the consequences of a transference object trying to fulfill the role assigned him?
3. To what degree would it be appropriate to say in TA terms that any interaction which is not adult–adult is transference?
4. What are the pros and cons for deliberately eliciting transference as a treatment vehicle?
5. How does ambivalence affect the likelihood of transference occurring in a counseling group?
6. What are the implications of the author's broader definition of transference for the treatment process?
7. How does the treatment of transference recommended in this chapter prevent acting out behavior? Why prevent it? Why not just use the consequences therapeutically?
8. To what extent may transference reactions be at least a response in part to the transference object?
9. How may a counselor differentiate between a client's justified reactions toward another member and transference reactions?

10. How does transference and/or countertransference effect communication between members?

11. Describe an instance in which transference or countertransference interfered with communication. To what degree did it also contribute to resistance and acting out behavior?

12. How do you feel about a counselor self-disclosing as a way of dealing with countertransference?

13. When a counselor notices transference being exhibited, what should he do?

14. Harold responds to Sam as a transference object, but Sam seems to accept Harold's reactions as deserved and real. What are the implications of Sam's behavior for Harold's growth? For Sam's growth? To what degree does it make any difference whether Harold treats Sam as a positive or negative transference object?

# References

Bach, G. R. Observations on transference and object relations in the light of group dynamics. *The International Journal of Group Psychotherapy*, 1957, *7*, 64–76.

Cohen, M. B. Countertransference and anxiety. *Psychiatry*, 1952, *15*, 231–243.

Durkin, H. E. *The group in depth.* New York: International Universities, 1964.

English, H. B., & English, A. C. *A comprehensive dictionary of psychological and psychoanalytical terms.* New York: Logmans, Green & Co., 1958.

Freedman, M. B., & Sweet, B. S. Some specific features of group psychotherapy and their implications for selection of patients. *The International Journal of Group Psychotherapy*, 1954, *4*, 355–368.

Fried, E. Some aspects of group dynamics and the analysis of transference and defenses. *The International Journal of Group Psychotherapy*, 1965, *15*, 44–56.

Fried, E. Basic concepts in group psychotherapy. Chapter 3A in H. I. Kaplan & B. J. Sadock (Eds.), *Comprehensive group psychotherapy.* Baltimore: Williams and Wilkins 1971.

Glatzer, H. T. Aspects of transference in group psychotherapy. *The International Journal of Group Psychotherapy.* 1965, *15*, 167–176.

Goodman, M., Marks, M., & Rockberger, H. Resistance in group psychotherapy enhanced by the countertransference reaction of the therapist. *The International Journal of Group Psychotherapy*, 1964, pp. 332–343.

Korner, I. J. Ego involvement and the process of disengagement. *Journal of Consulting Psychology*, 1950, *14*, 206–209.

Lieberman, M. A., Yalom, I. D., & Miles, M. D. *Encounter groups: First facts.* New York: Basic Books, 1973.

Maltsberger, J. T., & Buie, D. H. Countertransference hate in the treatment of suicidal patients. *Archives of General Psychiatry*, 1974, *30*, 625–633.

Patterson, C. H. *Counseling and psychotherapy: Theory and practice.* New York: Harper & Row, Publishers, 1959.

Wilson, J. Transference and counter-transference in counselling. *British Journal of Guidance and Counseling,* 1974, *2,* 15–26.

Wolf, A. The psychoanalysis of groups. In M. B. Rosenbaum & M. Berger, *Group psychotherapy and group function.* New York: Basic Books, 1963.

Wood, E. The need to make judgments. *Contact,* 1970, #30.

Yalom, I. D. *The theory and practice of group psychotherapy.* New York: Basic Books, 1975.

# Resistance

Failure to cooperate in the therapeutic process is resistance. In individual counseling a client may exhibit resistance by arriving late for an appointment, skipping sessions, postponing appointments, appearing unable to talk about problems, refraining from the definition of precise, behavioral goals, questioning whether or not he can be helped, dwelling on earlier events in his life, becoming preoccupied with side issues or small talk, acting distracted (or unconfused), acting out on his impulses, demanding or pleading for advice, being spontaneously cured (flight to health), and dropping out of treatment without getting help. In addition to all of the above which are exhibited in groups too, clients protect themselves and fellow clients by advice giving, protective talking, monopolizing, selective silences (and for an individual this can go unnoticed), talking about persons outside of their group, wondering whether or not the group is really a safe place to discuss personal problems, questioning whether or not confidences will be (or have been) kept, requesting further clarification on what is really expected of clients in a group, and acting overwhelmed about their responsibility for helping to develop and maintain therapeutic group norms.

## Client's Ambivalence

Sometime or other most clients experience ambivalence when they try to change: wanting and not wanting the services for which they have contracted (Osborn, 1949). Although clients who have heard the type of presentations and participated in the intake interviews described in Chapter 1 tend to exhibit less resistance and take more responsibility for coping with it than most clients, they still experience the type of ambivalence described by Osborn. Occasionally, even the highly motivated, confident client will (1) have difficulty admitting even to himself what really worries and upsets him, (2) wonder whether or not the other clients will continue to accept him when they discover what he is really like and/or what he has done, (3) question whether or not he is willing to suffer as much as may be required in order to solve his problem, (4) abhor the thought that opening himself up to some problems that also may uncover still others of which he is unaware, and (5) doubt whether or not he can really achieve the goals which he and his counselor defined cooperatively. Thus, resistance arises out of a broad spectrum of fears—not a desire to do battle with the counselor or therapist.

Perhaps, the most powerful source of help for assisting clients to deal with resistance is the genuine self-respect they experience as they struggle to discuss painful material, find that they can do it, and discover the extent to which they are admired by fellow clients for doing it. Moreover, discovering that their fellow clients can provide quality support (and where it is not forthcoming the counselor is able to detect their need for it and teach fellow clients to provide it) reinforces further risk taking behavior.

## Impact of Resistance on the Counselor

At one time or another most counselors and therapists have had difficulty accepting the resisting client, detecting precisely what he is feeling, and responding therapeutically to these feelings. When a counselor is most effective he can listen to the resisting client, detect the resisting client's underlying fear, reflect it, and enlist the other clients' assistance in these activities too. He also is able to enlist their assistance in trying to answer questions such as: "Why is this client having this impact on me right now? What unfinished business with whom does it suggest that I try to discuss? How can I use these data to respond to him now?" When a counselor is less effective, it is easy to react personally to the resisting client's behavior— to feel rejected, unappreciated, frustrated, and angry. On such occasions the counselor must try to determine the extent to which his techniques and/ or his own unresolved problems account for his client's resistance. Goodman, Marks, and Rockberger (1964) describe how they met together weekly for mutual supervision for two and one-half years and what they learned from these experiences:

> The focus shifted slowly, almost imperceptibly at first, from patient dynamics to exposing and exploring the irrational and distorted in our own perceptions of the therapeutic situation.

It became apparent that not only were our distortions interfering with our role as group therapists but that each one of us had specific islands of sensitivity (repetitive familiar situations) which had not been brought to light or resolved in his personal and control analysis. We found that the setting of peer group supervision permitted shades and nuances of emotional working through which contrasted with the authority-bound setting of the traditional supervisory experience.

The procedure in these sessions was for one of the therapists to choose for presentation and discussion the group which was not meeting his expectation for movement and in which he was encountering stiff resistance. The presenter would often present a tape recording of a session of his problem group, and his colleagues would question his interventions as well as the meaning of the interaction of group members. They would speak of the feeling they got as they listened to the session, and the presenting therapist would speak of what he saw as the resistance. The focus would then shift to some excess or lack of effective response in the presenter, a particular defensive attitude or position, and the feelings and reactions of his colleagues. . . . As we studied our countertransference to our groups, our patients, and each other, we became increasingly aware that these in turn induced reactions in our patients and led, at times, to seemingly impenetrable resistance phenomena within our therapy groups. (pp. 335–336)

We would, therefore, hypothesize that the phenomenon of a therapy group in a state of resistance which the therapist recognizes but is unable to deal with is likely to be related integrally to a countertransference distortion of the therapist. The therapist becomes bound up in affects related to his personal past, which are inappropriate to his current situation, and he cannot act constructively. We have no doubt that many premature terminations of treatment are based on such phenomena.

We have found the peer supervisory group an excellent setting in which to bring into consciousness many of the binding images which interfere with our work. As was noted in the clinical examples, the peer supervisory group often mirrors the complex forces operative in the therapeutic group situation, and as such may be more immediately helpful than the didactic supervisory relationship, which is more paradigmatic of the individual treatment situation. (p. 343)

These professionals helped each other recognize how lack of congruence influenced the therapist's ability to detect and respond helpfully to therapeutic material. As indicated in Chapter 2, their experience endorses peer supervision. Even better results can be achieved when peers use video rather than audio recordings as their source of data and help each other define precise, behavioral goals *for their professional growth*.

## Prevention

Of course the best method for coping with resistance is to do everything possible to prevent it, and when it occurs to recognize it early and deal with it (and to teach clients to recognize it and deal with it sensitively). Providing clients with the data they require to decide whether to participate; helping them accept responsibility for convincing themselves and their counselor that they are committed to discuss their problems openly, to formulate clear, behavioral goals, and to learn new behaviors; and helping them establish and maintain therapeutic group norms helps prevent resistance and to cope with it when it occurs. Furthermore, careful selection and assignment of clients to groups can help prevent group resistance (Chapter 1). With the type of structuring described in Chapter 1 most clients begin the first session by talking openly about what really worries them. The counselor takes note of their therapeutic client behavior, reinforces it, and helps clients reinforce it for each other: for example, "Dan, you are really impressed with the way Marjorie is able to discuss what really bothers her." Their norms encourage open discussion of problems, enhance self-respect, and reinforce those who do it first to such an extent that clients soon tend to perceive failure to admit resistance and try to cope with their own resistance as deviant behavior.

## Counselor Modeling

When clients are threatened in the ways described earlier they exhibit resistance. From the first time a client exhibits resistance the counselor models facilitating behavior and helps clients learn to do it too. He empathizes with the resisting client, tries to capture precisely what he is experiencing, helps him share his fears, and also his determination to face the problem and discuss it, and he reinforces the client's courage to deal with it. The extent to which the counselor can detect and reflect accurately in meaningful, concrete terms helps the resisting client proceed feeling that he has support on which he can rely. Thus, the counselor models acceptance of the client's struggle with resistance and encourages him to face the problem rather than excusing retreating from it.

After a resisting client has experienced some success in his struggle with resistance for the first time, the counselor may elect to review why he did what he did for the entire group, discuss the phenomenon of resistance and why it is important to help the client face whatever painful material there is involved (but not force him to do so), and help him to decide what he must do with whom to learn his desired new behaviors. Early in the treatment process he teaches clients to recognize and to help each other cope with it.

Sometimes when a client recognizes resistance in himself, he may request a private session with the counselor. To enable such a client to reap the full benefits from group counseling, the counselor should encourage him to discuss his reasons for such a request with fellow clients prior to the private session. Several benefits follow: (1) Other clients are more likely to accept the client's need for time alone with the counselor without the usual "sibling" rivalry. (2) In helping the client discuss why he is unable to discuss a certain topic, he discovers in others the support and encouragement he requires to discuss it, and without the private conference. (3) Such discussion enables the counselor to structure the private conference for other clients as well as this one. Here the writer agrees wholeheartedly with Bach (1954): that such private sessions should be group-centered—getting the client ready to discuss and resolve his problems in the group. As long as a client is a member of a treatment group, he should look upon the group as his primary source of help. This approach also prevents the drainage problem discussed by Bach, in which clients save personal material for the private conferences, allowing group sessions to degenerate into superficial material.

## Group Resistance

Occasionally most clients will exhibit resistance simultaneously (group resistance). This is most apt to occur when clients with similar problems (gifted underachievers) or similar motivating forces for their problems are placed in the same group (Freedman & Sweet, 1954). All or most of the clients are threatened by the same relevant, but feared discussion topics. Obviously, the counselor should have detected the problem in intake interviews and assigned no more than two of a type to the same group (Chapter 2). Even when clients have been selected and placed in groups with care there will be times when clients exhibit group resistance. On such occasions the counselor should merely note that several and perhaps all of them are faced with something that is difficult to discuss, suggest that each try to guess what he feels each of the others wants to discuss but is reluctant to discuss, convey his willingness to help each, and if that does not work, at least discuss why it is so difficult for each to discuss the problems with which he is struggling privately at that moment.

> I never cease to be awed by the rich lode of subterranean data which exists in every group and in every meeting. Beneath each sentiment expressed there are layers of invisible, unvoiced ones. How to tap these riches? Sometimes when there is a long silence in a meeting I express this very thought: "There is so much information that could be available to us all today if only we could excavate it. I wonder if we could, each of us, tell the group about some thoughts that occurred to us in this silence which we thought of saying but didn't." The exercise is more effective, incidentally, if the therapist himself starts it or participates. For example, "I've been feeling antsy in the silence, wanting to break it, not wanting to waste time, but on the other hand feeling irritated that it always has to be me doing this work for the group," or "I've been feeling torn between wanting to get back to the struggle between you and me, Mike. I feel uncom-

fortable with this much tension and anger, but I don't know, yet, how to help understand and resolve it." When I feel there has been a particularly great deal unsaid in a meeting, I have often used, with success, a technique such as this: "It's now six o'clock and we still have a half an hour left, but I wonder if you each would imagine that it is already six thirty and that you're on your way home. What kind of disappointments would you have about the meeting today?" (Yalom, 1975, pp. 137–138).

If the counselor happens to be making a video recording of such sessions, he may, after such comments, merely say, "Let's roll the tape back a few minutes and perhaps if we observe ourselves for a few minutes we will be able to figure out what we need to say to whom to make it easier for her or him to talk about what really bothers her or him." The counselor also may ask each to review what he thinks is expected of each on occasions like this, what he has accomplished, and what he has left to do. Usually, such a request calls forth a commitment from individuals to the group similar to that called for in the intake interview. It also may cause members to question whether certain members have the essential commitment required for memership. When this occurs the counselor may be tempted to schedule an intake for all or just those members about whom members have doubts. Inasmuch as this is a group decision, it is much better to help members get the problem out into the open and give the questionable members a chance to demonstrate their commiment to discuss their problems and to learn their desired new behaviors. Frequently, such discussions clarify doubtful members' goals and convey to them others' commitment to help them change. When, however, they choose to drop out or are asked the leave, the problem can be handled in such a manner that they leave with a clearer notion of what is required of them to change, the consequences of failure to change, increased confidence in their potential for learning new behaviors, and increased appreciation of why others cannot and should not allow them to block their growth. When the group permits the doubtful client to remain on probation, the counselor must help them state precisely what their new expected behaviors will be to remain and achieve full membership again. Usually when even reluctant clients are treated so honestly and are given a chance to demonstrate their readiness for growth they come through convincingly or voluntarily withdraw from the group. Thus, group cohesiveness is used to cope with group resistance. Within the basic treatment model described in Chapter 1, group cohesiveness need not be feared as Slavson (1957) suggested it is in psychoanalytic groups.

## Need for Structure

What in the early group sessions may appear to be group resistance may actually be clients' reaction to inadequate structuring. From their research with out-patient World War II veterans, Powdermaker and Frank (1953) concluded that intense competition results from too little structure and clients are inhibited by too much structure. For coping with resistance they recommended that:

1. The therapist give the group considerable responsibility for coping with resistance, especially when there is a patient with initiative with whom the resistant patient can identify. In such a case he can devote his efforts to facilitating the process of identification. Often this is best done by maintaining an interested silence. Therapy also is often facilitated when the therapist does not attempt to meet a challenge from a resistant patient but leaves it to the group.
2. In a newly formed group the therapist should not pressure a withdrawn patient to talk about himself until others have set an example. In a mature group he may not need to be concerned about this, since others will have already done so.
3. In a newly formed group the therapist should provide support to the resisting patient when the group fails to provide it. Essentially, support consists of taking the patient seriously and conveying the idea that members want to understand his problem and help him discuss it.
4. He should be alert for situations in which members of the group express feelings which seem to be similar to those of the resistant patient and call these similar feelings to the attention of the resisting client.
5. He should seize the opportunity to take advantage of a response by the resistant patient to any occurrence in the immediate situation related to his feelings.

## Client's Role

Bry (1951) also encourages the therapist to help the group deal with the resisting client. Early in the life of the group she encourages the therapist to devote considerable effort to helping patients understand why the phenomenon occurs, how it may be detected in oneself and others, and how they may respond to it. With such preparation she says that patients learn to manage it and to use it to detect therapeutic material. When, for example, patients exhibit protectiveness sooner or later the other patients detect what is happening and urge the resisting client to stop "beating around the bush."

On the other hand, Bry believes that there are situations in which the therapist must take over. She says that this is usually required in the early stages of the group, but it also may be necessary later when the resistance results from an unusually complex situation or when members of the group do not recognize it. Among those types which patients do not tend to recognize are intellectualization and advice giving.

Bry claims that the objective is to recognize and overcome resistance in order to proceed with the task of understanding the nature of the basic conflict and/or unfinished business with the significant other. Her interpretations are directed at the basic anxieties as well as toward the characteristic defense mechanism used. With reference to acting out, she interprets it immediately and focuses attention on the emotions displayed. Though she relies heavily on the use of interpretation, she realizes the therapist must take cognizance of his or her treatment goals and the patient's readiness to accept and use that which is uncovered by the interpretation.

Obviously, Bry is correct—clients can detect another client's resisting behavior and confront him. Moreover, clients can use confrontation productively with each other. For the writer better results tend to be achieved by teaching clients to empathize with the resisting client, to detect precisely what he is feeling, and to reflect these feelings to help him expose his resistance rather than to help them to dig it out with confrontation. Similar techniques are used to help clients recognize and to reflect resisting clients' underlying feelings associated with their tendency to act out (also resistance). They learn to accept readily why whenever possible they should try to detect and to reflect desires to act out and to help them discuss these feelings openly prior to acting out on them impulsively, and then having to deal with the resulting guilt. They also recognize readily why acting out decreases a client's motivation to face and resolve the problems associated with acting out. However, this type of discussion can become very attractive to clients and can be used by them to divert their attention away from relevant therapeutic material.

In any event, clients will pressure the resisting client to talk when they want to help him and when they are not certain they can trust him until he has shared his problems with them. However, it is questionable whether the counselor should encourage other clients to put the resisting client "on the hot seat." A few have even gone so far as to designate a given chair (such as the red chair) for the resisting client when it is his turn to face up to the problems which he seems to be resisting to face. Rather than trying to force such a client to talk, the counselor should help the other clients encourage him to talk. In order to profit fully from the therapeutic interaction within his group, every client must play two roles simultaneously—helper and client—listening very carefully to what other clients say, helping the speaker express himself, allowing the speaker's discussion to uncover therapeutic material within him, and dealing with his own problems as he becomes aware of them.

In psychoanalysis interpretation is the primary method used to cope with resistance. Perhaps better results can be obtained by use of reflection to help clients surface their feelings related to resistance, learn to manage them, and use them as energy for change. The four reasons which were presented in Chapter 1 for using reflection in preference to interpretation apply to management of resistance too: (1) clients are encouraged to assume more responsibility for their own growth; (2) they feel more like a partner in the process rather than someone who is treated by a superior; (3) reflection focuses upon underlying feelings and harnesses them for change rather than encouraging clients to intellectualize, and (4) clients often feel attacked when a counselor or therapist interprets their behavior. Adolescents are especially sensitive and vulnerable to any adult's judgment of their worth (Ackerman, 1955). Except for the dependent client, adolescents resent the air of superiority conveyed by interpretation. On the other hand, genuine participation in the recognition and management of their own resistance to growth enhances clients' self-respect, makes them more sensitive to underlying feelings in other situations which produce conflict and misunderstandings, and generally improves their relationship skills outside of their counseling group. They become more sensitive to their own inner feelings and learn to manage them more effectively.

## Summary

Resistance is a natural phenomenon in the therapeutic process which occurs when clients are threatened by change. Its impact can be minimized by carefully preparing clients for the therapeutic experience, by helping them accept responsibility for talking openly, by helping them learn new behaviors and by teaching them to help others change. Perhaps nothing reinforces these commitments as much as the increased self-respect they feel when they discuss their problems openly, discover that they can learn specific new behaviors, realize the extent to which they are admired and accepted for facing painful material early, and sense the degree to which members can learn to provide a quality support system.

When resistance is first observed by the counselor he tries to detect precisely how the resisting client feels, to reflect these feelings, and to provide quality support while the client discusses these feelings. Immediately after his first successful experience in helping a client cope with his feelings of resistance, the counselor describes the phenomenon, describes how it is exhibited, explains why it occurs, and describes what clients can do to help each other deal with it. The need to resist is further reduced when clients observe peers modelling self-disclosure and behavior change.

Resisting clients usually are reacting to the fear of change, the fear that the change will be too painful or the fear that the change will not be for the good. When, therefore, the counselor detects the resisting client's feelings behind the resistance, he is less inclined to feel rejected, unappreciated, frustrated, and angry. Consequently, he can more effectively use his energy to help the resisting client share his fears, sense the group's real support, and try to learn desired new behaviors. He also learns to use his responses to the resisting client to better understand the resisting client and to help him, and to teach others to help him. Clients do learn readily to recognize others' resistance and use it therapeutically, and to recognize and cope with their own resistance.

## Discussion Questions

1. To what extent, and in what specific ways, may effective structuring be used to prevent resistance? countertransference?
2. What happens when some clients fail to disclose and to participate therapeutically during the first several sessions? What may the counselor do when he discovers this problem?
3. What may the counselor do to establish group norms which call for regular attendance, promptness, and active participation by all members? How may such norms influence clients' effectiveness in coping with resistance?
4. Explain how the counselor's technique for dealing with clients' antitherapeutic behavior may prevent further resistance, may increase it, or may encourage clients to cope with it more effectively.
5. How may the inclusion of males and females in the same counseling group contribute to resistance or encourage clients to handle it more effectively?
6. What are some of the most effective techniques that a counselor may use to encourage clients to assume responsibility for therapeutic behavior from the beginning of the first session and for maintaining such a climate? Explain how these same techniques prevent resistance and/or help clients cope with it.
7. Under what circumstances would you encourage the counselor to have intensive intake-type interviews for resisting clients?
8. Assume that an agency, college, or school counselor has the competencies and the desire to introduce group counseling but meets resistance from the administration. How may he cope with such road blocks?
9. To what extent and in what specific ways may the resistance which you note in your counseling group be a function of the counselor's countertransference? How could you differentiate between the resistance which results from clients' fears and that which results from countertransference?
10. How may clients be encouraged to manage resistance in their group?
11. How may a counselor use resistance therapeutically in a counseling group?
12. Precisely how does encouraging clients to detect and reflect a fellow client's feelings which account for resistance produce substantially different results than encouraging them to interpret the behaviors related to resistance or to confront the resisting client?

13. How do you feel about the use of Perls' conversation with yourself as a technique to help a client cope with his own resistance? use of the Fiddler technique (Chapter 7) to cope with it? use of "top-dog under-dog" to cope with it?

14. Let us suppose that in the intake interview you discovered someone who exhibits behavior which suggests that he may be a resisting client, but he is the only client of that type and you feel that you need such a client in order to help one other particular client, what would you do? How would you feel about admitting such a client on probation?

# References

Ackerman, N. W. Group psychotherapy with a mixed group of adolescents. *International Journal of Group Psychotherapy,* 1955, *5,* 249–260.

Bach, G. R. *Intensive group psychotherapy.* New York: Ronald, 1954.

Bry, T. Varieties of resistance in group psychotherapy. *International Journal of Group Psychotherapy,* 1951, *1,* 106–114.

Freedman, M. B., & Sweet, B. S. Some specific features of group psychotherapy and their implications for selection of patients. *International Journal of Group Psychotherapy,* 1954, *4,* 355–368.

Goodman, M., Marks, M., & Rockberger, H. Resistance in group psychotherapy enhanced by countertransference reactions of therapist: A peer group experience. *International Journal of Group Psychotherapy,* 1964, *14,* 332–343.

Osborn, H. Some factors of resistance which affect group participation. *The Group,* 1949, *2,* 2–4, 9–11.

Powdermaker, F. B., & Frank, J. D. *Group psychotherapy.* Cambridge: Harvard University Press, 1953.

Slavson, S. R. Are there group dynamics in therapy groups? *International Journal of Group Psychotherapy,* 1957, *7,* 131–154.

Yalom, I. D. *The theory and practice of group psychotherapy.* New York: Basic Books, 1975.

# 7

# Role Playing

Role playing enables clients to communicate feelings and perceptions concerning problem situations which they have difficulty describing, and perhaps even admitting to themselves. It enables clients to improve communication, to experiment with and practice new ways of behaving, to test their readiness for and performance in new developmental tasks, to solicit feedback on proposed actions, and to see themselves as others see them. It is recommended here to enhance the effectiveness of group counseling, rather than as the primary treatment method. When clients are able to discuss their problems openly, discover new and better ways of behaving, and develop the self-confidence and commitment to apply what they have learned in daily living without further practice, dealing verbally with their problems is more efficient.

## Psychodrama vs. Sociodrama

Persons new to this field are often introduced to role playing in the literature under two other titles: sociodrama and psychodrama. When, for example, role playing is used by an elementary school teacher to help a child learn to cope with a common developmental task or by an employment counselor to help his clients practice essential skills for a job interview, it is usually labelled sociodrama because its purpose is to help persons cope with common social problems. When it is used by a counselor or therapist to help a client uncover and cope with a personal problem, it is usually called psychodrama.

Inasmuch as Moreno (1946, 1964, 1966, 1975) has contributed more than anyone else to the use of psychodrama in group psychotherapy his primary elements in the process are reviewed here (Moreno & Elefthery, 1975): (1) the *protagonist* (the client in the group with the most urgent need), (2) the *auxiliary ego(s)* (extensions of the protagonist who play the roles he requires to explore his private life), (3) the *director* or facilitator (who loosens up participants and prepares them for participation—he also is the producer, therapist, and analyst), (4) the *group* (who provides silent support, auxiliary egos, and most important of all, feedback), and (5) the *stage*.

> The setting is a stage for Psychodrama designed by Moreno. It is in a small auditorium equipped with seats like a theater but with no proscenium. The stage itself comes close to the first row of seats and is made up of three circles of increasingly smaller size placed on top of the other giving three different height levels. It has sometimes been described as looking like a three-tiered wedding cake. In addition, there is a semienclosed area in the back of the stage and a balcony. At the back of the auditorium there is a raised area with some simple lighting equipment.
>
> . . . Once the protagonist is on the stage, the director begins to set the scene. Let us take an example of a problem whose central focus is a work difficulty, a conflict between the protagonist and his immediate supervisor. The director should rely as much as possible on the protagonist to give directions on how to play the scene, making certain that the latter provides a description of the situation in which the conflict manifests itself with as much specificity as possible about the setting, how the furniture is arranged, and what other people, if any, are present. . . . The auxiliary ego should be chosen by the protagonist whenever possible, but may be chosen by the director, if he knows the members of the group well enough to decide who might fit the roles as described; or they may be selected in consultation of the two. Once all the participants have been chosen, the plot needs to be outlined in somewhat fuller detail. The roles of auxiliary egos have to be explained by the protagonist or the director. (Shaffer & Galinsky, 1974, pp. 112–113)

Moreno's *basic psychodrama techniques* are reviewed as follows (Moreno & Elefthery, 1975): (1) *self-presentation* is the protagonist's description of himself or the significant other whose role he has elected to play; (2) *self-realization* is the protagonist's vision of his past, present, and future life; (3) *direct soliloquy* is a monologue in which the protagonist steps outside the scene and speaks his thoughts freely to himself or the group; (4) *therapeutic soliloquy* (asides) is a technique which the protagonist uses to share hidden feelings and thoughts; (5) *doubling* is a technique which an auxiliary ego uses to help the protagonist sense his inner feelings more deeply, to detect his problems, and to evaluate them; (6) *multiple doubling* provides for several doubles to be on the stage with the protagonist (each portraying a different facet of his personality); (7) *mirroring* is used by an auxiliary ego to help the protagonist see himself and his pathology as others see them; (8) *role reversal* provides the protagonist an opportunity to play the part of his antagonist in a relevant scene; (9) *future projection* is designed to help the protagonist project himself into the future and to convey his deepest hopes and wishes; (10) *life rehearsal* is designed to help the protagonist practice in advance something he expects to encounter; (11) the *psychodramatic hallucination* technique is merely used to enable the protagonist to portray his own hallucinations; and (12 the *psychodramatic dream* technique is used to help the protagonist act out rather than tell about a dream.

Moreno's goal for patients is to make them more godlike—so creative, open, and in touch with their own feelings that they can extend themselves into the richest possible living. On one occasion Moreno (1946) spoke to Freud about use of dreams as follows: "You analyze their dreams, I try to give them the courage to dream again. I teach them how to play God."

A highly skilled counselor can use many of Moreno's psychodrama techniques to help his clients recognize possibilities for learning to cope with developmental tasks and to implement desired new behaviors. On the other hand, he must recognize that their use requires special professional preparation and that his clients *can be hurt* when they are used to expose problems for which clients are not ready to cope, when clients are pressured to use these techniques, and when clients are forced to play roles in which they feel very deeply threatened or uncomfortable.

## Role-Playing Techniques

So much of the literature stresses use of role playing to practice communicating negative feelings and coping with conflict. Perhaps it should stress more the usefulness of role playing in helping clients learn to recognize anger earlier and to cope with the situation while it still can be handled easier: for example, when Sally started to review their new bidding system for their duplicate bridge club the next night, Chuck thought she sounded as if she were belittling him, but he did not sit there and get angrier and angrier as he had previously, he said, "You're getting under my skin. Stop right there, let's talk about it. Let's suppose that you really want to help me, and I believe that you usually do. You be me and I'll be you. Then I'll try to talk to you playing me. (Following the role-played scene he drew upon experiences in assertiveness training to solicit and give feedback and to assess what they learned from the role playing.) Incidentally, they offered each other more effective suggestions and enjoyed bridge more the next evening.

Furthermore, clients have even more occasions when they need to practice expressing positive feelings toward a significant other: after dinner Nick sat looking at an old family picture thinking what he and his wife were like at that time (eighteen years earlier), how much he appreciated her as he thought about their family as they were then and how they are now, and how well the children had turned out. At first he thought, "I don't have to say anything. She knows how I feel." Then he remembered what they had learned in the marriage enrichment weekend and how he had practiced sharing such loving feelings. Then he said, "You are great. I was just thinking as I studied this picture what a good life we have had together." They hugged and their whole evening was enriched. Role playing helps clients learn to express such positive feelings to others in their counseling group and to significant others too.

Beginning with the presentation (Chapter 1), and throughout the entire process, the treatment model described in this book encourages clients to be open to their own therapeutic needs and to admit them when they become aware of them. Early in the process they are introduced to role playing and to functioning simultaneously as helper and helpee—for each to empathize with the primary client (the protagonist), to detect and reflect what he thinks the primary client is feeling, to try to recognize when another's therapeutic material has relevance for himself, to admit it, and to help each other learn new behaviors. The counselor enhances this process by using his understandings and observations of each to detect and reflect simultaneous needs and to make affiliation responses (Belonging, Chapter 3). When, therefore, a counselor uses role playing to supplement verbal interactions he must be conscious of these expectations and helping skills. Otherwise he may tend merely to treat the primary client (the protagonist) in front of the others. Moreover, the techniques described here are used to help clients uncover, present, and develop behavioral goals for therapeutic material rather than to diagnose and classify their problems (and obviously, it can be used effectively without a special stage).

**early recollections**    Early recollections are used by Adlerians to help a client understand his world. They also are used to help him advance toward his goals of safety, security, self-esteem, and success and to protect him from insecurity, danger, and frustration (Papanek, 1972). For our purpose here early memories are employed to enable a client to present himself, to uncover specific instances in which he may require assistance, and to define desired new behaviors. When a client is unable to respond openly to directions such as "Close your eyes, think about your early memories before age 10 that you can recall vividly, and tell us about them," a role-played scene may be developed as follows: "Perhaps it would be easier to share openly these memories if you would select a fellow client, believe that he is truly trustworthy, and that he would continue to accept you no matter what you or your family might have done in the past, and relate these early recollections to him (in person or on a telephone—two of which are made available for role playing). Clients who state that they cannot recall any early memories usually can recall some under these role-played conditions. Successful role-playing experience also tends to make it easier for them to share more spontaneously in the here and now too.

Teaching clients to relax and to fantasize (and to recall and discuss dreams) also enables them to uncover hidden feelings, hurtful critical incidents, and unfinished business in the here and now with significant others (Polster & Polster, 1973). Structuring similar to that illustrated above facilitates use of fantasy and discussion of dreams: "Select one of your fellow clients. Imagine that you have just awakened from a dream that you feel that you should share with someone. Close your eyes, visualize yourself at the beginning of the dream, and share it with this trusted confidant."

**expression of positive feelings**     Expression of positive feelings (life rehearsal) toward a significant other requires practice for many. Moreover such clients tend to rationalize not expressing these feelings verbally as Nick was tempted to do in the case cited earlier. Variations of the Human Potential Laboratory materials (McHolland, 1968; Otto, 1970) can be readily adapted for this purpose as was suggested for use of early recollections above: "For whom do you have good feelings which have not been expressed? What do you wish you could say to him or her? Who would you like to help you practice this scene?"

**magic shop**     Magic Shop (self-presentation) is used to help a client uncover therapeutic material and to encourage him to define meaningful treatment goals (Carpenter & Sandberg, 1973; Shaffer & Galinsky, 1974). Clients are invited to present themselves to the magic shop and barter, not for things but for personal characteristics or general desires: "A boy who had until then sat in total isolation without participation, asked to buy love and a perpetual high. Another boy asked to buy friendship (Carpenter & Sandberg, p. 246)."

Then they role played scenes in which each decided what stands in the way of his getting what he wants and what he would have to give up to get what he really wants.

**intimacy exercise**     When clients reveal the need for learning how to be closer and more intimate with someone, they are helped by intimacy exercise (life rehearsal) to discuss with whom they wish that they could express what. Frequently role playing is used to help them decide what they want to convey and to practice expressing it, including learning when and how to touch, to express desired feelings.

**pairing**     *Pairing* (Bach & Deutsch, 1970) provides some good case material which clients can use to develop scripts for role played scenes in group counseling.

Learning to touch appropriately and meaningfully is essential for learning to be intimate and genuine. Human beings need to touch and to be touched (Otto, 1971):

> Research in the teaching of reading indicates that not only is verbal facility—the ability to use words—not our primary mode of communication, but children who do not crawl, and touch, and handle things, almost invariably have difficulty with language. The thought and word are not our primary mode of communication. We are primarily animals who touch! Our deepest thoughts and feelings can only be communicated by touch—by physical intimacy. . . .
>
> We can become more aware of our bodies not only through loving, caring touch, but as a result of certain exercises and experiences. . . . Most of these exercises and experiences have been used for some time by Human Potentialities classes sponsored by various colleges and universities, and participants report excellent results. (Otto, 1971, pp. 36, 37)

Clients also can learn to practice touching as they talk, learn to request touching, and provide each other feedback in their efforts to learn to touch. They must and they can learn to touch meaningfully and appropriately in groups (Simon, 1974).

**approach-avoidance exercises**    Approach-avoidance exercises (self-presentation, experiencing self, and life rehearsal) are useful. Schutz (1967) labels this exercise *the encounter*:

> How: the two persons involved are asked to stand at opposite ends of the room. They are instructed to remain silent, look into each other's eyes, and walk very slowly toward each other. Without planning anything, when the two people get close to each other, they are to do whatever they are impelled from within themselves to do. They are to continue the encounter for as long as they wish. After it is completed the principals will ordinarily talk about their feelings, and the others will contribute their observations and identifications with the principals. It is essential to urge the principals to try to let their feelings take over and not plan what they will do when they meet.
>
> Caution: There are no special problems with this experience. It can be revealing and unsettling, but people usually know whether or not they are ready for it.
>
> Example: George had just been divorced and appeared to have much hostility as well as great attraction toward women. His feelings about women were apparently very confused, but he treated the whole area flippantly and with many jokes. Marla was very attractive and had very ambivalent feelings toward men. She was very dependent on them on the one hand, and very competitive on the other. She and George had avoided each other in the group until someone remarked their feelings toward the opposite sex seemed similar and wondered how they felt about each other. Characteristically neither could identify or verbalize how they actually felt toward the other. They said that they didn't feel anything. It seemed like an appropriate time for an encounter

since it might allow them to become aware of their feelings toward each other that were being blocked inside them. They approached each other slowly and when they met, George looked at Marla briefly and walked right by her, staring straight ahead. For fully five minutes both stood still, backs to each other, looking in opposite directions. The tension became too great for the observers and they began to urge the principals on to various resolutions of the impasse, but George and Marla accepted none. Then Marla stepped back, took George by the shoulders and turned him around so that she was facing his back. She then stepped back and the group waited anxiously for the next move. They didn't have to wait long, for Marla stepped up and delivered a tremendous kick in the rear of George, knocking him several feet across the room. Stunned, George just looked at Marla, who invited him to kick her back. He refused until she finally took a pillow and put it behind her. Reluctantly, George kicked her, but gently.

The effect of this interchange was different for the two participants. Marla felt elated and strong, her participation increased, and she became softer. Later in the psychodrama, she was able to work on her relations to her father, which helped her clarify her feelings toward men. George became depressed. His difficulties with women were serious and he was forced to face them directly, something he had successfully avoided up to that time. (Schutz, 1967, pp. 141–142)

Thus, the technique was used successfully for both. When the writer uses it he sometimes encourages clients to use therapeutic soliloquy to share those private or hidden feelings which they feel unable to own or express at that time.

Schutz also describes a number of other useful psychodrama techniques which can be adapted for group counseling. When, for example, a client is experiencing alienation, isolation, or loneliness he may use either of these break-in techniques.

The people identified as "in" stand and form a tight circle with interlocking arms. They may face either inward or outward depending upon whether the person trying to break in sees them as simply involved with each other and ignoring him (face in), or as deliberately attempting to keep him out (face out). The outsider then tries to break through into the circle in whatever way he can, and the group members try to keep him out. (Schutz, 1967, p. 131)

*Dance* and/or *movement* exercises (experiencing self or self-presentation) can be used with minimum structure to enable clients to express and experience "the connection between kinesthetic feelings and emotions, and—as Fritz Perls pointed out so effectively in Gestalt therapy—to stimulate awareness, and to help clients explore their creative abilities. Creative movement can be used in much the same way role playing is used to make words more fully experiential." (ibid, p. 97) . . . For example: Bob's stockiness is emphasized by the way he pulls his shoulders in and turns his feet inward. This is hardly the stance in which one would imagine to find a ten-year-old boy who is normally noticed by adults only when he is pinching, poking, or hitting another child. But for Bob, the posture is appropriate as an expression of how he feels about himself, for whenever he is confronted by his teacher or principal, he ends up on the bottom of everyone's list. Bob is not at all pleased with his disagreeable behavior, and he punishes himself most severely of all by imposing a sort of solitary confinement on his body and spirit. . . .

. . . The following exercise helps Bob: One person is placed standing behind Bob, who is seated cross-legged on the floor. Bob drops his torso forward, letting his head hang down toward the floor, and concentrates on deep, even breathing so as to relax completely. Then, starting at the bottom, Bob slowly brings his back into an upright position. The person standing behind him assists by firmly touching with his fingers each successive vertebra as it comes into alignment with those below it, while Bob imagines stacking them one at a time on top of each other. When Bob's head has returned to normal position, the standing person places his hand lightly under Bob's chin, pulls up on the head gently, and rolls it from side to side. If Bob has relaxed sufficiently, his head will rest loosely on his spinal column as if it were balanced on top of a pole.

In addition to this exercise, other improvisions calling for broad arm motions and long, stretching steps will help Bob expand the range of his movements. A good mental exercise in conjunction with these is to have Bob go through some of the movements with his eyes closed, trying to imagine what his body looks like. Then he can repeat his movements in front of a mirror.

. . . Though he has had a hard time finding or committing himself to alternate behaviors, his fellow clients now provide him with a place to discover and practice new ways of behaving. The counseling group also offers Bob a chance to see himself as others see him, to talk about his movement experiences, and to build up a vocabulary that includes the kinesthetic experiences in which he feels safe and proficient. Once labeled, these experiences can be introduced into Bob's everyday life, for use especially during times of anxiety and tension. That is, once Bob has learned to recognize and label his own body's early warning devices—hunched shoulders, tightened muscles, drawn-in neck—he will be alert to the crises at hand, and can then make a decision whether or not to lash out in the old destructive way or to put into practice his newly acquired and less alienating behaviors. (Ferreira, 1973, pp. 100–102)

**relaxation exercises**     Ferreira presents examples to illustrate how to use relaxation exercises (experiencing self) in group counseling with children—focusing attention upon various parts of the body in random order (Von Hilsheimer, 1970; Perls, Hefferline, & Goodman, 1951).

*Top dog* vs. *underdog* is one of the most famous of the Gestalt polarities. It conveys the struggle between the master and the slave:

The master commands, directs and scolds and the slave controverts with his passivity or stupidity, or ineptness or pretense of trying unsuccessfully to do the master's biddings. The polarities have infinite dimensions, however, like how my brother lives and how I live; my kindness and my cruelty; my affection and my cynicism. . . .

The task in resolving the polarity is to aid each part to live the fullest while at the same time making contact with its polar counterpart. This reduces the chance that one part will stay mired in its own impotence, hanging on the status quo. Instead, it is energized into making a vital statement of its own needs and wishes, asserting itself as a force which must be considered in a new union of forces. Whether one part is viewed as top dog and the other as underdog is not as important as the valid expression of each part articulating its own specific identity. (Polster & Polster, 1973, pp. 61–62)

Usually the writer has the primary client use two chairs of different sizes and heights in the treatment so that the client may sit first on one then on the other as he carries on the dialogue between his two opposing parts. As with other role playing the other members listen, encourage free expression, and discuss the scene after it has been played, preferably with a recording which can be used when desired either by the primary client or other members. Following these experiences usually the primary client accepts himself better and becomes a more active participant in the group: "This is solid respect for the self-regulation of the individual—not forcing or seducing him into behaviors which he himself has not largely set up (Polster & Polster, p. 68)."

**fiddler game**     Most will remember Tevye as he struggled to examine the pros and cons of an issue or decision in "Fiddler on the Roof." This technique can be used effectively in helping clients who either are experiencing ambivalence or struggling with a decision for which they may profitably examine both the pros and cons for proposed actions. For example, a female in her early twenties is trying to decide whether to marry the man who has just proposed to her. After her counselor described the Fiddler game (future projection) and explained its relevance for her, she began to play the game as follows (with her counselor and fellow clients listening, trying to detect hidden feelings and thoughts, and helping her express them): "I like Bill, and perhaps I even love him now. If not, I am quite sure that I could learn to love him. I respect him intellectually, and he respects me and would encourage me in my professional development. He is interesting and fun to be with, and he has a promising professional future. *On the other hand*, he is very ambitious, perhaps too ambitious. Sometimes I feel like I may be used to help him socially to achieve his goals in the corporation where he is employed. Though I feel he would be generous in his financial support for me and my children, I doubt that he would ever allow himself to become deeply involved with my children and care as deeply about them as I would like for the man I marry to do." And so she continued to state first arguments for and against her marriage to Bill. With the help of her fellow clients and counselor over several sessions, she clarified how she felt about Bill, identified the topics she felt she had to discuss with Bill, and developed the courage to discuss them openly with Bill. Eventually, she also identified what new behaviors she would have to learn to live successfully with Bill, explored whether she was willing to make those changes, and decided not only to discuss these changes with Bill (and his commitment to help her achieve them), but also what he would be willing to do to enhance their chances for a good marriage.

**self-appraisal exercises**    Self-appraisal exercises (self-presentation) were heretofore primarily used by adolescents and young adults who were struggling with questions such as: Who am I? What really interests me? What am I good at? What do I want to become? For what questions do I require answers about my interests, abilities, and aptitudes and about the opportunities available for me? Today increasing numbers of women are entering colleges and careers in their thirties and forties and men in their forties and fifties are considering changing their careers. Many counselors are organizing counseling groups for such persons. Early in their counseling, the counselor often teaches them to identify the questions for which they require answers and to initiate action to obtain their answers through use of tests and of self-appraisal techniques (Chapter 12, Ohlsen, 1974). Role playing is used to help them clarify what they need to know and from whom or what sources they may obtain desired information, and to practice making requests for it.

**autobiographies and autobiographies of the future**    Autobiographies and autobiographies of the future (self-presentation and future projection) are both used effectively to supplement the self-appraisal (Chapter 9, Ohlsen, 1974). Most clients can be taught to produce these between counseling sessions. The autobiography of the future is an extension of the autobiography designed to enable clients to project themselves ten years into a new role or to examine with considerable freedom their entire life's achievements (fifty years into the future). Where they have difficulty other clients can be asked to volunteer and model for them. The counselor also can utilize an adaptation of the directions used to help clients to produce early recollections.

Thus, a variety of techniques can be used to improve communication, to uncover new therapeutic material, to clarify goals, to encourage growth, and to generalize new behaviors to daily life. Most counselors tend to use primarily three of Moreno's basic techniques: life rehearsal (10), role reversal (8), and self-presentation (1). Fewer utilize mirroring (1), future projection (9), doubling (5), and variations of soliloquy (3). Some also are using two additional types of techniques to facilitate experiencing of self more fully (a) and feedback (b).

## Standard Roles

Some counselors use standard roles, encouraging group members to take various roles commonly encountered in everyday life. Boring and Deabler

(1951) developed twelve standard roles which they used in treating groups of from 12 to 16 veterans: mother-son (small boy), father-son (small boy), father-mother-son (small boy), siblings (two brothers), boy-girl (adolescent boy), mother-son (adult), father-son (adult), father-mother-son (adult), husband-wife (cold supper), neighbors in conflict, job-seeker versus personnel man, and childhood sex attitudes and experiences. "These basic situations allow the patient to be introduced to and to participate in more or less general roles which also prepare him for participation later in more personally structured ones related to his own conflict areas." (p. 373) They recommend, besides the group therapist, that two other professionals (or possibly coached clients) play the auxiliary male and female roles. Though there is value in this approach, and though the writer sometimes uses a similar one in group guidance for adolescents, and he teaches elementary teachers to use it for sociodrama in the classroom, nonetheless, in group counseling he prefers to use material from his clients' own lives.

Harth (1966) used a variation of this standard-role notion to treat failing lower-class third graders. He had them play the roles of various school personnel, so that they might change their attitudes toward school and better appreciate the attitudes of school personnel. His clients did improve their classroom behavior, but he failed to obtain significant changes in attitudes. Perhaps his tests were not sensitive enough to detect the attitude changes that occurred. However, he concluded that the students were not able to change their attitudes because they were unable to express their true feelings in these sociodramatic experiences.

Hawley (1974) developed another version of the standard role procedure for classroom use with adolescents. For the particular instance which he presented in his paper he arranged students' chairs in a large circle with two empty chairs standing facing each other in the middle of the circle: one is labelled "Sue" (adolescent) and the other is labelled "Dad" (but it could be either parent or another adult). The class developed case materials for Sue on a confrontation situation with which students that age are commonly faced. For the role-played scene both chairs are left empty but three students sit by Sue's chair and speak for her and three students sit by Dad's chair and speak for him. Usually they role play for five minutes or less, then discuss what they learned and react to proposed actions:

> The use of the open chairs and brainstorming allows students to bring their real concerns into the classroom with a degree of anonymity and a low level of risk. Since the material has been generated by members of the class, each student can take from the role play those elements which are relevant to his present life. (Hawley, 1974, p. 364)

Carpenter and Sandberg (1973) found that their juvenile delinquent clients required considerable structure to function well. They structured each session with music, poetry, fortune telling, art work or psychodrama techniques such as magic shop rather than permitting their clients to develop their own case materials as Hawley did. In part, they did this because sometimes their clients were reluctant to initiate role playing. Even for their more reluctant clients the emotional impact of role playing enables their clients to exhibit feelings of loneliness and to express their yearning for acceptance and love.

Haney, Banks, and Zimbardo (1973) studied the impact of role playing in a simulated situation. They used as their research subjects carefully assigned volunteer college students. Half of the subjects were randomly assigned to role play eight hour shifts as prison guards and half were confined and assigned to role play prisoners for a full week. Very careful observation of subjects led them to conclude that:

> The most dramatic of the coping behavior utilized by half of the prisoners in adapting to this stressful situation was the development of acute emotional disturbance—severe enough to warrant their early release. At least a third of the guards were judged to have become more aggressive and dehumanising toward prisoners than would ordinarily be predicted in a simulation study. Only a few of the observed reactions to this experience of imprisonment could be attributed to personality trait differences which existed before the subjects began to play their assigned roles. (Haney, Banks, & Zimbardo, 1973, p. 69)

Role playing does have an impact on subjects, and when subjects play negative roles in a damaging simulated situation, even carefully selected subjects can be hurt. Usually, however, the impact is positive because role playing is used to help clients, and even students in the classroom, explore problems and practice desired new behaviors. Paraprofessionals (persons from other professions such as teachers functioning in a therapeutic helping role as well as aides) often use standard roles when they assume leadership for help groups. For example, sensitive elementary school teachers can be readily taught to help children select from standard roles (such as the ones listed below) which enable them to deal with problems and/or developmental tasks with which they are faced, identify alternative actions and sources for assistance, and to practice the new desired behaviors and/or to practice requesting assistance from an appropriate source: a child feeling that he is too dumb to learn to read, succeed in arithmetic, and so forth, a lonely child, a child feeling afraid he is going to fail and doesn't know what to do, a child confronted with a bully, a grieving child, and a child who likes someone but does not know how to begin building a friendship. Likewise, secondary school teachers and youth leaders (such as YWCA and YMCA staff) employ role playing to help adolescents with common problems such as: initiating conversation with a stranger, making first contact to begin building a friendship, asking for a date, getting the floor and making a point in class discussion or youth leadership meetings, requesting assistance with school work, talking to a teacher about a grade, interviewing for a job, and interviewing for college admission. Shaftel and Shaftel (1967) and Chesler and Fox (1966) have produced very helpful materials for such leaders.

## Therapeutic Values of Role Playing

Most of the professional literature supports use of role playing in group counseling. Lippitt and Hubell's (1956) review of the research certainly supports it. Wallace, Teigen, Liberman, and Baker's (1973) work with a young adult supports its value when employed along with behavior therapy. On the other hand, Kradel's (1972) study suggests that role playing did not significantly improve his clients' growth. For the many who endorse it, their most commonly agreed upon values are reviewed below.

> To facilitate communication when a client is fumbling for words to describe his problem and the persons involved, or is having difficulty trying to clarify the nature of his relationship with a significant other, or is noticeably affected by another's problem and is having difficulty admitting that it is his problem too
> To detect unfinished business with significant others, decide what action is required, and to practice desired action
> To formulate and/or clarify a client's goals for counseling—to decide what he wants to learn to do differently with whom.
> To explore ways of strengthening relationships with significant others
> To solicit realistic and precise feedback concerning proposed actions and the ways the client tries to implement them
> To practice requesting assistance from significant others in defining desired new behaviors and in reinforcing these behaviors
> To generalize from successful experiences with the transference object in the client's counseling group by role playing with a fellow client proposed new behaviors (Chapter 5)
> To help a client re-live a moment when he first recognized resistance, admit it, and solicit the group's assistance in coping with it
> To increase a client's spontaneity, safe feelings, and freedom to talk openly and use his own creativity
> To increase members' involvement as both clients and as helpers
> To participate in a situation rather than just to talk about it—to experience more and to intellectualize less
> To facilitate participation for the action oriented—the doers as well as the talkers—for example, Riessman's (1964) lower class males
> To increase feelings of affiliation and/or identification with other members
> To provide a model for the primary client through another acting as his substitute in a role reversal or as an alter ego
> To increase a client's sensitivity to another's need and to motivate him to respond to these needs more fully and with greater empathy
> To increase a client's sensitivity to his inner feelings—to his physical as well as his emotional being and learn to influence even many autonomic functions
> To see himself more clearly as others see him
> To practice decision making
> To help clients identify specific questions for which they feel that they require answers about themselves and their opportunities and to decide how they may go about finding their own answers.

When a client projects himself into another's role and observes himself through another's eyes (especially during observation of a video recording of the role played scene), he comes to perceive their relationship differently, and usually more congruent with his significant other's perception. And when he observes another playing his role, he sees himself and his situation differently. But what happens when a client does not really try to empathize with his character and to project him as he is? What happens when the primary client merely tries to win his fellows clients' sympathy by portraying his adversary as "all bad guy." For example, when the primary client (the father) plays his son's role in a role reversal he projects only his son's arbitrary, worse side. In the first place this rarely happens. Moreover, even the father tends to be embarrassed when he examines a recording of the role played with fellow clients. And if he is not embarrassed about it, the group will usually detect such false portrayal and ask questions such as: "Is that the way your son really behaves when you try to talk to him?" In any case the father usually discovers some improved ways of responding to his son. Occasionally, the group will invite the primary client to bring the significant other to the group for further role-played scenes.

> Enactment is the one way of keeping alive the words a person uses to characterize himself or someone else. Keeping his language connected to action permits feelings of change and growth; the person is less likely to experience himself as stamped on the ass—indelibly this or that. (Polster & Polster, 1973, p. 245)

## Guidelines for Role Playing

A counselor should introduce role playing as a helpful technique when he describes group counseling for prospective clients. When, for example, a client (in session #2) fumbled for words as he tried to describe the problem situation in which he found himself, the counselor said, "I am not certain that we understand what is really bothering you—who is involved, how they are affecting you, how they contribute to your problem, and what you require of these significant others to cope with the situation better. Remember what I told you about role playing?" (He nods affirmatively.) "If you are willing, perhaps we could use it profitably here. With whom do you have a problem? Whose help would you like to enlist in solving it? Let's begin with you playing the part of the person with whom you are having the greatest difficulty. Whom would you like to play your part and the remaining characters' parts?"

In another instance an underachieving ninth-grade client was complaining about how unfairly he had been treated by his English teacher, who failed to notice how his behavior had changed for the better recently. The counselor's response was, "Jim, I guess it's pretty discouraging when you really try to get your assignments in on time and she doesn't even notice how you have changed. I also seem to pick up the feeling that you don't know how to tell her that bawling you out in front of everyone really discouraged you—made you feel like giving up even when you wanted to meet her expectations. If you like, maybe we can help you practice talking to her." After Jim described the scene and the active characters in it, the counselor urged him to select and brief characters for each role. First, Jim played the teacher's part, then his own role. Even before he played his own role, he acknowledged how he saw the situation differently and learned from the girl who played his role how he better could approach his teacher.

Nevertheless, Jim was still reluctant to speak to his teacher. Two students suggested that the counselor accompany Jim to see the teacher. In response to that suggestion the counselor said, "I guess you feel he needs someone to protect him, and perhaps make his teacher a little ashamed for the way she has treated Jim." Most of the clients agreed, but they also saw that it might start trouble between the teacher and the counselor, and then the teacher might make it even tougher on Jim. Eventually Jim decided to talk to her by himself. It turned out to be a rough experience, but Jim did it without "spouting off," and his relationship with that teacher did improve ever so slowly with much needed encouragement and support for Jim from his fellow clients.

Following the discussion of the first role playing, the counselor should review for the clients when role playing can be used effectively, describe its essential components, and suggest ways they may initiate it.

Whenever any member of a counseling group discovers a situation for which role playing seems to be appropriate he should suggest it and tell why he feels it would be helpful. If, however, the one suggesting it is not the primary client, the primary client (protagonist and/or director) has the right to reject or postpone it. When the primary client agrees with the idea he functions as director and prepares the group for the scene which is to be role played, does the staging and casting, and prepares actors for their roles (with the counselor helping, but giving the primary client maximum responsibility). Usually actors and any agreed-upon auxiliary egos are selected by the primary client from among the volunteers. Even reticent clients who have rarely participated in therapeutic interaction will often volunteer, and for roles that may be difficult, but relevant for them. When some roles are left unfilled clients are encouraged by the counselor to help the director identify needed actors. Inasmuch as some children find it easier to use puppets and/or dolls (and hence increase chances for volunteers) through which they speak their parts, these should be available in the counseling room.

The counselor assists the director, especially in preparing persons for their roles and in helping them put into words what they think their characters feel. Even here the counselor does not take the authoritarian role usually associated with the dramatic director. Instead he merely helps the director clarify a situation or a relationship and helps a player state a feeling.

Sometimes the counselor is asked to play a role. The role in which he is cast (perhaps that of an authority figure for the primary actor) often affects his relationship with certain clients long after the scene has ended. Although these problems can be worked out, they tend to distract clients from some of the benefits achieved in role playing. The counselor can prevent these problems by declining to play roles.

In most instances the primary actor profits most from first playing the role of the most significant other in the scene and then replaying the scene as himself. Regardless of the role he elects to play he learns much about the situation and the significant characters in casting, staging, and directing the others even before they role play the scene. Sometimes a primary client will report that his primary goals are achieved prior to the role playing.

The counselor must try to help role players grasp the notion that role playing is impromptu play. After he has briefed the group and had a chance to clarify his character's role, every player should feel free to portray it as best he can spontaneously. Even though he may have been given his character's words, the actor should not be concerned about remembering and stating them. Instead, he should try to capture his character's state of mind in the situation and to express his character's feelings as best he can, using his own words to speak spontaneously for his character.

The counselor also encourages his clients to use soliloquy whenever they believe that their characters will speak and behave differently from the way they really feel. For example, a nonconforming seventeen-year-old client, who was trying to learn to conform and accept certain limits, took the role of a boy much like himself. When he was put on the spot by a fellow student, he said: "Look, lay off, can't you see I'm trying to get along with Mr. Smith?" Then he turned his head to the audience, cupped his hand to the side of his mouth, and said in soliloquy, "That bastard is pushing me again. He can't stand to see me get along and stay out of trouble. I'd like to bash him in the mouth." The soliloquy not only helped the boy to convey his feelings, but it helped the entire group to empathize with him and enabled fellow clients to give him support while he was learning to live his new role.

Boring and Deabler (1951) were among the first to record role-played sessions and use playback to help clients recall their significant spontaneous verbalizations. Without a recording which can be played back as part of the discussion and feedback of the role-played scene, the primary client misses many of the significant interactions and is left with only general impressions of what happened: "In the playback, he is brought face to face with himself in a dynamic lifelike situation, and often for the first time, he sees himself more nearly as he is seen by others (p. 374).

Even better results tend to be achieved with video recordings. They provide important data on nonverbal behavior which otherwise tends to be overlooked. Furthermore, even clients who at first object to recordings usually accept them when the counselor explains that recordings are made primarily for three (or part) of these reasons: (1) to help clients discover how they are perceived by others; (2) to enhance the quality of their feedback for clients; and (3) to improve the accuracy and quality of feedback from clients, and the counselor's supervisors, for the counselor. Generally clients exhibit better acceptance of and empathy for fellow clients following study of a recorded session. When a client plays another's role he experiences more empathy for that client (Lippitt, 1947; Moreno, 1947). Taking another's role confronts himself with himself (Mann & Mann, 1958; Shaftel & Shaftel, 1967).

Just before a scene the counselor should assess whether all the players understand their roles. Anyone who has questions or wants help in playing his role should be encouraged to speak. While playing the scene every actor should feel free to stop whenever he feels unable to proceed, either because he has run out of material or because he is faced with behavior that he cannot act out. When he lacks material, he may use soliloquy to request it. When he cannot act out the behavior before him, he may wish to recess the interaction to enlist members' assistance. Such freedom makes the actors more secure in their roles; very likely it also increases their openness and spontaneity.

When someone (other than the primary client) terminates the role playing, he should first be given opportunity to request assistance or information or to react to whatever caused him to stop; then other actors and, finally, the audience should be given their chance to react to the interaction, to give feedback, or merely to ask questions for clarification. Usually the director stops the role playing when he has obtained the assistance he wants, or when he wants to restructure, or when he merely wishes to react to what has occurred. Here again the counselor should help clients focus on the feelings involved and on learning new ways of behaving.

Role playing produces powerful, realistic experiences for clients. Therefore, especially when it is first used, the counselor must teach clients to get out of their roles and return to the group as themselves. For clients who have had trouble getting out of roles (or letting others get out of their roles) the writer uses a ceremony in which players pretend to put masks on each other at the beginning and take them off after the role playing:

> Just before leaving the role playing, the counselor should assist actors in getting out of their roles. Effective actors often elicit feelings from the member-client, from group members in the observer position, and from all the counselor, all of which are not legitimate outcomes. That is, such feelings are appropriate to the role but not to the actor himself. It is important to the future functioning of the group that all members and the counselor have ample opportunity to distinguish and differentiate the feelings associated with the role and those feelings associated with the person who assumed the role. Such differentiation may be facilitated by "talking through" feelings, by having actors pantomime taking off makeup and costumes associated with the role, by having

actors take new chairs in the group, and by testing to see that everyone is relating person-to-person. Only when the counselor has clearly shed the role should the counselor move the group into another therapeutic venture. (Passmore, 1973, p. 281)

How may the director (primary client) benefit from discussion of the role-played scene? First, he has a chance to reveal his feelings about what happened during the role playing, to comment on whatever he may have discovered about himself and/or the relationships, and to consider the possible benefit of replaying the scene—possibly giving himself another role and soliciting new volunteers. From the comments of others he obtains new perceptions of the relationships and of his own function in the situation, feedback on how he behaved, and suggestions on how he could try to behave differently.

Other role players reap benefits, too: evoking others' reactions, experiencing new roles, and practicing approaches for coping with new or difficult situations (usually they volunteer for roles that have special meaning for them, though they are not always conscious of this fact). They also get feedback on the way they played their roles and the way they tried to cope with the problems with which their character was confronted. They should have an opportunity to express how they felt in their roles, how they felt about playing these particular roles, and what they learned from the experience. Sometimes such experiences enable them to solve problems without ever claiming them as their own. A more common reaction is for a client to see the relevance of the role for himself and to discuss the related problem with new openness.

Least benefited are the members of the audience. Even they, however, tend to become deeply involved as they observe and react to the scene. Some volunteer for roles when scenes are replayed. Usually those in the audience profit to the extent that they can and do become involved. Moreno (1966) stressed the importance of involving everyone present—looking upon everyone as a potential role player—and of giving everyone an opportunity to encounter with his real self and his problems.

## Summary

Role playing enables clients in groups to try out proposed new behaviors, to practice them, to improve their communication with members of their group, to obtain feedback, and to see themselves as others see them. Here it is endorsed as a supplement to verbal treatment rather than as a primary method to be used alone. When clients can discuss their problems openly, discover new ways of behaving, and implement these desired new behaviors through use of only verbal techniques, psychodramatic techniques are not needed.

Role playing is a valuable adjunct to group counseling. Clients should be introduced to the idea in the presentation and be taught to use it therapeutically in one of their early treatment sessions. When the counselor first observes a good situation in which role playing can be used effectively he should explain to clients how to use it; help the client whose problem revealed the need for it to describe the situation and the primary characters involved, select the role players, and brief them; and help them profit from the experience following the role playing. Furthermore, it is just as important to teach clients to disengage themselves from their role-played roles as it is to become deeply involved in them during the role playing. After clients have completed their first role-played session, the counselor should explain for what purposes they may wish to use role playing again, review what the basic components are in the process, and point out how they will be able to recognize when to use it next time.

## Discussion Questions

1. For what purposes have you seen role playing used effectively? In what ways is this similar to and different from how we have used it here?
2. In what significant ways have we used role playing differently than Moreno uses psychodrama in psychotherapy?
3. What are the pros and cons for a counselor playing a role in a counseling group?
4. How may role playing be used to manage resistance in a counseling group?
5. What unique advantages accrue to a primary client when he listens and/ or observes the role-played session in which he played another's role? Or when he plays his own role?
6. Why do clients require practice in expressing positive feelings? How does movement and touching add meaning to these role-played experiences?
7. What are some of the client behaviors that would indicate use of role playing to facilitate client growth?
8. Give an example of using soliloquy in group counseling.
9. What are the primary arguments for using standard roles in group counseling?
10. In our intake interview, and again during the second counseling session, Jane said that she is uncomfortable when she is touched by a man. Curt decides to role play a scene in which he will have to caress his wife. He asks Jane to play the part of his wife. What could the counselor

do to help Jane get ready for this experience or should he? If you were the counselor, how would you respond to Jane? What would you say to Curt?

# References

Bach, G. R., & Deutsch, R. M. *Pairing: How to achieve genuine intimacy.* New York: Avon Books, 1970.

Boring, R. O., & Deabler, M. L. A simplified psychodramatic approach to group psychotherapy. *Journal of Clinical Psychology,* 1951, *7,* 371–375.

Carpenter, P., & Sandberg, S. The things inside: Psychodrama with delinquent adolescents. *Psychotherapy: Research and Practice,* 1973, *10,* 245–247.

Chesler, M., & Fox, R. *Role playing methods in the classroom.* Chicago: Science Research, 1966.

Ferreira, L. Dance: An adjunct to group counseling. Chapter 5 in M. M. Ohlsen, *Counseling children in groups: A forum.* New York: Holt, Rinehart and Winston, 1973.

Greenberg, I. Audience in action through psychodrama. *Group Psychotherapy,* 1964, *17,* 104–122.

Haney, C., Banks, C., & Zimbardo, P. Interpersonal dynamics in a simulated prison. *International Journal of Criminology and Penology,* 1973, *1,* 69–97.

Harth, R. Changing attitudes toward schools, classroom behavior, and reaction to frustration of emotionally disturbed children through role playing. *Exceptional Children,* 1966, *33,* 119–120.

Hawley, R. C. Exploring student concerns through open-chair role playing. *The School Counselor,* 1974, *21,* 358–364.

Kradel, F. *Adlerian role playing for the reorientation and reeducation of high school students with behavior problems.* Unpublished doctoral disertation, West Virginia University, 1972.

Lippitt, R. Psychodrama in the home. *Sociatry,* 1947, *1,* 148–167.

Lippitt, R., & Hubbell, A. Role playing for personnel and guidance workers. *Group Psychotherapy,* 1956, *9,* 89–114.

Mann, J. H., & Mann, C. H. The effect of role playing experience on self ratings of personal adjustment. *Group Psychotherapy,* 1958, *11,* 27–32.

McHolland, J. D. From stress to release of human potential. Printed speech, Evanston, Ill.: Kendall College, 1968.

Moreno, F. Psychodrama in the neighborhood. *Sociatry,* 1947, *1,* 168–178.

Moreno, J. L. Psychodrama and group psychotherapy. *Sociometry,* 1946, *9,* 249–253.

Moreno, J. L. The third psychiatric revolution and the scope of psychodrama. *Group Pyschotherapy,* 1964, *17,* 149–171.

Moreno, J. L. The roots of psychodrama. *Group Psychotherapy,* 1966, *19,* 140–145.

Moreno, J. L., & Elefthery, D. G. An introduction to group psychodrama. Chapter 4 in G. M. Gazda. *Basic approaches to group psychotherapy and group counseling.* Springfield, Ill.: Thomas, 1975.

Ohlsen, M. M. *Guidance services in the modern school.* New York: Harcourt, 1974.

Otto, H. A. *Group methods to actualize human potential.* Los Angeles: Holistic Press, 1970.

Otto, H. A. *More joy in your marriage.* New York: Pocket Books, 1971.

Passmore, J. L. Role playing: A therapeutic adjunct to group counseling. Chapter 13 in M. M. Ohlsen (Ed.), *Counseling children in groups: A forum.* New York: Holt, Rinehart and Winston, 1973.

Papanek, H. The use of early recollections in psychotherapy. *Journal of Individual Psychology,* 1972, *28,* 169–176.

Perls, F., Hefferline, R. F., & Goodman, P. *Gestalt therapy.* New York: Dell, 1951.

Polster, E., & Polster, M. *Gestalt therapy integrated: Contours of theory and practice.* New York: Bruner/Masel Publishers, 1973.

Riessman, F. Role playing and lower socio-economic groups. *Group Psychotherapy,* 1964, *17,* 36–48.

Schutz, W. C. *Joy: Expanding human awareness.* New York: Grove, 1967.

Shaffer, J. B. P., & Galinsky, M. D. *Models of group therapy and sensitivity training.* Englewood Cliffs: Prentice-Hall, 1974.

Shaftel, F. R., & Shaftel, G. *Role playing for social values: Decision making in social studies.* Englewood Cliffs: Prentice-Hall, 1967.

Simon, S. B. Please touch! How to combat skin hunger in our schools. *Scholastic Teacher: Junior/Senior High,* 1974 (October), *35,* 22–25.

Von Hilsheimer, G. *How to live with your special child.* Washington: Acropolis Books, 1970.

Wallace, C. J., Teigen, J. R., Liberman, R. L., & Baker, V. Destructive behavior treated by contingency contracts and assertive training. *Journal of Behavior Therapy and Experimental Psychiatry,* 1973, *4,* 273–274.

# Counseling Children in Groups

Most professionals who do group counseling with children today are employed as elementary school counselors. Except for the good work that was begun over a quarter century ago by leaders such as Meeks (1963) and Wilson (1956), few school systems have employed elementary school counselors for more than a decade. When the 1958 National Defense Education Act was extended in 1964 to provide support for professional preparation of elementary school counselors and for states to develop pilot programs in local school districts, elementary school guidance programs began a rapid expansion. For example, Van Hoose and Vafakes (1968) reported that already there were 3,837 elementary school counselors employed in the schools. Just two years later (based upon a survey conducted during the 1968–1969 school term), Van Hoose and Kurtz (1970) reported that there were 6,041 employed in the schools. Carlson and Van Hoose (1971) appraised this growth as follows:

> The apparent shift in funding from federal to local sources is most encouraging. For several years large city school systems have experienced financial difficulties and have relied heavily upon federal funds for new programs and innovations. From 1965 through 1968, several large cities began to employ a few elementary school counselors in federally supported programs, and this policy accounts in part for a sizable percentage of counselors in large cities at the present time. As this investigation reveals, however, there is a trend toward

local support for elementary school counselors even in areas with severe financial problems. This new support suggests that elementary school counseling has gained recognition as a vital service and that efforts are being made to maintain and extend this service in large cities. (p. 45)

Moreover, the demand for well-qualified elementary school counselors remains in high schools. Increasingly they also are being employed as child therapists and as parent educators in community agencies (Ohlsen, 1974)

Two comprehensive research reports provide strong support for elementary school counseling services (Kaczkowski, 1972; Wellman, 1971). Furthermore, despite the relative newness of these programs and the counselor educators' disagreement over the extent to which these counselors should consult with teachers and parents rather than counsel children, the practitioners agree that elementary school counselors should counsel children and parents, consult parents and teachers, and coordinating pupil personnel services within their school buildings (Kaczowski & Patterson, 1975; McCreary & Miller, 1966; Mendelson, 1967; Smith & Eckerson, 1966). These surveys also revealed that those who counsel children must be competent to use group procedures to help parents and teachers as well as to counsel children in groups.

## Introducing Group Counseling for Children

To be most effective, elementary school counselors must be able to define their professional services, to describe them for teachers and parents as well as students, and to win acceptance and respect of parents and teachers. The principal can enhance this process by understanding and supporting the counselor's program and by arranging for the counselor to report periodically to the faculty and answer questions concerning his or her work (also to do the same for parents). At such meetings the counselor also describes his consultation services and explains why he likes to meet periodically with students in their classes to make presentations in preparation for group counseling, to answer their questions concerning his services, and to conduct guidance in cooperation with teachers' classroom guidance activities.

Within such a cooperative working atmosphere children often seek counseling on their own before either their parents or teachers recognize their need for counseling—even from trainees who are assigned to cooperating schools for practicum (Ohlsen, 1967). Such working relationships enable teachers and counselors to cooperate in helping children to cope with developmental tasks and for children to obtain assistance early and often prevent serious problems later.

Mayer (1967) also found that even kindergarten and first-grade children seek counseling on their own and profit from counseling. He concluded that the most important single source of information about a child is the child himself. McCandless and Young (1966) agreed that there is no substitute for information that can be gained from a child by observing him and interviewing him. To understand a child, an adult must understand how the child perceives his world, his own needs, his problems, and his behavior. Furthermore, counselors are just beginning to learn the extent to which even a young child can take responsibility for learning his own desired new behaviors and for helping his peers learn their desired new behaviors in groups. Since, however, expectations from him in group counseling call for new helping and learning skills, the counselor must take great care to communicate precisely how these expectations differ from other similar situations—for example, precisely how his relationship with his counselor differs from his relationship with his parents and teachers and how his working relationships with siblings and classmates differ from the way he works with, talks with, and helps fellow clients.

On the other hand, they also should be taught to apply their new listening and helping skills in daily living with friends, relatives, and classmates. When the classroom teacher and counselor respect each other they can best enhance the generalization from learning in the counseling group to the children's classroom—by having the members of a counseling group go back to their classroom and discuss how to cope with a developmental task. They can cooperatively lead classroom discussions to help children cope with common problems (Glasser, 1969; Hawes, 1973; Kaczkowski & Patterson, 1975; Sonstegard & Dreikurs, 1973) and to teach children to find the answers to their questions about themselves and their environment (Rogge, 1965). The counselor's parent discussion groups also help children to apply their new learnings in their homes (see last section of this chapter).

Generally regular consultation by a counselor with the parents and teachers of his clients provides them with the information they require to better understand their children's behavior and attitudes, helps them better accept their children, and enables them to encourage and reinforce desired new behaviors, without breaking confidences with the children (Chapter 1). When a counselor describes the nature of and his reasons for parent and teacher consultations, clients usually approve of consultation. They recognize the need for parents' and teachers' help in implementing desired new behaviors. Though Ohlsen and Gazda (1965) recognized they did not do sufficient consultation, they endorse it. One of their clients expressed the need for it as follows: "We are just kids and don't count for much; even our dogs are treated better than we are." Such a child usually requires the assistance of his counselor to convey such feelings and to request parents' assistance in improving his relationship with them. Similarly, many parents require the counselor's assistance in learning to express caring and to develop improved relationships with the child.

# Adapting Group Techniques for Children

Although most basic principles of group counseling apply to all ages, a counselor must adapt his techniques to his clients' social, emotional, and intellectual development, their previous experiences in groups, and their ability to communicate verbally. Perhaps children trust the counselor more readily than do either adults or adolescents, and they can communicate verbally better than many counselors and therapists thought they could until recently, but they do require more assistance than older clients do in communicating feelings and describing subtle relationships. To communicate effectively with children a counselor must understand his clients' vocabulary and language development and family background; be sensitive to their search for words to express themselves; be able to listen empathically and convey encouragement; and when appropriate, teach them the vocabulary that they require to express themselves adequately. When, for example, a counselor said, "You feel lonely," he meant that the client felt that he was without any warm, close relationships either at home or at school, but the client responded, "No, I am around lots of people both here and at home." Then he defined lonely as he was using it, and the client said, "If being lonely means that too, I'm lonely." Thus, the client learned to express the feelings he was experiencing. Moreover, the counselor was able to help his client express his feelings without embarrassing him or forcing him to verbalize material which could best be expressed through activities or play media.

Most of Ohlsen's (1973) contributors believe that children can interact verbally. Jefferies observes that some counselors have inaccurately concluded that inner-city children cannot communicate verbally because they do not use "Emily Post" language well. Actually, she believes that their "gutsy" language may enable them to communicate better than middle-class children in counseling groups. Some rely heavily on verbal communication. Sonstegard and Dreikurs believe that they can communicate with children adequately to help each uncover his real goals, discover whether or not he is pursuing them in ways that insure success or failure, ascertain whether his goals are factitious, examine the consequences of his behavior, and develop new goals when appropriate (or make him aware of his mistaken goals and reorient him to new goals that are likely to produce better consequences). Ellis helps his clients ferret out why they feel and behave as they do, and to discover more appropriate behaviors. Hawes argues strongly for verbal interaction in classroom discussions to accelerate language development, to help children learn to use language to cope with their environment, and to help children recognize the relevance of school for daily living as well as to teach them new behaviors. He also believes that the listening and talking which occur in his classroom discussion groups further higher thinking processes, and thereby enhances management of environment.

Gazda and Glass, on the other hand, tend most to question children's ability to interact verbally in a counseling group. Prior to the third grade Glass uses projective tests to uncover children's therapeutic material because he does not believe that they can reveal it verbally. Gazda seriously questions the use of verbal therapy for children from five through nine years, and believes that children from nine through thirteen years are uncomfortable discussing the topics that worry and upset them.

The younger the children are, the more structure they require. Associated with the need for more structure is the need for more counselor participation. Ohlsen and Gazda (1965) found that fifth-graders are sensitive to others' feelings, but without formal instruction in their client and helper roles they do not respond therapeutically as readily as adolescents. When, therefore, the counselor fails to provide essential structuring, especially during early sessions, children become restless, are easily distracted, and often compete for the counselor's attention. However, even with minimal structuring their helping skills improve during the life of the group.

Preparation for participation in group counseling should begin with the presentation and intake interview (Chapter 1). When, for example, he listens to a prospective client in the intake interview trying to convince himself that he is ready for group counseling, the counselor may respond to an uncertain child as follows: "You really have something to talk about, and I believe that you will discuss it in the group, but I wonder whether you are grown up enough to listen to others, to stay in your chair, not disturbing others, and to talk about it and try to help others. In order for me to help you and the others in the group, I must give all my attention to helping. I can't be scolding and disciplining those who do not behave." Then the counselor must detect what bothers the client and teach him to discuss it therapeutically, explain how he will teach him to be a helper, and help him make a commitment to function therapeutically in the group. When he feels that a client is questionable, he may admit him to the group on a trial basis with clearly stated expectations which are shared with other clients and used to evaluate performance at the end of the trial period.

Increasingly over the past five years the writer has come to teach his clients to function both as helpers and as clients and to solicit feedback from clients on his effectiveness as a counselor. Furthermore, especially during early sessions, he takes note of especially effective client and helper behaviors and calls the group's attention to them—even to the extent of stopping the recorder and replaying the effective behavior. When, for example, he observes a client make an accurate reflection, and subsequently it results in helping another discuss openly what really worries him. the counselor calls attention to the helpful behavior and sometimes even explains why this client's helping response was so effective. The counselor also notes and reinforces (and teaches clients to reinforce) productive client behaviors such as discussing openly his worries and concerns; clarifying his goals for counseling and stating them more clearly in behavioral terms; practicing the skills required to act; soliciting and using feedback productively; developing the skills, the self-confidence, and interpersonal skills to try new behaviors; reappraising failures in order to determine which call for practice of skills and which call for new alternative solutions; sharing successes and celebrating them; determining what new behaviors he will try between counseling sessions (homework); and assessing what he has accomplished and what he still has left to do.

Size of group and length of session also must be adjusted to the children's attention span, their ability to sustain interest in another's problem, and their general social maturity. Ohlsen and Gazda concluded that better results could have been achieved with their fifth-graders in smaller groups (five or six instead of seven or eight) and for shorter counseling periods (40–45 minutes instead of an hour). Perhaps most upper-grade elementary school children should be scheduled for even shorter periods (two sessions of 35–40 minutes per week) and then be increased in length as the children learn to use the time efficiently. Primary-school age children should be scheduled preferably for three periods per week of 5–10 minutes shorter duration.

The counselor who helps children effectively develops a safe relationship with them, can listen to them empathically, conveys respect for them, exhibits confidence in their ability to express themselves, is patient with them, communicates with them in their own language without condescension, and is able to control adults' tendency to evaluate them. He does not encourage a child to review his history, nor does he question why he behaved as he did in difficult situations. Rather than trying to help a client to understand why he behaved as he did in the past, he tries to help him learn desired new behaviors. When the child wants to or feels that he must discuss history, he listens and tries to discover how to help the child discover the relevance of that historical material for present problems and to define specific behavioral goals for each.

## Selecting Clients

Children who profit most from group counseling volunteer for counseling, have something to talk about, are committed to talk about it, are committed to change their behavior, and are interested in helping peers change their behavior. The counselor also may include some who have difficulty expressing themselves, but are committed to learn to do so—for example, the shy child who has difficulty making requests of significant others, participating in class discussion, or in making friends. Rarely is it advisable to include in a single group only one type of client, such as discipline problems or gifted underachievers. Usually underachievers can be treated most effectively with some other children who accept their ability, want to achieve, and are interested in learning to function better.

Children talk to their counselors about a variety of problems: coping with new situations and/or developmental tasks; grieving; school phobias; doubts about their ability to succeed in certain school subjects—especially reading and arithmetic; other learning problems; and expressing feelings toward or resolving conflicts with relatives, friends, and classmates. In the presentation and intake interview some clients seem to expect all adults to respond to them and to treat them as their mothers do. Group counseling helps such children to recognize individual differences and to relate to different individuals differently—to broaden their repertoire of human-relations skills and to adapt these skills to an ever enlarging environment.

When counselors are able to make presentations to groups of children and answer their questions that is usually sufficient to motivate most who are ready for group counseling. Wagner (1974) uses overhead projections of stick figures of children exhibiting problems on a screen to enrich her classroom presentations. Boy (1974) argues for a variety of media to introduce children to the counseling services—color slides with video recordings, motion pictures, video tapes, brochures, puppets, and student panels and so forth. The crucial points are to communicate what the services are like and who is helped by each so that each may select those which are most appropriate for him. For Dinkmeyer (1970) the key word is accessibility. It is not that every child needs counseling, but that every child should have access to counseling, especially assistance with developmental tasks.

If, therefore, the counselor does his job well he will try to select those who are ready and place each with the best possible combination of clients (Chapter 1). For children perhaps selecting clients who can define concrete goals and who can model for each other are the most crucial. From the pool of ready clients the counselor must in the final analysis ask as was suggested in Chapter 1: Who needs whom for what?

Most of Ohlsen's (1973) contributors use some selection procedures to screen their clients. Bosdell, Ferreira, Jefferies, and Passmore select their clients with considerable care, including an intake interview. Gazda and Glass recommend more use of diagnostic procedures to insure that disturbed children are not placed with normal children in counseling groups. Sonstegard and Dreikurs, Ellis, Gilbert, Hawes, and Mowrer believe that groups should be open to all volunteers.

Should boys and girls be treated in the same counseling group? Ginott (1961) reported that the prevailing practice in clinics was to separate boys and girls for treatment during latency period. Ohlsen and Gazda (1965) reported that girls in their fifth-grade groups were more mature, were more verbal, and tended to dominate the boys. They can be treated easier separately at that age. Gazda endorses it. Ohlsen disagrees; he believes that the counseling group may be the safest place in which boys and girls can learn to cope with the problems with which they are faced as a consequence of their differing rates of social-sexual development. Failure of adults to help them deal with these developmental problems at this time probably accounts for some of the problems with which adolescents, and even young adults, are faced in learning to develop wholesome heterosexual relationships.

## Goals

With reference to goals, Ohlsen's contributors addressed themselves to the following questions: What are your goals? What criteria do you use to assess effectiveness of counseling? How do you define your treatment goals? To what extent do you involve your clients and/or their significant others such as parents and teachers in developing goals? Where do you stand on the issue of helping clients adjust to their situation rather than trying to change it?

Of the authors, Patterson objected most strongly to specific behavioral goals. Those who agreed most strongly with the notion of specific behavioral goals were Sonstegard and Dreikurs, Ferreira, Hawes, Hosford, and Passmore.

Only Ferreira and Passmore gave specific attention to the notion of helping clients define criteria which they can use to appraise their own progress. Both indicated that they believe such criteria can be used by children to discover specific ways in which they are growing, and such discoveries reinforce further growth.

Although only Ferreira, Hosford, and Passmore state specifically how they encourage clients to participate in the goal-development process, most would seem to involve them in formulation of goals.

In general, Ohlsen's contributors help their clients adjust to their environment. Perhaps they do not feel that children could be expected to change either of the two institutions that seem to have the greatest impact upon them: home and school. Gilbert feels that it is unrealistic to expect children to exert influence when teachers and counselors have had so little success in changing either school policies or curriculum. On the other hand, contributors do encourage counselors to function as change agents in their consulting role for teachers and administrators (Dreikurs, Sonstegard, Ellis, Ferreira, Hawes, and Hosford) and for parents (Ellis, Sonstegard, and Dreikurs). They urge counselors to develop programs for helping teachers improve the learning climate and for helping parents develop a wholesome climate for rearing their children.

## Personal History and Insight

To what extent do Ohlsen's contributors encourage clients to discuss their personal history in group counseling? Of all the authors, only Sonstegard and Dreikurs make the most systematic use of history during their psychological investigation. Their purpose is to help each client understand the circumstances under which he developed his personal perspective and bias, his concepts and convictions about himself and his strategy for living. In particular, they try to obtain a picture of each client's family constellation and what conclusions he drew from it with reference to his perception of his problem and his behavior at present.

Interpretation is a basic part of the treatment process for Sonstegard and Dreikurs, and Ellis. They believe that clients must understand why they feel and behave as they do. However, Ellis helps clients achieve understanding of their irrational feelings and behaviors with minimal use of history. In the course of rational-emotive group counseling, he focuses almost entirely upon helping each client discuss what upsets him now, in order to help him understand and cope with his irrational self-statements. Even those who use interpretation as a basic component in their treatment process often question its use with children on the grounds that it requires sophisticated vocabulary which most children do not possess. Glass also warns that premature interpretation confuses children and inhibits their spontaneity. Instead he encourages children to help each other discover why they feel and behave as they do.

## Resistance

In general, Ohlsen's contributors agreed with the methods for dealing with resistance discussed in Chapter 6. When the approaches discussed in Chapter 1 are used much resistance in children's groups can be prevented.

A few exceptions are worth noting. For example, Ellis defines resistance as the client's refusing to learn or apply the A B C's of rational-emotive therapy. He shows the client how his irrational ideas interfere with his ability to profit from group counseling. When Sonstegard and Dreikurs, and Hawes, are confronted with resistance, they help the resisting client explore the natural consequences of his failure to learn and implement desired new behaviors.

## Use of Role Playing

Role playing can be used effectively with children when they have difficulty communicating what happened in some troublesome situation. When, for example, Wells (1962) tried to find out what happened when Tommy and Ray were dragged in from a playground fight (for help not for punishment), she found that both tried to talk at once and blame the other, but neither communicated very well so she asked them to reverse roles and *show her what happened*. Very quickly they were then able to convey what happened, how it got started, and how each had affected the other. With these data they were then able to resolve the conflict and to explore some better ways for coping with the problem in the future. Adaptations of this role reversal technique is very useful in counseling groups too. Of the other techniques discussed in Chapter 7, perhaps the most effective to use with children in group counseling are magic shop, break in and break out, role reversal, and role rehearsal (especially in making requests and in expressing positive feelings).

Furthermore, sometimes a child can use a play telephone in a counseling group to communicate to another client hurtful material that he seemed unable to express directly to another group member—even in ordinary role playing. Such a child also can use a combination of the two to express material which he does not appear to be able to do using either technique by itself: by having the child pretend that he is talking on the telephone to a trusted friend and having the other client assume that trusted friend's role in the role played telephone conversation. Children also can use puppets and dolls to speak for them to other puppets or dolls (for whom role players speak) to convey their perceptions of their problems, to present tentative solutions, and to practice social skills.

In cooperative classroom discussion groups which are co-led (at least to start with, but hopefully taken over by the teacher) by the teacher and a counselor, role reversal and role rehearsal can be used very effectively to help a child deal with a significant other and to practice coping with developmental tasks. Wells also used a psychodramatic career enactment technique in the classroom to encourage children to think about themselves as potential workers and to open up the exploration of careers. Children in upper elementary school grades were instructed to project themselves ahead into some specific job in pantomime. Some prefer to use a partner in the pantomime to function as a co-worker or to do a commentary on the worker following the pantomime. Children like it. Moreover, it encourages participants to do a lot of thinking in preparation for the scene and the discussion of it stimulates some very interesting reactions and questions concerning career development.

## Use of Play Media

Perhaps the strongest professional advocate for use of play techniques with children is Moustakas (1959). He believes that the child can participate in play activities on a mutual basis better than he can participate only verbally. He also endorses the use of play techniques for normal children:

> Perhaps the most important aspect of the play therapy experience for the normal child is the concentrated relationship with the therapist. In the busy life of children the opportunity rarely exists to be alone for one hour with an adult once or twice a week. Furthermore, it is rare for a child to have a relationship in which he is the center of the experience, where he can express his feelings and be understood as a person, where the adult is fully understanding of the child, watching, listening, making statements of recognition, and being present in a deeply human sense.
>
> Play therapy is a form of preventive mental hygiene for normal children. It is a way for them to grow in their own self-acceptance and respect, a way to explore feelings and attitudes and temporary tensions and conflicts that cannot be expressed easily and safely in school and at home. Often threatening feelings and disturbing experiences can be worked through in three or four sessions. (pp. 43–44).

In the kind of consultation groups which were mentioned in the section on goals teachers and parents can learn to listen, to use play media and role playing to give the kind of undivided attention described by Moustakas. Perhaps Guerney's (1964) play techniques for helping parents of disturbed children also can be adapted to enable parents of normal children to uncover their children's problems, to communicate with them, to enjoy them, and to enhance their personal development.

None of Ohlsen's (1973) contributors who write on the use of play, movement, and role playing endorse the use of play media with the enthusiasm exhibited by Gazda. He questions the use of verbal techniques below age nine and recommends only limited use of them before age thirteen. Bosdell, Ferreira, and Passmore believe that most elementary school children can discuss most of their problems, but Bosdell often uses play techniques to help children convey feelings and the purposes for which they require assistance. She endorses the counselor's selection of play materials that enhance a client's goals. Bosdell also uses play media as Ferreira uses dance and movement techniques to help children experience, own, accept, enjoy, and manage their feelings. Passmore uses role playing for similar purposes. In addition, he uses role playing to practice the interpersonal skills required to implement desired new behaviors.

Play media can be used to help children communicate and experience, own, manage, and even enjoy feelings which they have denied or been unable to express. Nevertheless, the counselor must be able to differentiate clearly between playing with a child and helping a client use play media to convey his needs and/or to achieve some specific goal. When children are taken into an unstructured play room they may waste time because they are overwhelmed with the wide choice of media, or they are inadequately prepared to chose the therapeutic material which is most productive for them, or the counselor has failed to differentiate between work in the therapy room and free play. Frequently, children can make the best use of the time when the counselor selects several media for each child to express himself and the group continues to meet in the regular counseling group room. When the latter is done the following materials tend to be adequate for most normal children treated in groups: clay, finger paints, paper, puppets, and a variety of dolls and doll clothing. For example, in this instance the five first- and second-graders relied on play media more than most children's groups. All five tended to be shy, and in fact, the counselor should have detected this in the screening process and included at least one spontaneous, more out-going client as a model (but someone who had real problems on which he wanted to work). Before the children came the counselor laid out the play media. On this particular day the children selected the following play materials as they entered the counseling room: one girl and two boys decided to play with finger paints, a third boy selected clay, and the remaining girl selected five dolls (the number in her family) and proceeded to dress them as two adults and three children. As each child played, the counselor moved about, responding to one child, then another, and encouraging them to interact with each other—both verbally and with play media. Occasionally, one shared with the entire group—a sort of show and tell. Gradually over several weeks they had learned to talk more about what bothered them and the new behaviors they wanted to learn. At the same time the counselor took great care not to put pressure on anyone to talk.

## Consulting Parents and Teachers

Increasingly, school counselors are learning to function as consultants to teachers and parents. Their goal is to help these significant others to enhance normal development. Most teachers and parents do care about youth, but they often require help in communicating their caring, in learning to encourage children and youth, in establishing and maintaining living guidelines, and in involving youth in developing and maintaining such norms. Instead they often become so bogged down in a power struggle that at first it is difficult to reach them and enable them to admit their need for consultation, but they can be reached.

For most parents and teachers the best way for a new counselor to initiate consultation is to describe his services to parents (perhaps through a PTA meeting) and to teachers (at a faculty meeting), including his consultation service and answer their questions nondefensively. On such occasions he describes consultation as a mutual relationship—one in which he often solicits their assistance in helping his clients learn new desired behaviors. Best results are achieved when the consultee feels that he can discuss a problem freely, make requests, and decide for himself the extent to which he uses the information and recommendations made by the consultant. Neither has any responsibility for or authority over the other.

For teachers and parents the counselor is a resource person in human growth and development. He has knowledge and special competencies which enable him to help teachers and parents decide what they may do to encourage a given student, to determine what quality of work they can expect from him, to try to figure out why he behaves as he does in specific situations, to describe the specific behaviors which they wish to change, and to develop a course of action for teaching and/or reinforcing desired new behaviors. For the counselor, teachers and parents help him understand his clients' interests, abilities, aptitudes, behaviors, and learning problems, what they may do cooperatively to encourage the development of clients' self-esteem, and what seems to work as reinforcers of desired behaviors. Moreover, the better teachers and parents understand his services, the more they are motivated to cooperate in helping his clients, and the better they are able to decide when to seek help for themselves and when to refer a student to the counselor for assistance. When they understand and accept his services they also seek out and participate in activities such as case conferences, affective education seminars, and parent education programs.

Nevertheless, the program will be built upon quality services and the counselor taking the initiative to request their assistance with his clients. For example, usually within a few days after a counselor seeks a teacher's assistance with one of his clients, the teacher requests the counselor's assistance with one of his students.

Although some individual consultation is necessary, much can be accomplished in group consultation, and sometimes such group consultation reaches individuals who may be reluctant to seek individual consultation (and this has proven to be true for agency personnel as well as school counselors). Those who respond are encouraged to help design sessions which best meet their needs. Moreover, participation is voluntary, members keep confidences, they perceive the leader as someone who will not be called upon to evaluate them, and they respect the leader's knowledge and professional skills. Two such groups are described here.

For the first group a school counselor agreed to lead a professional growth group on adolescent psychology for a group of high school teachers for fifteen weeks. Basically they used a technique similar to Powell's (1948) seminar on great books. At the close of each session they agreed on the discussion topic for the next week and he suggested readings that might help them prepare for their next discussion. The teachers wanted to learn more about adolescents' needs and interests and what they could do to encourage their development and to enlist their cooperation in the learning process. They also wanted help in applying their new knowledge in the classroom. They shared new ideas, reacted to the readings and others' ideas, shared their successes and failures in implementing their new knowledge and skills, and used role playing to practice skills and to provide data for feedback. Often their discussions were very similar to a counseling group. In another sense their discussion differed sharply from a counseling group:

instead of talking about their personal problems, they discussed the problems they were meeting in trying to relate more personally to their students, to further emotional and social development as well as their intellectual development, and to involve their students in developing and in maintaining improved group norms. Nevertheless, the counselor felt that members' responses called forth from him his very best counseling skills. Moreover, their parting recommendation for him to limit future such groups to a dozen or so participants suggests that they wanted the personal attention provided by effective counseling groups.

Professionals also have used small groups effectively for parent education. These groups tend to be more productive when they are organized for parents with similar age children (pre-school-age children, primary school-age children, upper-elementary school-age children, junior high school or middle school students, and senior high school students). Ideally the group should be limited to five or six couples, and parents of younger children tend to be more responsive than those of older children. Many parents of adolescents have given up on their children, but are willing to try to do a better job with their younger children. Like prospective clients for a counseling group they want to know what will be expected from them and whether they can genuinely expect to be helped prior to joining a group. Listed below is a counselor's presentation for prospective members:

> These groups are designed to help parents discuss the child rearing problems with which they would like assistance, to share ideas and to discover new techniques for coping with them, to decide precisely what new behaviors each wants to learn, and to enlist the assistance of his or her spouse in implementing these desired new behaviors.
>
> In order to help members discover new behaviors that they would like to learn, they are encouraged to read books such as Dreikurs and Soltz's *Children: A Challenge* and Ginott's *Between Parent and Child*. Early in the discussion couples are encouraged to help each other to restate the good ideas which each obtained from books in behavioral terms and then to help each choose from his (her) entire list of six or fewer new behaviors that he would like most to implement.
>
> Usually the leader tries to select for a group five or six couples who have children about the same age with whom they would like help. The discussion groups will meet for an hour and a half, once a week, for six to eight weeks. Now I would be happy to answer any questions about the process and the kind of help you can expect from it. I am passing out two cards for each couple. On the first you will find a brief review of what I have said and my telephone number. On the other, please write your name, check whether you want to join a group, and if you checked "yes," please record your address and telephone number.

Counselors of children in both agencies and schools tend to spend more time consulting significant others than do most counselors who work with adolescents and adults. Counselors are increasingly using group techniques for parent education and for encouraging teachers to assume a more active role in affective education.

Even without the assistance of a consultant the effective teacher furthers children's social and emotional as well as intellectual development. He helps each discover what he can expect from himself, to recognize and develop his special aptitudes and interests, to understand and accept himself, and to help each learn to play and work with his classmates. With the assistance of effective consultants teachers also are learning to help their students detect, share, own, enjoy, and manage their feelings (Henderson, 1972).

With the assistance of an effective consultant elementary school teachers can learn to use role playing to help their students convey subtle feelings, to practice human relations skills, and to learn to deal with significant others (Chapter 7). When, for example, Robert's teacher learned that a bully, Mike, had beaten Robert up on the playground, she used role playing in the classroom to help Robert (as well as the other children) cope with Mike. From the description of the event, role playing the scene several times, and discussing it, Robert's classmates learned to cope better with bullies too. They also learned to provide support and encouragement to each other.

Teachers also are able to use the role reversal technique described earlier in this chapter (Wells, 1962) to help children reveal what really happened, to discover new alternatives for coping with conflict, and to practice implementation of selected alternatives.

Much useful material is now available to help elementary school teachers provide meaningful affective experiences in the classroom: Ojemann, Hawkins, and Chowning (1961), Dinkmeyer (1972), and Ball (1972).

Glasser (1969) and Sonstegard and Dreikurs (1973) have developed useful classroom discussion techniques to help teachers enrich their affective education programs. In general, teachers are more apt to use these classroom techniques when they have a competent consultant from whom they can request assistance when they feel that they require it. As a consultant to teachers Rogge (1965) taught teachers by demonstrating his technique for them, recording and criticizing his demonstrations, and finally recording and criticising their first efforts to use the technique. Briefly his technique consists of giving children a chance to ask any questions (or turn in their questions on slips of paper for upper elementary school grades) that they have wanted to ask, but were reluctant to ask or did not feel anyone could answer. Rather than to merely answer their questions, the leader encourages the children to share their ideas concerning where or from whom they could turn for the desired information. Frequently several classmates function as a committee to obtain the desired information and report back to the next classroom discussion.

The research and the marked increase in behavioral therapy techniques also has encouraged teacher and parent consultation with counselors. Rather than to merely extinguish unacceptable behaviors or to use relaxation methods to cope with anxiety producing events, Wells (1962) proposed a very useful ego-building technique which enabled an almost incorrigible second grader to replace his unacceptable attention getting behavior with commendable behavior. She initiated it with a classroom discussion in which the class, the teacher, and she concluded that Michael required some special help to get along in that class. Rather than sending Michael to the principal's office several times daily for misbehaving, the new plan called for everyone to note and report good school work and/or especially considerate acts which Michael did. Then at the close of each day the group would select the description of the good behavior, and send Michael to the principal with that description. This along with a variety of similar techniques have been developed cooperatively by the teacher and counselor and used successfully to help disruptive students and students with learning disabilities. Similar techniques have been developed cooperatively and used successfully by parents and counselors.

In order to benefit from a consultation a consultee must believe that he can discuss his needs openly without the fear of being put down, criticized, evaluated, or let down by having his confidence broken. Wolfe (1966) described the crucial elements in this relationship as follows:

> Consultation is concerned with the giving and taking of help in an interpersonal relationship. The outstanding feature of the relationship is its permissiveness. However, regardless of the setting, there are common features of consultation. The consultee is free to seek (or not to seek) the consultant's assistance. After receiving advice or information, the responsibility and decision for using or rejecting such advice remains with the consultee. The consultant has no responsibility for, or authority over, the action of the consultee. Implicit in the relationship, however, is the the authority of the consultant's knowledge, special competence, and professional conscience. Like most human relationships, consultation is a two-way process. Although the balance is usually weighted toward giving by the consultant and receiving by the consultee, both should give and receive. . . . The consultant should serve as a catalyst, stimulator and motivator of ideas. (p. 132)

The mutual nature of this relationship is perhaps more crucial to the counselor than any other consultant to teachers. He requires parents' and teachers' assistance as much as they require his. He often requires their assistance to understand his clients' needs and behaviors, to help his clients define behavioral goals, and to enlist parents' and teachers' assistance in reinforcing his clients' desired new behaviors. For many parents and teachers their first request for consultation follows the counselor's request for help from them. However, he must not use the pretense of needing a parent's or teacher's assistance to reach them when his real purpose is to set them up for a consultation. They will see through such a facade and resent it.

When a teacher seeks a consultation, the counselor uses his counseling skills to develop the same quality of relationship as in counseling, but the content of their interaction is different. Rather than help the teacher discuss his personal problems, the counselor uses his counseling techniques to help the teacher describe the student for whom he seeks help, and when additional information is required they decide together what shall be collected and by whom; to discuss how he feels toward the child; to describe the specific behaviors and attitudes he would like to change; and to plan specific procedures for achieving the desired changes.

The same general principles apply to parent consultations. Many parent consultations follow a counselor's request for assistance from parents. Others result from the counselor describing his services, including consultation, for parents at PTA meetings and at open houses for parents at the beginning of the school year. Usually he encourages them to ask questions concerning his services. The way he fields their questions, listens to their requests, and relates to them following the meetings help to make him a safe consultant. Usually these contacts result in individual consultations which in turn open the doors for group consultations and parent education groups.

## Summary

Most professionals who do group counseling with children are employed as elementary school counselors. They counsel children and parents, consult parents and teachers and coordinate all pupil personnel services within their school buildings. They must be competent to use group procedures. Although they try to make their services available to all students, they focus upon normal development and early recognition of children's problems.

They make a special effort to communicate the nature of their services to children as well as to parents and teachers. Consequently, normal children often seek counseling on their own before either parents or teachers recognize their need for assistance. Under these circumstances children also understand what is expected of them and are able to discuss their worries and concerns better than many counselors and therapists had previously thought that they could.

Children tend to trust the counselor more quickly than do either adolescents or adults, but the counselor must possess a special knowledge of his clients' background and language development to enable them to communicate adequately in groups. Children also require more structure. They require more assistance than older clients do in learning to be good clients and good helpers. Size of group and length of attention span also must be adjusted to the children's attention span, their ability to sustain interest in another's problem, and their general social maturity. The younger the clients the more frequently they should meet and for shorter periods of time. At the beginning, upper-grade elementary school children should be scheduled for 35–40 minutes twice a week and be increased up to ten or fifteen minutes when children learn to use additional time well. Primary school-age children should be scheduled for 5–10 minutes shorter sessions three times a week.

Best results are obtained with children when the counselor can enlist their parents' and teachers' cooperation. Such assistance helps children implement new behaviors back in their classrooms and in their homes. It also encourages mutual consultation among counselor, teachers, and parents. When, for example, a teacher consults a counselor, he is encouraged to describe the student; to tell how he feels about the child; to describe precisely how he would like to see the child's behavior change; and together they develop specific plans for helping the child learn the desired new behaviors.

## Discussion Questions

1. How can a counselor determine when a child requires assistance in expressing himself verbally in a group? What may the counselor do to help the child without pressuring him to talk?
2. What are the most important adaptations that a counselor who has been successful with adults must make to function well with a group of children?
3. With what common problems are counselors faced when they adapt their adult techniques to children?
4. Under what circumstances should a counselor use play techniques in group counseling with children? Why would you function differently in using play material for diagnosis rather than for treatment in a counseling group?
5. For what reasons may a counselor initiate a family conference for a client treated in a group? What problems do you foresee in carrying out such a conference?
6. What are the advantages of the counselor helping teachers adapt group techniques for use by the teacher in the classroom?
7. Let us suppose that you initiated a consultation with a parent and then he requested a consultation with you and then asked you how your relationship with him would differ from his relationship with his therapist. What would you say?
8. What are some of the typical problems of normal first graders, fourth graders, and sixth graders?
9. Would you prefer to treat fifth grade boys and girls in the same group? Why, or why not?
10. In your counseling group a fifth-grade boy told how much he loved

his mother and wanted to please her, but complained about her being much too strict and expecting him to make perfect grades. Last week he became sick and was given permission to go home early. He surprised his mother with her lover. Now she is trying to bribe him by letting him do as he pleases.

a. How should the counselor respond to this new complaint in the group?

b. What may the counselor do to insure that confidences are kept in the group?

# References

*ACES Sub-Committee Report on the Preparation of Elementary School Counselors.* Washington, D.C.: American Personnel and Guidance Association, 1968.

Ball, G. *Magic circle at school.* LaMesa, Calif.: Human Development Training Institute, 1972.

Bosdell, B. J. Counseling children with play media. In Ohlsen, M. M. (Ed.), *Counseling children in groups: A forum.* New York: Holt, Rinehart and Winston, 1973.

Boy, A. V. Motivating elementary school pupils to seek counseling. *Elementary School Guidance and Counseling,* 1974, *8,* 166–172.

Carlson, J., & Van Hoose, W. H. Status of elementary school guidance in large cities. *Elementary School Guidance and Counseling,* 1971, *6,* 43–45.

Dinkmeyer, D. Developmental group counseling. *Elementary School Guidance and Counseling,* 1970, *4,* 267–272.

Dinkmeyer, D. Duso D-1C and D-2C kits. Circle Pines, Minn.: American Guidance Services, Inc., 1972.

Dreikurs, R., & Soltz, V. *Children: A challenge.* New York: Duell, Sloan and Pearce-Meredith Press, 1964.

Ellis, A. Emotional education at the living school. In Ohlsen, M. M. (Ed.), *Counseling children in groups: A forum.* New York: Holt, Rinehart and Winston, 1973.

Ferreira, L. Dance: An adjunct to group counseling. In Ohlsen, M. M. (Ed.), *Counseling children in groups: A forum.* New York: Holt, Rinehart and Winston, 1973.

Gazda, G. M. Group procedures with children: A developmental approach. In Ohlsen, M. M. (Ed.), *Counseling children in groups: A forum.* New York: Holt, Rinehart and Winston, 1973.

Gilbert, J. Counseling black inner-city children. In Ohlsen, M. M. (Ed.), *Counseling children in groups: A forum.* New York: Holt, Rinehart and Winston, 1973.

Ginott, H. G. *Group psychotherapy with children.* New York: McGraw-Hill, 1961.

Ginott, H. G. *Between parent and child*. New York: Macmillan, 1965.

Glass, S. D. Practical considerations in group counseling. In Ohlsen, M. M. (Ed.), *Counseling children in groups: A forum*. New York: Holt, Rinehart and Winston, 1973.

Glasser, W. *Schools without failure*. New York: Harper & Row, 1969.

Guerney, B. Filial therapy: Descriptions and rationale. *Journal of Consulting Psychology*, 1964, *28*, 304–310.

Hawes, R. M. Getting along in the classroom. In Ohlsen, M. M. (Ed.), *Counseling children in groups: A forum*. New York: Holt, Rinehart and Winston, 1973.

Henderson, T. L. *The impact of an affective discussion group on prospective teachers*. Unpublished doctoral dissertation, Indiana State University, 1972.

Hosford, R. E. Behavioral group counseling with elementary school children. In Ohlsen, M. M. (Ed.), *Counseling children in groups: A forum*. New York: Holt, Rinehart and Winston, 1973.

Jefferies, D. Counseling ghetto children in groups. In Ohlsen, M. M. (Ed.), *Counseling children in groups: A forum*. New York: Holt, Rinehart and Winston, 1973.

Kaczkowski, H. R. *An appraisal of the elementary school counselor's role behavior*. Springfield (Ill.): Office of the Superintendent of Instruction, 1972.

Kaczkowski, H. R., & Patterson, C. H. *Counseling and psychology in the elementary schools*. Springfield (Ill.): Thomas, 1975.

Mayer, G. R. An approach for the elementary school counselor: Consultant or counselor? *The School Counselor*, 1967, *14*, 210–214.

McCandless, B. R., & Young, R. D. Problems of childhood and adolescence. In Pennington, L. A., & Berg, I. A. (Eds.), *An introduction to clinical psychology*. New York: Ronald, 1966.

McCreary, W. H., & Miller, G. Elementary school guidance in California. *Personnel and Guidance Journal*, 1966, *44*, 494–498.

Meeks, A. Elementary school counseling. *The School Counselor*, 1963, *10*, 108–111.

Mendelson, R. L. *The elementary school counselor: Description of professional preparation, actual work experiences, and personal qualifications*. Unpublished doctoral dissertation, University of Illinois, 1967.

Moustakas, C. E. *Psychotherapy with children*. New York: Harper & Row, 1959.

Mowrer, O. H. Group counseling in the elementary school: The professional versus peer-group model. In Ohlsen, M. M. (Ed.), *Counseling children in groups: A forum*. New York: Holt, Rinehart and Winston, 1973.

Ohlsen, M. M. *An evaluation of a counselor program designed for prospective elementary school counselors enrolled in 1965–1966 NDEA Institute*. Project #6-8087, U. S. Office of Education, College of Education, University of Illinois, 1967.

Ohlsen, M. M. Community guidance services. Chapter 4 in *Guidance Services in the modern school*. New York: Harcourt, 1974.

Ohlsen, M. M., & Gazda, G. M. Counseling underachieving bright pupils. *Education*, 1965, *86*, 78–81.

Ojemann, R. H., Hawkins, A., & Chowning, K. *A teaching program in human behavior and mental health*. Iowa City: University of Iowa Press, 1961.

Passmore, J. L. Role playing: A therapeutic adjunct to group counseling. In Ohlsen, M. M. (Ed.), *Counseling children in groups: A forum.* New York: Holt, Rinehart and Winston, 1973.

Patterson, C. H. The group relationship in the elementary school. In Ohlsen, M. M. (Ed.), *Counseling children in groups: A forum.* New York: Holt, Rinehart and Winston, 1973.

Powell, J. W. The dynamics of group formation. *Psychiatry,* 1948, *11*, 117–124.

Rogge, W. Building professional behavior. Chapter 11 in *Elementary school guidance in Illinois.* Springfield: Office of State Superintendent of Instruction, 1965.

Smith, H. M., & Eckerson, L. O. *Guidance services in the elementary school: A national survey.* Washington, D.C.: U. S. Office of Education, 1966.

Sonstegard, M. A., & Dreikurs, R. The Adlerian approach to group counseling of children. In Ohlsen, M. M. (Ed.), *Counseling children in groups: A forum.* New York: Holt, Rinehart and Winston, 1973.

Van Hoose, W. H., & Kurtz, M. Status of guidance in elementary schools: 1968– 1969. *Personnel and Guidance Journal,* 1970, *48*, 381–384.

Van Hoose, W. H., & Vafakas, C. Status of guidance and counseling in elementary schools. *Personnel and Guidance Journal,* 1968, *45*, 536–539.

Wagner, C. A. *Selected characteristics of children differentially referred for group counseling.* Unpublished doctoral dissertation, Indiana State University, 1974.

Wellman, F. E. *Final report of Project Success.* Columbia: University of Missouri, 1971.

Wells, C. G. Psychodrama and creative counseling in the elementary schools. *Group Psychotherapy,* 1962, *15*, 244–252.

Wilson, F. M. Realities in guidance programs in elementary schools. *Personnel and Guidance Journal,* 1956, *3*, 41–44.

Wolfe, H. E. Consultation: Role, function and process. *Mental Hygiene,* 1966, *50*, 132–134.

# Counseling Adolescents in Groups

Adolescents are engrossed in their search for identity, in establishing themselves in adult roles, and in achieving their independence. At the same time they are trapped by dependence. They do not want to give up their parents' financial assistance for education, or even their help in establishing themselves in adult roles, but they resent the controls which they associate with the assistance. Many adolescents also openly admit that they want and value parents' and relatives' emotional support and guidance. But they would prefer adult friendships and adult consultations which would allow them to request information, feedback, and even advice, but with the mutual understanding that as adults they are free to accept or reject their consultant's advice. They would appreciate adult relationships with parents—in transactional analysis terms (Steiner, 1974), adult-to-adult transactions rather than child-to-parent transactions.

McCandless (1970) believes that many adolescent problems involve frustrations in achieving major goals: status, adequate sexual adjustment, and self- and socially-fulfilling values and morals; and that rapid social changes and relaxation of moral values have complicated adolescents' lives even more than it has adults':

> Status may be more highly valued for boys, sociality for girls. Both are
> probably more important in the long run than sex although the importance of

175

sexuality is likely to be underplayed within the core, middle-class culture. While often neglected by scholars an individual's moral values development is likely to be more important than anything else in determining the quality of his life. These four major goals are achieved in all life settings, whether family, school, community groups, or job.

The point that needs greatest emphasis in a psychology of adolescence is that a drive-change theory predicts that the period is one in which great personal change can occur. Such change can be malign or benign, and it is society's responsibility to maximize the latter while minimizing the former. (p. 36)

## Adolescent Needs

The adolescent is trying to determine who he is, what he would like to do, what he can do, and to develop the will and self-confidence to do it. At the same time he is changing his referent group from family to peers. Because of rapidly changing times, and peers' consuming demands for independence, they encourage him to question many of his parents' values.

Unlike Hall (1904), who described adolescence as a period of storm and stress, Hurlock (1967) cited Gesell, Ilg, and Ames' (1956) findings to support the notion that the period could better be described as a period of heightened emotionality. Ausubel (1954) characterizes adolescence as a period for testing the adequacy of the personality structure laid down during childhood. Ackerman (1955) believes adolescents tend to be extraordinarily sensitive to others' judgment of their worth. Being caught between the twin horns of conformity and defiance explains their trigger-edge irritability. Nowhere is their rawness and their need to prove themselves more vivid than in their relationships between the sexes. Each is acutely aware of the other, is highly sensitive to the other, and lacks the confidence of the more experienced, mature adult. They do tend to get excited more easily and are more easily threatened than mature adults. When, therefore, their significant others' treatment vacillates from treating them as children to treating them as adults and trying to get them to fulfill their significant others' unfulfilled needs, adolescents often lack the self-confidence and interpersonal skills to react maturely. On the other hand, Ausubel found that although personality defects appear to be more glaring during this period, they tend to be only transitory disturbances. Even when the personality defects are more basic, he concludes that the appearance of the most serious personality disorders occur after, rather than during adolescence. Except for those who experienced markedly deviant sexual development, Hurlock concludes that most learn to cope with the problems with which they are confronted as adolescents. Adolescents often give their parents and teachers a hard time and thereby cause these adults to wonder whether they will ever find themselves; Kirkpatrick (1952) agrees that most do, and without any permanent scars.

Garrison's (1965) review of the research on adolescents suggests that much of adolescents' anger results from frustration of some goal-seeking activity. Adolescents feel that they are pressured to work for others' goals for them, that they are not allowed to make their own important decisions, and that they are expected to work for goals which are not appropriate for them. On these occasions they often feel that their significant others bully them. Lacking the verbal and social skills to cope with these limitations, they tend to strike back as a restrained and tormented animal would.

Adolescents want to be participating members of society (Ayer & Corman, 1952). Their interest in national and world affairs has long been fostered by high school and college teachers, and it has been greatly increased by television. Adolescents are more concerned about social problems than most adults realize. They appreciate support and encouragement from significant adults when they try to solve social problems (and under these circumstances they will listen to adults' suggestions). They thrive on genuine opportunities to solve social problems and on recognition for real accomplishments. On the other hand, when adults ignore obvious social problems, they tend to become disappointed, disillusioned, and even cynical with adults' complacency (Neidt & Fritz, 1950). Some feel that they must protest with demonstrations, strikes, and even riots to get adults' attention and to bring about desired changes. Others give up and withdraw by ignoring or running away from significant adults, by turning to drugs, by quitting school, or by staying in school but withdrawing from the learning process.

The adolescent's needs may be stated as general goals for group counseling as follows:

1. Search for identity by defining meaningful goals for various facets of life
2. Increased understanding of his interests, abilities, and aptitudes
3. Improving skills for identifying opportunities and for evaluating them in terms of his own interests, abilities, and aptitudes
4. Increasing interpersonal skills and self-confidence to recognize and solve his problems
5. Improving interpersonal skills and self-confidence to recognize when decisions are required, how to make them, and how to implement them
6. Increasing sensitivity to others' needs and improving skills for helping others satisfy their needs
7. Improving communication skills for conveying his real feelings directly to relevant persons, and with considerations for their feelings
8. Independence to examine what he believes, to make his own decisions, to take reasonable risks, to make his own mistakes, and to learn from his mistakes
9. Improving interpersonal skills to deal with authority figures in a mature manner, for example, employers, police, government officials as well as parents and teachers
10. Meaningful participation in developing and maintaining limits on his own behavior

11. Growing knowledge and skills for coping with his physical and emotional changes associated with maturation
12. Improving skills for living adult roles

Much as adolescents want their independence from parents, there are times when they feel very dependent upon them. They are ambivalent about their financial dependence; they resent it, and at the same time they are reluctant to relinquish it. When they want to lean on adults they must know they can count on them. For example, they are willing to act out of deference to their parents to cope with peer pressure to do something which they do not want to do anyway, and perhaps feel is wrong to do. They feel more secure when they realize that their parents have the ego strength to enforce limits when they do not feel able to do so for themselves.

Some adolescents feel that no one has ever tried to teach them to behave independently. Others feel that they are forced to rebel to escape from their parents' control. Though at some times most adolescents rebel to avoid conformity, the rebellious tend to conform more than the conformists. The difference is that they are controlled by peers rather than by their family's values and traditions. Sometimes the rebellious are used by unprincipled demagogues who may be approximately their own age, but more likely are adults who pretend to understand them in order to use them.

When rebellion serves no purpose except to fight conformity or to revolt against the establishment and its traditions, it is a neurotic reaction to authority. Healthy rebellion arises out of love for something—a recognition that something must be changed and a commitment to change that which is wrong. Healthy rebellers have goals. Furthermore, they want to participate in the planning and the implementing of specific changes, and most are willing to accept adults' assistance.

Unfortunately, many adults seem to assume that adolescents must rebel to earn their independence, and hence parents must learn to tolerate it. When parents, teachers, and employers learn to empathize with adolescents, to listen to them when they want to talk openly, to respect adolescents' ideas, and to enlist their assistance in solving problems and in defining meaningful limits and enforcing them (and changing limits as the adolescents are able to function more responsibly), many of the heartaches and conflicts with which adolescents (and their parents) are confronted in their growing up can be resolved without rebellion. Adolescents can accept from strong, understanding adults the assistance which they require to meet their increasing responsibilities. They are searching for meaning *in their daily lives* (here and now) in their communities as well as in their schools and homes. They cherish meaningful group experiences with peers in student government, leadership training, personal growth groups, and in counseling groups. Competent counselors, whom they perceive as unequivocally trustworthy confidants, are required to provide them with counseling and to provide their parents with child-rearing education.

## Meeting Adolescents' Needs in Groups

Described below are some ways in which group counseling contributes to fulfillment of *some* of the adolescent's special needs.

*Search for identity* is a central theme for the adolescent. He wants to know who he is, what he can become. Most adolescents know many things about themselves and they know that they are important to some people. At the same time they have many doubts about themselves—often more than they think most other adolescents have, and certainly more than the adults they know and admire had when they were adolescents. For some these feelings can be dispelled by good reading material on adolescent psychology and by voluntary discussion groups, but neither of these can provide the warm, accepting atmosphere that a college freshman portrayed in describing her group-counseling experiences as a high school senior (five girls and a young male counselor):

> As the weeks passed, I learned to talk about more facets of me and to make more daring decisions. The relationship I had with the girls was unique because, for one, I could talk about the real me with no fear of being attacked. . . .
>
> We all talked about our abilities to express emotion, about our role as women in a working world, and about our work as students. I was more concerned than other girls about my role as a career woman. I wanted a career and a home. . . .
>
> We all found ourselves growing up in the group. . . . We had gained self-confidence regarding social situations and our abilities to achieve our goals. We were more sure of accomplishing our goals because we had learned to set realistic goals. Our confidence in social situations was inspired by the open, honest relationship we had in the group. Finally we had taken on some decision-making responsibility in the group; we were treated like adults there, so we wanted to act like adults. (L. Ohlsen, 1966, pp. 401–402)

Within such a group (especially with both boys and girls present) an adolescent discovers that he is someone special. He also discovers that other teenagers whom he admires and respects have problems, some perhaps more serious than his own. Furthermore, in spite of his faults, they really accept him and they are committed to help him learn to relate to important others outside the counseling group as well as to richly relate to him within their group. Experiencing such genuine acceptance strengthens his ego—gives him the self-confidence and the courage to face up to his problems and to solve them.

*Increased understanding* of his special interests, abilities, and aptitudes should have begun prior to adolescence. Very early in life understanding parents and teachers should have helped him discover what he has a right to expect from himself. Even when this has been done well, the adolescent tends to face many questions about his interests, abilities, and aptitudes that will require thorough self-appraisal with the individual assistance of a competent counselor, and often with some special testing, carefully interpreted by a counselor for the individual. Possessing this kind of information, the adolescent is better able to explore his real self with fellow clients, sharing his positive feelings about his strengths, explaining why he cannot accept and use certain strengths, and revealing his areas of doubt—wondering to what extent his weaknesses will block certain plans. His fellow clients' ability to empathize and to accept him provides the support he needs to face up to his weaknesses—and then correct them if he can with reasonable effort or accept them and adapt his plans accordingly.

*Improving skills in obtaining adequate information* about his options and environment is a problem for everyone, but especially for adolescents. Who should go to college? What does one need to know to choose a college? How can one get ready for scholarship and admission-testing programs? What can one do to increase his chances for getting off to a good start in college or on a job? What problems do young people meet on their first job? How may they cope better with them? How does one get a job? How can one make the most of his opportunities? How can one best meet a girl (or boy) whom he would like to date? How can one decide when he is really in love?

Though adolescents may sometimes appear to be flippant, they are seriously concerned to learn more about their opportunities and to improve their understanding of their environment. Many of them are naive and they know it, and they are embarrassed about it. Many of their questions can be answered by directed reading—especially when they are given an opportunity to discuss and clarify what they learned in small voluntary discussion groups or in counseling groups where they feel it is safe to ask their questions and say what they think. Within the safe atmosphere of a counseling group, they also *enhance their own self-respect by helping others*.

Rarely do today's adolescents feel as genuinely needed and appreciated as they do in counseling groups. (They also can experience this feeling of genuine worth when their family council deals with its problems and the parents exhibit genuine respect for their children's needs and ideas.)

*Improved skill in assimilating and appraising information* about one's opportunities can be acquired in the ways just discussed. However, one must also learn where to find validating information and how to make decisions. When an adolescent fails, he can profit from the assistance of fellow clients in appraising his decisions and actions and in planning for new ones. Failure alone teaches the adolescent nothing except how one can be hurt, but with the assistance of accepting others (especially peers) he can discover why he failed and how he may attack the problem again, discuss openly how he was hurt, why he may be reluctant to try again, and discover why he must try again. Where the problem involves new or threatening relationships, he can even practice his new approaches by role playing the encounter.

Understanding teachers also can do much to help youth assimilate and appraise information. They can look for and take note of instances in which youth displayed good judgment in class discussion and in written work. They also can try to limit their discouraging behavior, trying to help youth learn from their mistakes rather than merely criticizing them. A conscientious teacher appreciates the assistance of an accepting counselor in learning to play his supportive role more effectively. Techniques that a counselor can use to do this were discussed in Chapter 8.

*Increasing interpersonal skills and confidence in his ability to recognize and solve an adolescent's problems* develops in a counseling group. When an adolescent discovers that other teenagers have problems, are willing to deal openly with them, and can solve them, he develops more confidence in himself and the treatment process. Good models have a tremendous impact on adolescents and can teach them how to relate openly and to help others. Ackerman (1955) found that adolescents catch on quickly to the notion of reaching behind mere talk to respond to genuine feelings. They learn how to pick up the real feelings revealed by such nonverbal behavior as body posturing, facial expressions, and motor behavior. Ackerman also found that he could foster the use of these nonverbal cues by sharing his bases for his interpretations.

*Improving sensitivity to others' needs and improved skills for helping others* are developed in a counseling group in the ways discussed above.

Adolescents also learn, in the ways just discussed, to communicate their real feelings and needs. A family conference can be used effectively to further this process. If, even after role playing a scene in a counseling group, the adolescent does not feel adequate to face and deal with a family conflict, the counselor can arrange a family conference (or one for only the client and his parents) in which the adolescent is given an opportunity to reveal how he feels about them (and usually he feels much more positive toward them than he has let them know), how he has been hurt in the home, and what he would like from them (and usually his most important wants are much more acceptable than they realized). During such a family conference the counselor helps the other members listen to the adolescent while he expresses his feelings and requests. The counselor also helps the adolescent listen to his family as they discuss their feelings for him, thereby increasing his sensitivity to others' needs. Finally, he helps them to agree at least on some tentative solutions. Often he helps them establish a family council, providing them with a technique for dealing with family problems and for helping adolescents improve communication skills. Such a structure also enables adolescents to help parents function more effectively as parents, accepting and fulfilling their roles as models for their children. *Improved communication* is also engendered by consultation with parents and teachers.

*Improving relationship skills* learned in such meaningful groups as family councils, classroom discussions, voluntary discussion groups, and counseling groups can be used to improve social skills. Ohlsen (1974) described meaningful programs that have been developed in agencies and schools.

*Independent behavior* can be observed, practiced, and reinforced in a counseling group. With this atmosphere adolescents discover that their ideas are respected, that they as well as others do foolish things in trying to achieve independence, and that their fellow clients can provide helpful feedback and suggestions for improving their behavior. They also learn, by role playing as well as talking, to communicate feelings directly to relevant persons and to be assertive yet considerate in communicating directly with authority figures such as employers and police as well as parents and teachers.

Important as these experiences are for adolescents, perhaps even more can be accomplished in separate discussion groups for parents and teachers. In such groups the adults learn to accept adolescents and their responsibilities for them when they discover for themselves, not only from reading but also from observing adolescents and talking frankly with them, (1) what really bothers the adolescents with whom they are involved; (2) how they feel and how much they really want acceptance, understanding, and assistance in coping with their new selves; (3) how much they appreciate assistance in developing independence in preference to fighting for it; (4) what it means to adolescents to be respected, to have their ideas seriously considered and at least sometimes accepted; (5) the extent to which they will try to get along with authority figures who try to empathize with them; and (6) the extent to which they use important adults as models—copying bad characteristics as well as good ones. However, it still will not be easy for adults to help adolescents learn to be independent, because most of the adults' models have used authoritarian approaches in trying to cope with adolescents. Beleaguered adults also recognize and appreciate the type of consultant's assistance provided in such discussion groups.

The rationale has already been presented for giving adolescents an opportunity *to participate in developing and maintaining limits for their own behavior*. Obviously, it helps teach them to accept the responsibilities that accompany increased independence. Equally crucial are the experiences that develop meaningful values and reasonable expectations and provide good models. When important others failed to provide such essential positive influence, Gadpaille (1959) noted from his experiences in treating delinquent adolescents that:

> The great majority of such adolescents I have interviewed came from such disrupted and rejecting homes that they were never able to feel their needs could or would be fulfilled by their parents. There was no real benefit to be gained by "being good" and conforming to the demands of their parents, and the resentment of this state of affairs spread to include all authority. The only way to get what they wanted was to take it by force, considering only themselves. Since this learned pattern is associated with considerable pleasure-impulse gratification, they become fixated on it.

It should be stressed here that the delinquent population from which the observations of this communication are drawn is, I think, a typical one. Most of these adolescents were not the products of criminal subcultural groups or of rigid, punitive societies. They were primarily products of homes in which social values were, at least, verbally stressed, but were stressed without adequate parental reward for adherence to those values. (p. 277)

These important others who should have helped these adolescents develop meaningful values and served as models for them in their daily lives were phonies, and hence adolescents rejected both the people and their values. Adolescents need models who try to live the values they preach. However, youths' models need not be perfect. In fact, many good models have their greatest impact when they discuss with adolescents the significance of their values for themselves, the problems they are facing in trying to be the kind of adults they would like to be, and enlist the adolescents' assistance in reinforcing the behavior they are trying to learn to practice. Significant others also must possess the ego strength to enforce the limits that adolescents have helped to define. Unfortunately, many authority figures do not possess the ego strength, the knowledge of adolescents, the human-relations skills, and the confidence in their adolescents to fulfill these roles. Many are afraid to do what is necessary lest the adolescent challenge their authority or reject them and their love.

Within an effective counseling group, adolescents discover fellow clients who are good models. They also discover their peers' models and how models have shaped these fellow clients' behavior. (Good books, especially biographies, also can provide powerful models for youth. Once they discover the value of such models, they often suggest relevant books for each other.) They observe their peers' search for reasonable compatibility between real selves and ideal selves; they help others change their attitudes and behaviors; and they help them learn to convey their new selves to important others outside their counseling group. Eventually they conclude that they can achieve these goals, too. Observing others solve their problems increases the adolescent's confidence in his ability to solve his own problems.

*Growing knowledge and skills to understand and to cope with physical and emotional changes* is achieved in group counseling for the very reasons stated above. In this meaningful relationship with admired and trusted peers adolescents can learn to discuss their new feelings, how to cope with these feelings, and others' expectations of them (for example, what a date expects). They discover that they can talk about their concern about their size, personal grooming, condition of skin, appetite, health, sexual development, social development, and attractiveness to the opposite sex.

Counselors also can enhance normal development by preparing teachers and parents to answer adolescents' questions. In discussion groups a counselor can help teachers and parents discuss, and role play coping with, such communication problems as (1) their own discomfort and embarrassment with their adolescent's questions; (2) their sensitivity to his emotional readiness for the information; (3) their intelligent use of good reading material to answer his questions and to open up topics for discussion; (4) their good sense to stop when they have answered his questions to his satisfaction; (5) their ability to accept his questions seriously—no matter how naive or irrelevant they may find them; (6) their ability to answer *his* questions for him *now* rather than answer the related questions that they wished someone had answered for them; (7) their own maturity to recognize and admit when they lack adequate information to answer his questions; and (8) their ability to recognize and help him discuss the feelings behind his questions, and when appropriate to refer him for assistance that they have not able to give.

*Improving skills to learn and live new roles* ties in directly with the previous paragraphs. Fulfilling this need also relates directly to the adolescent's search for identity, increased understanding of himself, and improved social skills. To discover that others are struggling with familiar problems makes his own more acceptable; seeing others learn to cope with their problems is encouraging; and helping them increases his respect for himself. Thus group counseling is especially appropriate for adolescents. It enables them to satisfy some of their strongest needs, especially in providing real assistance to peers while obtaining assistance from them.

## Special Considerations for Adolescents

Adolescents are often brought to counseling and therapy under duress. They are made to feel that they are to blame for whatever happened at school, at home, or at work. Even when they elect to seek help on their own, they often harbor some misgivings about it because of the way they have been blamed by significant adults. Therefore, the counselor must be very sensitive to adolescents' underlying feelings and doubts, to detect and reflect their unique feelings, to answer nondefensively their questions about expectations, and to help them formulate precise, behavioral goals. Unless the school counselor is very careful, he can portray himself as defending authority figures at school, at home, or at work, and thereby markedly reduce his chances of being accepted as a trustworthy helper. On the other hand, his task is not to defend the adolescent's actions; his task is to help the adolescent function more effectively.

For junior and senior high school groups the counselor tends to be more active than he normally is for groups of college students and adults. Although they appreciate the opportunity to help define working relationships and to take an active role in developing and in maintaining a therapeutic climate, adolescents seem to have less tolerance for ambiguity than college students and adults. Adolescents want to know precisely what they are getting into, what will be expected from them, and how it will help them. Therefore, the counselor's presentation should include examples of problems that adolescents have discussed in groups (including some which are obviously the problems of prestigious youth), how they were helped, and how fellow clients as well as the counselor contributed to their growth. Clearly stated expectations, nondefensive counselor responses to clients' efforts to clarify them, and a working atmosphere in which they believe that they can shape the structure are all important to adolescents. They also appreciate an informal setting with space so that they can shove the chairs back and sit on the floor and/or use movement and exercises. The drama of relating genuinely to each other and trying to be themselves is enticing and exciting for adolescents. It encourages them to respond most openly and helpfully. They are intrigued with the counselor's helping behaviors and the way he teaches clients to be helpers as well as clients. They learn readily from models. As they grasp and integrate what is expected of them, the counselor gradually becomes less active.

> Because of the adolescent's emotional volatility, his propensity to quickly transform feeling and impulse into action, and his exquisite developmental sensitivity to anxiety and discomfort, it is necessary to help him put into language, as early as possible, his ambivalent feelings toward the group. The verbal expression of negative affect toward the group is the best guarantee against precipitous withdrawal. The group therapist can alert the group to a disgruntled and potentially withdrawing member by asking, "Do you think John is planning to return next week?" On a group level, the extension of opportunities to evaluate the group experience and the therapist's performance are fruitful. A question such as, "How do you feel this group is going or not going?" is fertile on several levels; it elicits unspoken negative feelings and demonstrates that the therapist's ego can sustain their criticism. (Rosenthal, 1971, p. 358)

The writer agrees with Rosenthal's general suggestion, but he prefers to use a reflection rather than the type of questioning which he used to surface the adolescent client's volatile feelings—for example, "John, you seem to be so upset with us that you are wondering whether you want to return for our next session;" or "John, you aren't completely satisfied with this session so far today. Perhaps it would help to replay the tape in order to give you a chance to point out to me, and to your fellow clients, where we missed something with which you wanted help, or tried to help, but weren't effective. It also would be useful to have you point out where you wanted to talk about something, but you were kind of afraid or embarrassed to do so." Similar responses also can be used to surface impulses to "act out" and to encourage clients to cope with such feelings prior to acting out (Chapter 6).

Given the adolescent's peer orientation and his need to be acceptable in their eyes, the attractiveness of the group is more important to adolescents than to most clients. Its attractiveness is further increased by the fact that everyone who volunteers is not admitted—that each client is selected with care to maximize the chances for obtaining the best possible combination of clients for success. Moreover, a presentation which stresses the client's right to decide for himself whether to participate and the client's responsibility for getting himself ready for counseling and for convincing himself and his counselor that he is ready to talk openly and to learn new behaviors seems to convey both responsibility and caring to adolescents: "We want you in our group. Are you ready? *Can you make the necessary commitments to learn your desired new behaviors?"*

Inasmuch as acceptance by peers is so crucial for adolescents, the presentation notes precisely how group counseling helps clients to improve their relationships with significant others and to develop new relationships— even with those whom they believe that they could like but have been reluctant to seek out and try to build a relationship with. In the intake interview the counselor is encouraged to help prospective group members to explore with whom they would like to be placed and with whom they would prefer not to be placed. Moreover, role playing is introduced early in the therapeutic process in order to help clients improve their relationships *with specific persons* and to practice meeting specific developmental tasks, especially those pertaining to functioning in relevant adult roles. In addition to helping adolescents practice building and/or improving relationships with specific persons through role playing, a number of relationship-building techniques described in Chapter 7 can be used profitably with adolescents: human potential lab exercises for teaching them to give positive feedback, breaking into and out of a group for dealing with membership needs, intimacy exercises, touching exercises, and the approach-avoidance exercise. Since the last two can be used to help adolescents express their feelings toward peers of the opposite sex and to manage their related fears and insecurity, their use with adolescents is discussed again here. Although their expression of these intense feelings is enhanced by an informal atmosphere and the use of nonverbal techniques (Olsson & Myers, 1972), these exercises can be used more effectively when the purposes of each exercise and the clients' participation in it are spelled out carefully prior to its use.

When, for example, the counselor detects skin hunger, he helps clients discuss their need, wish, or desire to touch and be touched, and usually clients discover that others share this need—that even most adults have not learned to satisfy this need satisfactorily. Perhaps they are still afraid, but it is now tolerable fear. They come to accept it as a normal desire for which they can learn appropriate and considerate responses, and practice them in their counseling group. Frequently the counselor defines with their assistance some specific situations with which most members of the group would like to learn to cope. Then the counselor selects from volunteers the members who do the prescribed touching (described in the situations they developed cooperatively), share their feelings as they approach and touch each other (and use soliloquy to express those feelings which they do not feel able to express directly), and learn from the feedback which they are given during subsequent discussions. The counselor reinforces their risk taking and successful touching experiences; and when they fail, he helps them decide what they are willing to attempt next and teaches fellow clients to provide encouragement and support for their next trial efforts. Thus, with sensitive consideration for individual's rights, he uses the exercises to desensitize clients to touching as well as to practice touching.

The approach-avoidance exercise consists of two volunteers looking at each other and walking toward each other, sharing their feelings as they approach (and using soliloquy to express those feelings that they are unable to express directly), touching each other as they meet, and discussing their experiences, including the feedback from observers. Best results tend to be achieved when it has been preceded by the touching exercises. Furthermore, the counselor usually finds that it is profitable to help them review what they learned from the touching exercises: for example, that others want to learn to deal directly with each other, to express their real feelings to others, and without threatening or hurting to touch significant others too; that this is something that can be learned; that their partner in the scene must be as interested in learning to be close to significant others as the primary client is; that the volunteer is committed to help the primary client— that he will not laugh at the primary client even when he makes a dumb boner, and that he will not tell anyone about these boners. In other words, the primary client is provided with safe practice situations. After clients have utilized the technique successfully they often use a variation of it to practice expressing positive feelings to significant others and to practice making requests of such persons. Adolescents have a great need to prove themselves to opposite sex peers, and consequently they find it difficult to express tender feelings to opposite sex peers; nevertheless, they recognize quickly that the counseling group is a place where they can develop these skills.

Although adolescents often act as though they are confident, and even spurn significant adults' efforts to protect them from their needlessly careless behaviors, they admit readily in a safe counseling group that they are not very confident, and that they need to practice (role play) dealing with peers as well as their significant adults. When therefore the counselor helps them explore with whom they want to learn to do what he conveys empathy and understanding of their real inner needs. Thus, clearly stated behavioral idiosyncratic goals increase the security and attractiveness of a counseling group. Role playing facilitates these essential learnings, alerts them to developmental tasks with which they require assistance, and enables them to discover that others whom they accept and admire are struggling with similar problems. Frequently, even the adolescent who has demonstrated the commitment for membership in a counseling group may have difficulty accepting a problem as his own until he has helped another in role playing to cope with a similar problem. Use of role reversal, accompanied by tape recordings of the role-played scene (and preferably video recordings), enables a client to understand better his impact on others and their expectations of him, and helps him grasp what they must experience as they try to relate to him. As suggested earlier some clients require a session with parents and/or the entire family in which the counselor helps the client communicate how he really feels toward them, how they have hurt him, and what he requires of them to implement desired new behaviors. At such sessions parents tend to be deeply touched when they discover that he does still care about them and that he genuinely wants their help in implementing desired new behaviors. Moreover, he is touched deeply as he listens (and perhaps for the first time) to his family members answer the same questions.

> It is important, if not imperative, for the group therapist to discuss with group members the question of how the inevitable approaches and contacts from parents should be handled. Parental phone calls requesting information on a member's group functioning or the unsolicited transmission of information which the member is not yet ready to share with the group create potentially thorny problems for group leaders of adolescent groups. The therapist's early willingness to consult with the group on this matter not only gives him practical operational guidelines with individual members but also enhances group self-esteem and aids in creating a climate of trust and respect. (Rosenthal, 1971, pp. 360–361)

Since quality membership in an attractive group of peers is valued so highly by adolescents, the counselor's presentation stresses the quality of membership in group counseling, clients' responsibilities for obtaining it, and specific new types of behaviors learned by clients. They are impressed too by the genuine opportunities provided in group counseling to help peers. Hodgman and Stewart (1972) strengthen this feeling by involving previously successfully treated out-patients in a community mental health center in screening clients for groups.

This counseling model's emphasis on each client's acceptance of responsibility for getting himself *ready* for counseling and for defining precise behavioral goals helps to satisfy adolescents' need for independence and enhances their feeling of security in their group. They accept their responsibility for learning to trust. They also are comforted by the emphasis on their learning new behaviors rather than on their making basic personality changes.

Meaningful *participation* in developing and in maintaining therapeutic norms is essential for all clients, but for adolescents it is crucial. Since discovering others' as well as their own growth is so satisfying to them, they require clearly stated criteria for evaluating fellow clients as well as their own growth.

On the other hand, the counselor must be wary lest adolescent clients resist termination of a wonderful, accepting relationship. Rather than to seemingly attack them with a penetrating interpretation, better results seem to be achieved with a reflection such as: "You really like each other, and even though most of you have achieved your goals, you are reluctant to say your goodbyes." Termination exercises which focus on growth one or two sessions before termination also help them accept termination when it seems to be indicated: "Perhaps each of us could think about which of his goals he has achieved, what he still has left to do, and what each of you think the others have achieved and what they have left to do. After we have discussed these perhaps we will be able to decide how much more time we will require and be able to figure out how to say our goodbyes to each other."

Obviously, adolescents thrive upon responsibility for their own growth. Frequently, however, they require instruction in decision making, assertive training,[1] and conflict resolution and the opportunity to practice these skills in their counseling group prior to implementing them with significant others. Clients can be involved in such a manner that they accept responsibility for their own growth—for example, by helping them accept responsibility for getting themselves ready for counseling, by helping them define behavioral goals and criteria for their own growth, by soliciting feedback from them on the counselor's helping skills as well as peers' helping skills (Chapter 2), by teaching them to help each other (in role playing), and by reinforcing specific helping behaviors. For adolescent clients, the counselor also must watch for and reinforce their therapeutic norm development and therapeutic norm maintenance behaviors. Again this last point is true for all clients, but adolescents require it more than most, and it certainly helps prevent clients banding together against the counselor and/or therapist (group resistance) in ways that have concerned some therapists (Hauserman, Zweback, & Plotkin, 1972; Redl, 1948; Slavson, 1957).

*Openness* is contagious in a group of adolescents. Although most adolescents find that it is easier to discuss their problems with a group of peers than alone with a counselor, being given responsibility for getting themselves ready for counseling further strengthens this openness (Chapter 1). Both the meaningful participation in defining precise behavioral goals and the emphasis which the model places upon learning new behaviors enhances adolescents' feelings of security and willingness to be open with fellow clients (Chapters 1, 2, 3, and 4). Furthermore, membership in an attractive group of motivated peers provides the adolescent client with much needed good peer models for self-disclosure, for developing behavioral goals, for discovering and celebrating growth, and for soliciting and using feedback required to implement new behaviors outside the group.

Finally, helping adolescents learn new behaviors and implementing them is not sufficient. Best results are achieved when adolescents learn to share their goals, to solicit encouragement and reinforcement from significant others, to communicate their new selves to significant others, and to request assistance in maintenance of new behaviors. When the counselor detects an adolescent's discouragement because significant others such as teachers and

---

[1] When they are bullied by significant others such as parents, teachers, or employers, or even if they just think that they are being oversupervised, adolescents become aggressive. Sometimes they appear aggressive when they merely lack the skills to cope adequately.

parents continue to treat him as he used to be, and unknowingly reinforce rejected old behaviors, he can alert the entire group to this problem with a reflection such as: "You get pretty discouraged when you try so hard to change and your mom continues to distrust you for what you used to be. I guess you need help in conveying to her precisely how you have changed, how she hurts you and makes you want to give up when she continues to be critical of you, and what instead you require of her to further your growth." Such a reflection usually surfaces several clients' need for such assistance and encourages all of them to discuss precisely how they have changed, how they may best communicate their new selves to their significant others, and how they may solicit reinforcement for their continuing growth.

## Peer Helpers

A popular trend is to augment the services of professionals in community agencies, schools, and colleges with the services of paraprofessionals and peer helpers. They are often used effectively in crisis centers to prevent suicides and to assist drug addicts. Furthermore, there is evidence to support use of paraprofessionals (Carkhuff, 1969; Lamb & Clark, 1974; Pyle & Snyder, 1971) and of peer helpers (Carkhuff, 1968; Ohlsen, 1974; Tucker & Cantor, 1975). From his review of the research on treating drug addicts Ohlsen (1974) concludes that Synanon groups provide some of the most effective treatment for drug addicts, including alcoholics. Although this peer counseling technique has been used primarily with institutionalized patients, he encourages counselors in out-patient settings to serve as consultants and to help youth adapt the Synanon model for club-type groups which would meet for an hour a day five days a week. Obviously, the success of such groups would be enhanced by participation of successfully treated former drug users who had lived in a Synanon house.

Peer helpers also are being used successfully with children and adults. Mowrer (1973) endorses their use to aid the emotionally disturbed as well as to enrich the quality for normal, healthy adults.

Hamburg and Varenhorst (1972) have developed a very carefully designed program to train peer helpers to provide very specific services for secondary school students. Biehn (1972) describes her experiences in helping college students housed on one floor in a dormitory to create a therapeutic community. Living with them, she helped them to determine what and how they wanted to learn, to develop a structure for learning to accept the responsibility for learning, to cope with the conflict within their group, and to develop the skills which they required to help each other develop socially and emotionally as well as intellectually. She found that as she learned to be truly herself and less concerned about being the counselor she became a better helper and trainer of helpers.

Perhaps two of the writer's experiences can be used to illustrate further how adolescent peer helpers can be used. Both types of clients tend to be difficult to help, especially when the counseling groups are made up entirely of either type. In the first instance gifted underachieving ninth graders were invited to tutor, and generally encourage, gifted underachieving seventh graders. Soon the helpers requested assistance in doing tutoring. Informal seminars with eight to a group were organized for this purpose. The seminar leaders possessed reasonably good background in learning disabilities and study skills, and were very effective counselors of groups. The tutors were encouraged to request specific help with specific seventh graders, to discuss their feelings toward their helpees, to practice their desired new helping behaviors in the seminar, and to share their successes and failures. As they learned to empathize with these seventh graders, to encourage them, to help them seek encouragement from significant others, and to feel better about themselves as a consequence of providing significant help for others, their own school achievement improved markedly, and perhaps more than it would have had the counselors organized a counseling group for them.

The other group of helpers were institutionalized delinquent males. After several attempts to develop a productive group counseling program, an effective counseling group was finally developed. As these clients terminated their group they reviewed precisely how the group had helped them. When they had finished the counselor said, "You have demonstrated that you can help each other. There are many others in this institution who also need help but don't know how to request it or would be ashamed to admit it; I wonder how we could reach them. I wonder whether each of you know of such fellows whom you would be willing to help if I were to help you learn how to do it." This generated a discussion of such clients. Each identified at least one such person whom he would like to help individually. Then a seminar was planned for them. The first session was devoted to helping them plan and practice their approach to their helpees. Thereafter the sessions were used primarily for their sharing successes, examining failures, and identifying new approaches. Those who were most successful in helping their clients helped them to define specific desired new behaviors. About half of their clients were helped individually and enough clients were identified and referred for two more effective counseling groups.

## Summary

Adolescents are engrossed in their search for identity, in establishing themselves in adult roles, and in achieving their independence. At the same time they are changing their referent group from family to peers. On the other hand, most parents still have a great deal of influence on adolescents.

Perhaps the two most important elements provided in a counseling group are genuine acceptance and encouragement offered by peers who are committed to help them and a trustworthy adult who seems to trust and respect them. Such a safe, therapeutic group encourages adolescents to talk openly, to seek essential information about themselves and the opportunities open to them, to appraise the information and feedback they obtain, to develop an essential repertoire of social and human relations skills, to formulate essential life goals, to become more aware of significant others' needs, to learn to satisfy their own needs and to help their significant others satisfy their needs too, to learn to live with the increasing number of adult roles, and to develop the confidence, skills, and ego strength to cope with life problems as they meet them.

Most of the ideas presented in the first seven chapters apply to adolescents as well as to adults. Since adolescents are often brought to counseling under duress and made to feel that they are to blame for whatever went wrong at home, school, and work, the counselor must be very wary of these feelings, help clients discuss them, and convey that his task is not to prove who is wrong, but instead his task is to help the adolescent function more effectively. Furthermore, adolescents are impressed more than most clients with the reasons why clients are selected with such care for each group, why they must accept responsibility for getting themselves ready for counseling and proving their readiness, and why they must define precise behavioral goals and growth criteria.

Many adolescent problems result from significant others' failure to try to empathize with them, to understand their unique needs, and to help them fulfill these needs during this period of rapid maturation. Therefore some of the counselor's time should be devoted to helping significant others further adolescents' wholesome development. Though individual consultations with significant others are essential too, much can be accomplished through group consultation with significant others such as parents and teachers. Examples of such consultations were presented in Chapter 8.

## Discussion Questions

1. Why is the adolescent's need to prove himself so strong? How does this need affect his behavior in daily living, and in his counseling group?
2. Why does the adolescent react to interpretation as he does? What are the advantages and disadvantages of using it with adolescents?
3. Think about the adolescent's needs and then explain precisely how a counselor would have to treat adolescents differently than he does adults in group counseling.
4. Why does group counseling usually appeal more to adolescents than individual counseling?
5. How may a counselor structure role playing in a group of adolescents to make it appealing for them?

6. In what ways would you expect adolescents to formulate different group treatment norms than do adults?

7. What may a counselor do to enable an adolescent to make a strong commitment to learn new behaviors in a counseling group?

8. What would you do differently in organizing a group for hostile youth and/or delinquents than you would do for most adolescents?

9. Some authorities have suggested that adolescents exhibit little transference in their counseling groups. Why do you suppose such authorities have so grossly misunderstood adolescents?

10. What may a counselor do that could cause adolescents to wonder whether he was defending the authority figures in their lives with whom they were having trouble? What could he do to minimize such suspicions?

11. What special precautions could a counselor take in his presentation that would encourage adolescents to volunteer for group counseling?

12. What criteria would you use to screen adolescents for group counseling? Would you use different criteria in a school, a community agency, and a state hospital for adolescents? If so, tell what criteria you would use differently for each. If not, explain why you would use the same for each.

# References

Ackerman, N. W. Group psychotherapy with a mixed group of adolescents. *International Journal of Group Psychotherapy,* 1955, *5,* 249–260.

Ausubel, D. P. *Theory and problems of adolescent development.* New York: Grune & Stratton, 1954.

Ayer, F. L., & Corman, B. R. Laboratory practices develop citizenship concepts of high school students. *Social Education,* 1952, *16,* 215–216.

Biehn, J. Community as counselor. *Personnel and Guidance Journal,* 1972, *50,* 730–734.

Carkhuff, R. R. Differential functions of lay and professional helpers. *Journal of Counseling Psychology,* 1968, *15,* 117–126.

Carkhuff, R. R. *Helping and human relations: A primer for lay and professional helpers,* Vol. I. New York: Holt, Rinehart and Winston, 1969.

Gadpaille, W. J. Observations on the sequence of resistances in groups of adolescent delinquents. *International Journal of Group Psychotherapy,* 1959, *9,* 275–286.

Garrison, K. C. *Psychology of adolescence.* Englewood Cliffs, N.J.: Prentice-Hall, 1965.

Gesell, A., Ilg, F. L., & Ames, L. B. *Youth: The years from ten to sixteen.* New York: Harper & Row, 1956.

Hall, G. S. *Adolescence.* New York: Appleton, 1904.

Hamburg, B., & Varenhorst, B. Peer counseling in the secondary schools. *American Journal of Orthopsychiatry,* 1972, *42,* 566–581.

Hauserman, N., Zweback, S., & Plotkin, A. Use of concrete reinforcement to facilitate verbal initiations in adolescent group therapy. *Journal of Consulting and Clinical Psychology,* 1972, *38,* 90–96.

Hodgman, C. H., & Stewart, W. H. The adolescent screening group. *International Journal of Group Psychotherapy,* 1972, *22,* 177–185.

Hurlock, E. B. *Adolescent development.* New York: McGraw-Hill, 1967.

Kirkpatrick, M. E. The mental hygiene of adolescents in the Anglo-American culture. *Mental Hygiene,* 1952, *36,* 394–403.

Lamb, D. H., & Clark, R. J. Professional versus paraprofessional approaches to orientation and subsequent counseling contacts. *Journal of Counseling Psychology,* 1974, *21,* 61–65.

McCandless, B. R. *Adolescents: Behavior and development.* Hinsdale, Ill.: Dryden, 1970.

Mowrer, O. H. Group counseling in the elementary school: The professional versus peer-group model. In M. M. Ohlsen (Ed.), *Counseling children in groups: A forum.* New York: Holt, Rinehart and Winston, 1973.

Neidt, C. O., & Fritz, M. F. Relation of cynicism to certain student characteristics. *Educational and Psychological Measurement,* 1950, *10,* 712–718.

Ohlsen, L. A student's perception of group counseling. *Clearing House,* 1966, *40,* 401–403.

Ohlsen, M. M. *Guidance services in the modern school.* New York: Harcourt, 1974.

Olsson, P., & Myers, I. Nonverbal techniques in an adolescent group, *International Journal of Group Psychotherapy,* 1972, *22,* 186–191.

Pyle, R., & Snyder, F. Students as paraprofessional counselors at community colleges. *Journal of College Student Personnel,* 1971, *12,* 259–262.

Redl, F. Resistance in therapy groups. *Human Relations,* 1948, *1,* 307–313.

Rosenthal, L. Some dynamics of resistance and therapy management in adolescent group therapy. *Psychoanalytic Review,* 1971, *58,* 353–366.

Slavson, S. R. Are there group dynamics in therapy groups? *International Journal of Group Psychotherapy,* 1957, *7,* 131–134.

Steiner, C. *Scripts people live.* New York: Grove, 1974.

Tucker, S. J., & Cantor, P. C. Personality and status profiles of peer counselors and suicide attempters. *Journal of Counseling Psychology,* 1975, *22,* 423–430.

# Challenging Clients: The Emotionally Debilitated

This is the first of three chapters on challenging clients. Each of these clients has been difficult and/or challenging for some counselors enrolled in group counseling practicum. Almost all of these counselors except the clinical psychology students had some public school teaching experience. Many also had successful public school or college counseling experience.

Whenever a counselor discovers that a particular client is difficult for him, he should ask himself what that reveals about himself. He must try to answer questions such as (1) Why does this particular client make me uncomfortable? (2) How may I use these data to detect and to respond to his feelings? (3) What has been his impact upon me? (4) What clues suggest countertransference? (5) Am I reacting to being used as a transference object? (6) What is his impact on the other clients in the group? and (7) If he is having an antitherapeutic impact, what may I do to cope with it?

As with other clients, a counselor must try to discover the answers to these questions about a difficult client: (1) What is unique about him? (2) Where does he hurt? (3) What unfulfilled needs does his behavior suggest? (4) How may I facilitate open discussion of these therapeutic materials? (5) How may I make a reflection which relates his pain and unsatisfied needs to desired new behaviors? (6) What may I do to sensitize the other clients to his therapeutic material and involve them in the therapeutic process? and (7) If I am experiencing countertransference, what must I do to disengage myself and once again become therapeutically re-engaged (Chapter 5)?

In order to involve the other clients in treating a difficult client, a counselor must search for the answers to questions such as: (1) How does he make them feel? (2) What feelings does he have in common with other clients? (3) How may I respond to these common feelings and facilitate affiliative feelings among them? and (4) How may I prepare him to request and use feedback from his fellow clients?

For this chapter the counselor's attention is directed to emotionally debilitated clients: the grieved, dying, anxious, or crisis victim, the hostile, the depressed, and the learning disabled.

There are times when everyone is at least temporarily disabled by debilitating emotions such as anger, anxiety, embarrassment, depression, disappointment, distress, failure, fear, grief, hate, loneliness or self-doubts. On such occasions one is tempted to blame others or the establishment, to give up, or to act irresponsibly. Furthermore, it is tempting to feel sorry for and wallow in self-pity with these clients. That does not help them. Those who are most effective with such clients are able to detect the suffering client's debilitating emotion, to reflect it accurately, to help that client discuss it, and to decide what he must do to manage it more effectively. Usually, debilitating emotions involve significant others. Consequently, the client must decide precisely what he must do with whom in order to cope with his debilitating emotion. Furthermore, he must come to believe that he can cope with them and make the commitment to himself and to his group to behave responsibly. Some also must express their hopeless feelings or explain what a rotten deal they got, or even explore whether or not they must express more revenge before they can take the risks required to honestly try to cope with the relevant persons involved and learn the required new behaviors (Chapter 14). In order to define the desired new behaviors and act responsibly eventually each must decide: (1) What are his alternative behaviors (to get him off his dead center anxiety state)? (2) Which of the alternatives are most appropriate for him—fit his life style? (3) What special satisfactions would each alternative action provide? (4) For which does he have the most confidence to act? and (5) What new interpersonal skills must be learned to implement each alternative solution?

During the course of the above events some will appear too disorganized or too discouraged to participate meaningfully and to accept responsibility for their behavior. Even when they are grieving the counselor would do well to help them express their grief and to begin exploring what they are willing to attempt now and when they will be willing to take more responsible action in managing their own lives. Encouragement to act with the known support of the counseling group (and their help is developing a support system outside of their counseling group) is preferred to self-pity and no action. It is surprising what debilitated persons can do with such support. Nevertheless, some may still be unwilling to do anything for themselves until the group helps them explore the consequences of their failure to act (or to stop their irresponsible behavior). For example, a seemingly psychotic middle-aged woman refused to accept any responsibility for her lot, and consequently to do anything to improve it, until her fellow clients pushed her to explore the consequences of continuing her behavior. At first her irresponsible, dependent behavior seemed to get her everything she wanted from her family and friends. As she discussed her lot with the group members' assistance, and penetrating reflections, she began to detect the impact of her behavior on those she genuinely loved—that her behavior was depriving her of the three things she wanted most of all, even if she had to accept normal adult responsibilities to achieve them: self-respect, genuine acceptance and love from her family and most valued friends, and quality companionship with these significant others. Obviously, these efforts to help her did not change her behavior immediately, but it was a beginning. Thereafter, it was easier for her fellow clients and her counselor to detect her crazy, irresponsible feelings, to help her assess their impact, and to help her decide with whom she was ready to do what now. With very clear, precise criteria for evaluating her own growth, she was able to detect and celebrate her own growth. Fortunately, she also had a daughter and husband with whom she learned to share her goals and to request specific reinforcement of desired new behaviors. The members of her counseling group also helped her to enlarge her support system for responsible, enriched living.

## Griever

How does he feel? Why does he grieve? Clients seem to grieve for a number of reasons. Most experience loneliness and hopelessness for the future. Many feel helpless. Often, after a long illness of a loved one, the response to his death may be relief—followed by feelings of guilt. Many also feel guilt and self-condemnation because they wish they had treated the deceased better or differently, or because they wonder whether everything possible had been done to save his life. On the other hand, if he really rejected the deceased, a griever may at first feel relief and possibly even pleasure, but a guilt reaction may follow. Most counselors and therapists believe that the principal feeling is one of self-pity.

Children often experience feelings like those described above when a much-loved neighbor, friend, or relative moves away. They also experience real grief over the loss of a pet.

When someone denies the loss or is not helped to grieve, related problems may be exhibited years later. This is what happened to Frances, a fifty-year-old widow who sought counseling. In her intake interview she said she wanted to learn to cope with her grieving sister. Her sister's husband had been dead a year, but her sister still refused to go out with their friends and relatives, often cried herself to sleep, would not return to work, and seemed to be completely helpless. In response to another client's reflection Frances admitted reluctantly that she resented her sister very much. Early in the next session she cried and discussed the death of her own husband. Though she had lost her husband five years earlier, Frances felt that she had to be strong and to deny her deep feelings over the loss of her husband, but the group helped her discover that they could accept her grief, provide quality assistance in working it through, and help her to decide how she could learn to live without him. Once she had worked through her own grief, she was able to help her sister obtain the treatment she required and to accept the affection of an old friend and neighbor who had recently lost his wife.

Lindemann (1944) studied psychoneurotic patients who lost a relative during treatment; the relatives of patients who died while hospitalized; disaster victims from the Coconut Grove fire and their relatives; and the relatives of servicemen. For acute grief he reported a common syndrome:

> . . . sensations of somatic distress occurring in waves last from twenty minutes to an hour at a time, a feeling of tightness in the throat, choking with shortness of breath, need for sighing, and an empty feeling in the abdomen, lack of muscular power, and an intense subjective distress described as tension or mental pain. The patient soon learns that these waves of discomfort can be precipitated by visits, by mentioning the deceased, and by receiving sympathy. There is a tendency to avoid the syndrome at any cost, to refuse visits lest they should precipitate the reaction, and to keep deliberately from thought all references to the deceased. (Lindemann, 1944, p. 141)

He also found that reaction to grief could be delayed, and that morbid grief reactions represented distortion of normal grief. These distorted reactions included (a) overactivity, (b) acquisition of symptoms of the deceased, (c) a recognized medical disease, (d) alteration in relationships to friends and relatives (patient is irritable, does not want to be bothered, and gradually isolates himself), (e) hostility toward specific persons, (f) efforts to hide hostility, giving appearance of schizophrenia, (g) a lasting loss of social interaction, (h) actions detrimental to his own social and economic existence (he behaves in foolish ways that damage friendships, and he wastes financial resources or permits himself to be cheated out of them by unscrupulous persons), and (i) agitated depression (his grief is exhibited with insomnia, feelings of worthlessness, bitter self-accusation, and self-punishment—he may become dangerously suicidal).

Unknowingly, his friends and relatives often protect the griever from facing reality and dealing with grief. Rather than letting him discuss his real feelings and weep, they block his grieving with empty reassurances. They may even be so stupid as to suggest that he will soon forget—that time heals all wounds. Even the suggestion that he will soon forget is perceived by him as an attack: it seems to challenge the sincerity of his love for the deceased, when in fact he feels his loss so keenly that the whole future looks bleak. Until they learn to react more therapeutically, even fellow clients also tend to respond in these nonhelpful ways.

With reference to these nonhelpful ways in which persons try to help, Kubler-Ross (1969) wrote as follows:

> Once the patient dies, I find it cruel and inappropriate to speak of love of God. When we lose someone, especially when we have had little time to prepare ourselves, we are enraged, angry, in despair; we should be allowed to express these feelings. The family members are often left alone as soon as they have given their consent for autopsy. Bitter, angry, or just numb, they walk through the corridors of the hospital, unable often to face the brutal reality. The first few days may be filled with busywork, with arrangements and visiting relatives. The void and emptiness is felt after the funeral, after the departure of relatives. It is at this time that the family members feel most grateful to have someone to talk to, especially if it is someone who had recent contact with the deceased and who had anecdotes of some good moments toward the end of the deceased's life. This helps the relative over the shock and the initial grief and prepares him for a gradual acceptance. (p. 177)

What the griever needs to know is that friends and relatives care about him—that though they cannot understand fully how much his loss hurts, they want to help him express his grief and to discover the strength to deal with it. Furthermore, they provide real support when they exhibit confidence in his ability to cope with it by helping him express it, rather than deny or conceal it. Even though he may prefer to withdraw, they patiently involve him appropriately in their relationships. They also help him to move back into other meaningful social relationships and to reestablish himself in his work. With such considerate responses they may be given opportunities to protect him from leeches who would take advantage of him during his grieving period.

Lindemann describes this grief work as follows:

> The duration of a grief reaction seems to depend upon the success with which a person does the grief work, namely, emancipation from the bondage to the deceased, readjustment to the environment in which the deceased is missing, and the formation of new relationships. One of the big obstacles to this work seems to be the fact that many patients try to avoid the intense distress connected with the grief experience and to avoid the expression of emotion necessary for it. The men victims after the Coconut Grove fire appeared in the early psychiatric interviews to be in a state of tension with tightened facial musculature, unable to relax for fear they might "break down." It required considerable persuasion to yield to the grief process before they were willing to accept the discomfort of bereavement. . . . They became willing to accept the grief process and to embark on a program of dealing in memory with the deceased person. As soon as this became possible there seemed to be a rapid relief of tension and the subsequent interviews were rather animated conversations in which the decreased was idealized and in which misgivings about the future adjustment were worked through. (p. 143)

To illustrate how a patient moved out into the stream of life and developed a future for herself, Lindemann described the case of a forty-year-old widow: ". . . She then showed a marked drive for activity, making plans for supporting herself and her little girl, mapping out the preliminary steps for resuming her old profession as secretary, and making efforts to secure help from the occupational therapy department in reviewing her knowledge of French." (p. 143) For some persons (like this griever) counseling includes assistance in choosing a vocation.

Group counseling provides a climate in which clients experience more readily than in individual counseling the genuine encouragement to discuss the intense pain associated with the loss of the loved one, to cry, to learn to make requests of significant others, to accept others' love and companionship, and to decide what they must do to begin a more meaningful life. In addition to helping the primary grieving client, the counselor watches for clues which suggest that other clients also have unfinished grieving problems and helps them admit their problems and deal with them. When one client deals with a grief problem this usually uncovers unfinished grieving problems for several clients who did not request help originally with grieving.

Often adults do not realize that most children experience grief. They fail to notice how deeply a child feels about the loss of a pet or how much he misses that friend or relative who moved away. He also worries about what may happen to loved ones. Beginning elementary-school counselors are often surprised about the number of children who seek assistance with grieving problems—especially when they mention grieving in their presentation. They also tend to be impressed with the sensitive way in which children can help each other. Counselors also are encouraged to help teachers and parents of a grieving child. Seminars and discussion groups can be used effectively to help teachers and parents work through their own grieving problems and prepare themselves to help children cope with such problems. Counselors also are encouraged to conduct small discussion groups in the community (for example, churches) to help adults to cope better with the phenomenon of grieving and to refer those who require treatment for grieving.

## Dying

When those closest to the terminally ill can be helped to accept death, to face death with the dying, to help the dying accept it, and to help the dying person complete his most important unfinished business, *the griever* is motivated to face death, to decide what he wants most from life for himself, to look at his failures and lost opportunities in a new light, and to complete his unfinished business with significant others, including the dying. Hopefully the griever will be encouraged hereafter to express beautiful positive feelings when they are first experienced. In counseling groups clients learn to express positive feelings when they are experienced, to express angry feelings less hurtfully, to recognize the problem's underlying conflict, and to cope with conflict. Thereby, they reduce the amount of unfinished business to be dealt with as one faces death. In order to help others learn to face death, the counselor must learn to face it himself.

Kubler-Ross (1969) found that most of the terminally ill patients whom she interviewed knew that they were terminally ill (even before they had been told) and appreciated her help in facing death. Her patients moved through five stages in learning to accept death: (1) denial and isolation, (2) anger, (3) bargaining, (4) depression, and (5) acceptance. She described this last stage as follows:

> If a patient has had enough time (i.e. not a sudden, unexpected death) and has been given some help in working through the previously described stages, he will reach a stage during which he is neither depressed nor angry about his "fate." He will have been able to express his previous feelings, his envy for the living and healthy, his anger at those who do not have to face their end so soon. He will have mourned the impending loss of so many meaningful people and places, and he will contemplate his coming end with a certain degree of quiet expectation. He will be tired and in most cases quite weak. He will also have a need to doze off to sleep often and in brief intervals, which is different from the need to sleep during times of depression. This is not the sleep of avoidance or a period of rest to get relief from pain, discomfort, or itching. It is a gradually increasing need to extend the hours of sleep very similar to that of the newborn child in reverse order. . . .
>
> Acceptance should not be mistaken for a happy stage. It is almost void of feelings. It is as if the pain had gone, the struggle is over, and there comes a time for "the final rest before the journey" as one patient phrased it. This is also the time during which the family needs usually more help, understanding, and support than the patient himself. (pp. 112–113)

Children as well as surviving adults must be considered in helping the dying person's significant others. Moreover, Kubler-Ross' findings suggest that those who attempt to help the grieving (and dying) child must know how children perceive death: (1) up to age three he is concerned primarily with separation, (2) next age group is concerned about fear of decay and mutilation (from seeing pets killed by cars or birds mutilated by other animals), (3) around age nine children begin to understand the permanence of death, and (4) during adolescence the loss of a significant other such as a beloved parent appears to be too much to endure. All should be listened to and encouraged to express whatever they feel, and after they have expressed their grief, discovered their sources for support, and developed the strength to endure it they should be able to find a new life without the loved one. Working through the grief also should be used to help the griever, and especially the young griever, to understand and accept death. With the assistance and cooperation of a child's teacher and parents, a counselor can use such a technique as classroom discussions (Chapter 8) to enlist classmates' assistance to help the grieving child and to help his classmates deal with the death taboo.

> Becoming aware of the death taboo, confronting the facts and reality of its existence, and working through the distortions and emotions which surround it are the counselor's responsibility if communication is to remain open. Adults must especially allow children to inquire about death, share their memories and anxieties about it, and encourage them, when necessary, to accept the naturalness of their feelings without guilt or embarrassment. One hopes that as we all learn to acknowledge and accept our deepest feelings unashamedly, we are creating a philosophy of life that promotes equal regard and respect for the value and rights of others' feelings. In helping children develop wise and beautiful ways of coping with death, we may hopefully provide them with a new and stronger dimension to life. (Berg, 1973, p. 32)

## Anxious

Being anxious is not the same as experiencing tension. An individual experiences tension when he anticipates some exciting or challenging event—for example, when he waits in the wings to go on stage to perform, when he waits for the whistle to begin an athletic contest, or even when he effectively studies for an examination. In this last instance one would expect the tension to be discharged by the completion of the examination. Furthermore, when he is functioning well, such experience creates a minimum of anxiety. On the other hand, when he doubts his ability to perform well on the examination to an extent that it interferes with his preparation or his performance during the examination, he is experiencing debilitating anxiety. Whereas anxiety tends to interfere with effective action, tension tends to focus attention on action.

Sometimes the anxious will frighten the other clients, and even the inexperienced counselors, with his tears, apprehensions, and disorganized behavior. They are afraid that he will talk too freely and expose more material than he can manage. Under these circumstances, especially during the first few sessions, clients are tempted to reassure the anxious one. Though such efforts are meant to provide support, the underlying attitude conveys doubts concerning the client's ability to cope with his problems and possibly lack of confidence in the treatment process. Thus, the precise feelings of the reassurer as well as the anxious one must be detected and reflected in order to get them out into the open where they can be managed.

Actually, even anxious crisis victims rarely uncover material which they cannot handle. However, anxious clients can be hurt by penetrating interpretations and by the feeling that they may be abandoned when they reveal very disturbing material. Usually they feel safer in the type of group described in Chapter 1 than they do in everyday interactions at home, at school, or at work when they are confronted with hurtful demands, probing, and nagging. Although clients face and relive hurtful events during counseling, and they are pressured to change their behavior and attitudes, fellow clients learn to provide genuine support during painful moments. Even when another uncovers painful material with a penetrating reflection, the anxious one realizes that his helper is trying to help him face and learn to cope with relevant therapeutic material rather to confront him with his maladaptive behavior; the helper is trying to empathize with the anxious one, to convey confidence in his ability to solve his own problems, and to provide support while the anxious one is learning desired new behaviors. Not only is the counselor able to convey that he cares and dares to suffer with the suffering client, and will not abandon him in distress or "chicken out" and try to minimize the extent of the hurt, he is able to teach the other clients to provide this quality support.

Some readers may wonder, nonetheless, what they can do when they believe in an early session that a client is revealing too much too fast; they are afraid that later the client may regret what he revealed, or that he may continue to self-disclose too freely outside of the counseling group. When a counselor begins to feel uncomfortable with such a client he should listen to the client and try to assess whether he is worried about the client or himself (Chapter 5). If he suspects that the client may continue to reveal inappropriately private thoughts and feelings to others outside of counseling and be hurt by it, the counselor is obligated ethically to clarify expectations— differentiating between what is appropriate behavior in a counseling group and what is appropriate elsewhere. If he feels later that a client regrets what he shared, the counselor reflects these feelings, helps the anxious client discuss them, and helps fellow clients respond to the threat. When doubts about keeping confidences or continuing to be accepted by a certain fellow client arise, the counselor and the other clients too help the anxious one express his feelings and resolve his problems with that particular fellow client.

Sometimes a member cannot follow what the anxious one is saying. He may be talking too fast or incoherently. By making a reflection which clarifies, the counselor can convey that he is interested, slow the client down, and encourage him to clarify what he is trying to communicate: "Pardon my interruption, but I'm afraid I did not understand what you are trying to convey. I'm not sure whether you tried to speak to your Latin teacher and failed to get help, whether you are afraid to speak to her, or you don't think that it will do any good." When the counselor merely wants to slow the client down he may say something like: "I'm having difficulty keeping up with you—trying to understand everything you are telling us. Apparently, a number of things are upsetting you. Perhaps we could understand you better if you could select one or two of the problems with which you would like help first and discuss them a little more slowly." In any case, the counselor must try to identify the anxious client's therapeutic material and respond to it helpfully; enlist the other clients' support and assistance; help them cope with any threatening material which the anxious one uncovers in them; and help the anxious one implement his new discoveries and learnings with his significant others outside the counseling group.

With the structuring, careful selection of clients, and the definition of precise behavioral goals described in Chapter 1, clients come better prepared to help the anxious client than most readers may realize. The counselor also tends to have more confidence in the anxious client's ability to face his threatening material and deal adequately with it. When clients realize that they have been selected with care to maximize their chances for getting help in the group, their counseling group becomes more attractive, and they are able to respond more spontaneously to each other. They are able to let the anxious one cry and talk out his feelings. The better they accept each other, the more they believe in each other, and accept the fact that it is worth the pain experienced to achieve the benefits of counseling, the more productive their group is. Talland and Clark (1954) found that their patients were helped most when they discussed their most painful topics. Clients can accept essential pain to learn and implement their desired new behaviors.

## Hostile

When clients and especially adolescents are pressured by others to accept counseling, they often appear hostile. Even when they seem to cooperate in the intake interview, they spend an undue amount of time complaining about their significant others who require treatment more than they do. Before adolescents are encouraged to join a group, the counselor should try to convey that he understands how they feel and that perhaps the group is not appropriate for them unless they are willing to discuss how they have been hurt and learn specific new ways of relating to these significant others in addition to whatever else they would like to work on.

Another similar client may appear to be hostile when he actually feels inadequate or lacks the human-relating skills to cope with some specific persons and/or situations. Frequently, he is "badgered" by an employer, a co-worker, a spouse, a parent, or a teacher who is an intellectual bully, and he strikes back (or is afraid that he will explode and hurt his adversary) because he feels trapped, cornered, or overwhelmed. Like a trapped animal who is tormented, he would run away if he could, but he is caught and forced to deal with the threatening situation. He needs to learn to widen his repertoire of human relations and verbal skills in order to deal with his hurtful adversary.

Still another type is the client who has had a very strict, moralistic upbringing. He may seek relief from obsessional thoughts concerning normal reactions to a target person for justified anger (or similar guilt-arousing sexual thoughts toward appropriate sex objects). Helping such a client define precise behavioral goals and obtaining feedback from peers that these are normal reactions helps such a person, but usually these are not sufficient. He must practice expressions of anger to relevant target persons in role playing and listen to feedback from fellow clients. Some also require assertiveness training in order to cope with such feelings. Rosen (1975) believes that such clients must be taught systematically to accept these normal feelings.

Finally there is the genuinely hostile client who has been rejected, hurt, let down, or abandoned by someone whose love and acceptance he requires. Whereas the aggressive may accidentally step on others as he moves toward his goal with minimum regard for others' rights, he hurts others accidentally; the really hostile person, however, is often distracted from his goal in order to hurt others. He tends to be demanding, brutal, sullen, and defiant. Even when he turns to a counselor for help, it is difficult for the counselor and fellow clients to prove to him that they want to understand him, accept him, and help him. Consequently, the counselor who helps him must be strong and have the courage to help him make a genuine commitment to change, to define precise goals, and to disclose hurts openly in the group, and perhaps even admit him to the group on a probational status. When such a client tends to gloss over the depth of his pain, it takes courage, on the part of the fellow clients as well as the counselor, to be assertive, empathic and demanding—that is, to state the wish to help and not to let the hostile client's anger and defensiveness keep them from hanging in there—patiently, caringly insisting that he own his pain and decide what unfinished business he has with whom; what he is going to do about it; and if these significant relationships cannot be salvaged, to decide what new behaviors he must learn to function more effectively with those with whom he replaces the unsatisfactory significant others. Expressing empathy through accurate reflections is important for every challenging client, but for this client it is especially important, and it requires a great deal of courage.

Difficult as it is for the hostile client to accept other members' efforts to empathize with him, this is what he requires. When they refuse to let him brush them off and respond helpfully with warmth, trying to detect how he really feels and to help him express these feelings, and conveying their willingness to help him cope with those who hurt him, their confidence in his ability to learn desired new behaviors, and their expectation for him to change, he is motivated to change. Previously, he has learned to expect and to deal with hostility. When he does not get it, he looks for it anyway. Though he may be surprised, he does not feel like attacking them. As he gradually discovers the extent to which the others can detect and reflect how he feels and are able to provide encouragement for him, he is motivated to help others rather than to push them away and attack them. As he learns to play the helping game, he feels better toward himself and is able to accept help from others more readily.

Hostile clients are especially threatening to beginning counselors who were formerly teachers. When hostility was expressed in their classrooms, they did not feel confident in coping with it, and in their efforts to manage it they often became caught up in power struggles. Hence, they tend to perceive the expression of hostility as a personal defiance of them. When such a counselor discovers: (1) that such a client is attempting to deal with him as a transference object, and thus, the feelings may not be directed toward him as a person; (2) how different these various types really feel and how each requires different assistance; and (3) that a hostile client does express much significant therapeutic material to which a counselor can respond, he begins to learn to relate to the hostile client.

## Depressed

Many reasonably healthy persons who are coping with life successfully become deeply discouraged when they lose a significant other through abandonment, death, divorce, or conflict; they are confronted with a serious health problem; they experience career problems; they suffer severe financial losses, or they are very angry with themselves for something they did or failed to do that they should have done. Some who normally manage most disappointments meet several at once and give up—by becoming psychotic or by committing suicide.

With improved counseling services in the schools and the community agency outreach programs hopefully increasing numbers of children and youth will be helped to deal with their early disappointments as they occur. Elementary school counseling programs are designed to help children and to help teachers and parents assist children (Chapter 8). Community mental health agencies and school adult education programs in personal growth, parent education, and family education are designed primarily for adults. Hopefully these programs also will help individuals develop strong personal support systems. Nevertheless, there will be times when most persons require the help of a counselor or therapist when they become depressed. Most who have not learned to deal with serious hurtful experiences and disappointments can be helped by group counseling. Often they can be helped best with those who contribute to their depression (and frequently unknowingly). They require the assistance of that person and/or persons in their counseling group (or family therapy) to determine what they can expect from their significant others, what others expect from them, and what new behaviors must be learned to fulfill the expectations, to renegotiate these expectations when necessary, and to make requests of significant others. Frequently, these significant others unknowingly reinforce sick behavior.

Some also lack the skills to communicate how they feel toward the depressed, and to develop and to enjoy quality companionship with them. On the other hand, some depressed already have reasonably good relationships with significant others, but they have such a low opinion of themselves that they twist even these good relationships into confusion, frustration, and disappointments. Those who help them must teach them to recognize and enjoy the quality relationships already available to them and when necessary to develop new ones. Others require assertiveness training in addition to group counseling in order to make reasonable requests of significant others and/or to stand up for themselves when the occasion calls for it.

## Learning Disabled

Kirk and Bateman (1962) defined a learning disability as follows:

> A learning disability refers to a retardation, disorder, or delayed development in one or more of the processes of speech, language, reading, writing, arithmetic, or other school subjects, resulting from a psychological handicap caused by a possible cerebral dysfunction and/or emotional or behavioral disturbances. It is not the result of mental retardation, sensory deprivation, or instructional factors. (p. 73)

As for every other difficult client, the counselor must be able to detect and reflect the pain and hurt this client is experiencing. Very early in his formal education, the child with learning disabilities tends to conclude that school success will be difficult, if not impossible, and that he has less ability than his real potential. When, for example, a happy, confident five-year-old was given a Stanford Binet her I.Q. score was 115. Later when she developed a serious reading problem in second grade and lost a great deal of her self-confidence her score on the same test was 98. Following remedial reading instruction and a full year of school success, she was retested on the same test by the same psychologist and scored 123.

Not only do learning disabilities influence children's performance on tests and their academic expectations of themselves, but they often continue to have a negative impact on their personal and career development as adults. They are reluctant to attempt special on-the-job training which could result in promotions, to consider new employment opportunities, and to accept leadership roles in community programs. When, however, they profit from remedial instruction for their learning disabilities and are provided with counseling, hard core unemployed obtain employment, underemployed seek and obtain promotions, and adults return to college to complete preparations for much desired professional careers.

Obviously, space cannot be allocated here to deal adequately with treating learning disabilities, but counselors and therapists must be sensitive to those behaviors which suggest learning problems (Anderson, 1970; Kacz-kowski & Patterson, 1975). Furthermore, every effort should be made to identify children with learning problems early and initiate appropriate treatment. Where classroom discussions include descriptions of learning disabilities in children's language, and where clients are encouraged to discuss such problems and to help identify learning disabilities, discussion leaders have been impressed with children's ability to identify children with these problems. Furthermore, counselors should enlist children's, parents', teachers', and school psychologists' assistance in identifying and correcting learning disabilities.

Bills' (1950) early work demonstrated that nondirective group play therapy can improve the performance of retarded readers. Just a couple of more recent examples also are cited to confirm his early findings (Sonstegard, 1961; McCollum & Anderson, 1974). McCollum and Anderson reported that elementary school students in counseling groups improved significantly both oral and reading vocabulary skills, but not their vocabulary development.

Perhaps Ferreira's[1] discovery most influenced the writer to include this type of client in this chapter: that the counselor's and fellow clients' acceptance of and confidence in the learning disabled's ability to succeed encourages "successfully" counseled clients with learning disabilities to merely accept themselves better and work enough harder to succeed in school without recognizing and correcting their learning handicaps. Both counseling and correction of learning disabilities are essential for efficient learning.

## Summary

This is the first of three chapters on difficult clients. It discusses the following clients with debilitating emotions: the grieved, dying, anxious, hostile, depressed, and learning disabled.

Every counselor must try to understand why some clients are difficult for him, what their impact is on him and how he may cope with it, what each difficult client's unique troublesome feelings are, how he may respond to these feelings and detect relevant behavioral goals for each, and how he can involve clients in helping each other. Most counselors require recordings of counseling sessions and the assistance of a trusted colleague or supervisor in order to learn to cope with difficult clients.

When members discover an emotional debilitated client they must detect the suffering client's pain, reflect it accurately, help that client discuss it, and decide what he must do to manage it more effectively. He must come to

[1] Personal communication with Linda Ferreira.

believe that he can learn to cope with his debilitating emotions and make the commitment to himself and to his group to behave responsibly. Sometimes he may appear so disorganized and discouraged that members of the group are tempted to pity him when instead they must encourage him to explore the consequences of failure to act and to move ahead and learn new behaviors.

## Discussion Questions

1. How may the counselor assess the impact of a difficult client on fellow clients?
2. What may the counselor do in the intake interview to increase the chances that each of the difficult clients discussed in this chapter will use the group productively?
3. What may you do to help a grieving friend? What would you do differently to help a similar client in group counseling?
4. A client in your counseling group frequently complains about the way he is treated by his girl friend. Finally, several members become angry with him and tell him to decide what he must do and do something now. He gets angry and leaves. What would you do?
5. How may you determine prior to beginning your group which clients will be difficult for you?
6. After you discover what type of clients are difficult for you, how may you use those data in organizing and beginning a group?
7. What may a counselor do when a client appears completely discouraged and unwilling or unable to do anything for himself?

## References

Anderson, R. P. *The child with learning disabilities and guidance.* Boston: Houghton-Mifflin, 1970.

Berg, C. D. Cognizance of the death taboo in counseling children. *The School Counselor,* 1973, *21,* 28–32.

Bills, R. E. Nondirective play therapy with retarded readers. *Journal of Consulting Psychology,* 1950, *14,* 140–149.

Kaczkowski, H. R., & Patterson, C. H. *Counseling and psychology in elementary schools.* Springfield, Ill.: Thomas, 1975.

Kirk, S. A., & Bateman, B. Diagnosis and remediation of learning disabilities. *Exceptional Children,* 1962, *29,* 69–79.

Kubler-Ross, E. *On death and dying.* New York: Macmillian, 1969.

Lindemann, E. Symptomatology and management of acute grief. *American Journal of Psychiatry,* 1944, *101,* 141–148.

McCollum, P. S., & Anderson, R. P. Group counseling with reading disabled children. *Journal of Counseling Psychology,* 1974, *21,* 150–155.

Rosen, M. A dual model of obsessional neurosis. *Journal of Consulting and Clinical Psychology,* 1975, *43,* 453–459.

Sonstegard, M. *Group counseling methods with parents of elementary school children as related to human growth and development.* State College of Iowa, 1961, mimeographed report.

Talland, G. A., & Clark, D. H. Evaluation of topics in therapy discussion groups. *Journal of Clinical Psychology,* 1954, *10,* 131–137.

# Challenging Clients:
# The Other-Controlled

One variety of other-controlled client is described by Grater (1958) in his paper "When Counseling Success Is Failure." Such a client is very sensitive to others' needs. He tries very hard to determine what is expected in counseling and to do it. Consequently, he tends to elicit positive transference. If, for example, other clients discuss sex problems, he discusses sex problems. He discusses his problems very openly, and he makes others feel close to him because he shares common problems with them. Usually when counseling ends, he is picked by fellow clients and the counselor as the one who has helped most. Actually, he is often helped with all his problems except the one with which he requires assistance most—being controlled by others.

He treasures others' acceptance so much that he discusses whatever others seem to want to discuss and opens himself up to pressure to do whatever others prefer to do. Consequently, he is often used by others and he resents it, but he is reluctant to express his resentment because he questions his own worth—doubts whether he can win others' love and acceptance any other way.

Not all such clients will recognize this problem as their own. Whenever the counselor detects in the intake interview (or even during counseling) that a client is unduly sensitive to others' needs and exhibits unusual desire to please others, he may make a reflection such as, "You are quick to detect what others need and want very much to please them, but sometimes I'll bet it makes you a little angry when they take advantage of you. At such times

I'll bet you wish you were strong enough to stand up for your own rights and ask your friends to do just once what you'd like to do." As the client discusses these feelings, it is important for the counselor to enlist the other group members' assistance in teaching such a client to be more assertive—to identify specific significant others with whom he must learn to be more assertive and to practice in role playing being more assertive. The counselor also should encourage the other clients to watch for instances in which this submissive client reacts submissively to them and to help him practice being assertive with them. In group counseling the task is to help everyone to obtain assistance with those problems with which he wants help most. In any case, helping such a client recognize and express his feelings of doubt about his self-worth and resentment about being used exposes his needs to others so that they can help him deal with his needs, gives others a chance to express their positive feelings toward him and their commitment to help him, and enables him to explore what he would like to do differently with whom.

## Silent or Withdrawn

The silent one and the withdrawn one may be one and the same; on the other hand, they may perceive themselves very differently and have very different reasons for remaining silent. Hence, a counselor must observe the silent one very carefully to detect how he feels about himself.

Some clients have learned to become deeply involved in interacting with others with a minimum of talking. When others express their feelings or deal with their problems, they convey empathy and support nonverbally; they experience feelings with others, learn from others, and adapt what they learn to solve their own problems. Others serve as their mouthpiece. Usually these silent ones openly reveal their problems early, so they are not looked upon with suspicion. Some clients who fall into this category recognize that their school performance or their proficiency at work is underrated. Hence, even though they can be helped within their counseling group with minimum verbal participation, they recognize that they must improve their verbal-interaction skills in order to gain the recognition they deserve.

Another infrequent verbal participator within a counseling group is the deliberate, slow-moving person who takes his time to figure out how he feels and what he wants to say. He also may be reluctant to interrupt others to express himself. If the counselor watches him carefully, he will note that repeatedly he nearly gets the floor and then loses it to another. Merely observing that once again he has lost out is usually sufficient to sensitize other clients to his need for assistance in capturing the speaker's role. He also may need to be encouraged to express himself more assertively and to discuss underlying resistance.

The withdrawn one tends to have a more negative self-image than either of the silent ones described above. He tends to be less confident that he can be helped by counseling and that he can say anything that really will help others. Carefully timed reflection conveys empathy and helps him reveal his problems. When he tries to express his feelings, he discovers that the other members really care and that they want to help him change. Furthermore, he discovers that they can be very patient in helping him face his problems.

Most counselors want every client to interact verbally, and some, especially former teachers, are made to feel uncomfortable by the silent one. They are tempted to call upon him as they did in class recitations. This tends to put him on the spot. Fellow clients also tend to put him on the spot because they are suspicious of him. Helping him discuss precisely how he feels not only increases his readiness for change, but it increases others' acceptance of him. Participating in such interaction also provides him the practice he needs in developing his social skills.

## Scapegoat

The scapegoat is the focus of displaced aggression. Some masochistic persons set themselves up for this role. They derive pleasure from being insulted, offended, or mistreated. Others permit it in order to have relationships with others; they doubt their ability to be genuinely loved and accepted, and they would rather be a scapegoat than have no relationships at all. Some others are naive: they lack the social skills to cope with those who hurt them. Scapegoating is a common phenomenon, which can be observed even in a group of animals. Usually one finds a scapegoat who is the victim of jokes, is teased, is confronted with probing questions or hurtful interpretations, or is kept on the "hot seat." When these behaviors occur in a counseling group, the scapegoat may be victimized by a sadistic person who pretends to be trying to help.

Since the disadvantages of putting someone on the "hot seat" and treating one client at a time have already been discussed in Chapter 6, it will suffice to state here that such methods tend to encourage clients to use the scapegoat as an object for their displaced aggressions. Instead, when a counselor observes a client being used as a scapegoat, he should reflect the feelings that he feels the scapegoat is experiencing. Usually he has feelings of hurt plus some of the others described above. Such a reflection enables the hurt one to express how he feels and rallies support and understanding from the others. It also helps the hurter discover his impact on others and encourages him to search for new ways of relating to others. Sometimes when he has hurt others, the hurter will experience the role of scapegoat. Then his feelings of hurt also must be reflected. However, this is not sufficient. Members of the group should expect, and assist, both the scapegoat and the hurter to learn new ways of relating to others. Careful structuring may be needed here, lest clients become so afraid of hurting someone that they lose their spontaneity, or for fear of hurting them they grow reluctant to put pressure on each other to learn new ways of relating. However, they can learn to distinguish between sadistic hurting and helping one another deal with hurtful material during the course of getting help.

## Socializer

The socializer is the one who wants to extend the counseling relationships into social relationships outside the group. He wants his fellow clients and the counselor to be his best friends. He so thoroughly enjoys the quality of his relationships with the members of his counseling group that he may wish to substitute these relationships for those with his important others. Rather than allowing this to happen, the members of his counseling group should help him perceive the counseling group for what it is—a temporary relationship in which he learns to cope with his important others and when essential to build new relationships with others outside his counseling group. Failure to deal openly with this problem often leads high school and college youth to resist termination of their counseling group. It also encourages clients to socialize with fellow clients during counseling.

Some counselors question the extent to which a counselor can or should control socializing of members outside of the counseling group. As a consequence of his experiences in treating more disturbed patients, Bach (1954) discussed this controversial point as follows:

> Clinical management of the natural tendency of emotionally disturbed patients to socialize with and to seek further support from each other outside the official clinical meetings is a controversial point among group therapists. Most group therapists accept their patients' socializing needs, but few make it an official part of the clinical program as we do. Classically oriented psychoanalysts see in socializing outside the therapeutic setting only obstruction to the therapeutic process. (p. 114)

Bach encourages his patients to socialize. He feels that it relieves some of the tensions that build up during group sessions and enables clients to discover that in spite of their problems they can relate effectively to each other socially. Furthermore, he believes that they do reveal things about themselves within the relaxed social atmosphere that they may not reveal in the treatment group. He also expects his patients to bring back into their group the new material revealed during socializing. He believes that their custom of sharing and communicating all interpersonal interaction that occurred during the socializing tends to prevent misuse of acting out.

Nevertheless, there are at least four reasons for discouraging socializing: (1) it increase chances for confidences to be broken; (2) it tends to increase acting out; (3) it encourages clients to become dependent upon fellow clients for meaningful relationships, when instead they should learn to relate to their significant others or develop new relationships; and (4) it enables them to escape from their responsibility for coping with resistance within their treatment sessions. Furthermore, socializing seems to increase drainage —the revelation of private material in social sessions rather than in the therapy session.

## Dependent

Most dependent clients feel relatively inadequate. Some feel inadequate in most situations, others in only a few. Within these situations they lack the confidence both to make decisions and to act upon them. Dependent clients have had their dependent behavior reinforced by persons who needed to have someone dependent upon them or by important others such as parents and teachers who did not bother to teach them, during the normal process of growing up, how to behave independently. Hence, these clients require opportunities to learn and practice independent behaviors. They also need the understanding and support that a group of peers can provide when they approach independent action and retreat from it, and when they try it, seem to fail, and must re-evaluate what they tried before they can develop the courage to try again. Some profit from systematic instruction in the decision making process—using real case materials from their own lives to practice decision making. For these occasions the use of the "Fiddler Game" (Chapter 7) also is very helpful—especially when they can listen to a recording of their own struggle: for example, "I must decide now on a college major. I am quite certain that I would like teaching English at the high school level. I enjoy adolescents' spirit, and I can manage them, but on the other hand, what will my mother and my fiancée think about me just being a school teacher? Perhaps I am kidding myself too, and I wouldn't really be as good at it as I think." Perhaps he does require more information about his chances for success in high school teaching, the nature of the work, the income, and the employment opportunities, but even more he requires assistance in deciding things for himself and in asking his significant others to accept his decisions—not only to mature but to experience some real self-respect. Here his fellow clients can encourage him, help him practice presenting his case in role playing scenes with specific significant others, and serve as a model for him during the role reversal phases of role playing. They also can help him discover and use others as models. Certainly good models are more powerful than advice for such a client. Such experiences encourage dependent clients to behave more independently.

On the other hand, dependent clients are not easily helped. They have learned many effective ways of manipulating others into doing things for them: for example, (1) by appearing so helpless that they convince other clients and the counselor that at least for the present some specific advice or assistance is essential; (2) by getting themselves into situations in which they seem to lack any coping resources; (3) by appealing to the strength, wisdom, and maturity of others and thereby seducing others into taking responsibility for them.

Usually it helps to place a dependent client in a group with someone who is trying to learn to cope with a dependent other. With role-playing scenes in which the client who is possessed by a significant dependent other expresses how negatively he feels toward his dependent significant other the dependent discovers how his significant others must feel when he uses them. This also encourages him to explore why some friends have deserted him and how perhaps others who have stuck with him must resent him at certain times. The counselor detects and reflects how significant others must feel toward each and what each must learn to do to cope *with his own* significant others. Without this confrontation with their own dependent behavior and their own recognized need for self-respect, dependent clients often are difficult to motivate to change. Usually they have surrounded themselves with some friends and relatives (and even counselors) who enjoy being needed by dependent persons.

## Advice Giver

Advice giving fulfills some important unmet, and perhaps unconscious, needs of the advice giver such as need for recognition (Bach, 1954). It also implies and conveys mutual interest and caring (Yalom, 1975). Some clients believe genuinely that giving advice is the way to help fellow clients. Others use advice giving as a way to solicit feedback on alternative solutions which they would like to try. Advice giving also may occur when a client is experiencing resistance; he uses it (1) to cover up his own dependency feelings, (2) to shift focus of attention to another, and (3) to encourage another to take some action rather than to continue to discuss material which is painful for the advice giver. Powdermaker and Frank (1953) present two additional reasons: (1) to exhibit superiority to the doctor ("I can help him better than you can.") and (2) to conceal the contempt for the one who seeks advice. Freud (1933) notes an underlying sadism in the person who exhibits an overzealous desire to help another. Yalom (1975) calls attention to the symbiotic nature of the relationship between some advice seekers and the advice giver (and comments on its value):

> The patient who, for example, continuously pulls advice and suggestions from others only to reject it ultimately and frustrate others is well known to therapists as the "help rejecting complainer" or the "yes, but" patient. Other patients may bid for attention and nurturance by asking for suggestions about a problem which is either insoluble or which has already been solved. Others soak up advice with an unquenchable thirst yet never reciprocate to others equally needy. Some group members are so intent in preserving a high status role in the group or a facade of cool self-sufficiency that they never ask directly for help; some are effusive in their gratitude; others never acknowledge a gift, but take it home, like a bone, to gnaw on it privately. (p. 12)
> ... Direct advice from members occurs without exception in every therapy group. . . . Despite the fact that advice giving is common in early interactional group therapy, I can recall few instances in which a specific suggestion concerning some problem was of direct benefit to any patient. (p. 11)

Clients see readily the folly of advice giving, but they can be seduced by the dependent client's helplessness and/or request to be rescued. When the advice giver is tempted to rescue the dependent client, the counselor may be tempted to interpret his advice giving behavior. By itself that is rarely effective. Usually better results are obtained by reflecting the feelings of both, and encouraging the other clients' participation—for example, "Let's all try to capture how each of you two feel and then help you (the advice giver) decide what you can do to help him (advice seeker) without giving him advice. You (the advice giver) are deeply touched by his helplessness and you want to rescue him and tell him what to do. And you (the advice seeker) would like that. You think that those who really care about you should rescue you when you are hurting—even though it may prevent you from discovering for yourself what you could do to help yourself." Such a response tends to stop the advice giving, encourages both parties to think about what they are doing, and encourages the other clients to help both find new improved ways of coping with their dilemma.

Sometimes the advice giver cannot stand to see even a client who is dealing with his problems well, but is exhibiting a lot of pain, suffer. On such occasions the counselor may respond to the advice giver as follows: "When Tom suffers like that in order to convey how he feels and to decide what he must do to achieve his goals it's too painful for you. Consequently, you suggest some things that Tom can do in order to push him quickly into some action and to spare him, and perhaps you, some pain. I wonder whether Tom has talked enough about how he feels, whether he would like to decide for himself what he would like to do, and how he feels toward you for pushing him away from this painful material that he has just now developed the strength to face." Again the primary focus of the response to help the advice giver examine his own needs and to involve the other clients in helping him deal with the problems which motivate him to block therapeutic discussion by another.

Similarly some beginning counselors also have trouble letting a client suffer, especially those who have come out of work assignments in which they had an authoritarian role and perceived themselves as champions of the hurting and the underdogs. They too are tempted to rescue the hurting dependent client. On the other hand, they can be very impatient with the clients who are too quick to give advice.

Thus, readers can see readily that even some of the other-controlled clients such as the advice giver and the advice seeker (dependent) may try to control others. They feel controlled, but they want to learn to assert themselves—to be real and genuine and at the same time considerate.

## Summary

Just as was said in Chapter 10, every counselor must try to detect why some clients are difficult for him, to learn to use his understanding of their impact upon him to respond to them therapeutically, to search for each one's unique feelings, to facilitate open discussion of these feelings, and to help each learn his own desired new behaviors. When a difficult client does not sense his impact upon others, the counselor helps him request feedback and use it to define goals and to learn new behaviors.

The chapter began with the other-controlled client who is so sensitive to other's needs and is so controlled by them that he has difficulty requesting assistance in learning to cope with his tendency to let others take over his life. It also discusses the shy, silent, withdrawn, scapegoat, socializer, dependent, and advice giver.

Though the latter two do have problems with others controlling them, they also tend to control their significant others.

## Discussion Questions

1. How do these other-controlled clients really differ from debilitated clients? What special help does each require from the counselor?
2. To what extent is each really other controlled?
3. Which of the other controlled has the greatest impact on his significant others? What is the nature of his impact?
4. How may a counselor differentiate between the shy and the withdrawn?

What difference does it make in the way the counselor responds to him in group counseling?
5. What are the primary arguments for and against encouraging members of a counseling group to socialize during counseling?
6. If a counselor encourages socializing, with what ethical problems may he be confronted?

## References

Bach, G. R. *Intensive group psychotherapy.* New York: Ronald, 1954.

Freud, S. *New introductory lectures.* New York: Norton, 1933.

Grater, H. A. When counseling success is failure. *Personnel and Guidance Journal,* 1958, *37,* 233–235.

Powdermaker, F. B., & Frank, J. D. *Group psychotherapy.* Cambridge: Harvard University Press, 1953.

Yalom, I. D. *The theory and practice of group psychotherapy.* New York: Basic Books, 1975.

# 12

# Challenging Clients:
# The Reluctant

The reluctant client is often coerced into seeing a counselor or therapist by a parent, spouse, teacher, friend, employer, probation officer, or judge. He is made to feel that he is to blame for whatever happened at home, at school, or at work. Even when he recognizes that he has problems with which he requires assistance, he is reluctant to try to change, probably doubts his own ability to learn essential new behaviors, and certainly questions the likelihood of being helped by this person whom he is forced to see.

To accept treatment is often perceived by such a client to mean that he accepts the blame for a problem with a significant other. At least it means that he must admit to himself that he has some weakness with which he requires assistance: "Acquiescing to the counseling enterprise can become symbolic of failure by his having to internalize the notion, 'I'm inadequate'. Reluctance becomes a shield against this kind of assault on one's sense of well-being. (Vriend & Dyer, 1973, p. 242)"

On the other hand, those who threaten the status quo in the establishment may be referred for counseling—not so much to help them become more self actualizing as to protect the referrer or the establishment against their threatening demands for change. "The counselor, thus confronted, remains the institutional representative of the system, the eminently distrustful authority figure by virtue of his very role; the one who is paid to straighten out conscientious objectors. (Vriend & Dyer, p. 242)"

Futhermore, counselors tend not to be prepared emotionally to deal with the reluctant client—they tend to perceive the client's antitherapeutic behavior as personal rejection and to blame themselves for their client's failure to cooperate in the therapeutic process. Instead, a counselor must detect and reflect what his client is feeling, help him express his feelings (including his feelings about himself, how he can learn to cope with the one who coerced him to come for counseling, and with what he would like help), describe the treatment process, and help him to decide whether or not to genuinely accept the treatment for himself. Until such a client discovers that he has a real choice concerning participation in counseling and accepts responsibility for demonstrating his own readiness and commitment to learn essential new behaviors, he is not likely to profit from counseling. Even when he decides for the present *not* to participate, such an approach tends to increase the chances that he will seek help from this counselor in the future and that he will explore openly the natural consequences of his failure to accept help at this time. Sometimes such a client also maybe is willing to make a commitment to try group counseling on a trial basis. Then the group must decide whether or not he is a sufficiently good risk to be trusted and be admitted on some sort of probationary basis which they define for him in behavioral terms.

Vriend and Dyer present another somewhat different but effective approach, which relies more on the use of confrontation and interpretation than the one described above, which relies primarily on the use of reflection.

The effective counselor questions the source of the reluctance. What rewards does the client receive from his obvious resistance? Is this behavior typical for this person? Despite his overt rejection of my helping efforts, can I allow him this behavior and continue to accept him as a person of worth who can be taught to benefit from counseling? Is the resistance due to my being a symbol of authority? Would he see cooperation as an admission of his own weakness? Does resistance protect him from having to admit it? These questions help the counselor to avoid the trap of projecting the client's reluctance into himself, thus creating strong possibilities for ultimately giving up on the client.

. . . Dealing with the reluctant behavior as it is manifested, rather than ignoring it, communicates to the client that (a) his feelings are acknowledged and understood, (b) counseling is not a process that pretends that feelings do not exist, (c) counseling does not avoid feelings, (d) the counselor has an integrated personality and is strong enough to handle resistance in any form without being personally threatened, (e) by looking at the client and his behavior openly and directly the counselor is full of attention and respect for the importance of what is going on in him and in his world, and (f) the counselor is capable of avoiding moralization by showing the client that he is entitled to his behavior, even when it is antisocial, ineffective, and does not have the import it was generated to produce.

... Reliable interpretation of silence, hostility, or excessive acquiescence tend to (a) provide the client with greater self-understanding, (b) demonstrate counselor competency and capacity as a resource for further help, (c) help the client learn the nature and causes of his own resisting behavior, (d) teach the client that counseling is not a one-sided effort in which one party does all the work, and (e) show the client that counseling does not skirt behavior just because it makes most people feel uncomfortable. ...

The client who encounters the accepting goal-centered counselor, committed to helping and willing to go right to work at eliminating barriers to the mutual task, can hardly maintain his pose for long. Resistance is seriously challenged when a client is asked, "Are you ready for us to do some things together to make your current life a happier one?" Or, "Can we agree to meet for three sessions and set up a goal for the end of that time?" Or, "Can we establish as a goal that you tell all you can about yourself in relation to this kind of difficulty? (pp. 244–245)

Thus even those who do not volunteer for group counseling can be helped by it providing that such clients are helped to express their feelings concerning the external pressure to participate, that they understand what will be expected from them in the group (Chapter 1), that they accept these expectations, that they ask to participate, and that they accept the responsibility for developing trust of the counselor and fellow clients, for convincing themselves and their counselor that they are ready for group counseling, and for learning desired new behaviors. Pressuring such clients to participate can have serious consequences for all concerned: success for them is unlikely and they may prevent other clients from obtaining help; reluctant clients also may conclude, quite properly, that counselors do not respect others' privacy—that they can and do invade others' private world—whether or not they are wanted there. Such a complaint not only damages the counselor's relationship with reluctant clients but with other prospective clients too. A counselor must be strong enough to help a reluctant client uncover his real reasons for avoiding counseling and still respect the client's right to decide for himself whether to accept counseling in order to learn desired new behaviors.

## Nonclient

Sethna and Harrington (1971) found that clients who did not discuss their problems openly and participate actively within the first several sessions tended either to drop out or to become nonclient members—participating very little and appearing to be easily threatened. Similarly Lieberman, Yalom, and Miles's (1973) casualties did not feel safe and close to fellow clients. As casualties perceived it, their group failed to provide the support, security, and cohesiveness which most helped clients experienced. Perhaps their drop-outs withdrew to protect themselves against attack and threat.

In contrast, Lieberman, Yalom, and Miles's (1973) most helped (high learners) experienced the pleasure of feeling close to others, of trust, and of feeling secure in seeking and giving feedback. They felt that they were quality participants—seeking help and giving it. They experienced caring and being cared for. They felt that they were encouraged to take risks and try new behaviors. They felt that they were members of cohesive groups. Consequently, they talked openly, gave others honest, considerate feedback, and felt secure in requesting feedback from others. Moreover, they developed increasing tolerance for others' views and foibles and became more self-directed and less other-directed.

In other words, the care taken to select clients and to prepare them for their responsibility as clients and as helpers described in Chapter 1 should encourage even reluctant clients to participate effectively. Even those who learn much from letting others speak for them and from observing the behavior changes in their good models could profit more by learning to speak up for themselves—by openly describing where they hurt, with what they require assistance, and what they must do to define and implement desired new behavior. They must practice active participation for more effec-tive living with co-workers, classmates, relatives, or friends; they must learn to make requests, to actively help others, and to be more assertive.

Clients who profit most from group counseling know what will be expected of them prior to deciding whether to participate in group counsel-ing (including how to participate as clients and as helpers), have some specific behavioral goals, and are committed to discuss their problems openly and to learn some desired new behaviors. They expect to participate from the beginning as active, responsible members of their groups.

## Disruptive Student

Frequently parents, teachers, or juvenile officers seek help with such clients. When this happens the counselor must decide who is the client (and/or con-sultee, Chapters 8, 9). First the counselor should help the referrer describe the misbehaving person's disruptive behavior, tell how he feels toward this person, tell precisely how he would like to see the person's behavior change and cooperatively decide the extent to which the referrer and the counselor wish to involve the disruptive person in achieving these desired new behaviors, including whether he will be referred for counseling and by whom. Within an institutional setting, such clients may be helped by various behavior modifica-tion techniques, without counseling (Azrin & Powers, 1975; Azrin & Weso-lowski, 1974; Foxx & Azrin, 1972; Lobitz, 1974; Matson & Cahill, 1976;

Matson & Horne, 1975; Tyler & Brown, 1967; Wells, 1962). The type of disruptive, brain-damaged children whom Werry and his associates (1966, 1967) have treated successfully by behavioral modification techniques rarely respond to either individual or group counseling (or therapy).

What was said about the reluctant client at the beginning of this chapter concerning the use of counseling to force clients to comply certainly applies to this type. In the classroom, and even in prison work forces, their disruptive behavior serves two useful purposes for them: (1) it attracts attention to them (something they probably have not learned to earn more honorably) and (2) it demonstrates that no one can make them do anything that they do not want to do (of course, criminals may be forced to give up their lives to prove this point). Even when such clients can genuinely accept group counseling in order to learn desired new behaviors, the cooperation of significant others such as parents and teachers is essential. Best results are obtained when such clients are able to describe their desired new behaviors for their significant others and to enlist their assistance in recognizing and reinforcing their efforts to implement these new behaviors. Frequently significant others also require assistance in managing such persons. Adlerians have produced some of the best management guidelines for them (Dreikurs & Soltz, 1964; Dreikurs, 1972; Dreikurs & Grey, 1968).

Usually even adult clients of this type have difficulty postponing gratification to earn big goals—for example, the charlatan who mastered some medical skills as a military medic and practices medicine after he is discharged, or the bright bank robber who cannot wait to earn enough money to afford big cars and expensive living. Until such clients hurt enough and have decided that they probably never will achieve their most important goals behaving as they have previously, they probably will not become good clients.

When an effective counselor is able to use the approach described at the beginning of this chapter, and these clients are beginning to question anyway whether their approach will ever enable them to achieve their goals, some disruptive clients will try seriously to commit themselves to behavior changes in group counseling. Usually such a counselor is most successful when in addition to their own idiosyncratic goals he is able to detect and reflect their underlying needs which get them into trouble and to help them define some behavioral goals such as: (1) to earn recognition from specific significant others with specific, more readily acceptable behavior; (2) to work out with specific significant others what they can expect of each other and live these expectations rather than try to prove that no one can make them do what they do not want to do; and (3) to define mini-goals for each long-term goal, and thereby experience some quick satisfaction with achievement of mini-goals. Some who are treated successfully in counseling groups also can be trained to function as peer helpers for those who cannot accept group counseling (Chapter 9).

## Drug Addicted

With the very poor rehabilitation of drug addicts, schools and community agencies must give serious attention to prevention. Wherever possible young people, including addicts, should be encouraged to help plan and evaluate such programs. If these prevention programs are to be effective Grant (1972) believes that drug educators must listen to youth, discuss openly how they feel about drug use, exhibit commitment as change agents to current glaring social injustices, and be able to help youth work constructively for social change. Moreover, most youth know quite a bit about drugs and are quick to catch authors' and teachers' half-truths and personal biases. To merely provide information alone is not sufficient (Swisher & Crawford, 1971). Youth must be given the opportunity to share findings on drugs, to compare them, and to react to the information provided. Perhaps this can best be done in classroom discussion groups of the type described by Glasser (1969), and Sonstegard and Dreikurs (1973).

Rarely is either group counseling or group psychotherapy effective with drug addicts. They have given up and so have their significant others given up on them. At a meeting with heroin addicts one member who even realized that he could break the habit described his plight as follows: "I can kick the habit, but all of my friends are drug addicts. Most of the nonaddicts I know won't have anything to do with me, and I don't know how to make new friendships. I have no regular job, and I don't see much of a chance of getting a decent job." Although Krawinski, Fowler, Rotenberg, and Boyson (1972) contend that drug use is the symptom, not the problem, nevertheless, it prevents the drug user from working on his original problems.

Markoff (1966) concludes that once persons become addicted to hard drugs, there are no good rehabilitation risks. He reports that most addicts tend to be weak, immature, irresponsible people who see themselves addicted for life. Frequently they were pampered by parents who rescued them when they got into trouble, and perhaps unknowingly reinforced the unacceptable behavior by exhibiting deep caring then and only then. Perhaps these same parents have such high aspirations for them that they doubt that they can live up to the expectations, and they are too weak to deal with the problem of significant others' unreasonably high goals for them.

Except for Synanon groups, most traditional methods for treating addicts are ineffective. Whereas a 2 percent cure rate is common for most drug programs, Gateway House (a Synanon group) reported 80 to 85 percent success (drug abstinence for the two-year follow-up period after finishing the program) for those who completed their two-year program (Martin, 1972). These peer counseling groups have some features which are similar to the procedures for earning membership described in Chapter 1 but are much hrasher: (1) a prospective member must convince a committee of current Synanon residents in an intake interview that he is committed to substitute a new, meaningful way of life for his irresponsible, selfish, stubborn, and self-pitying drug-addicted existence (Higgins, 1972; Martin, 1972). (2) He must convince the committee that he can and will accept responsibility for himself (arrive at appointed places on time, do his work, keep himself clean, and agree not to use drugs, fight, or smoke, and break all ties with all former associates). (3) After he is admitted he is expected to obey the rules for the group, do his work, help others grow, and serve as a good model for others. During treatment each member is expected to discuss his problems openly and to react to others honestly, but with compassion. Discussions focus on feelings, behavior, success, and futures. Members learn to extinguish undesirable behaviors and to reinforce desired new behaviors. Up until now most of those treated in Synanon groups have been in-patients. The work with out-patients in mental health centers and schools also looks promising.

Bratter (1974) has had more success than most therapists in treating the addict. With more courage than most he also describes his failure with a methadone addict (Bratter, 1975). Occasionally a drug addicted client can be helped when he elects to join a counseling group following the type of presentation described at the beginning of this chapter for reluctant clients. Sometimes several intake interviews are required to communicate precisely what will be expected of him and answer his questions concerning the extent of his commitment to talk openly, to define precise behavioral goals, to assume responsibility for his own recovery and for developing meaningful relationships with significant others, and to convince himself as well as the counselor that he is ready and committed to change his behavior now. If the counselor is not completely convinced on these grounds, he is ethically obligated to convey to the addict's family that he cannot help the client at this time, discuss with them the natural consequences of the addict's failure to fully accept treatment now, and discuss with them what they must do to protect him until he can accept treatment. When such a client detects the extent of such caring he may accept treatment unconditionally and be treated successfully. Even then he is most apt to be treated best with strong clients who can learn to believe in him and will have the patience to help him change. Usually his chances for help are best in a group which is made up of primarily nonaddicts, and which includes at least one good model for him (Nye, 1973).

## The Monopolist

Most group therapists and counselors agree that the monopolist is a resister and a poor treatment risk. In many ways he behaves like a pampered child. He appears to be highly threatened whenever anyone moves in to compete with him for the limelight—he really feels inadequate and unloved. Perhaps he feels that he must control the situation because he has so little to offer as a human being. Bach (1954) believes that fear of attack and isolation accounts for the monopolist's defensive overreaction and his struggle to maintain the center of the stage for himself. Yalom (1975) believes that his compulsive speech is an attempt to deal with his anxiety. As the tension and resentment in the group increase, Yalom notes that he becomes increasingly anxious and speaks more compulsively. Perhaps he merely wants to prove that he is superior to everyone in the group, including the counselor. He is certainly skilled in capturing and holding the speaker's role. Hence, he is able to focus discussion on his preferred topics and to divert attention from the topics he dislikes.

Usually the monopolist draws attention to himself in some way during the presentation and when he is faced with threatening material during the intake interview he speaks compulsively. It is most productive to respond to this behavior immediately: "When you are faced with something scary or difficult, you are tempted to talk compulsively. That will interfere with you getting help in counseling. Hence, I (and your fellow clients in the group) will try to guess what you are trying to cover up or run away from and will help you discuss it. When I said ————, you changed the subject and started to talk very fast. Let's go back to that topic right now and I will help you learn to discuss it." It also helps to explore with him in the intake interview whether he can listen to others, share time with them, be sensitive to others' feelings and needs, encourage them to discuss openly what bothers them, and discuss openly what really bothers him. It is important for him to recognize the negative social consequences of his monopolizing behavior and to develop some specific, behavioral goals with reference to it. Generally, he requires more assistance in defining and in accepting specific behavioral goals than do most clients. Sometimes it helps in the intake interview to encourage him to describe his models, and to identify with his assistance the prospective clients who could serve as models and who are strong enough to interrupt his compulsive talking and to help him profit from feedback. Placing him in a group with older, more mature clients helps too.

Bach's (1954) recommendation that the monopolist be accepted for group treatment on a probationary basis has merit. Then at the opening of the first group session he should be expected to speak first, describe his monopolizing problem, tell what he requires of fellow clients to change, and discuss some criteria which they may use to decide whether or not he be allowed to continue beyond an agreed upon probationary period. High on this list must be his ability to listen to others without interrupting and to accept and use feedback. Perhaps the most telling feedback for him to accept is an observation and critique of a videotaped role-played session in which he observes another take his role in a role reversal (Chapter 7). It can be further enriched by asking the monopolist to play the alter ego for the person who is trying to cope with his self-centered, controlling behavior and to supplement what he says and does. This becomes even more potent when the person who is trying to cope with the monopolist also is encouraged to use soliloquy to express the private anger, frustrations, and disappointments that he experiences in trying to get the monopolist to listen, share time, and to work on relevant therapeutic material.

Even before he gets into the group the monopolist should be helped to examine the natural consequences of his behavior. When therefore he can be admitted to the group on the condition that he have as a goal to change this particular behavior, he is better accepted by others and this increased acceptance enables him to accept others' efforts to cope with his nontherapeutic behavior. Without such understanding and commitment Yalom (1975) observes that he will get feedback only in a disjunctive, explosive manner which in turn elicits a defensive posture on the monopolist's part. The counselor must try to prevent this (as suggested above), or intervene early, to prevent the monopolist from committing social suicide in the group.

When, for example, the counselor first notices the other clients reacting negatively to Frank's monopolizing behavior, he says, "You get upset with Frank when he interrupts and takes over. It is pretty difficult for you to believe that he really wants to listen to you and help you decide what you can do when he interrupts you and talks about something else." Though he tends to be shocked and hurt when he first learns how others respond to his monopolizing in the group, he listens to their feedback providing that he has made a commitment to change prior to admission and reiterated this commitment to fellow clients at the beginning of treatment. Fellow clients also can be taught to detect and reinforce his developing listening and helping skills. Sometimes they also decide to set up a system for insuring some time for everyone every session: a minimum time for the shy and reticent and a maximum for those who tend to use more than their share of time (usually, this is enforced best by assigning each a partner who helps the former get the floor and serves as a monitor for the latter). Whereas the monopolist learns to share his difficulties in living up to the group's expectations of him, he appreciates their considerate efforts to help him control his monopolizing. He does not want to be perceived as a deviant within a group of fellow clients whom he respects and admires. Furthermore, learning to listen to others' problems and experiencing success in helping them tends to be highly satisfying and reinforcing for him. Consequently, though he is difficult to manage within a counseling group, a counseling group is probably the best place for him to learn to manage this behavior.

## Acting-Out Client

Acting out may be expressed as transference: a client may inappropriately express toward a group member feelings that he has for some important other person. Obviously, too, clients may act out with others outside their treatment group. Acting out also may be resistance—a substitute for remembering and coping with the problem within one's counseling group.

Ziferstein and Grotjahn (1957) described a patient for whom acting out was resistance. Escaping from the pain of remembering and dealing with relevant material, she fled to the pleasure of her sexual acting out:

> As long as this deep oral longing is not understood, interpreted, worked through, and integrated, it will lead to acting out. It would appear, then, that not only in the case of acting-out characters, but also in the case of acting out in the course of therapy, the basic cause of acting is the patient's repressed orality, and that acting out is essentially a defensive maneuver against orality. . . .
>
> Acting out is a form of activity whereby a patient unconsciously discharges repressed, warded-off impulses and relieves inner tension. Instead of remembering certain traumatic and therefore repressed experiences, the patient relives them. However, the patient is unaware of this fact, and to him his actions seem appropriate to his present situation. . . .
>
> There are people in whom the tendency to act out is prominent throughout life. There are the "acting-out" characters, who are frequently found to be oral individuals, with low tolerance for frustration or postponement of gratification, and with defects in superego and ego formulation. . . .
>
> Acting out is only a temporary, and not a satisfactory, solution. This analytic handling of acting out, as of any resistance, is prompt interpretation. With the help of interpretation, "acting out" is changed into "working through."
>
> Acting out may involve the patient in realistic troubles, sometimes of a serious nature. This may complicate the treatment if the therapist reacts with anxiety and tries to restrain the patient, by exercising his authority rather than by understanding and interpreting. The patient may then take advantage of the therapist's anxiety and punish him by further acting out, or he may react as to a forbidding parent with castration fear or submissive compliance. The result may be a chaotic situation, aggravated in part by the countertransference of the therapist and the other group members. Most important: the therapist and the group may vicariously enjoy the patient's acting out and unconsciously encourage him, perhaps rationalizing it with the idea that it's good for the patient to develop the courage to gratify impulses, test reality, learn in the school of life, etc. etc. In this situation the therapist and the group members are behaving like parents of delinquent children (Johnson & Szurek, 1952) who unwittingly encourage their children to act out the parents' own repressed impulses. (pp. 81–83)

This type of encouragement to act out occurs also in groups of reasonably healthy clients. Two examples are described here. The first was an attractive college freshman who joined a group of college undergraduates for assistance in relating to peers. At the first session she revealed that she had been married and divorced the previous summer. From her description of her husband he seemed to have considerable sex appeal, but they experienced poor sexual adjustment and she left him after a few weeks. She also discussed a man whom she was dating and with whom she was tempted to have intercouse. During this discussion she solicited sympathy from the group, cleverly, but subtly, attracted special attention from two of the men, and seemed to appeal for her group to condone her acting out. Though the members offered verbal objections to her having an affair, they did condone it by their nonverbal behavior and their laughter. A well-timed reflection by the counselor, concerning her desire to have this behavior condoned and members' willingness to enjoy it vicariously, alerted everyone to what was going on so that they all could state openly what they felt. Consequently, they refused either to condone or reject her wish to act out; they conveyed that she must decide what was right for her and accept responsibility for her own behavior.

An eleventh-grade boy (Ralph) told the members of his high school counseling group about the way his unreasonable father nagged him. Ralph had been very open in discussing some other problems and had been very helpful to the others during the six previous sessions. Everyone, including the counselor, grew obviously angry with Ralph's father. When Ralph concluded that he would "smash him in the mouth" the next time his father nagged him, they obviously supported the idea, and no one picked up these feelings and helped the members deal with them. Consequently, no one was surprised when Ralph had a fight with his father.

Wolf (in a panel discussion by Durkin, Glatzer, Kadis, Wolf, and Hulse, 1958) stated that acting out is always destructive and irrational but that it can be used therapeutically. In Ralph's case the counselor did use the acting out therapeutically, but had he detected what was going on earlier, he could have helped Ralph deal with these feelings without hurting either himself or his father as he did.

"Acting out is a dramatic means of discovering persistent problems and then discovering the means to deal with them. (Wolf, p. 92)" In the same panel discussion Glatzer said:

> A therapist must not be involved in encouraging this blind, irrational behavior or in overstressing its possible benefits as abreaction any more than he would encourage resistance in any other form, instead of analyzing it. . . . What is needed, then, is not the opportunity to act out, to solidify the unwillingness to learn, but to stimulate understanding of its motivation and inappropriate quality so that it becomes ego-alien. Acting out seems to me like the hard core of resistance, and like all resistance it must be repeatedly worked through in order to attain what Fenichel (1945) describes as "the union with ego of what was previously warded off by it." . . .
>
> I don't think that an extended period of acting out makes it fuller or richer. It is still blind, driving behavior and it seems to me, nothing therapeutic is gained by permitting it to continue unanalyzed. Constant interpretation as soon as the therapist becomes aware that his patient is acting out and understands what he is doing (and this often gives the patient sufficient time to act out) tends to promote insight into his destructive behavior and seems to mini-

mize its frequency. I cannot see why acting out should be permitted to remain unanalyzed any longer than it takes the therapist time to recognize it and see its significance. . . .

One of the advantages of immediate handling of acting out in the group situation is that a spontaneous interpretation of acting out in a fresh setting seems to have a more dynamic effect. Permitting a patient to act out, make a fool or nuisance of himself, when the therapist is aware of what is going on, may constitute a greater narcissistic injury to the patient than early interpretation and help to further encapsulate his repressed memories. . . . (pp. 93–94)

The writer agrees with most of the excellent ideas quoted above:

1. A patient should be helped to recognize the phenomenon of acting out as early as possible.
2. Whenever possible it should be prevented by prompt action.
3. The acting-out patient should discover early that it is a kind of activity in which he or others can be hurt. (Whereas the authors quoted above would accomplish this by a well-timed interpretation, the writer would use reflection—for the reasons stated in Chapter 6. As suggested in Chapter 6, he would teach clients to recognize and cope with this phenomenon just as they do other forms of resistance.)
4. When acting out does occur, it can be used therapeutically within the group.

A counselor should not accept the notion that acting out is inevitable. Of course, it may happen sometimes, but much of it can be prevented. Perhaps it is more easily prevented with less disturbed clients than those of the authors quoted above. A carefully timed reflection brings the material into the open where it can be dealt with. The client tempted to act out is helped to understand his motivations better, learn new and better ways of solving his problems, and discover how fellow clients react to his irresponsible behavior. His fellow clients, in turn, often discover how they encourage and condone such behavior. Sometimes they discover that an acting-out client takes advantage of his being in treatment, using it to justify things he has wanted to do but ordinarily would not do. When the one who is or may be hurt as a consequence of a client's acting out is a member of the counseling group, or someone plays the part of the hurt one in re-enacting the scene, the counselor can reflect the hurt one's feelings and help both the hurt one and the hurter deal with the resulting problems. If, however, the counselor does this merely to shame the acting-out client, his response will be seen for what it is.

In any case, role playing (see Chapter 7) can be used effectively to deal with acting out and to prevent it. Involving the one who is tempted to act out in describing the tempting setting, in selecting the role players from his counseling group, assigning them appropriate roles, acting out the scene, and listening to the reactions to the role playing provides him with rich feedback. Role playing also can give him practice in coping directly with such situations rather than evading them.

Although acting out can uncover repressed material to be dealt with in the treatment group, the counselor should try to prevent it whenever possible in order to protect those who may be hurt. Note also Glatzer's point that allowing a client to act out can further encapsulate repressed material—thus making it less accessible to treatment. Moreover, it is easier to help a client express and cope with his feelings for a transference object (or the real person) before he acts them out than it is to deal with the shame and embarrassment, as well as the underlying motivations for acting out, afterward.

## Summary

For every difficult client, the counselor must ask himself why this particular client is difficult for him, how he can use his reactions to the client to detect and reflect significant therapeutic materials, assess the extent to which his reaction is a countertransference one, help him define precise, idiosyncratic goals, and help him develop the trust to share openly with fellow clients and to implement his own desired new behaviors.

Even reluctant clients for whom expectations and possible benefits are communicated well can learn to be good clients and be treated successfully. However, they must accept the treatment expectations, must truly want to be members of a counseling group (and without any coercion from the counselor), be committed to talk openly and to define precise behavioral goals, and exhibit genuine willingness to listen to and to help fellow clients.

## Discussion Questions

1. Why do counselors tend to be evaluated on the basis of their failures rather than their successes?
2. How do counselors' personal characteristics and needs influence difficult clients' behavior during treatment and following?
3. What are the unique advantages of a client listening, observing, and criticizing a video recording of a role-played session in which role reversal was used and then repeated with the client playing his own role?
4. What special considerations must a counselor keep in mind in treating a client whom he recognizes to be difficult for him?
5. For which of the three types of difficult clients (Chapters 10, 11, and 12) would Perls' top-dog underdog be most appropriate? For which would the "Fiddler Game" be most appropriate?
6. Which of the clients discussed in this chapter would be most difficult for

you to detect prior to placing him in a group? Discuss this type with two colleagues for the purpose of *identifying specific behaviors* that may help you to identify him prior to the first group counseling session.

# References

Azrin, N. H., & Powers, M. A. Eliminating classroom disturbances of emotionally disturbed children by positive practice procedures. *Behavior Therapy,* 1975, *6,* 525–534.

Azrin, N. H., & Wesolowski, M. C. Theft reversal: An overcorrection procedure for eliminating stealing by retarded persons. *Journal of Applied Behavioral Analysis,* 1974, *7,* 577–581.

Bach, G. R. *Intensive group psychotherapy.* New York: Ronald, 1954.

Bratter, T. H. Helping affluent families help their acting-out, drug abusing adolescent. *Journal of Family Counseling,* 1974, *2,* 22–31.

Bratter, T. H. The methadone addict and his disintegrating family: A psychotherapeutic failure. *The Counseling Psychologist,* 1975, *5,* 110–124.

Dreikurs, R. *The challenge of child rearing.* New York: Hawthorne, 1972.

Dreikurs, R., & Grey, L. *Logical consequences: A new approach to discipline.* Des Moines: Meredith, 1968.

Dreikurs, R., & Soltz, V. *Children: A challenge.* New York: Duell, Sloan, and Pierce-Meredith, 1964.

Durkin, H. E., Glatzer, H. T., Kadis, A. L., Wolf, A., & Hulse, W. C. Acting-out in group psychotherapy. *American Journal of Psychotherapy,* 1958, *12,* 87–105.

Fenichel, O. *The psychoanalytic theory of neurosis.* New York: Norton, 1945.

Foxx, R. M., & Azrin, N. H. Restitution: A method of eliminating aggressive-disruptive behaviors of retarded and brain damaged patients. *Behavior Research and Therapy,* 1972, *10,* 15–27.

Glasser, W. *Schools without failure.* New York: Harper & Row, 1969.

Grant, R. H. Drug education: What it is and isn't. *Journal of Drug Education* 1972, *2,* 89–97.

Higgins, A. Synanon is for people who never learned to live. *Dodge News Magazine,* August, 1972, 21–23.

Johnson, A. M., & Szurek, S. A. The genesis of anti-social acting out in children and adults. *Psychiatric Quarterly,* 1952, *21* 323–343.

Krawinski, W., Fowler, F. S., Rotenberg, L. A., & Boyson, W. A. Workable community concepts in drug abuse. *Journal of Drug Education,* 1972, *2,* 125–138.

Lieberman, M. A., Yalom, I. D., & Miles, M. D. *Encounter groups: First facts.* New York: Basic Books, 1973.

Lobitz, W. C. A simple stimulus clue for controlling disruptive classroom behavior. *Journal of Abnormal Child Psychology,* 1974, *2,* 143–152.

Markoff, E. L. Synanon in drug addiction. In J. H. Masserman (Ed.), *Handbook of psychiatric therapies.* New York: Grune & Stratton, 1966.

Martin, P. M. Is God at Gateway House? *Christian Century,* September 20, 1972, 933–936.

Matson, J. L., & Cahill, T. Overcorrection: A technique for eliminating resistant behaviors. *JSAS Selected Documents in Psychology,* 1976.

Matson, J. L., & Horne, A. M. Overcorrection and extinction-reinforcement as rapid methods of eliminating the disruptive behavior of relatively normal children. Paper presented at Northcentral Association for Counselor Education at Kansas City, 1975.

Nye, L. S. Obtaining results through modeling. *Personnel and Guidance Journal,* 1973, *51,* 380–384.

Quay, H. C., Weery, J. S., McQueen, M., & Sprague, R. L. Remediation of the conduct problem child in the special class setting. *Exceptional Children,* 1966, *32,* 509–513.

Sethna, E. R., & Harrington, J. A. A study of patients who lapsed from group psychotherapy. *British Journal of Psychiatry,* 1971, *119, 59*–69.

Sonstegard, M. A., & Dreikurs, R. The Adlerian approach to group counseling of children. In M. M. Ohlsen (Ed.), *Counseling children in groups: A forum.* New York: Holt, Rinehart and Winston, 1973.

Swisher, J. D., & Crawford, J. L. An evaluation of a short-term drug education program. *The School Counselor,* 1971, *18,* 265–272.

Tyler, V. O., & Brown, G. The use of swift, brief isolation as a group control device for institutionalized delinquents. *Behavior Research and Therapy,* 1967, *5,* 1–9.

Vriend, J., & Dyer, W. W. Counseling the reluctant client. *Journal of Counseling Psychology,* 1973, *20,* 240–246.

Wells, C. G. Psychodrama and creative counseling in the elementary school. *Group Psychotherapy,* 1962, *15,* 244–252.

Werry, J. S., & Wollersheim, J. P. Behavior therapy with children: A broad overview. *Journal of American Academy of Child Psychiatry,* 1967, *6,* 346–370.

Yalom, I. D. *The theory and practice of group psychotherapy.* New York: Basic Books, 1975.

Ziferstein, I., & Grotjahn, M. Group dynamics of acting out in analytic group psychotherapy. *International Journal of Group Psychotherapy,* 1957, *7,* 77–85.

# 13

# Marriage Counseling in Groups

Humans require meaningful, intimate relationships with individuals for whom they care deeply and from whom they sense mutual caring. Today most adults accept marriage as the best way to contract for this relationship, but increasing numbers question the appropriateness of marriage for themselves. Though marriage is challenged more openly today, Zorbaugh (1929) discovered that during the first quarter of this century marriage vows were ignored by many rural and small town youth who moved to the big cities to seek their fame and fortune—living together unmarried until they were prepared financially to get married. They reported that they wanted "someone to talk to, someone to tell their troubles to, and someone to come home to." Obviously, they also wanted someone with whom they could experience sexual satisfaction.

Landis (1975) supports the validity of marriage as contributing to normality, which is, at least to a large degree, determined by the opportunity one is given for constant, meaningful communication with other persons.

One of the best indices of the effect of social isolation and a sense of anonymity on personality is the suicide rate. Data for a three year period indicate that the married are by far the least likely to suicide. Of white males, only 21 per 100,000 of those married commit suicide, compared to 80 of these divorced, 76 of those widowed, and 44 of those single. Comparable rates for the white female are 7 of those married, 19 of those divorced, 13 for those widowed, and 8 for those single. (Landis, 1975, p. 6)

> Marriage is modern man's best arrangement for avoiding the solitariness of adulthood. . . . The need for the companionship of a marriage partner in the industrial world cannot be written off as a spurious value. The human being, to remain human, needs someone with whom he can interact on a continuing basis, expressing his deepest joys and fears, plans and failures, hopes and needs. (Landis, 1975, p. 5)

Nevertheless, some authorities question whether marriage and family life as we know it today can or should survive. Davids (1971), for example, suggests limited term marriage contracts that may or may not be renewed. Others endorse marriage contracts that provide for extramarital sex relations, and for some commune living. However, Rogers (1972) found that meaningful continuing extramarital sexual relationships required more time and energy than his couples were able to give, and consequently, they returned to a monogamous relationship. Furthermore, Mowrer (1973) discovered that these special contracts were difficult to develop—individuals often wanted freedom for themselves that they were reluctant to give their mates. He also discovered that secret contract breakers hurt themselves as well as those they deceived.

Even those who prefer some living arrangement other than marriage must be able to communicate to prospective living partners what they will expect from them, what they are willing to contribute to the relationship, and to respect the prospective partner's rights in developing a mutually acceptable contract.

O'Neill and O'Neill (1974) encourage helpers to facilitate the development of their clients' potential for responsible decision making and actions:

> Change we must, but it should be a change we choose to make, in a direction we choose to go. Instead of being carried along powerless and without control by the constant pace of change, we can elect to take hold of our lives and design a life strategy to help us meet change. Instead of following someone else's life plan or getting lost in the shuffle, we can learn the skills to help us make change work for us in a creative and challenging way. And if we choose not to change in some areas, we at least know it is our own choice. If we know how to internalize our growth plan we can then not only make a selective adaptation to external change but we can also be in touch with ourselves and with our own growth. This is the only way in which change can lead to sense of personal security. (p. 16)
>
> . . . trying to capture the joy of sex which we are told should be ours, we mechanically practice new techniques. Eventually all the external stimuli pall and we end up feeling more bereft than before. Without internal change, the spontaneous feeling is lacking. The spontaneous feeling of a merging wholeness which characterizes sexual expression as our greatest medium for sharing can only come from inside ourselves. The externals just don't do the trick. (p. 17)
>
> Yet if we really examine the situation, we may realize that most of our unhappiness with decisions we make stems from the fact that we have relinquished our autonomy—our own part in making them. We give up this auton-

omy in many ways: by being influenced by others than ourselves, by not seeking adequate information relevant to our needs, by not knowing our values and priorities, by stubbornly resisting change or by sinking in a rut and making a "decision" by default. (pp. 159–160)

Deciding between marriage and its various alternatives is a crucial decision, and one that the individual must make for himself in order to be comfortable with it, and to make the essential commitments for its success. Sometimes clients are afraid to reveal their true values and priorities lest they be scoffed at by others whose love and acceptance they value highly. For such persons group counseling can help them learn to be more assertive, and also to respect and to exhibit tolerance for views different from their own. It helps them to discover what they value, to learn to make requests of significant others, and to decide for themselves whether or not they can learn to live with particular significant others who have values very different from their own. Hopefully increasing numbers will have such opportunities to participate in such groups prior to deciding with whom they would like to live and within what type of life style. When individuals realize that they can make certain crucial decisions for themselves they are less threatened by change. They learn to develop and use their support system, their self-respect is increased, and they exhibit more genuine commitment to implement desired changes.

## The Need

There is great demand for competent marriage counselors today. Masters and Johnson (1975) estimate that over half of the married couples have not learned to function effectively sexually. In addition there are many who have good marriages but are seeking marriage counseling to enrich the quality of their relationships.

Most church-related couples turn first to their pastors for assistance with their marriage problems. Although increasing numbers of pastors are seeking professional preparation in marriage counseling and in human sexuality, most are not adequately prepared to provide the professional services required. Even the couples who turn to community mental health agencies and family services agencies are often allowed to waste precious time fighting and complaining about the spouse's shortcomings. Thus many couples continue to be victimized by charlatans and by conscientious but unqualified helpers:

Never have so many couples needed outside help with their marital problems. Never have so many qualified marriage counselors been available to lend valuable assistance. And yet, more than ever before, distressed couples are being fleeced, demeaned, and hurt by inept marriage counselors and by charlatans. (*National Observer,* October 30, 1971, p. 1)

Instead of encouraging couples to spend their time complaining about each other, each partner must be encouraged to discuss what really worries and upsets him, to decide what new behaviors he must learn, and to solicit his spouse's assistance in learning these new behaviors. In addition to helping each become a better person each must learn to recognize and manage conflict.

Koch and Koch's (1976a) new book *The Marriage Savers* and a *Psychology Today* article: "A Consumer's Guide to Therapy for Couples" (1976b) are also addressed to management of conflict.

Professionals doing marriage counseling have a great opportunity to help persons in trouble. However, they must be competent; they also must support legislation to protect the public from the charlatans and the unqualified; and they must affiliate with a strong professional organization which is committed to help them continue their professional growth and to discipline the incompetent and unethical.

## Help Seekers' Problems

Those who seek assistance usually have not learned how to develop and maintain close intimate relationships. Often they are afraid to be open and genuine. They do not realize that their real private selves are more lovable than any of the false faces they wear to impress others.

Another common problem that those who seek marriage counseling have, but usually one with which they do not request assistance, is learning to share with their partner even the beginnings of tender, loving and/or grateful feelings. When they learn to detect them and put them into tender language, they are delighted to experience the increased strength of such feelings. For example, Ralph discovered that Jan (his overweight wife) had joined a weight watchers' and jogging group. Heretofore, she had always resisted his encouragement to deal with the problem. It really thrilled him that she was willing to do something to like herself better. After practicing what he wanted to say with the help of the group (and in front of her), he finally spoke as follows: "I am really glad that you decided that to do something for yourself. I have always known that you are a beautiful person, but now you seem to be willing to try to believe it about yourself. What may I do to reinforce your successes?" Then he asked her to stand and he hugged her. Afterwards he said, "That was great. Now I mean it even more than I did when I spoke earlier."

Other more common feelings expressed at first by couples seeking counseling are boredom, anger, deceit, neglect, lack of closeness, inadequacy, and lack of sexual satisfaction. With reference to sex they often have not learned to accept their sexuality, to express it tenderly, and to give each other pleasure outside of sex as well as with it. Neither have they learned that each is responsible for his own satisfaction—that his mate cannot provide it for him. Those who believe that their problem is primarily a sexual one and seek assistance from a competent team like Masters and Johnson (1970, 1975), usually discover that sexual dysfunction is a function of a relationship problem—that each must become sensitive to the other's needs, to communicate more effectively, to discover ways of giving each other special pleasure, and to enjoy giving each other pleasure both sexually and in many ways.

> One basic conflict characterizes all marriage neuroses: need for closeness and fear of it. People whose fear is greater than their need for closeness do not get married. Those who do not experience closeness as a threat to their identity are able to establish satisfying relationships with their spouses, with mutual respect and understanding of their differences. (Papanek, 1971, p. 697)

> Two people form a bond in the mistaken expectation of finding security, trust, understanding, and intimacy. They hope that on the basis of such a relation they will be able to develop autonomy, competence, and a feeling of self-worth. If marriage partners distrust each other and lack understanding, intimacy is replaced by anger and hostility. Each feels undermined by the other. (Papanek, 1971, p. 721)

Rarely have they learned to plan together as partners, to recognize conflict early, to cooperate in resolving conflicts, and to make cooperative decisions. Frequently, their effort at cooperative planning has resulted in a power struggle. Even their intended requests sound like demands.

Similarly Koch and Koch (1976a) report that certain common marital complaints of ten or fifteen years ago are still reported today: lack of communication, unfulfilled emotional needs, problems with kids, sexual problems, infidelity, money, in-laws, alcoholism, and physical abuse. They also describe three new problems: (1) the woman is breaking out of her cocoon and suddenly demanding her rights of a husband who is not prepared to cope with the demands; (2) neither can accept sex-role stereotyping, but men have not learned to express the newly required tenderness and women are having difficulty giving up the self-effacing emotional support role; and (3) neither has learned to deal with the self-sacrificing demands of marriage and parenthood. Young couples require assistance in dealing with postponement of these responsibilities and the older couples require assistance in freeing themselves from them.

## Group Counseling

Papanek (1971) believes that Mittelman (1944) was the first to propose treating the husband and wife together in marriage counseling. Prior to that time psychoanalytic theory and practice had established that each should be treated separately and by different therapists. Ackerman (1970) contends that such separate treatment can result in divorce rather than prevent it. Instead, like Mittelman, he believes that the couple should be treated as a couple or as one of several couples in a group. Today there is growing support for group marriage enrichment programs too. (Calvo, 1973; Deutsch, 1967; Gallagher, 1975; Gurman, 1971; Hopkins & Hopkins, 1976; Jones, 1967; Lebedun, 1970; Olson, 1970; Pew & Pew, 1972; *React*, 1973).

From his experience with behavioral approaches, Liberman (1970) concludes that clients can learn to define specific goals, to practice desired new behaviors and to reinforce a spouse's adaptive rather than maladaptive behaviors. In other words, successful treatment reverses the discouraging interaction pattern within many families:

> Typically, families that come for treatment have coped with the maladaptive or deviant behavior of one member by anger, nagging, babying, conciliation, irritation, or sympathy. These responses, however punishing they might seem on the surface, have the effect of reinforcement of deviance, that is, increasing the frequency or intensity of the deviant behavior in the future. Reinforcement occurs because the attention offered is viewed and felt by the deviant member as positive concern and interest. (Liberman, p. 107)

With the type of structuring described in Chapter 1 and the next section, marriage counseling clients learn to accept responsibility for *talking openly about their own worries and concerns* rather than criticizing their spouses, for defining specific behavioral goals, for implementing desired new behaviors —both within the group sessions and with spouse between sessions, and for reinforcing spouse's desired new behaviors. They learn to listen to their spouse, to communicate, to make requests, and to share warmly private feelings. They learn to recognize the early signs of conflict, to help each other reveal early what is annoying, and to cooperate with each other in resolving conflict; and they do all these things better in the presence of others who see through their unproductive games, give them considerate but precise feedback, and even put pressure on them to discuss their problems openly and try some new alternative solutions. They also discover good models for themselves as couples and as individuals, and they discover too that others whose problems probably are more serious than their own have been able to learn desired new behaviors. They learn to differentiate between rescuing another and providing him with quality support. Many generalize from these experiences to develop meaningful support groups with friends outside group counseling.

## The Triad Counseling Model

Most laymen recognize that it is difficult for three persons to develop an effective working relationship. Even a child learns quickly to use this group to his advantage—pairing up first with one parent (or friend) then with the other and playing them off against each other. Some counselors have had similar difficulties when they have tried to counsel a couple. Perhaps that is why so many have questioned whether it could be done.

What this treatment model does is to teach two to pair up to help the third rather than to hurt him. In the presentation of the model the counselor teaches clients that the best way for a client to grow as a person and to enhance the enrichment of his marriage is to talk about what really worries and upsets him about himself. When, for example, the wife speaks first the counselor listens very carefully, tries to detect precisely how she feels, encourages her to discuss what really bothers her about herself, rather than about her husband, helps her decide precisely how she would like to change her own behavior, encourages her to practice desired new behaviors, and helps her solicit specific reinforcement when she successfully exhibits new behaviors. Instead of criticizing her husband and complaining about his faults, as spouses usually do in most marriage counseling, she is encouraged to discuss her own guilt, frustrations, shortcomings, and feelings of inadequacy and to develop her own plans to implement her desired new behaviors. While the counselor is helping her he also is watching for opportunities to teach all the other clients but especially the speaker's husband to be his special helper. In particular, he teaches her husband to listen empathically, to help him guess how he thinks she really feels, to formulate reflections which facilitate her discussion of her feelings, to provide reinforcement and quality support as she practices in the group and implements outside the group the desired new behaviors, and to reinforce desired new behaviors and attitudes. She learns to do the same for him when he functions as a client, and both have these norms reinforced by the other couples in the group. As each partner listens (with the encouragement and reinforcement of the other clients as well as the counselor) she (he) gradually experiences increased empathy and compassion for her (his) spouse, learns to check out her (his) hunches (especially those conclusions that were drawn from nonverbal behaviors and previously acted on without checking them out), and learns to communicate better with her (his) spouse. Each also learns to recognize earlier the clues for conflict, to identify the sources of annoyance, to face the conflict, and to deal with it more effectively with the help of both fellow clients and the counselor. The desire to learn new behaviors is substituted for fighting, hurtful criticism, and self pity. Couples with children[1] also  obtain assistance in child rearing and in establishing and maintaining a family council.

When the writer first talks to a couple about marriage counseling in the intake interview, he helps them to discuss briefly what their problems are and whose cooperation is required to solve them. Very quickly he directs

[1] From time to time when a couple struggles with a child rearing problem an extra treatment hour is scheduled for the counselor to meet with the couple's family just prior to the regular marriage counseling session in order to help the family identify their primary problems, to help them decide what they can do cooperatively to solve the problems, and, if they do not already have one, to help them introduce the family council. For these sessions the counselor follows the Adlerian model (Dreikurs, 1972a). During the family counseling the other three or four couples observe. Following the family session they provide feedback to the family.

each partner's attention to what really worries and upsets him about himself that he wants to change. As each talks he teaches the other from the beginning to be a good listening helper and to assist his spouse formulate very precise behavioral goals. Then he describes the triad, tells how it works, explains why he uses it, and asks each to convince the other and himself that he really is committed to talk openly, to learn specific new behaviors, and to help the other clients, and especially his spouse, learn new behaviors. The client is given responsibility for proving his own readiness and for demonstrating his willingness to change (Chapter 1). When a prospective client cannot make such a commitment, he is helped to explore why he cannot do this and what are the natural consequences of such a decision. For instance, a client may not have had sufficient opportunity to get even with the mate; reflecting back to him his need for more revenge tends to be somewhat shocking, but highly productive. Another may be fearful of change or fearful that willingness to change will call forth more demands for change. (This is minimized when each client defines his own desired new behaviors in terms of his own goals for himself rather than to meet the mate's needs.)

After the couple has talked about their problems, and how each wants to change, the counselor helps them discuss their goals as a couple. Some who are good prospective clients for marriage counseling cannot express these needs in the intake. They require considerable self-disclosure in the group before they can define their goals as a couple. Others are willing to join a couples group for their own personal growth but are not willing to define their goals until they have definitely decided that they are committed to a successful marriage with this particular spouse.

In such a case the counselor schedules time alone with each to explore any problems that each cannot yet discuss in front of his (her) spouse, to practice discussing these and other difficult problems, and to explore the extent of his (her) commitment to this marriage. Finally, they meet as a triad again to share any new information they decided to share and to decide cooperatively whether or not to participate. If affirmative they decide on what grounds they will participate and if they are to be admitted to the group on probation what they will say to the group about it. Further they decide what criteria they would like to have the group use to decide whether they will be permitted to continue treatment in the group.

Even though the counselor seems to communicate well in the presentation and in the intake interview what is expected of clients in this treatment model a few clients may begin counseling by griping about his (her) mate. This must be dealt with at once, but kindly and considerately: for example, "I can understand why you want to point out your spouse's faults and complain about her (him), but that will interfere with your own, her (his), and the other clients' growth. Furthermore, you will discover that others will accept you better and try harder to help you when you *discuss what really bothers you about yourself.* Begin with those worries and concerns that you discussed in the intake interview. We will give you our undivided attention and help you discuss them."

Dealing promptly with such deviations from the model, and where necessary asking other members to clarify expectations, helps establish therapeutic norms and encourages clients to accept responsibility for establishing them.

Dreikurs' (1972b) rationale for his conflict management model also makes a very good case for this marriage counseling model:

> Change yourself and thereby others. . . .
>
> To explain a conflict situation I use the example of a dialogue. Tragically and surprisingly, I venture to say, we simply know only the lines which our opponent speaks, but not ours. And his lines alone do not make any sense. When the mother comes complaining, it is about what children are doing; the children complain about the mother; husband and wife complain about each other. Everyone is full of good intentions, provided that the other one will change.
>
> We all try to change the other one and have no luck. Stop thinking what the other should do; the only one we can change is ourselves. . . .
>
> And this, my friends, is one of the strongest statements I can make in my whole approach to pyschology and human nature. If, as you feel weak and hopeless when you are confronted with somebody who doesn't behave properly, you stop thinking about what *he should do,* and begin to think about what *you could do,* and the doors open wide. You suddenly become aware of the power which you never dreamt you had. Then you can use encouragement, logical consequences, persuasion, all these ways to helping him to change—merely by changing yourself. I think this is the most important lesson, namely, that we begin to see what we are doing and could do differently, and stop thinking about what he should do.
>
> . . . we must reach agreement on shared responsibility.
>
> So the fourth point for solving conflicts is leadership which brings people together to listen to each other, to realize the reality of their common problem, and to share responsibility. (pp. 204–206)

# Adapting Group-Counseling Techniques for Couples

Generally, the material presented in the earlier chapters applies to couples' groups. For each of the exceptions the writer supplements the general principle to adapt it for couples' groups. Recently, he has discovered that these adaptations also apply to counseling groups designed for parts of families: mother-daughter, father-son, mother-son, father-daughter, and sibling-sibling groups (Depressed, Chapter 10).

Selecting good prospects for marriage counseling is more difficult than selecting other clients for a group. Developing a therapeutic relationship is complicated by the fact that both partners are rarely equally committed to counseling. When, therefore one partner agrees reluctantly to participate in marriage counseling, additional intake interviews may be required to help the reluctant one (Chapter 12) discover that he can talk openly about what really worries and upsets him, to practice discussing his disappointments and guilt, to explore the extent of his commitment either to improve his own personal adjustment and/or to improve the marriage, to define specific behavioral goals for self and marriage, and to review the natural consequences of refusing to accept help now. Sometimes additional sessions for couples are required to help each share his own goals, to define cooperatively their goals as a couple, and to use the materials from at least their primary sources of conflict to provide a practical lesson in conflict management.

The counselor is caught in a dilemma when one of the partners is highly committed and the other is only partially committed or possibly indifferent to treatment. On such occasions he owes it to both to help the committed partner model good client behavior by talking openly about how she (he) would like to change, to express her (his) disappointment, and to explore the possibilities and consequences of treatment in a regular adult group without her (his) spouse; and finally to help the reluctant one examine the consequences of her (his) failure to accept help now. Rather than to admit an uncommitted client, the counselor would do better to admit the committed one to a regular adult group in which she (he) could learn desired new behaviors, solicit her (his) partner's assistance in reinforcing her (his) desired new behaviors, and request his (her) assistance in resolving the problems which are the primary obstacles to their successful marriage. On the other hand, sometimes the partially committed client will agree to admission to the marriage counseling group on a probationary basis. When this is done he (she) must be given a limited number of sessions in which to learn to discuss his own problems openly, to define precise behavioral goals, to solicit feedback from the group, and to use it therapeutically rather than to merely react against it (and, of course, such a reluctant client should be expected to share with the group at the beginning of the first session why he is being admitted on probation, the criteria which he would like the other members to use to decide whether he be allowed to continue beyond a specified number of sessions, and the extent to which they will give him feedback on his performance as a client and helper before they vote).

On the other hand, there is always some danger that the group will take sides against the reluctant client and favor his (her) committed spouse. In this case the reluctant client may be the hurt one, and hence, the counselor must help him (her) express his (her) hurt and solicit the group's assistance in teaching him (her) to be a good client and helper. In any case, as long as they are both members, the counselor as well as the other members must be committed to help each learn his own desired new behaviors, and when they feel that they no longer can do that they must decide what must be done to maximize the therapeutic worth of the group for each member, including helping a dismissed member locate new sources for treatment. When members learn to act so responsibly, rarely do they have to force out even a reluctant client. Instead he is impressed by their sincere desire to help and to prevent anyone from destroying the effectiveness of the group. Poorest prospects tend to have difficulty discussing their own problems openly, defining precise behavioral goals, and avoiding complaining about their spouses.

Usually most marriage groups can profit from some *systematic instruction in cooperative decision making and in conflict management* in which case material from their own lives is used to help relevant couples apply the principles in their current problem solving. Most couples also profit from systematic instruction in developing a support system (and one that clearly differentiates between a support system and a rescue service).

Group size can be five couples instead of three or four as one would tend to have in regular groups. The additional couple can provide more variety with reference to types of marriage problems, more persons with whom to identify and from whom to seek support, and more models for the improvement of both a couple's marriage and of each partner's personal adjustment. For models' input, and sometimes for feedback, the "N" in a statistical sense seems to be the number of couples in a marriage counseling group rather than the number of clients. On the other hand, a top limit of five couples seems to be necessary so that each client as well as each couple obtains some help in each session.

In order to accommodate the large group and to provide room for the various exercises recommended for relationship development in Chapter 7, the *counseling room (group setting)* should be somewhat larger than most group counseling and/or therapy rooms. It also should be carpeted and arranged so that couples can arrange for informal seating arrangements, role playing, and moving around.

*Initiating client talk* in the intake interview may be shoved aside by one or both partners' need to complain about the partner's inconsiderate and/or hurtful behavior, to complain about partner's unwillingness to change, to express the need for revenge, or to push for a decision on whether the marriage is worth saving. When this happens the counselor should describe the treatment model again, explain why it works, encourage both to practice client talk, and help them decide whether they can make the necessary commitment to profit from the treatment. If they decide to make the commitment then they should be encouraged to identify their primary marriage problems briefly, to discuss what changes each believes he must make in order for the marriage to succeed, and to continue client talk with the definition of specific behavioral goals.

When they accept the treatment model and realize that its purpose is to help each *improve his own personal adjustment as well as to improve the quality of their marriage,* they usually are able to postpone the decision on whether to try to make it or to split until they have had more therapeutic experiences. They also tend to see the advantages of making that decision in the group with the assistance of fellow clients (and the chances are greater that they will decide to stay together when they make this decision in the group with the assistance of fellow clients). In other words, they are taught good client behavior and are reinforced for it from the first contact.

*Helping clients define specific criteria* which they can use to appraise their own growth is not different from other groups, but perhaps it is more important because it provides other clients (and especially the partners) with the guidelines they require to detect growth. Like other clients, detecting one's own growth encourages further growth, but in marriage counseling it also is crucial that one's spouse recognize and reinforce that growth. When, therefore, a client discovers that he has achieved real growth and his (her) spouse fails to detect it and reinforce it, precise criteria of growth help him (her) to present the supporting evidence for growth and to request help from the spouse in celebrating it.

*Teaching clients to be good helpers as well as clients is crucial for this model.* It is designed to substitute empathic listening and other encouraging behaviors for the usual discouraging behaviors of most unhappy marriages. Within such an atmosphere every possible effort is made to teach partners to plan cooperatively, to substitute mature, helpful support for a rescue service, and to achieve both a meaningful independent fulfillment and a close partnership in which they share responsibility for managing their home, family, finances, and the development of an ever-increasing richer companionship.

*Learning to request, accept, and use feedback* (Chapter 3) is essential for all groups but it is even more important for unhappy marriage partners. Frequently, they have not truly learned to listen to feedback. Even couples for whom this is a problem can learn to help others listen to feedback from fellow clients' as well as their mate, and to explore the implications of the feedback for new behaviors to be learned. Especially when accompanied by the use of role-played scenes in which other members act as alter ego to help another to express his (her) deep, unexpressed feelings, such discussions tend to open up communication between partners, to encourage them to check out impressions, and to teach them to make requests which are truly requests rather than thinly veiled demands.

*Helping clients to practice the interpersonal skills* required to make requests, to solicit feedback, to express loving, tender feelings, to develop intimacy, to teach, and to celebrate peak experiences are essential in all group counseling, but needed even more in marriage counseling. Even the most insensitive spouse can be deeply touched as he (she) sees his (her) mate struggling in role playing to verbalize a deeply felt, but awkwardly expressed tender feeling and observes a fellow client patiently help him (her) express these feelings. Mates also tend to be touched by the extent of their spouses' skin hunger, loneliness, and need for intimacy. As was suggested in Chapter 7, couples can read *Pairing* (Bach & Deutch, 1970), select case materials from the book for which they need practice, use the material in role playing in their group, and solicit feedback. They also can use other intimacy and touching exercises (Chapter 7) productively in marriage counseling groups. Much of the intimacy deficiency and loneliness which many couples describe in marriage counseling can be corrected by the clients with the assistance of their partners by owning their needs, expressing them to partners, and learning to enjoy them. When, however, persons have not learned to satisfy these needs adequately in growing up, and/or their earlier efforts to express them to their partners have produced negative consequences, they require much practice and patience to learn to satisfy them. This they can learn to do in counseling groups.

## Managing Conflict

Whether consultees are marriage partners, or the members of a local board of education who believe that the schools have been unfairly criticized by the chamber of commerce when they failed to attract a significant new industry to the community, they must be helped to answer questions such as: What is the problem as you perceive it? Whose cooperation do you require to solve it? How may the cooperation of these persons be enlisted to solve the problem? Who will contact each? What must the one making the contact keep in mind as he solicits assistance in solving the problem?

Rarely does it do any good to try to help disagreeing parties prove who was at fault. Sometimes, however, one party (or group in a conflict) has been hurt so much that he wants revenge for his hurt—or at least he would like to prove for his "significant public" who is responsible for the "obvious unfair treatment." When the counselor (consultant) detects such feelings he reflects them, helps the members of the counseling group (or other consultees) discuss them, and helps them explore the natural consequences of revenge. Usually after they have discussed the natural consequences of revenge, the other clients are able to help the revengeful one(s) move on to decide (1) what their primary sources of conflict are, (2) what they can do as a couple to cope with these problems, (3) whose cooperation is required to make essential changes, (4) how to solicit the assistance of these other persons, (5) what new behaviors each of them must learn, (6) how each can reinforce each desired new behavior with what precise reinforcers, and (7) how they can appraise and celebrate their growth.

Early in the conflict-management process marriage partners must learn to become increasingly sensitive to clues which suggest irritation and learn to deal with them before they develop into deep hurt and/or anger. Each also must help the other differentiate between anger which arises from within as a result of disappointments in one's self for sins of omission as well as commission, and anger which results from others' inconsiderate acts. When it is the former a client must discuss what he does not like about himself and/or his behavior and decide precisely how he will learn to behave differently, including learning to accept himself as imperfect. When it is the latter he must learn to face the hurter and to enlist his cooperation in applying the steps outlined above for resolving conflict. Usually such clients profit from assertiveness training to supplement their group counseling.

As Dreikurs indicated, each must learn to behave more effectively himself, and when he can decide precisely how he would like to change, share these goals with his significant others, request their assistance in learning these desired new behaviors, enlist their help in deciding what is reinforcing, and agree upon appropriate reinforcement of successes. To the degree that the committed one learns desired new behaviors and models them effectively (or in a religious sense witnesses for his community of believers), he will encourage his partner to learn new behaviors. Incidentally, Lerner (1964) discovered that both normal youth and disturbed youth experienced conflict within their families, but that a statistically significantly greater number of normal youth came from families in which conflict was faced and resolved, whereas a significantly greater number of disturbed youth came from families in which conflict was ignored or denied.

## Summary

Today most adults accept marriage as the best way for them to develop continuing, quality companionship, including sexual satisfaction. Nevertheless, some continue to question the appropriateness of traditional marriage and family for them: (1) First there are those who are genuinely searching for a better method than the nuclear family; (2) Then there are those who are unable to make the essential commitments for a successful marriage; and (3) finally there are those who are attracted to an alternate life style out of deference to others whom they admire.

Deciding between marriage and its various alternatives is a crucial decision that each person must develop the courage and skills to make and implement for himself. Otherwise he will not be able to make essential requests of his living mate(s), to participate meaningfully in developing adequate contractual agreements, and to make essential commitments to insure success in whatever arrangement he chooses.

Today there is growing need for marriage counseling. Unfortunately, many who provide this service are not adequately prepared to provide quality services and to use modern techniques. Increasingly the best prepared counselors treat couples in groups.

This chapter emphasizes the advantages of the triad model in which husband and wife are treated together in a group in which each discusses his own worries and unfilled needs, defines specific behavioral goals, and enlists his (her) spouse's assistance in learning and reinforcing desired new behaviors, and when his (her) spouse is functioning as a client he (she) becomes the counselor's special helper for his (her) spouse. What this method does is teach the two to pair up to help the third rather than gang up on him to hurt him.

The final section of the chapter is devoted to a method used to help couples recognize sources of conflict early, to marshall their resources, and to learn to cope with conflict. Best adjusted youth grow up in families in which parents have developed the courage and skill to cope with conflict.

## Discussion Questions

1. What would you do if the circumstances suggested that the counselor arrange for a family counseling session just prior to the marriage counseling session as is recommended in the chapter and either husband or wife refused to participate in the family session?

2. Some counselors for families have observed that individuals play very different roles outside the family than within it. How may you discover these differences and use the data in the therapeutic process in family counseling? In marriage counseling?

3. With what unique ethical problems may a counselor be confronted in doing marriage counseling? In doing family counseling?

4. With what pitfalls is an individual confronted in trying to decide between marriage and its various alternatives? What may a counselor do to maximize the chances that a client makes the best choice for himself?

5. What are the advantages and disadvantages of Guerney's (1964) training couples in small groups to conduct play therapy sessions at home for their own children?

6. What are the primary advantages and disadvantages of treating both husband and wife in the same group?

7. What may a counselor do to increase the attractiveness of a marriage counseling group or a family counseling group?

8. After thirty-one years of marriage that have been plagued with serious health problems and different life styles, the wife decides that she would like a divorce, but agrees to come to marriage counseling. What could you do to facilitate therapeutic talk? With what problem do you think each may be faced in becoming good clients in a marriage counseling group?

# References

Ackerman, N. W. *Family therapy in transition.* Boston: Little, Brown, 1970.

Bach, G. R., & Deutch, R. M. *Pairing: How to achieve genuine intimacy.* New York: Avon, 1970.

Calvo, G. *Marriage encounter.* St. Paul: National Marriage Encounter, 1973.

Davids, L. North American marriage: 1990. *The Futurist,* 1971, *5,* 190–194.

Deutsch, D. Group therapy with married couples: The birth pangs of a new life style in marriage. *Individual Psychologist,* 1967, *4,* 56–62.

Dreikurs, R. Family counseling: A demonstration. *Journal of Individual Psychology,* 1972a, *28,* 207–222.

Dreikurs, R. Technology of conflict resolution. *Journal of Individual Psychology,* 1972b, *28,* 203–206.

Gallagher, C. *The marriage encounter: As I have loved you.* New York: Doubleday, 1975.

Guerney, B. Filial therapy: Description and rationale. *Journal of Consulting Psychology,* 1964, *28,* 304–310.

Gurman, A. S. Group marital therapy: Clinical and empirical implications for outcome research. *International Journal of Group Psychotherapy,* 1971, *21,* 174–189.

Hopkins, P. E., & Hopkins, L. Marriage enrichment and the churches. *Your Church,* 1976, *22,* 49–52.

Jones, W. L. The villain and victim: Group therapy for married couples. *American Journal of Psychiatry,* 1967, *124,* 107–110.

Koch, J., & Koch, L. A consumer's guide to therapy for couples. *Psychology Today,* 1976a, *9,* 33–40.

Koch, J., & Koch, L. *The marriage savers.* New York: Coward, McCann, 1976b.

Landis, P. H. *Making the most of marriage.* Englewood Cliffs, N.J.: Prentice-Hall, 1975.

Lebedun, M. Measuring movement in marital counseling. *Social Casework,* 1970, *5,* 35–43.

Lerner, P. M. *Resolution of intrafamilial conflict in families of schizophrenic patients.* Unpublished doctoral dissertation, University of Illinois, 1964.

Liberman, R. Behavioral approaches to family and couple therapy. *American Journal of Orthopsychiatry,* 1970, *40,* 106–118.

Masters, W. H., & Johnson, V. E. *Human sexual inadequacy.* Boston: Little, Brown, 1970.

Masters, W. H., & Johnson, V. E. *The pleasure bond: A new look at sexuality and commitment.* Boston: Little, Brown, 1975.

Mittelman, B. Complementary neurotic reactions in intimate relationships. *Psychoanalytic Quarterly,* 1944, *13,* 479–485.

Mowrer, O. H. Group psychotherapy. Speech at Indiana State University, 1973. *National Observer,* October 30, 1971, p. 1.

Olson, D. H. Marital and family therapy: Integrative review and critique. *Journal of Marriage and Family,* 1970, *32,* 501–538.

O'Neill, N., & O'Neill, G. *Shifting gears: Finding security in a changing world.* Philadelphia: M. Evans and Co., 1974.

Papanek, H. Group therapy with married couples. In H. I. Kaplan & B. J. Sadoch, *Psychotherapy*. Baltimore: Williams and Wilkins, 1971.

Pew, M. L., & Pew, W. L. Adlerian marriage counseling. *Journal of Individual Psychology*, 1972, *28*, 192–202.

*React: A marriage survival kit*. Family Concerns, Inc. (Box 14249, Omaha, Nebraska 68114), 1973.

Rogers, C. R. *Becoming partners: Marriage and its alternatives*. New York: Delacorte Press, 1972.

Zorbaugh, H. *Gold Coast and the slum*. Chicago: University of Chicago Press, 1929.

# 14

# Appraisal of Group Counseling

Recently there has been a marked increase in the use of group procedures. With this increase has come the development of interesting and promising innovations by competent leaders of groups on one hand and poorly conceived procedures developed by unqualified leaders on the other. Both types have often failed to describe adequately the treatment process, to indicate precisely what is expected of participants, and to communicate who is most apt to be helped by the treatment under what conditions. Leaders must provide prospective participants with this type of information for them to decide whether they can be helped in groups and by what treatment. Leaders also must screen participants and help them define reasonable, achievable goals.

Most of the critics have focussed their attack on encounter, sensitivity, and marathon groups rather than on counseling or psychotherapy groups. Hartley, Roback, and Abramowitz (1976) report that evaluations vary from Rogers' (1968) "most significant social intervention of this century" to Maliver's (1973) "a multi-million dollar business—a callous exploitation and a sham of group therapy."

The charismatic pull of encounter groups is attracting an increasing number of persons who are ill-suited for interpersonal confrontation and for whom thorough treatment may be appropriate. This situation has intensified mental health professionals' expression of concern about possible psychonoxious effects of encounter groups. Such diverse organizations as citizen groups, the U.S.

Congress, and national organizations of psychiatrists and psychologists have also voiced alarm at the growing faith vested in spokesmen for the encounter cult. In contrast, many encounter leaders deny the existence of undue risk to participants. (Hartley, Roback, & Abramowitz, 1976, p. 247)

> Anyone following the history of modern psychotherapy cannot fail to be impressed by the depth and vehemence of feeling attending introduction of new theories and techniques, the acrimony of the ensuing debates, and the powerful emotional reactions generated in professional and lay circles alike. (Strupp, 1973a, p. 115)

Even though they are not as apt to feel the sting of public criticism, counselors and therapists must be able to define their treatment more clearly than they have previously (and tell precisely how it differs from other similar techniques), to describe their expectations of participants, and to characterize the type of clients for whom the treatment is most appropriate (and for whom it may be hurtful). The popularity of the group movement is attracting clients for group counseling and group psychotherapy, but it is also encouraging more clients to question their prospective counselor (or therapist) concerning its worth. Recent emphasis on accountability and increasing competition for tax dollars has caused administrators in public institutions to call for improved evaluation of services.

For school counselors Kefauver and Hand (1941) stress the importance of counselors' soliciting periodic feedback from students, staff, and parents. Similarly, Dressel (1961) concludes that decision makers, whether they are conscious of it or not, judge the worth of a product, an idea, or a service. When the professional fails to define specific criteria and to collect essential data for evaluating his services, Dressel believes that he runs the risk of being evaluated unknowingly on the basis of prejudice, tradition, or rationalization rather than on the worth of the idea, the service, or the product.

Increasingly, counselors are learning to help their clients, at the beginning of counseling, to define specific goals in terms of observable or measurable changes in behavior, interpersonal skills, feelings, or attitudes. Even the counselor who does not believe that he has the skills and/or time to do systematic research, but does help his clients develop precise goals, can assess outcomes of counseling and solicit systematic appraisal from clients and their significant others. When, for example, a kindergarten girl told her counselor that she was worried about her three-year-old brother becoming her mother's favorite child, the counselor helped her define these counseling goals (and the criteria for assessing each is listed parenthetically): (1) to tell her mother she was afraid that, when she was not home all day, her mother would learn to like her brother more (to report back to her counselor on whether or not she told her mother and what happened); (2) to tell her mother how much she loves her (to report back when she did it and what happened); and (3) to request time alone with her mother every day to do something special (to report back how many days each week she succeeded). The counselor's notes showed these three items: (1) her mother listened to her and hugged her; (2) the mother began at once to spend some time at least once every day alone with the girl; and (3) the mother called the counselor to tell especially what item #2 meant to her. Even such specific case notes can be used very effectively to convince administrators, clients' significant others, and colleagues that specific treatments do help clients.

Important as the type of case notes described above are, they are not sufficient. The counselor must determine how efficacious his treatment methods are for whom under what circumstances. In order to meet the ethical standards of his profession, he must ask himself in selecting each client for a group: Is this a client whom I can help best by this method? During the course of treatment he must continue to ask himself this same question. After terminating treatment, he must ask: Who was helped most by this technique? Who failed to profit from it? Who was hurt by it? What information about these clients might have enabled me to predict who would have been hurt or helped? In what specific ways did my behavior contribute to or interfere with each client's growth?

In other words, an investigator must ask more precise questions than "Was group counseling effective?" or "Did group counseling really change clients' attitudes and behaviors?" Instead, an investigator must ask: For whom was this particular group counseling effective, and with what clients and under what kinds of circumstances? Were some counselors more effective than others? How did the successful counselors differ from the others? What professional preparation and experience are required to provide it? Who profited most from it? Who may be hurt by it? How was readiness for counseling assessed? To what extent were clients committed to change their behavior and to help fellow clients change their behavior? To what extent were they convinced that they could be helped, and that their fellow clients could be helped? To what degree did each participate in defining his treatment goals and accept these goals as reasonable for him? To what extent did the actual treatment focus upon each one's own idiosyncratic goals? To what degree was the counselor able to develop a therapeutic relationship with each client, to help each to relate therapeutically to the others, and to help each accept responsibility for developing and maintaining a therapeutic climate within the group? Were adequate criteria developed to appraise each client's growth in terms of his goals? Were adequate appraisal techniques used to appraise each client's growth in terms of relevant criteria for him? Was the research design adequate to fulfill the researcher's purposes? Did he use appropriate statistical methods?

Obviously it is difficult for researchers to meet all of these conditions in appraising outcomes of group counseling. When one considers the practitioner's commitment to service, the limited time and financial support available to him for research, and the difficulties involved in appraising counseling outcomes, one can readily understand why some practitioners avoid systematic appraisal, and why some who attempt it overlook avoidable errors in their research design. Though no study even approaches perfection, counselors must improve their techniques for appraisal of clients' growth, and design much better studies for formal appraisal of group counseling, conducted for specific clients under specified conditions by adequately described treatment methods and counselors. Within its limited space, this chapter merely tries to identify the most serious problems involved and offers some practical suggestions for solving them. Relevant outcome studies also are reviewed briefly. For readers who work in a school setting and would be interested in soliciting systematic feedback on counseling services from teachers, parents, and students, Ohlsen (1974) describes a cooperative self-study procedure.

## Definition of the Problem

Stating a research problem clearly and developing a rationale for it is a slow and painstaking process. As the investigator develops his ideas he may find that it is helpful to begin with a question for which he would like an answer. Usually it helps to record the question and keep notes on all the various approaches that he could use to answer it. Although he can obtain valuable feedback from friends and colleagues on even such tentative ideas, usually he will obtain more useful feedback when he has developed a four- or five-page typewritten mini-proposal in which he has answered these questions: What is the question (or the research problem)? Why is it worth investigating? How will I do it? From whom will I collect what data? When? How? If, indeed, the idea proves to be a good one eventually the investigator must also be able to incorporate into a proposal the answers to questions such as: What is the central problem? Does the proposal focus primary attention on the central problem? Has the study been delimited sufficiently to answer the central research question? Are hypotheses stated clearly? Can adequate data be collected to test essential hypotheses? Will the order in which the data are collected influence subjects' responses? What pilot studies are required to clarify the treatment, to appraise the competencies and the commitments of the treaters with reference to each treatment, and to solicit feedback from similar subjects with reference to each of the selected criterion measures? Is it perfectly clear which are the *dependent* and which are the *independent* variables? How will the data be analyzed? Are the hypotheses stated in clear, testable language? Do the hypotheses indicate clearly a logical statistical test? Does the investigator defend adequately his use of these statistical analyses with these data? Does the investigator seem to be prepared to explain either significant or nonsignificant findings? What are practical implications of each significant (or failure to obtain significant) finding? How may each be accounted for? Though clearly stated answers to these questions are important in obtaining support from a funding agency, such answers are even more important for the investigator; they insure that the investigator understands precisely what he has contracted to do prior to beginning the research.

Goldstein (1959) contends that much of the laxity with respect to error and hasty decisions for which the research on counseling and psychotherapy has been criticized applies to all applied psychology. Rather than ask, "Have I done adequate pilot studies and solicited adequate feedback to control every possible error?" Goldstein contends that too many applied psychologists ask, "How much sloppiness can I permit and still have something?":

> It must be granted that scientific discoveries can be made, on occasion, in spite of abundant error. . . . Nonetheless, error must be properly viewed as a matter for discomfort and admitted only when there is no alternative. (Goldstein, p. 275)

> . . . We should do a compulsive job of planning our research: how the data will be collected, how they will be analyzed, and even how they will be interpreted. Lacking careful planning, we may be tempted to improvise as we go along. This can lead us far afield from our original hypotheses. Pilot studies are strongly recommended. (Pepinsky, 1953, p. 293)

Fortunately some counselors are beginning to ask important questions and to formulate carefully stated hypotheses to evaluate the impact of clearly defined treatments provided by competent professionals on clearly described subjects in specific settings. Others could do significant research with the help of competent research consultants who are committed and able to help the potential researcher define his research problem. However, even some well-funded agencies have failed to produce good research because they employed uninvolved research specialists as consultants who did not listen to the researcher and help him develop his own research (and either they forced him to do a study that appealed to them or they left him feeling even more unsure of his research competencies). In order for research to have meaning for the practitioners in an agency and for them to try genuinely to apply it, they must participate in the formulating of the research, help carry it out, and feel safe in asking questions about the results.

Finally, in defining a research problem there is no substitute for a thorough review of the related research. It can help the investigator clarify and sharpen the statement of his problem, identify and separate interacting variables, clarify the unique features of the treatment process, discover problems which may occur in appraising and/or supervising the competencies of the treaters, discover variables to be controlled and/or observed carefully during treatment, clarify hypotheses to be tested, discover clever methods for evaluating change in subjects, and identify new, improved statistical methods for analyzing his data. Every beginning graduate student should know this, but even many experienced researchers fail to do it carefully, or they have it done by inexperienced assistants who merely identify results and miss subtle design errors which could be detected by sophisticated researchers and corrected rather than repeated again.

## The Treatment Process

In order to generalize another's findings and apply them to his own situation or to replicate a study, a counselor must know the answers to the following questions: "What are the primary features of the treatment? Precisely how does it differ from other similar treatments? What unique professional skills must the treater possess in order to provide it? What did the investigator do to insure mastery and use of these skills during the course of the experiment? Who were the clients? Was there anything special or unique about them? Was there anything about the setting in which the treatment was administered that should be considered in applying it in other settings?" Unfortunately, researchers often fail to provide the answers to such questions. Furthermore, they often use the term "group counseling" to label very different treatments. For example, the titles assigned to the following three studies suggest that they are similar treatments, but they were not:

1. Teacher-counselors who had very little specialized preparation for counseling gave educational and vocational information to students in guidance classes of approximately thirty students each.
2. Well-qualified counselors interpreted tests to students in small groups— usually less than ten in each group. The counselors also encouraged each group to discuss the relevance of the information for vocational planning. Nothing in the paper suggested that students were encouraged to discuss their feelings concerning what they learned about themselves.
3. A well-qualified counselor conducted intensive group counseling for one semester within a highly favorable setting for carefully selected clients. The treatment process and the size of groups were clearly defined.

Obviously, there are many reasons why what was found in any one of the above three cannot be generalized to apply to situations similar to the other two. If, however, the relevant elements in each study had been described in sufficient detail, a reader could determine for himself whether any of the findings could be applied to his situation.

For purposes of discussion in this chapter it is assumed that the counselor has mastered at least the facilitative behaviors described in Chapter 2, that he understands the unique features of group counseling described in Chapter 1, and that he can provide the crucial elements in the helping process reviewed in Chapter 1. When, therefore, the writer reviews outcome studies he asks himself whether they could possibly apply to these kinds of counselors doing group counseling.

## The Treater

Rarely have researchers adequately described the counselors (and psycho-therapists) used in their studies. For example, in one study, well designed in most of its aspects, the researcher compared the efficacy of the same counselors providing individual and group counseling for a specific type of client, but failed to describe the professional competencies of the counselors. Correspondence with the researcher revealed that the counselors were trainees who had had formal course work and supervised practicum in in-dividual counseling, but neither course work nor practicum in group counseling. In other words, their minimal professional preparation and inadequate professional experience makes them questionable performers in individual counseling and completely unprepared to provide group counseling. Neither those treated in individual and group counseling im-proved significantly more than the control subjects. Had those treated individually improved significantly more than those treated in groups, read-ers would have assumed that individual counseling was superior for this type of client when treated within that particular setting. Obviously, such a con-clusion would have been unwarranted.

The counselor is an important variable in the therapeutic process. When he presents himself for professional preparation he must be screened care-fully and humanely. His preparation must help him to develop the essential competencies to enable him to facilitate behavior change and encourage him to continue his professional growth on the job (Chapter 2). When he does not develop these essential helping skills during professional preparation and accept the responsibility for his continuing growth, his profession must be prepared to discipline him. Clients can be hurt as well as helped by treatment (Bergin & Garfield, 1971; Carkhuff & Berenson, 1967; Truax & Carkhuff, 1964). Those who prepare counselors and therapists must select carefully for training and develop counselors and therapists of types 4 and 5 defined below by Carkhuff and Berenson's five point scale:

1. Describes the severely disturbed client who is essentially immune to human encounter, and the retarding therapist.
2. Describes the distressed client who distorts reality but lives in the world of reality, and the moderately retarding therapist.
3. Describes the situationally distressed client who functions moderately well, and the minimally facilitative therapist.
4. Describes the more potent client who relates effectively—has a positive influence on others—and the therapist who facilitates change in those he tries to help.

5. Describes the person who is involved in a lifelong search for self-actualization for others as well as himself.

Using this scale, Carkhuff and Berenson reported that their typical client was slightly lower than 2, with a range between 1 and 3, and that counselors and therapists varied in their facilitating functioning from 1 to 4, with a mean of approximately 2.

> At the highest levels, these facilitators communicate an accurately empathic understanding of the deeper as well as the superficial feelings of the second person(s); they are freely and deeply themselves in a nonexploitative relationship; they communicate a very deep respect for the second person's worth as a person and his rights as a free individual; and they are helpful in guiding the discussion to personally relevant feelings and experiences in specific and concrete terms. (p. 45)
>
> . . . The average discrepancy, then, between the counselor and the client would appear to be minimal, with the main difference being the higher levels of functioning to which counselors may range. (p. 52)
>
> . . . Patients who received low conditions throughout psychotherapy tend to show clear negative change in personality functioning. This seems to say, that with schizophrenia at least, low conditions lead to a deterioration in personality functioning. This latter finding has a special significance since, if comparisons had been made only between combined therapy group and the control group, no differences in outcomes would have appeared. That is, while high conditions lead to positive change, low conditions lead to negative change so that the overall net result of "good" and "bad" therapy combined is comparable to that seen in matched control groups. (Traux & Carkhuff, 1964, p. 862)[1]

In other words, there are far too many treaters who do not possess the professional competencies to help their clients and patients. Those who provide professional preparation for counselors and psychotherapists must appraise their programs with care and develop new improved programs—especially improved in-service programs for practitioners. They must search for the answers to questions such as (Chapter 2): How may we improve our screening and selective admission-retention techniques in order to identify the good prospects early and encourage them (and identify the poor prospects and help them define new more appropriate goals)? On the basis of research findings concerning which techniques are most effective with whom (and which are rarely effective in bringing about behavior change), what should be taught to prospective treaters? What crucial questions must be answered on treatment techniques? How may students in training, recent graduates, and employers of recent graduates be involved in appraising

---

[1] There are also many other instances too in which researchers failed to obtain significant differences in means between groups and concluded that chance may account for their findings when in reality they obtained significant changes in standard deviations, which in turn usually means that some clients are hurt while others are helped by the treatment.

preparation programs, including early human relations skill training, personal therapy, and practicum and intern experiences as well as didactic preparation? What may be done to encourage the staff to do cooperative field studies with practitioners and trainees in field placements? What can be done to encourage and to reinforce continued growth in the field as practitioners?

A treatment can be fairly appraised only when it is provided by competent treaters, and various treatments can be compared only when treaters accept each method's worth, are committed to provide the treatment under specified conditions, and feel confident to provide each effectively. It is to be hoped that increasing research will be done in the field with experienced, competent counselors and therapists serving as treaters.

## Goals for Group Counseling

Failure to define specific goals for counseling in precise measurable or observable terms for each client is one of the most serious weaknesses of the research designed to appraise counseling outcomes. Such goals are necessary in order to define precise criteria for selecting or developing instruments and observational techniques to appraise changes in clients. Without such behavioral goals, researchers are tempted to use whatever evaluation techniques are readily available, and consequently, often use vague, general measures that cannot be defended as relevant, reliable, or valid. Specific goals also help clients understand and recognize the specific ways in which they change during and subsequent to counseling and such discoveries tend to reinforce further growth.

Hill (1975) contends that all too frequently when specific behavioral goals are not defined at the beginning of treatment, neither clients nor counselor has any real idea upon termination whether or not the treatment was helpful. She believes that clearly stated goals enable them to decide which problem areas require attention, to develop strategies for change, and to make necessary commitments for change.

Seligman (1975) believes that the helplessness of the depressed is learned behavior. He also believes that depressed patients can be helped to develop goals and be guided through specific situations in which they learn to exert progressively greater control over their environment. As the depressed patients discover that they can have some impact on the forces in their lives, their depression dissipates. Assertiveness training also helps such clients (Chapter 10).

Broad knowledge of one's clients that can be gleaned from observation of them, listening to them, and review of the literature about clients in that state of life helps the counselor understand his clients and detect the therapeutic material upon which he can help them define behavioral goals. More and more counselors are accepting their clients' reasons for seeking counseling, helping them translate these reasons into specific goals stated in terms of specific behaviors, attitudes, or skills, and helping them develop new goals during treatment. When such goals are developed cooperatively they encourage client growth. Obviously, doing it is much more difficult than it is to discuss, but effective counselors are learning to do it.

From the point of view of the funding agency as well as the researcher, specific treatment goals are important too. Meade's (1972) appraisal of Ford Foundation projects revealed that the most successful school-improvement projects were those for which specific goals were carefully defined prior to funding; another crucial factor was good, continuing leadership by a committed project director.

## Criteria

After specific goals have been defined for each client in behavioral terms, the counselor helps each decide how he will recognize when he has achieved them. Basically these must be used to select or develop criterion measures to appraise changes in clients.

When one examines the literature by practitioners one is impressed with their commitment to help their clients with their distressing problems, with their concern about helping clients achieve their own goals, and with their practical suggestions for helping clients, but when it comes to appraising outcomes of counseling they tend to accept very general, vague criteria for appraising clients' growth: for example, improved interpersonal functioning or increased self-acceptance. Frequently failure to obtain significant growth can be traced to use of vague, general criteria. Edwards and Cronbach (1952) argue against such global criteria as follows:

> Some investigators have tried to keep broad measures and yet stay within conventional statistics by pouring their data into a single overall index of adjustment. This is not recommended, for such an index blurs together the strengths and weaknesses of each method and provides no guide for improvement. Experience in predicting teacher success is a case in point. Hundreds of studies produced negligible correlations or contradictory results so long as a global rating of success was the criterion. As soon as investigators went to a more specific criterion which dealt with aspects of the teacher's performance, they began to get appreciable validities, where a mixed criterion lumping intellectual, emotional, and administrative contributions is not predictable. In therapy an overall index is not a good criterion if progress of a patient away from anxiety is concealed by negative scores assigned for an increase in expressed aggression. (p. 56)

As the counselor examines the behavioral goals for each client he must not only ask, "What data must I collect to assess each client's growth?," but "Is there a likelihood that some clients may be hurt as well as helped by this technique?" and "Are individuals apt to move in opposite directions on the same criterion measures, and if, therefore, we combine the data for these clients, cancel out each others' growth?" When the first of the latter two can occur the counselor must try to identify the two types of clients, observe them during treatment, and analyze their responses to criterion measures separately.

For the second of the latter two questions in which the researcher is suspicious that clients' movement on criterion measures may be in opposite directions and thus cancel out each others' growth, signed numbers must be used to prevent cancelling out of opposite change. If, for example, a counselor treats in the same counseling groups underconforming and overconforming clients (and increase in test scores indicates increased conformity), then signed numbers could be used to convert the negative change in overconforming clients' scores into positive change and thereby prevent their negative (but appropriate) movement from cancelling out the positive movement of underconformers.

Inasmuch as the worth of counseling must be appraised in terms of its impact upon individual clients, perhaps the counselor should help clients define significant growth for each prior to counseling. When, for example, George, a very bright tenth grader, asked to join a counseling group to improve his grades and his relationships with teachers and parents, the counselor helped him decide how he (and his parents and teachers) would know when he had achieved these relationship goals. With reference to grades he had a GPA of 3.4 the previous semester. He decided that he could raise it to a 4.5 (on a 5-point scale). After eight or nine weeks George decided he should revise his GPA goal to 4.0 to enable him to spend more time on a physics project and to do some special reading in psychology and literature. When two of his fellow clients raised a question about a similar change in GPA goal George argued against it on the grounds that they required scholarships in order to finance their college education. Had the counselor used change in mean GPAs as a primary criterion measure rather than achieving the client's goal, the change would have posed a threat to his chances for success.

When prior to treatment a counselor helps each client decide what would be judged to be significantly changed behavior with reference to each of his idiosyncratic goals, then all the researcher must do is compare the number of instances in which experimental subjects achieved their goals with the number of instances in which control subjects (or clients treated by other methods) achieved theirs. Although there is no way to prove that these achievements are of equal worth, this approach does take account of individual clients' needs, makes them responsible for helping to decide what would be significantly improved behavior, involves them in both the treatment and the appraisal process, and conveys respect for their personal judgments.

# Criterion Measures

Even after researchers have helped clients to define goals and criteria for appraising change in behavioral terms, they must select or develop measures that detect and appraise the exact nature of clients' growth or negative movement. When the researcher fails to follow these steps he may be tempted to make some of the errors discussed earlier: (1) to use whatever appraisal measures are readily available, (2) to collect the same data on all subjects even when they are pertinent *for only part of the research subjects* (for example, use improvement in GPA for all subjects when it can be defended as relevant for half or less), (3) to overlook use of signed numbers for subjects for whom the researcher can predict movement in opposite directions, and (4) to use vague, global measures to assess precise behavioral change. In selecting criterion measures researchers also frequently make two other common errors: (1) they select criterion measures which are insensitive to change and (2) they use techniques which they cannot defend as either reliable or valid.

Bereiter (1962) contends that present standards for test construction tend to produce stable measures of status and mastery of concepts, skills, and knowledge. However, such measures tend to be insensitive to the differential changes that guidance and counseling services tend to produce. If, therefore, such changes are to be detected and appraised criterion measures must focus on change rather than on status.

Without reasonably good reliability, an instrument cannot be valid. Although more researchers could establish reliability on their criterion measures more readily than validity, far too many do not bother to do so. Jensen, Coles, and Nestor (1955) make a case for four methods for guidance workers who are concerned with demonstrating the reliability of their instruments: internal consistency, stability, equivalence, and agreement between two or more raters. With increasing emphasis upon observation of behavior outside the treatment setting by significant others and judges, the last of the four takes on increased importance. Although computations of correlation coefficients among raters' scores is still most often used, the writer's experience suggests that percentage of agreement between pairs of judges' ratings on each decision is a more severe test of reliability. Moreover, Forgy and Black (1954) concluded that agreement between experts' responses to criterion measures was sufficient evidence of content validity. In addition Jensen, Coles, and Nestor also argue for the use of construct validity for such instruments.

Leary (1957) provides a system which the writer will use for discussing the common types of instruments used to appraise counseling outcomes. His five levels of personality are determined by the sources of data: (1) concerns the person's impact on others—his public communication level; (2) his conscious description (self-report) level; (3) the person's autistic, projective-fantasy, preconscious-symbolization level; (4) unexpressed unconscious level; and (5) ego level. The last two have no practical value for researchers at this time.

Level 1 appraisals are usually labelled as external measures of change. Typically sociometric tests, behavior inventories, Q-sorts, and check lists are used to obtain data from significant others such as classmates, friends, teachers, siblings, parents, and employers (and occasionally trained judges). In marriage counseling, for example, the best data concerning clients' growth seems to be provided in response to Q-sorts or behavior inventories which are developed out of the goal and criterion statements for the members of each group and responded to by fellow clients and spouses. Self-reports generally agree less with expert judges than either of the two named above, and counselors generally overestimate clients' growth. Except for Hilkey's (1975) findings in which inmates in a federal prison rated their own growth as greater than their counselors' rated growth, counselors (and therapists) tend to exaggerate clients' growth. Sethna and Harrington's (1971) therapists' ratings of their patients' improvement also was less than what the patients reported for themselves.

> Therapeutic progress of 41 clients was assessed by the clients, their therapists, and two independent judges. The clients' evaluations were unrelated to their therapists' evaluations, but they were highly related to the evaluations made by independent judges. Further analyses suggested that the disagreements between clients and therapists stemmed from the therapists' inaccuracy in perceiving clients' problems and the therapists' tendency to overestimate the progress of therapy relative to clients and independent judges. (Horenstein, Houston, & Holmes, 1973, p. 149)

With self-referred clients Hornstein, Houston, and Holmes question whether the counselor's or therapist's opinions should be used to evaluate outcomes. They believe that clients know better than they can articulate why they came for assistance and whether they were helped. Their findings on the therapists' inaccurate perceptions of clients' problems certainly helps make the case for therapists using reflections to check out their perceptions of clients' problems and to involve clients in helping them develop precise behavioral goals early in the treatment process (Chapter 1).

> The fulcrum for therapeutic change is the *affective relationship* which becomes the vehicle for therapeutic change. Through the medium of that relationship the therapist exercises his power as a better socializer and change agent. Thus, therapy seeks to effect a better (more adaptive) balance between the need for self-expression, self-fulfillment, and freedom, on the one hand, and the demands for self-control, socialization, conformity, and self-discipline, on the other. (Strupp, 1973b, p. 117)

> The criteria of improvement most helpful for our purposes and used in this study were those evolved by Hartley and Rosenbaum (1963). They were

derived from the responses of 81 psychotherapists to questionnaires in which they had to indicate their criteria for judging improvement. These criteria were (a) improved interpersonal functioning in and out of therapy group, (b) ability to cope with and adapt to a variety of experiences, (c) self-acceptance, self-confidence, self-reliance, (d) insight, self-awareness, and (e) symptom reduction. (Sethna & Harrington, 1971, p. 652)

Even though they run the risk of biasing their reports from significant others Broedel, Ohlsen, Proff, and Southard (1960) strongly encourage clients to share their treatment goals with relevant significant others and to solicit from them systematic reinforcement of desired new behaviors. Otherwise these very persons either may not notice the desired new behaviors when they are exhibited (and the hard-working client will feel let down and disappointed) or, worse still, they will unknowingly reinforce the undesirable behaviors which the clients are trying to extinguish or replace.

Rickard (1965) also endorses the involvement of significant others in the treatment and evaluation of its outcomes. In order to minimize biased reporting he trains his judges to solicit appraisal information on the basis of precise criteria:

> It seems feasible to select a board of judges, not necessarily psychologists, who might interview important figures in the patient's life, examine case material, and interview the patient more precisely to identify stable, sensitive, relevant behavior to be changed. After psychotherapy or the experimental treatment, the same judges without knowledge of which patients were experimental Ss, would again examine sources of evidence which would bear upon whether the behavior had, in effect, changed. Rickard and Brown (1960) have demonstrated that judges may show a high degree of agreement as to whether or not a specific behavior changes as therapy progresses. An additional function of the judges would be to consider the stability of the behavioral change over time. (p. 65)

Horenstein, Houston, and Holmes obtained interjudge reliabilities of clients' behavior: .92 and .97 pretherapy and .97 and .98 posttherapy.

Meehl (1959) recommends that the type of data obtained from others described by Rickard *be recorded* on a standard form for more effective statistical treatment. He prefers to have observers and interviewers use the Q-sort for recording their findings. The writer prefers to use a behavior inventory whose items consist of precise, behavioral descriptions that were developed out of the goal statements for the members of the counseling group. Observers (or interviewers) are required to indicate for each item the degree to which the behavioral description describes each subject (and without knowing which subjects were treated and which were the controls). Where a criterion involves an event that can be observed and counted, such as the number of times each week a student completes his homework on time, it should be reported as a specific number so that it can be compared with the relevant behavior during the baseline period.

Even though Broedel, Ohlsen, Proff, and Southard's clients complained that significant others often failed to notice and reinforce desired new behaviors, they found that parents and trained observers did detect and report significant changes on a behavior inventory. Very likely even better results would have been obtained had the items in the inventory been designed especially for these clients and developed out of their behavioral goals. Unless significant others can detect and describe the desired new behaviors, they will tend to discount the worth of counseling, and certainly will not be able to reinforce the desired changes.

Most investigators who attempt to evaluate the worth of counseling solicit appraisals from clients' significant others and trained observers (Level 1) and from self-reports (Level 2). In addition to behavior inventories, Q-sorts, semantic differentials, sociometric tests, and checklists which are used for both Levels 1 and 2, clients are administered personality tests and asked to write autobiographies. In general, Berg (1952) noted that the major virtue of all rating scales is their convenience, accessibility, and capacity to provide quickly a comprehensive estimate of adjustment not readily available by other methods. Unfortunately such devices are often thrown together carelessly and little effort is made to establish reliability and validity. Such carelessness must not be tolerated.

Earlier, the limited worth of vague, general measures such as personality tests was discussed. Ohlsen (1974) concludes that there is no solid supporting evidence for the use of personality inventories to help clients identify specific problems or to accept them, and to define goals for counseling and to help their counselors appraise the outcomes of counseling. Although Pattison (1965) also criticizes all global measures of change in clients, he concludes that personality tests are especially disappointing for appraising outcomes of counseling and psychotherapy. Paul (1967) points out that subjective measures are notorious for their lack of reliability and validity and that personality inventories in particular hold little promise for appraising the outcomes of counseling and psychotherapy.

When a counselor has established a good relationship with clients, they are tempted to report what they think their counselor wants to happen. On the other hand, when clients do not volunteer for counseling and never fully accept its worth or develop a good relationship with their counselor, some may deny even the precise, behavioral changes that a trained observer detects. Nevertheless, when most clients are given the opportunity to describe their own growth in terms of specific changes in behavior their reports tend to agree with independent judges (Horenstein, Houston, & Holmes, 1973). In any case, counselors cannot afford to ignore clients' evaluations of their services. Their evaluation determines to some extent the support for these services. Furthermore, even young clients can give valuable feedback that can be obtained only from them.

Limited data for appraising outcomes of counseling are obtained from

Level 3 data (autistic, projective fantasy, or preconscious views). Leary (1957) used primarily TAT and Rorschach to obtain these data. Just as content analysis can be used to determine whether or not clients actually discuss the topics related to their goals and to identify from their reports on successes and failures how they were helped, it also can be used to obtain answers to specific questions from projective tests (which clinicians can use to complete behavior inventories and Q-sorts). If, for example, a client's goal pertained to increased acceptance of self, one would expect him to discuss the identification figure with considerably more positive affect during posttesting on the TAT than he did during pretesting. Moreover, when Wigell and Ohlsen (1962) did a content analysis of the first several sessions for groups of underachieving adolescents they discovered that these clients discussed authority figures with significantly more frequent use of negative affect than either ambivalent or positive affect, and during the last several sessions discussed this same topic with significantly less negative affect. When the counselor is able to schedule several follow-up sessions (usually 60 to 90 days following termination), content analysis can be used to determine whether gains identified in posttesting were maintained. During the follow-up sessions clients are encouraged to discuss the problems for which they sought help. They also may be encouraged to discuss: what they accomplished or how they were hurt; with whom they learned to do what; what is left to be done; whose help is required to learn these unlearned new behaviors; and how that assistance may be requested.

## Research Subjects

When a researcher has defined the prescribed treatment for whom, under what conditions, and by whom, he should have his basic criteria for selecting his research subjects. Nevertheless, he also must have the answers to these questions: What is my population? How may I best sample it in order to be able to generalize? In order to use the desired statistical analysis, what must I consider in selecting my sample? How large a sample will I require in order to appraise adequately this technique, under these circumstances, and especially with these evaluation techniques? What control subjects do I require? What are my obligations to controls? What can I do to encourage (and insure) that controls not seek some other treatment while they are serving as controls? What must I do to insure that all data are obtained on all subjects (including follow up data)?

Although most researchers seem to accept the need for control subjects and use some technique for randomly assigning subjects into experimental and control groups, they often fail to determine whether by chance the groups differed prior to treatment. Moreover, they must monitor the behavior of control subjects to ensure that they do not seek treatment elsewhere while they are serving as control subjects. When researchers have made a convincing presentation and screened prospective clients carefully, they tend to accept treatment, and often seek it during the control period. Bergin (1963) concludes that one reason why experimental subjects have failed to improve significantly more than their controls is that controls had obtained treatment too. Consequently, researchers must investigate the daily life experiences of both control and experimental subjects in order to identify influential experiences other than counseling that could have influenced behavior change. For this reason the researcher also should explain to controls how chance determined which were treated first, convey his continuing interest in them, and tell precisely when their treatment will begin. Researchers also should seriously consider budgeting to pay all for posttreatment and follow-up testing; it markedly enhances cooperation.

With careful planning the control subjects can be treated later, and have their scores during treatment compared with their scores during the control period. This design ensures treatment for controls as well as experimental subjects (and thereby improves cooperation with institutions as well as with research subjects), increases the number of experimental subjects, and ensures that at least part of the experimental subjects are like control subjects. On the other hand, this method does not permit the investigator to obtain follow-up data on these subjects as control subjects. After they are tested at the beginning and end of the control period, they are given the prescribed treatment (and the posttesting for the control period also serves as pretesting for the treatment period). Whether the investigator uses subjects as their own controls or uses only other subjects as controls, some clients who have accepted the need for specific treatment must be forced to postpone treatment, and this tends to reduce their readiness for treatment.

Three methods are commonly used to select control subjects who are comparable to experimental subjects: (1) select subjects, test them, have them wait the length of the treatment period, and serve as their own controls (as suggested above for part of the experimental subjects); (2) match experimental and control subjects on the basis of relevant variables; and (3) statistical controls—for example, analysis of covariance. Prior to deciding which sampling as well as statistical analysis he will use, the researcher must determine which will enable him to test his hypotheses. If, for example, he decides to match experimental and control subjects, then certain statistical tests that require random sampling cannot be used. When he draws a large sample, however, he may be able to divide the experimental and control groups by use of random number techniques, and feel reasonably certain that they are similar. Nevertheless, he may wish to use appropriate statistical analyses to determine whether or not chance can account for observed differences in experimental and control subjects' scores prior to treatment.

Some scholars have developed long-term cooperative working relationships with school systems and community agencies for training centers. Such cooperative relationships have been especially effective in providing student teaching in public schools. The writer believes that similar cooperative continuing relationships could provide a pool of research subjects for the evaluation of counseling services. Although university researchers have usually taken the initiative for short-term projects, guidance directors should be encouraged to initiate such continuing working relationships. For individual projects, the guidance director must try to assess the researcher's acceptance by the cooperating school staff and his ability to state clearly what he expects to do, why it needs to be done, and how the results may be used to improve the particular service involved. The guidance director also should try to assess the researcher's commitment to help cooperating school staff implement the findings of the research. When these conditions have been met, cooperating school personnel achieve genuine satisfaction from helping solve professional problems, and research scholars are encouraged to do their own research in the practitioners' work setting; school personnel obtain assistance in appraising their services; and the research findings tend to be more readily accepted and used by practitioners.

Where university training centers have been developed to provide clients for practice and internships and have earned a reputation for good service to schools and community agencies, a wide variety of clients tend to be referred to these centers (and could open the way for using these centers for cooperative research as well as for service and training). From such a large pool of clients, a researcher can identify appropriate clients, treat them as they become available, and markedly increase the number of subjects available over a period of time for a particular project. When the particular type of clients which are needed for a project are described carefully, counselors in cooperating institutions will help identify and refer them for the project too. In addition to obtaining a large pool of appropriate clients, this approach tends to have the further advantage of clients coming to the project knowing what is expected and accepting the need for treatment.

## Statistical Analyses of Data

The process begins with identifying the questions for which the researcher is seeking information. After he decides what the research questions are, he can develop his hypotheses and select the essential statistical analyses to test his hypotheses. Early in the process he must review the assumptions which he makes when he reviews each of the possible ways of analyzing his data and determine which must be met. He also must be certain that he has collected his data in a form that lends itself to his statistical analysis.

Two of the most common mistakes researchers make in selecting statistical procedures are: (1) the use of statistical tests for which the basic assumptions for their use have not been met and (2) a consultant's assistance with statistical analyses of the data is sought *after* the data have been collected. When consultants are employed during the planning stage the researcher can obtain help in stating hypotheses more clearly, in collecting essential data to test his hypotheses, in arranging to have at least some instruments machine scored, and in selecting or writing a computer program (and in scheduling his computer analysis of data). Such arrangements not only save precious time but such assistance encourages some who are unsure of the quantitative skills to do research.

With better qualified counselors, the need to compare several alternative treatment methods, and the sophisticated computer program that can be made available to counselors, researchers are able to tackle much more complicated problems: To what extent is the effectiveness of a technique a function of the type of clients treated, of the circumstances under which the treatment is administered (including elements such as type of clients combined, place of treatment, length of counseling session, number of times per week, and so on), and of the competency level of treaters? What elements within the group seem to have the greatest impact on the counselor and clients? Do counselors and clients who are members of effective groups play different roles than they do in ineffective groups? How do those clients who profit most from group counseling differ from those who profit least from counseling? Are some methods most productive for certain types of clients, and possibly when provided by a certain type of counselor? Several of the above questions would require a three-dimensional analysis of variance. Others would require a factorial design as suggested by Edwards and Cronbach (1952). Cohn (1967) and his team of researchers strongly encouraged researchers to use multivariate statistical methods to investigate process and outcome variables simultaneously.

Edwards and Cronbach conclude that those who appraise outcomes of counseling must be sufficiently suspicious and tough-minded to recognize proven fact and sensitive enough not to discard unproven ideas for which their experiments were not powerful enough to detect significant results.

> If this tender-minded soul is gullible, believing in what has met no significance test, he will end up with a science stuffed with superstitions. But if he holds these yet-unproven ideas in the air, as notions which may guide him in the next experiment or the treatment of the next patient, he is more likely to be correct than the man who casts the idea from his mind as soon as one experiment fails to provide significant confirmation. (p. 57)

## Results of Studies with Children

Selected studies in which relatively healthy children were counseled in groups are reviewed here.

Even though it involves too few subjects, Davis' (1948) study is reviewed here because it is one of the better early studies for which relevant criterion measures were used. She counseled nine first grade children in two groups twice a week for ten weeks. She photographed her subjects periodically during free play and obtained pretreatment, posttreatment, and follow-up sociometric testing to appraise changes in classmates' social acceptance of clients. She concluded that their social acceptance was improved.

Barcai, Umbarger, Pierce, and Chamberlain (1973) compared the effects of three group treatments on low socioeconomic fourth and fifth graders: (1) group counseling (which was cognitively oriented), (2) group remediation, and (3) art activity. They concluded that activities which reward the use of language and focus on specific interventions were the more effective methods. They also concluded that teachers' personality, expectations, and attitudes may enhance or retard the impact of an intervention.

Crow (1971) compared the effects of three types of group counseling with varying degrees of structure. She provided each group of sixth graders with group counseling once a week for 45 minutes for 12 weeks. Although she obtained no significant differences among treatment groups, the combined clients for all three treatments made significantly greater growth than her control subjects on all but one of the criterion measures (improved grades). On one variable, improved self-concept, boys exhibited significantly greater growth than girls. No follow-up data were obtained.

Although they used a small number of subjects (and usually GPA tends to be difficult to improve by short-term treatment), Deffenbacher and Kemper (1974) found that counseled sixth graders suffering from test anxiety improved their grades significantly more than control subjects. They used group desensitization with two groups of sixth graders for 40–45 minutes once a week—one group for five weeks and the other for six.

Hansen, Niland, and Zani (1969) investigated the effectiveness of model reinforcement and reinforcement group counseling with elementary school children using sociometric status as a criterion. They compared three combinations of clients, each consisting of 18 subjects: (1) low sociometric status students counseled with those of high sociometric status; (2) low sociometric students counseled by themselves; and (3) a control group which met for an activity period. All groups met twice a week for four weeks (usually considered too short a period). This discussion focused on learning to get along with others. The counselors consciously reinforced desired behaviors. Low sociometric status students in the model reinforcement groups made significantly more gain in social acceptance than did those counseled without models and the controls. Moreover, the gains were maintained in the two-month follow-up.

Hinds and Roehlke (1970) appraised the effectiveness of a learning theory approach to group counseling with third, fourth, and fifth graders who were referred by classroom teachers as disruptors of learning. They used co-counselors (the authors) for 20 sessions over a 10-week period. Prior to counseling a base rate for disruptive behaviors was established.

Counselors used systematic reinforcement in groups to shape each client's behavior and to extinguish disruptive behaviors. When each group earned the desired points, they selected the game they played. Perhaps the same results could have been obtained had the counselors functioned as consultants and helped the classroom teachers learn to be behavior modifiers. Nevertheless, like .the previous study reviewed above, this is a good example of a well-designed study in which competent counselors provided the treatment and obtained significant results.

Kelly and Mathews (1971) adapted Glasser's (1969) classroom meeting model for group counseling. Even though they seemed to have designed their study with care, they failed to obtain significant results. Possibly their limited experience with the model, their small sample, their limited treatment period, and their criterion measures account for their negative results. Perhaps also some children who have adapted well to school who desire counseling for other reasons could be combined with this type of child and improve the chances for success in the group. In any case the study should be repeated with the suggested changes.

Kern and Kirby (1971) compared the effects of a counselor-centered group counseling procedure with one in which trained peer helpers were used to assist the counselor. Groups of five to eight fifth and sixth graders met for 50-minute periods once a week for 9 weeks. In those groups in which peer helpers were used, clients exhibited significantly greater improvement on personality measures than did either the controls or the ones treated in counselor-centered groups. These results should encourage counselors to invite (and even train) clients to serve as helpers as well as clients. Unfortunately no follow-up data were collected to determine whether gains were maintained.

In spite of their brief treatment and their small number of subjects, Kranzler, Mayer, Dyer, and Munger (1966) obtained significant results. Eight fourth graders, counseled twice a week for six weeks, improved (and maintained their growth in a follow-up) more than similar students who were provided group guidance by their classroom teacher.

Mayer, Kranzler, and Matthes (1967) compared changes in pupil–teacher relationships for two types of groups: (1) one was given a combination of individual and group counseling and (2) the other participated in teacher-led guidance groups (and both were compared with controls). They found that counseling enhanced pupil–teacher relationships in the more pupil-centered classrooms but that it had less apparent effect in the more teacher-centered classrooms. With a larger sample and more experienced counselors perhaps stronger results would have been obtained.

Moulin (1970) assessed the effects of client-centered group counseling with play media on intelligence, achievement, and psycholinguistic abilities of underachieving first, second, and third graders, largely black and educationally deprived children. Significant changes were noted following treatment for nonlanguage sections of the mental test and for the psycholinguistic ability test.

Novick (1965) compared the results obtained for good and poor prospects treated as outpatients by individual and group counseling in a community mental health center. Groups varied in size from three to five. Clients were behavior problem cases. Observers rated each client on 19 behavioral characteristics such as bullying, cheating at school, and so on at 3 different intervals: precounseling, after 10 sessions, and after 20 sessions. No significant changes were noted after 10 sessions, but significant changes were noted after 20 sessions. Good prospects responded to treatment better than poor prospects. Chance could account for any differences in scores for those treated individually and in groups. This last point is also supported by Meltzoff and Kornreich's (1970) review of the research on psychotherapy.

Ohlsen and Gazda (1965) appraised the impact of group counseling upon bright, underachieving fifth graders. Twenty-two students were counseled twice a week for eight weeks in groups of five or six. Compared to their controls they increased congruence between perceptions of self and ideal self, increased acceptance of peers, markedly decreased instances of psychosomatic illnesses such as asthma attacks, stomach cramps, and headaches, but failed to improve their grades, achievement test scores, acceptance of self, and behavior inventory scores. Perhaps selection of more highly committed clients with clearly defined behavioral goals and the use of a behavior inventory based upon their goals would have increased their chances for greater success.

Randolph and Saba (1973) designed a study to compare the relative effectiveness of four group experiences for off-task fifth and sixth grade pupils: (1) modeling, (2) modeling with behavioral consultation, (3) control (no attention), and (4) a placebo (they were provided with a career development experience). Four groups of six each received group counseling. The precise nature of the treatment for each was described exceptionally well. Both treatments improved on-task behaviors significantly better than either control. For grade point average only the modeling with consultation group improved significantly over first controls but not second controls (placebo). Neither treatment group improved attitude toward school more than controls.

Sonstegard (1961) found that group counseling for fifth grade underachievers improved reading achievement, classroom behavior, and work habits when parents and teachers also were actively involved in the treatment program.

Thombs and Muro (1973) compared the gains obtained by social isolates (second graders in a rural Maine school) treated in two ways (play media and verbal group counseling) with controls. Although both counseled groups improved significantly more than controls, best results were obtained with play media.

Tosi, Swanson, and McLean (1970) appraised the impact of social reinforcement in group counseling on verbal output of nonverbalizing sixth graders and concluded that the treatment changed behavior. They also observed that clients and teachers learned to reinforce desired new behaviors. In a similar study Tosi, Upshaw, Lande, and Waldron (1971) found that systematic reinforcement was the more effective of their two reinforcement models.

Winkler, Teigland, Munger, and Kranzler (1965) identified 121 underachievers in 22 classrooms. These children were assigned to one of five types of groups: group counseling, individual counseling, remedial reading, Hawthorne effect, and control group. Six beginning counselors provided 14 half-hour counseling sessions. The fact that they were beginners with limited counseling experience with children probably accounts for their failure to obtain significant results. Hence, the study should be replicated with qualified, experienced counselors.

Based upon their review of the research concerning counseling children in groups, Howard and Zimpfer (1972) concluded that group counseling is effective, but that group approaches with parents and teachers appear to be even more promising. Inasmuch as many children's problems develop prior to school enrollment and during primary grades they urge elementary school counselors to devote more of their time to primary school children and their parents and teachers. They concluded that group counseling with children improved affective learning, sociometric status, attitudes toward school, and reading performance, but that it often failed to improve grades. With reference to achievement the writer believes that in order to improve grades the counselor must focus more therapeutic attention on improved achievement; help clients to assess the degree to which they want to improve their grades and for whom, and (for those who accept the need to improve their grades) to define precise behavioral goals related to improved achievement; place underachievers with achieving clients who are worried about good achievement; obtain remedial instruction for those who require it (and possibly by peer teaching, especially by fellow clients); and enlist parents' and teachers' encouragement and reinforcement of desired new behaviors.

In general, positive results were obtained, but perhaps better results would have been obtained had the researchers helped counselors identify and focus upon the problems which brought the children to counseling, involved the children in defining specific, behavioral goals, and appraised outcomes in terms of ᶜlients' idiosyncratic goals. Increased use of role playing probably also would have helped clients learn to behave more effectively with specific target persons. Possibly clients should have been helped to communicate their desired new behaviors to significant others, especially parents and teachers, and to enlist their assistance in reinforcing desired new behaviors. The most carefully designed studies in which highly competent persons served as counselors produced the best results.

## Results of Studies with Adolescents

Chapter 9 makes a psychological case for the use of group counseling with adolescents. During the past decade there has been a marked growth in its use. There also has been an increase in research designed to appraise its efficacy for adolescents.

Bates (1968) investigated clients treated by two methods: (1) weekly meetings for a class period for thirteen weeks and (2) continuous session meetings during school hours for two consecutive days. The 36 students who were treated by each method were divided into three groups for counseling. Except for the responses to the Rotter sentence-completion test (for which their responses improved over those of the controls), the marathon groups failed to exhibit any significant change over controls. For the regular counseling groups changes over controls were obtained with reference to school attendance, citizenship, vocational choice, acceptance of self, and acceptance of others. They also maintained their GPA whereas the GPAs of those treated by marathon and controls deteriorated. Bates concluded that treatment over a longer time provided the continuing reinforcement which is required to sustain change.

Baymur and Patterson (1960) compared outcomes of individual and group counseling for underachieving high school students and failed to obtain significant change for either. However, the counselor was unsure of her helping skills and had limited experience with American adolescents.

Benson and Blocher (1967) appraised the effectiveness of developmental group counseling for low-achieving tenth grade boys. This technique is primarily concerned with helping clients master developmental tasks and develop a more adequate repertoire of coping behaviors. In spite of their small $N$ (12 students treated in two groups) their counseled students improved their grades, decreased discipline referrals, improved feelings of adequacy, and persisted in school better than controls.

Broedel, Ohlsen, Proff, and Southard's (1960) gifted underachieving ninth grade clients were provided group counseling twice a week for eight weeks. Their counseled clients improved significantly more than their controls with reference to achievement test scores, acceptance of self and others, ability to relate to peers, siblings, and parents, but failed to improve their GPAs significantly. Follow-up data in 15–18 months indicated that they maintained their growth. Three-year follow-up also indicated that the treated underachievers tended to improve their grades slightly whereas the general trend for bright students was for grades to decrease gradually. More careful selection of clients and greater care in helping them develop precise, behavioral goals probably would have increased these gains.

Bush (1971) did the first of four studies designed to appraise the efficacy of the model of group counseling described in Chapter 1. His primary concern was division of time among clients during each session. Bartell

(1972) appraised the effect of the intake interview on client outcomes. Hilkey (1975) assessed the impact of video-tape training in client and helper roles on counseling outcomes. Generally, all three concluded that group counseling was effective but that no one of these elements by itself had a significant effect on outcome—especially in the latter two instances; they concluded that though the element that each studied influenced the quality of interaction during the first few sessions, competent counselors were able to compensate for the fact that it was not provided. However, at first counselors felt more comfortable with the clients who had completed careful intake interviews or had been trained as clients and as helpers by the video tape. DeEsch (1974) counseled disruptive secondary school students and obtained significant changes with reference to decreased deviant sign scores on the Tennessee Self-Concept Scale, improvement in GPAs, and decreased referrals to the principal's office for disruptive classroom behavior. He also noted that on several variables controls also improved their performance. De Esch concluded that the carefully conducted intake interviews in which specific, behavioral goals were established enabled controls to decide how they wanted to change and to develop the commitment to do it. Davis and Sanborn (1973) also demonstrated that counselors who help high school students develop specification contacts and encourage them to take responsibility can produce change with brief contacts.

Caplan's (1957) unruly, antisocial junior high school clients who were counseled in groups improved significantly their congruence between self and ideal self and their citizenship grades, but not their GPAs.

Catron (1966) appraised the impact of group counseling by cocounselors in training upon thirteen groups of high school students. Though the clients' stated purpose was educational-vocational planning, they exhibited much more interest in discussing (and were permitted to discuss) parent–child relationships, variation in quality of their teachers, peer relationships, and social attitudes. In addition to helping them discuss their feelings related to personal problems, counselors helped them surface underlying feelings concerning decision making. Catron's clients improved significantly perception of self, but exhibited no significant changes in either ideal person or ordinary others.

Clements (1966) evaluated the efficacy of group counseling to reduce anxiety of college-bound high school seniors. Counseling sessions (six while in high school, and additional ones for those who volunteered as college freshmen) focused on attitudes, fears, and aspirations. The counseled students exhibited significantly less anxiety both prior to college entrance and after beginning college.

Finney and Van Dalsem (1969) used GPAs and scores from California Study Methods Survey to compare results from underachieving high school tenth graders who were counseled for four semesters and from similar students who were not counseled. Although the counseled students did not perform significantly better on the above two criteria, they were rated by teachers as more cooperative in class and they were absent less, but they were not referred to the office less for poor deportment.

Gilliland's (1968) black high school students who were counseled for a year in groups improved more than controls with reference to vocabulary, reading, English usage, vocational maturity, and occupational aspirations.

Hansen, Zimpfer, and Easterling (1967) investigated the relationship between changes in self-concept and therapeutic climate in their counseling groups (six groups of eight or nine in six high schools). They found that students' perceptions of the relationship was important to achieving increased congruence between real and ideal self-concept.

Hansen and Sanders (1973) identified extreme cases of "overshooting" and "undershooting" unrealistic vocational choices and compared the impact of individual and group counseling on eleventh and twelfth graders. Chance could account for any observed differences between those treated and their controls, but they obtained a significant interaction. The "overshooters" who were counseled in groups and the "undershooters" who were counseled individually developed more realistic choices.

Jesness (1975) conducted a very carefully designed study for the treatment of delinquent boys aged 15–17 in two institutions; clients were randomly assigned to one of two similar institutions which differed only in the treatment provided: behavior modification in one and transactional analysis in the other. In addition to the twice weekly small group-therapy sessions for the latter, large community meetings were held two or three times a week. TA principles also were applied daily in coping with the delinquents' management. With reference to parole criteria the two techniques were equally effective. However, each treatment generated some specific advantages. Behavioral programs resulted in greater gains noted on specific observer ratings whereas TA programs resulted in greater changes in attitudinal and self-report appraisals. Moreover, the data showed that delinquents in both programs' recidivism rates for the experimental period were significantly lower than the base rate for the year prior to the research project.

Krumboltz and Thoresen (1964) assessed the effect of both individual and group behavioral counseling on volunteer eleventh graders from six high schools near Stanford University. Two types of treatment were used on both individual and group basis: reinforcement counseling (for information-seeking behavior) and model-reinforcement counseling. They also provided for a special control for the Hawthorne effect. Individual and group counseling were both effective, but males who received model-reinforcement counseling were stimulated more by the group than by the individual setting. Model-reinforcement counseling was generally more effective for males than females. However, the model was a male, hence it may have been easier for the male students to identify with him. This is another unusually well-designed study.

Laxer, Quarter, Isnor, and Kennedy (1967) failed to obtain significant gains when they counseled disruptive junior high school boys in groups. Inasmuch as DeEsch obtained significant results with similar clients who were given an opportunity in their intake interviews to demonstrate their readiness and commitment to learn new behaviors and were helped to define precise behavioral goals, perhaps these conditions made the difference. Moreover, the writer has achieved best results with misbehaving students when he places them in groups with strong conforming students rather than treating them by themselves.

Lodata, Sokoloff, and Schwartz (1964) modified with group counseling the attitudes of slow learners: three groups from grades 7 and 8, one from grades 4 and 5, and two groups from grade 3. On the basis of teachers' ratings they improved students' attitudes toward learning and authority figures, school attendance, and teachers' tolerance of students.

McCarthy (1959) divided 24 bright, underachieving ninth grade boys into four groups (two experimental and two controls) and provided six one-hour treatment sessions in which subjects' attention was focused on disguised case materials based on the boys' own problems. The clients' task was to try to diagnose the reasons for failure and to plan ways of helping these boys. Though they were not told that these were their own problems, they became defensive when their own case materials were discussed, and perhaps insufficient attention was given to helping them discuss these feelings. In any case, significant changes were not obtained. This study reminds the writer of a pilot project in which he provided a seminar for ninth grade underachievers, who served as tutors for seventh and eighth grade children who requested assistance with arithmetic and English. As these underachievers talked about the problems with which they were confronted in helping others, they also often discussed what they could do to improve their own performances. In other words, the seminars became counseling for them. During their struggle to figure out how to help these younger students like themselves, they seemed to grasp the negative consequences of their underachieving behavior and to increase their commitment to improve their school achievement.

Mezzano (1967) discovered a statistically significant relationship between investment in group counseling and improvement in GPA. His subjects were low-motivated high school students (18 received individual and group counseling, 18 received group counseling only, and 28 served as controls).

Sarason and Ganzer (1973) investigated the relative effectiveness of two group methods: (1) relied on modeling and required subjects to imitate roles which they observed their models perform, and (2) employed structured discussion of the same material, but without modeling or imitation. Both types (groups of four or five) were attended by two models or discussion leaders. There were 64 subjects for each type of group: 15½–18 years old with a mean IQ of 95. Modeling appeared to be superior to discussion only. The study also makes a case for the practice of interpersonal skills in role playing advocated in Chapter 7 and the use of video tapes for feedback.

Smith and Evans (1973) compared results achieved with experimental group guidance with individual counseling to facilitate vocational development. Significantly better results were obtained by those treated by group procedures than controls and individually counseled.

Thoresen and Krumboltz (1967) investigated the relationship between counselor reinforcement of certain responses and specific behaviors with volunteers from six high schools near Stanford University. Model reinforcement produced significantly more information-seeking behaviors than reinforcement alone did.

Warner and Hansen (1970) used verbal-reinforcement and model-reinforcement group counseling to help alienated eleventh grade students. Both treatments reduced feelings of alienation in only six sessions.

In most instances researchers obtain significant results, but unfortunately counselors did not seem to take account of adolescents' special needs in counseling. With more carefully selected helpers perhaps more clients would have been helped and fewer would have been hurt.

## Results with College Students and Adults

In the final group of selected studies investigators used primarily college students, but a few used reasonably healthy out-of-school adults as research subjects.

Abramowitz, Abramowitz, Roback, and Jackson (1974) used 26 mildly distressed college students to evaluate the differential effectiveness of directive and nondirective group therapies with internally controlled clients (those who believe that the events that occur in their lives are results of their own initiatives) and externally controlled clients (those who believe that events in their lives are determined largely by luck or powerful outside forces). They found that internally controlled clients were more responsive to the nondirective therapy whereas externally controlled clients tended to be more responsive to directive therapy.

Brown (1969) tried to determine whether the degree of structure had differential impact on high- and low-anxious students. He found that high-anxious underachieving college students benefited more from an unstructured approach than low-anxious underachieving students. Furthermore, he recommended less structure for high-anxious and more structure for low-anxious students even in remedial courses such as study skill courses.

Chestnut (1965) evaluated the effect of structured and unstructured group counseling for gifted college underachievers. Whereas those assigned to the unstructured group were permitted to discuss whatever originated spontaneously in their group, the counselor for the structured group encouraged clients to discuss, and to develop skills for coping with, the genesis of poor achievement. By the end of treatment only those in the structured group had improved grades significantly more than their controls. At the three-month follow-up their grades were still significantly better than those of the unstructured group.

Dickenson and Truax (1966) assessed the efficacy of time-limited group counseling for underachieving college freshmen. By comparison with their controls counseled students tended to earn passing grades and to improve thir GPAs more than noncounseled students. Futhermore, those clients who experienced relatively high levels of therapeutic conditions (accurate empathy, unconditional positive regard, and genuineness) showed the greatest improvement.

Fiedler (1949) provided preventive group psychotherapy for college students faced with comprehensive exams at the University of Chicago. Three of his four groups profited from Fiedler's psychotherapy, but one powerful resisting client in the fourth group was so threatened by therapeutic interaction that he blocked it and that group failed to make significant growth.

Gazda and Ohlsen (1961) appraised the effects of group counseling on four groups of prospective counselors (34 clients). By comparison with their controls those counseled improved significantly their manifest needs in the predicted direction: increased autonomy and decreased abasement and succorance for all four groups, but other changes for only two groups; increased heterosexuality for two groups and decreased nurturance for two groups. Changes assessed by the picture-story test and the behavior inventory failed to achieve significance for either posttesting or follow-up. When, however, the interviewer (in a 14-month follow-up) requested clients to describe specific ways in which they had been helped or hurt, all but two clients were able to describe some specific ways in which they had been helped.

Gilbreath (1967) reported on a study in which he assessed changes in underachieving first- and second-year college males. Two counselors participated in the group counseling projects; each counseled two groups by the high-authority, leader-structured method and two groups by the low-authority, group-structured method. Those counseled by the leader-structured method experienced a higher rate of increase in GPAs and greater ego strength than did either the group-structured clients or the controls. At the three-month follow-up the leader-structured group's rate of increase in GPAs was not significantly greater than that for those counseled by the group-structured method. Furthermore, the investigator concluded that his dependent clients improved GPAs in leadership-structured groups but not in group-structured groups. By contrast, his independent clients seemed to improve GPAs more in group-centered groups than in leader-centered groups.

Gorlow, Hoch, and Teleschow (1952) counseled 17 graduate students in three groups twice weekly for 18 to 20 sessions. After prospective clients volunteered, the counselors used an intake interview to determine whether or not they were deeply concerned about some problems on which they were willing to work. After counseling, all clients perceived themselves and their fellow clients in a more favorable light. The investigators also developed a reliable method for dividing clients into two groups: most profited and least profited. Most-profited clients exhibited a significant decrease in negative behavior and increase in positive behavior, whereas no significant change was noted in the behavior of least-profited clients.

Graff, MacLean, and Loving (1971) compared results obtained by reactive inhibition and reciprocal inhibition therapies for anxious college freshmen with results obtained from similar clients who participated in a neutral discussion group and obtained significant gains with both methods. Futhermore, their gains were maintained in the eight-week follow-up.

Leib and Snyder (1967) compared the effectiveness of group counseling and of experiences in a lecture discussion course on reading and study skills for underachieving undergraduates. Those treated by both methods improved their GPAs significantly, but chance could account for any observed differences in growth between the treatment methods.

Lieberman, Yalom, and Miles (1973) completed the most carefully designed and conducted study of the decade. They compared ten treatment methods for which, in most instances, two top advocates for each system were chosen to lead a group. For two systems no leaders were required: Synanon and Bell and Howell Peer Tape. Each system and the way the group functions are described in detail in Chapter 2 of their book. Of those completing the groups 50–70 percent (depending on the method of evaluation) experienced some positive change; 61 percent thought that they had learned a great deal. For those who changed positively, three out of four maintained their gains. All in all, experimental-control differences were modest, but probably meaningful and positive. For almost 80 percent of both participants and controls, specific positive changes were noted by their significant others. In general, these researchers concluded that their encounter groups were less effective than the results for psychotherapy reported by Bergin and Garfield (1971). Moreover, results for a technique varied markedly with different leaders—for one leader a technique proved to be one of the best whereas with another it proved to be one of the poorest (least gains for clients and most casualties).

Muro and Ohnmacht (1966) investigated the effects of group counseling on college freshmen enrolled in teacher education. One group was counseled once a week and the other was counseled twice a week. Compared to the controls, neither group improved significantly on acceptance of self, the dogmatism scale, or preference for complexity.

Ofman (1965) tried to appraise the impact of group counseling on college students. Owing to the design of the experiment and the statistical methods used, it is difficult to assess the impact of counseling. The investigator's study should alert future researchers to some of the differences between experimental subjects and those who are selected as controls. He made a good case for a baseline group and for researchers' making a greater effort to control motivational factors. At the beginning of his study there were no significant differences between volunteers in his treatment and control groups, but his subjects in the baseline group earned significantly higher GPAs than the volunteers. By the end of the experiment his treated subjects had improved their grades sufficiently so that there was no longer a significant difference in GPAs between treated and baseline subjects. Furthermore, his treated subjects earned significantly higher GPAs at the end of his experiment than did his control group.

Roth, Mauksch, and Peiser (1967) provided group counseling for bright, underachieving undergraduates (52 counseled in groups of from 7 to 12, and 52 controls). Counseling groups met twice a week for approximately one hour. The investigators concluded that these students do poorly in order to avoid risk taking and to maintain a dependent relationship with their family. Hence, the counselor tried to provide help with both study skills and these dynamics. Those counseled improved their GPAs more than their controls, and the follow-up appraisal revealed that they maintained their gains.

Spielberger, Weitz, and Denny (1962) evaluated the effectiveness of group counseling for anxious college freshmen. Volunteers who were provided group counseling showed greater improvement in GPAs than did the controls, who volunteered for group counseling but were not provided it. The investigators also found a significant relationship between the number of sessions clients attended and the improvement in their GPAs (a Pearson $r$ of .63). From their analysis of MMPI scores they concluded that high attenders may be tentatively described as active-repressive, middle attenders as passive-rebellious, and low attenders as passive-withdrawn and ruminative. In their later study Spielberger and Weitz (1964) appear to have added subjects from another group of freshmen and to have made additional analyses of their data. Besides finding additional support for the findings reported above, they found proportionately fewer severe underachievers among the anxious than among the nonanxious underachievers; failure dropout rate for anxious volunteers in 1959 was less than for nonanxious students; and failure dropout rate in 1960 was lower for anxious volunteers and anxious nonvolunteers than for nonanxious students. Their rationale for providing counseling at the very beginning of college for these students is quoted below:

> There is little evidence, however, that personality problems are direct and immediate causes of poor academic performance. It seems more likely that, in response to the pressures of college life, students with personality problems are predisposed to develop maladaptive study habits and attitudes which, in turn, interfere with the learning process and lead to underachievement. For college students identified as having personality problems, preventive measures implemented at the beginning of the freshman year would come at a time when the potential for serious maladaptive behavior is heightened by new environmental stresses. (p. 1)

Tavormina (1975) evaluated the relative effectiveness of behavioral counseling and reflective group counseling with mothers of mentally retarded children. Compared to his waiting list controls, clients in both treatment groups improved significantly, but those treated by the behavioral technique made significantly greater growth.

Teahan (1966) evaluated the effects of group psychotherapy on first-semester college sophomores who were in the top quarter of their high school class, but were not successful as freshmen. Because he believed that certain aspects of their personality interfered with college success, the counselor focused attention on personal and emotional problems. He obtained significant improvement in GPAs. Those whose GPAs improved described their fathers as more dominating and ignoring than those whose grades did not improve. Those who improved most also tended to obtain high Ma scores on MMPI. The high F scores on MMPI suggest, the investigator concluded, that those most helped were more ready to discuss their personal problems, and their Si scores suggest that they were drawn into the group to satisfy their need for social interaction.

Thelen and Harris (1968) identified and contacted by letter 127 under-achievers: 52 did not respond; 38 responded and completed the 16 PF, but were not interested in group psychotherapy; and 37 completed the test and volunteered for group psychotherapy. The latter were divided randomly into treatment subjects and controls—with dropouts these became C = 13 and E = 19 (four counseling groups). Those counseled improved their grades. The investigators concluded that those helped had less apprehension about treatment, were more self-accepting, and accepted the notion of obtaining assistance. Those who volunteered for group psychotherapy have the most to gain from it and the most to lose from not obtaining it.

The primary focus of Wetzel, Kinney, Beavers, Harvey, and Urbanuk's (1976) treatment was to help each patient develop his own effective and satisfying means to get out of the hospital and stay out. From the beginning the staff emphasized development of specific target behaviors for each, establishment of priorities, rapid pursual of target behaviors, and short-term treatment. Inasmuch as Veteran Administration patients were released as soon as they achieved their goals, there was a rapid turnover in membership. The outcomes appear to be promising, but the results were based upon informal questionnaire follow-up from patients after discharge. Nevertheless, the treatment seems to be promising and hence it should be evaluated more carefully.

## Generalizations about Research Outcomes

During the past decade the research on outcomes of counseling as well as the helping skills of counselors and therapists has improved markedly, especially in group counseling, but all the helping professions must learn to cooperate more effectively in order to protect the public from unscrupulous persons who offer professional services which they are unqualified to provide —especially in various group techniques. The helping professions also must screen prospective helpers with greater care, improve the quality of professional preparation, and encourage practitioners to grow on the job. Much also must be done to help liaison workers and referrers such as teachers and clergymen to provide quality support and encouragement and use peer helping techniques, but without attempting to provide therapeutic service for which they are not qualified. The professionals must recognize that even qualified helpers can hurt as well as help certain clients under certain circumstances (Bergin & Garfield, 1971; Lieberman, Yalom, & Miles, 1973).

Meltzoff and Kornreich (1970) also concluded that the quality of research has improved:

> From every point of view (design, sampling, criteria, nature of controls, data analysis), the quality of research has improved along with the quantity. . . . Among the adequate studies, 84 percent showed positive effects of psychotherapy that were statistically significant. Similarly 75 percent of the questionable studies reported significant results. (p. 174)
>
> The weight of experimental evidence is sufficient to enable us to reject the null hypothesis. Far more often than not, psychotherapy in a wide variety of types and with a broad range of disorders has been demonstrated under control conditions to be accompanied by postive changes in adjustment that can significantly exceed those that can be accounted for by passage of time alone. (p. 175)
>
> There is little existing evidence of any systematic differences in efficacy between group and individual therapy. Studies that purport to show advantages of combination of the two methods are not sufficiently conclusive, either in design or analyses, to permit such conclusions. (p. 183)

Strupp (1973b) draws a similar conclusion:

> During the past 30 years the quantity as well as quality of research contributions has grown, and there is every reason to believe that the coming decades will see intensification of this effort. (p. 734)
>
> . . . New treatment methods in this area, it may be observed, do not arise from the efforts of researchers or as the result of experimentation in the laboratory; instead, they emerge in response to social needs that are met by the ingenuity or inventiveness of charismatic therapists whose individual temperment and philosophy of life are thoroughly intertwined with the therapeutic approach they espouse. (p. 794)
>
> From everything that has been said, it follows that significant increments in knowledge, at least within the therapeutic framework, are likely to come from intensive study of individual cases in which disciplined observation is complemented by, and takes account of, the complex interaction of variables, a task that cannot be accomplished by statistical manipulations, although certain statistical techniques may be helpful in other respects. (p. 799)

Inasmuch as there is clear evidence that individuals can be hurt as well as helped, practitioners as well as researchers must continue to look for the answer to the questions: Who was helped and hurt by this method, with whom, under what conditions, and with what kind of a treater? It also means that researchers must develop better criterion measures (an area in which the profession is seriously deficient at this time) to assess change and use multivariate statistical analysis to examine the interaction of process variables and outcome variables. Finally, since the treater is such an important variable in process (Truax & Carkhuff, 1964; Lieberman, Yalom, & Miles, 1973; Grunebaum, 1975), researchers must do everything possible to produce selection techniques which will enable them to select and prepare the best possible helpers. Furthermore, when they appraise a technique they must make every effort to insure that they have chosen treaters who accept it and are committed to use it effectively to help these particular subjects under these circumstances.

## Summary

Both the quality and quantity of outcome studies have improved in the last decade. Moreover, investigators are asking increasingly difficult questions. It is no longer sufficient to ask: "Was group counseling effective?" Today researchers are asking: "For whom was group counseling effective with what quality level of leadership, with what type of clients, with what types of problems, and under what circumstances?" Increasingly researchers are encouraged to use multivariate analyses to investigate process and outcome variables simultaneously.

Research questions and hypotheses must be formulated with greater care. Such careful planning identifies weaknesses that can be corrected prior to beginning the research, helps to insure that the investigator collects the data required to test his hypotheses with statistical methods chosen, and helps to insure that a well-designed plan is followed. If research consultants are to be used they should be involved early in order to improve the design, to select the best possible criterion measures, to ensure that proper methods are used to select research subjects and controls, to collect the data in manageable form, and to analyze the results appropriately.

These common weaknesses of outcome studies were discussed: (1) Researchers commonly fail to define and defend a clearly stated, researchable problem. (2) The treatment process is not defined with sufficient care and detail for another to replicate the study or even to determine whether similar results were obtained. (3) Treaters often are trainees with minimal experience and training. In order for methods to be compared, researchers must use treaters who are competent to provide the designated treatment(s), and where the experiment calls for the same treaters to use more than one technique they must be equally competent in each and feel equally committed to provide quality service with each. (4) Researchers often fail to help each client define specific behavioral goals in precise measurable or observable terms. (5) Without adequate treatment goals, it is very difficult to define adequate criteria to appraise outcomes. (6) Even after researchers have helped their clients to define behavioral goals and clear criteria, they still must select or develop adequate criterion measures (and unfortunately they often use poor criterion measures). (7) Research subjects and control subjects are not selected with sufficient care (and often the sample is too small). (8) In addition to selecting appropriate statistical methods required to test the hypotheses, the researcher often fails to take necessary precautions to insure that data were collected and subjects were sampled in a manner to justify the use of desired statistical analyses. (9) It is not sufficient to demonstrate that desired changes occurred during treatment. Follow-up studies are essential to determine whether gains achieved were maintained. Suggestions for coping with each of these weaknesses were discussed.

During the last decade research has improved, but many of the weaknesses described above still have not been adequately corrected. Nevertheless, perhaps the most serious problem with which the helping professions are faced today is improving the competencies of the helpers. Increasingly, however, researchers are selecting competent treaters to provide the prescribed treatment, are helping clients to define meaningful, relevant, behavioral goals, helping them define criteria to appraise outcomes, selecting improved criterion measures, and obtaining better results than previously. The best designed studies conducted by the most competent professionals are obtaining the best results. Although clients may be hurt as well as helped, there is supporting evidence that competent professionals can help clients in groups.

## Discussion Questions

1. Why have critics directed their attacks on encounter, sensitivity, and marathon groups more than on group counseling and group psychotherapy?
2. What is the natural consequence of professionals' failure to evaluate the worth of their services?
3. What are the clues that may suggest to a researcher that clients have been hurt as well as helped?
4. With which of the types of criterion measures do you feel most comfortable? Why?
5. What do you conclude from the research on group counseling with children? What could have been done to increase the chances for obtaining significant results?

6. Eysenck's (1952) paper is often cited by those who doubt the value of counseling and psychotherapy. What were the primary weaknesses of that study? To which of his conclusions should the helping professions give special attention?
7. What are the most promising advances that could improve the quality of research on counseling outcomes?
8. How may a counselor use the techniques discussed in this chapter to determine whether a client is making sufficient growth to continue treatment?
9. To what extent does the research on adolescents and young adults counseled in groups confirm how they are different from either children or older adults?

## References

Abramowitz, C. V., Abramowitz, S. I., Roback, H. B., & Jackson, C. Differential effectiveness of directive and nondirective group therapies as a function of client internal-external control. *Journal of Consulting and Clinical Psychology*, 1974, *42*, 849–853.

Barcai, A., Umbarger, C., Pierce, T., & Chamberlain, P. A comparison of three group approaches to underachieving children. *American Journal of Orthopsychiatry*, 1973, *43*, 133–141.

Bartell, W. *The effect of the intake interview on client perceived outcomes of group counseling.* Unpublished doctoral dissertation, Indiana State University, 1972.

Bates, M. A test of group counseling. *Personnel and Guidance Journal*, 1966, *46*, 749–573.

Baymur, F., & Patterson, C. H. A comparison of three methods of assessing high school students. *Journal of Counseling Psychology*, 1960, *7*, 83–90.

Benson, R. L., & Blocher, D. H. Evaluation of developmental counseling with groups of low achievers in high school setting. *The School Counselor*, 1967, *14*, 215–220.

Bereiter, C. Use of tests to measure change. *Personnel and Guidance Journal*, 1962, *41*, 6–11.

Berg, I. A. Measures before and after therapy. *Journal of Clinical Psychology*, 1952, *8*, 46–50.

Bergin, A. E. The effects of psychotherapy: Negative results revisited. *Journal of Counseling Psychology*, 1963, *10*, 244–249.

Bergin, A. E., & Garfield, S. L. *Handbook for psychotherapy and behavior change.* New York: Wiley, 1971.

Broedel, J., Ohlsen, M., Proff, F., & Southard, C. The effects of group counseling on gifted underachieving adolescents. *Journal of Counseling Psychology*, 1960, *7*, 163–170.

Brown, R. D. Effects of structured and unstructured group counseling with high-

and low-anxious college underachievers. *Journal of Counseling Psychology,* 1969, *16,* 209–214.

Bush, J. *The effects of fixed and random actor interaction on individual goal attainment in group counseling.* Unpublished doctoral dissertation, Indiana State University, 1971.

Caplan, S. W. The effects of group counseling on junior high school boys' concept of themselves in school. *Journal of Counseling Psychology,* 1957, *4,* 124–128.

Carkhuff, R. R., & Berenson, B. G. *Beyond counseling and therapy.* New York: Holt, Rinehart and Winston, 1967.

Catron, D. W. Educational-vocational group counseling: The effects on perceptions of self and others. *Journal of Counseling Psychology,* 1966, *13,* 202–207.

Chestnut, W. J. The effects of structured and unstructured group counseling on male college students' underachievement. *Journal of Counseling Psychology,* 1965, *24,* 388–394.

Clements, B. E. Transitional adolescents, anxiety and group counseling. *Personnel and Guidance Journal,* 1966, *45,* 67–71.

Cohn, B. *Guidelines for future research on group counseling in the public school setting.* Washington, D.C.: American Personnel and Guidance Association, 1967.

Crow, M. L. A comparison of three group counseling techniques with sixth graders. *Elementary School Guidance and Counseling,* 1971, *6,* 37–42.

Davis, J. L., & Sanborn, M. P. Getting student action on guidance goals. *Journal of Counseling Psychology,* 1973, *20,* 209–213.

Davis, R. G. Group therapy and social acceptance in first grade. *Elementary School Journal,* 1948, 219–223.

DeEsch, J. B. *The use of Ohlsen's model of group counseling with secondary students identified as being disruptive to the educational process.* Unpublished doctoral dissertation, Indiana State University, 1974.

Deffenbacher, J. L., & Kemper, C. C. Counseling test-anxious sixth graders. *Elementary School Guidance and Counseling,* 1974, *9,* 22–29.

Dickenson, W. A., & Truax, C. B. Group counseling with college underachievers. *Personnel and Guidance Journal,* 1966, *45,* 243–247.

Dressel, P. L. (Ed.) *Evaluation in higher education.* Boston: Houghton Mifflin, 1961.

Edwards, A. L., & Cronbach, L. J. Experimental design for research in psychotherapy. *Journal of Clinical Psychology,* 1952, *8,* 51–59.

Ewalt, P., Cohen, M., & Horwatz, J. Prediction of treatment acceptance in child guidance clinic applicants. *American Journal of Orthopsychiatry,* 1972, *42,* 857–864.

Eysenck, H. J. The effects of psychotherapy: An evaluation. *Journal of Consulting Psychology,* 1952, *16,* 319–324.

Fiedler, F. E. An experimental approach to preventive psychotherapy. *Journal of Social and Abnormal Psychology,* 1949, *44,* 386–393.

Finney, B. C., & Van Dalsem, E. Group counseling for gifted underachieving high school students. *Journal of Counseling Psychology,* 1969, *16,* 87–94.

Forgy, E. W., & Black, J. D. A follow-up after three years of clients counseled by two methods. *Journal of Counseling Psychology,* 1954, *1,* 1–8.

Gazda, G. M., & Ohlsen, M. M. The effects of short-term group counseling on prospective counselors. *Personnel and Guidance Journal*, 1961, *39*, 634–638.

Gilbreath, S. H. Group counseling, dependence, and college male achievement. *Journal of Counseling Psychology*, 1967, *14*, 449–453.

Gilliland, B. E. Small group counseling with negro adolescents in a public high school. *Journal of Counseling Psychology*, 1968, *15*, 147–152.

Glasser, W. *Schools without failure*. New York: Harper & Row, 1969.

Goldstein, M. Some characteristics of research in applied settings. *American Psychologist*, 1959, *14*, 272–278.

Gorlow, L., Hoch, E., & Teleschow, E. *The nature of nondirective group psychotherapy*. New York: Bureau of Publications, Teachers College, Columbia University, 1952.

Graff, R., MacLean, G. D., & Loving, A. Group reactive inhibition and reciprocal inhibition therapies with anxious college students. *Journal of Counseling Psychology*, 1971, *18*, 431–436.

Grunebaum, H. A soft-hearted review of hard-nosed research on groups. *Group Psychotherapy*, 1975, *25*, 185–199.

Hansen, J. C., Niland, T. M., & Zani, L. P. Model reinforcement in group counseling with elementary school children. *Personnel and Guidance Journal*, 1969, *47*, 741–744.

Hansen, J. C., Zimpfer, D. G., & Easterling, R. E. A study of the relationships in multiple counseling. *Journal of Educational Research*, 1967, *60*, 461–462.

Hansen, J. T., & Sanders, D. L. Differential effects of individual and group counseling on realism of vocational choice. *Journal of Counseling Psychology*, 1973, *20*, 541–544.

Hartley, D., Roback, H. B., & Abramowitz, S. I. Deterioration in encounter groups. *American Psychologist*, 1976, *31*, 247–255.

Hartley, E., & Rosenbaum, M. Criteria used by group psychotherapists for judging improvement in patients. *International Journal of Group Psychotherapy*, 1963, *13*, 80–83.

Hilkey, J. H. *The effects of video-tape pretraining and guided performance on the process and outcomes of group counseling*. Unpublished doctoral dissertation, Indiana State University, 1975.

Hill, C. A process approach for establishing counseling goals and outcomes. *Personnel and Guidance Journal*, 1975, *53*, 571–573.

Hinds, W. C., & Roehlke, H. J. A learning theory approach to group counseling with elementary school children. *Journal of Counseling Psychology*, 1970, *17*, 49–55.

Horenstein, D., Houston, B. K., & Holmes, D. S. Clients', therapists', and judges' evaluations of psychotherapy. *Journal of Counseling Psychology*, 1973, *20*, 149–153.

Howard, W., & Zimpfer, D. G. The findings of research on group approaches in elementary guidance and counseling. *Elementary School Guidance and Counseling*, 1972, *6*, 163–169.

Jensen, B. T., Coles, G., & Nestor, B. The criterion problem in guidance research. *Journal of Counseling Psychology*, 1955, *2*, 58–61.

Jesness, C. F. Comparative effectiveness of behavior modification and transactional analysis programs for delinquents. *Journal of Consulting and Clinical Psychology*, 1975, *43*, 758–779.

Kefauver, G. N., & Hand, H. C. *Appraising guidance services in secondary schools.* New York: Macmillan, 1941.

Kelly, E. W., & Mathews, D. B. Group counseling with discipline problem children at elementary school level. *The School Counselor,* 1971, *18,* 273–278.

Kern, R., & Kirby, J. H. Utilizing peer helper influence in group counseling. *Elementary School Guidance and Counseling,* 1971, *6,* 70–75.

Kranzler, G. D., Mayer, G. R., Dyer, C. O., & Munger, P. F. Counseling with elementary school children: An experimental study. *Personnel and Guidance Journal,* 1966, *44,* 944–949.

Krumboltz, J. D., & Thoresen, C. E. The effects of behavioral counseling in group and individual settings on information-seeking behavior. *Journal of Counseling Psychology,* 1964, *11,* 324–333.

Laxer, R. M., Quarter, J. J., Isnor, C., & Kennedy, D. R. Counseling small groups of behavior-problem students in junior high schools. *Journal of Counseling Psychology,* 1967, *14,* 454–457.

Leary, T. *Interpersonal diagnosis of personality.* New York: Ronald, 1957.

Leib, J. W., & Snyder, W. W. Effects of group counseling on underachieving and self-actualization. *Journal of Counseling Psychology,* 1967, *14,* 282–285.

Lieberman, M. A., Yalom, I. D., & Miles, M. B. *Encounter groups: First facts.* New York: Basic Books, 1973.

Lodato, F. J., Sokoloff, M. A., & Schwartz, L. J. Group counseling as a method of modifying attitudes in slow learners. *School Counselor,* 1964, *12,* 27–29.

Maliver, B. L. *The encounter game.* New York: Stein & Day, 1973.

Mayer, G., Kranzler, G. D., & Matthes, W. Elementary school guidance and peer relations. *Personnel and Guidance Journal,* 1967, *46,* 360–365.

McCarthy, M. V. *The effectiveness of a modified counseling procedure in promoting learning among bright underachieving adolescents.* Research Project #SAE-6401, Washington, D.C.: Department of Health, Education, and Welfare, 1959.

Meade, E. J. *A foundation goes to school.* New York: Ford Foundation, 1972.

Meehl, P. E. Some ruminations on the validation of clinical procedures. *Canadian Journal of Psychology,* 1959, *13,* 102–128.

Meltzoff, J., & Kornreich, M. *Research in psychotherapy.* New York: Atherton, 1970.

Mezzano, J. A. A consideration for group counselors: Degree of investment. *School Counselor,* 1967, *14,* 167–169.

Muro, J. J., & Ohnmacht, F. W. Effects of group counseling in dimensions of self-acceptance, dogmatism, and preference for complexity with teacher-education students. *Journal of Student Personnel Association for Teacher Education,* 1966, *5,* 25–30.

Moulin, E. K. The effects of client-centered group counseling using play media on the intelligence, achievement, and psycholinguistic abilities of underachieving primary school children. *Elementary School Guidance and Counseling,* 1970, *5,* 85–89.

Novick, J. I. Comparison of short-term group and individual psychotherapy in effecting changes in nondesirable behavior children. *International Journal of Group Psychotherapy,* 1965, *15,* 366–373.

Ofman, W. Evaluation of a group counseling procedure. *Journal of Counseling Psychology,* 1965, *11,* 152–159.

Ohlsen, M. M. *Guidance services in the modern school.* New York: Harcourt, 1974.

Ohlsen, M. M., & Gazda, G. M. Counseling underachieving bright pupils. *Education,* 1965, *86,* 78–81.

Pattison, E. M. Evaluation studies of group psychotherapy. *International Journal of Group Psychotherapy,* 1965, *15,* 382–393.

Paul, G. L. Strategy of outcome research in psychotherapy. *Journal of Consulting Psychology,* 1967, *31,* 109–118.

Pepinsky, H. B. Some proposals for research. *Personnel and Guidance Journal* 1953, *31,* 291–294.

Randolph, D. L., & Saba, R. G. Changing behavior through modeling and consultation. *Elementary School Guidance and Counseling,* 1973, *8,* 98–106.

Rickard, H. C. Tailored criteria of change in psychotherapy. *Journal of General Psychology,* 1965, *72,* 63–68.

Rickard, H. C., & Brown, E. C. Evaluation of a psychotherapy case in terms of change in a relevant behavior. *Journal of Clinical Psychology,* 1960, *16,* 93.

Rogers, C. R. Interpersonal relationships: Year 2000. *Journal of Applied Behavioral Science,* 1968, *4,* 265–280.

Roth, R. M., Mauksch, H. O., & Peiser, K. The non-achievement syndrome, group therapy, and achievement change. *Personnel and Guidance Journal,* 1967, *46,* 393–398.

Sarason, I. G., & Ganzer, V. J. Modeling and group discussion in the rehabilitation of juvenile delinquents. *Journal of Counseling Psychology,* 1973, *20,* 442–449.

Seligman, M. E. *On depression, development and death.* San Francisco: Freeman, 1975.

Sethna, E. R., & Harrington, J. A. Evaluation of group psychotherapy. *British Journal of Psychiatry,* 1971, *118,* 641–658.

Smith, R. D., & Evans, J. R. Comparison of experimental group guidance and individual counseling as facilitators of vocational development. *Journal of Counseling Psychology,* 1973, *20,* 202–208.

Sonstegard, M. *Group counseling methods with parents of elementary school children as related to pupil growth and development.* State College of Iowa, 1961 (mimeographed report).

Spielberger, C. O., Weitz, H., & Denny, J. P. Group counseling and academic performance of anxious college freshmen. *Journal of Counseling Psychology,* 1962, *9,* 195–204.

Spielberger, C. O., & Weitz, H. *Improving academic performance of anxious college freshmen.* Psychological Monograph #590, Washington, D.C.: American Psychological Association, 1964.

Strupp, H. H. The experimental group and the psychotherapeutic enterprise. *International Journal of Group Psychotherapy,* 1973a, *23,* 115–124.

Strupp, H. H. *Psychotherapy: Clinical research and theoretical issues.* New York: Jason Aronson, 1973b.

Tavormina, J. B. Relative effects of behavioral and reflective group counseling with parents of mentally retarded children. *Journal of Consulting and Clinical Psychology,* 1975, *43,* 22–31.

Teahan, J. E. Effect of group psychotherapy on academic low achievers. *International Journal of Group Psychotherapy,* 1966, *16,* 78–85.

Thelen, M. H., & Harris, C. S. Personality of college underachievers who improve with group psychotherapy. *Personnel and Guidance Journal,* 1968, *46,* 561–566.

Thombs, M. R., & Muro, J. J. Group counseling and the sociometric status of second grade children. *Elementary School Guidance and Counseling,* 1973, *7,* 194–197.

Thoresen, C. E., & Krumboltz, J. D. Relationship of counselor reinforcement of selected responses to external behavior. *Journal of Counseling Psychology,* 1967, *14,* 140–144.

Tosi, D., Swanson, C., & MacLean, P. Group counseling with nonverbalizing elementary school children. *Elementary School Guidance and Counseling,* 1970, *4,* 260–266.

Tosi, D., Upshaw, K., Lande, A., & Waldron, M. A. Group counseling with nonverbalizing students. *Journal of Counseling Psychology,* 1971, *18,* 437–440.

Truax, C. B., & Carkhuff, R. R. The old and new theory and research in counseling and psychotherapy. *Personnel and Guidance Journal,* 1964, *42,* 860–866.

Warner, R. W., & Hansen, J. C. Verbal reinforcement and model reinforcement group counseling with alienated students. *Journal of Counseling Psychology,* 1970, *17,* 168–172.

Wetzel, M. C., Kinney, J. M., Beavers, M. E., Harvey, R. T., & Urbanuk, G. W. Action laboratory: Behavior group therapy in a traditional context. *International Journal of Group Psychotherapy,* 1976, *26,* 59–70.

Wigell, W. W., & Ohlsen, M. M. To what extent is affect a function of topic and referent in group counseling? *American Journal of Orthopsychiatry,* 1962, *32,* 728–735.

Winkler, R. C., Teigland, J. J., Munger, P. F., & Kranzler, G. D. The effects of selected counseling and remedial techniques on underachieving elementary school children. *Journal of Counseling Psychology,* 1965, *12,* 384–387.

# Index of Names

# Index of Subjects